There Is No Making It Out

There Is No Making It Out

Stories-So-Far and the Possibilities of New Stories

Romeo García

Utah State University Press
Logan

© 2025 by University Press of Colorado

Published by Utah State University Press
An imprint of University Press of Colorado
1580 North Logan Street, Suite 660
PMB 39883
Denver, Colorado 80203-1942

All rights reserved

 The University Press of Colorado is a proud member of Association of University Presses.

The University Press of Colorado is a cooperative publishing enterprise supported, in part, by Adams State University, Colorado School of Mines, Colorado State University, Fort Lewis College, Metropolitan State University of Denver, University of Alaska Fairbanks, University of Colorado, University of Denver, University of Northern Colorado, University of Wyoming, Utah State University, and Western Colorado University.

ISBN: 978-1-64642-676-8 (hardcover)
ISBN: 978-1-64642-677-5 (paperback)
ISBN: 978-1-64642-678-2 (ebook)
https://doi.org/10.7330/9781646426782

Library of Congress Cataloging-in-Publication Data

Names: García, Romeo, 1987– author.
Title: There is no making it out : stories so far and the possibilities of new stories / Romeo García.
Description: Logan : Utah State University Press, [2024] | Includes bibliographical references and index.
Identifiers: LCCN 2024017608 (print) | LCCN 2024017609 (ebook) | ISBN 9781646426768 (hardcover) | ISBN 9781646426775 (paperback) | ISBN 9781646426782 (ebook)
Subjects: LCSH: Archives—Social aspects—United States. | Archives—Political aspects—United States. | Archives—Philosophy. | Rhetoric—Social aspects. | Memory—Social aspects. | Collective memory. | Decolonization.
Classification: LCC CD971 .G37 2024 (print) | LCC CD971 (ebook) | DDC 973—dc23/eng/20240923
LC record available at https://lccn.loc.gov/2024017608
LC ebook record available at https://lccn.loc.gov/2024017609

Sections of chapters were originally published in different forms and are reprinted with pemission or are open-access from the following publications: *Across the Disciplines* (2022), *Community Literacy Journal* (2018), *Composition Studies* (2022), *Constellations* (2019), *Journal of Multimodal Rhetorics* (2018), *Open Words* (2017), *Peitho* (2023), *Reflections* (2019), *Rhetoric, Politics, Culture* (2022), and *Writing Center Journal* (2024). More detailed information can be found in the permissions section after the references.

Cover art: "Paranoia Quilt" by Celeste de Luna, color reduction woodcut on fabric, 37" x 64", 2019

Contents

List of Figures vii

Use of Archives, Interviews, Conversations, and Words ix

Shorthand and Key Phrases xi

Acknowledgments xiii

Prologue xv

Introduction: (Decolonizing) Archival Impressions 3

Section 1: An Archival Interruption: The Analytic

    Reflexión-Meditación: That Which Lives in the Bones 37

1. An Epistemic System and Modern/Colonial and Settlerizing Designs 41

    Reflexión-Meditación: A Reflection on Moving to Utah 63

2. Corrido-ing the Idea of Utah and Mormon/ism 67

    Reflexión-Meditación: A Reflection on Corridos 103

3. Corrido-ing the Idea of Texas-LRGV and the Settler 107

    Reflexión-Meditación: Haunted/Haunting Peoples and the Im/Possibilities of a Prospective Vision 171

Section 2: Decolonizing Archival Impressions: The Im/Possibilities of a Prospective Task

4. Making It Out of Haunting Mentalities 177

    Reflexión-Meditación: Returning Home 225

5. Making It Out of Haunted Mentalities   229

Section 3: The Demand for Something Else

    Reflexión-Meditación: Joining the Band   259

Conclusion: Being-and-Becoming Recognizable to "We/arth"   263

References   283
Permissions   329
Index   331

Figures

0.1. Grandma with my primos and me   xxi
0.2. Literacy   xxii
3.1. A verse from a W. E. Stewart Land Company pamphlet   113
3.2. A verse from a W. E. Stewart Land Company pamphlet   114
3.3. Song from a W. E. Stewart Land Company pamphlet   115
3.4. Song from a W. E. Stewart Land Company pamphlet   116
3.5. Song from a W. E. Stewart Land Company pamphlet   117
3.6. Song from a W. E. Stewart Land Company pamphlet   117
3.7. Tweet by Elon Musk   119
3.8. Tweet by Elon Musk   119
3.9. Depiction from TRA   127
3.10. Depiction from TRA   127
3.11. Page from a book showing a jacal   130
3.12. A new "attractive" home in the Mission style   130
3.13. Map of the LRGV   131
3.14. Cover of a settler advertisement   135
3.15. Settler advertisement   136
3.16. Prosperity   137
3.17. Primitive homes   139
3.18. Harlingen Once a Blur on Map Called "Six-Shooter Junction"   143
3.19. 36 Dead Bandits   144

3.20. Sharyland advertisement 146
3.21. Harlingen Gateway to the Valley Wants You 150
3.22. The Gaze 153
3.23. Harlingen Proud of Its Modern School System 155
3.24. The Magic Valley myth 156
3.25. A White-Washing 165
4.1. Snapshot of Norma's email 186
4.2. Snapshot of Norma's email 186
4.3. UofU first pair of responses 188
4.4. UofU first pair of responses 189
4.5. UofU second pair of responses 190
4.6. UofU second pair of responses 191
4.7. UofU third pair of responses 191
4.8. UofU third pair of responses 192
4.9. UofU trio of responses 192
4.10. UofU trio of responses 193
4.11. UofU trio of responses 194
4.12. A snapshot of UofU student blog posts 203
4.13. A snapshot of UofU student blog posts 203
4.14. A snapshot of UofU student blog posts 204
4.15. A snapshot of UofU student blog posts 205
4.16. A snapshot of Candace's blog post 206
4.17. Candace's response post 217
5.1. We Await 233
5.2. A student essay on the coming of the railroads 234
5.3. Conveniently forgetting 235
5.4. A student poem 244
5.5. No Papeles 245
6.1. En Esta Dirección 267

Use of Archives, Interviews, Conversations, and Words

When working with the archives, all names and spellings (including spelling mistakes and the parlance of the English grammar) are used as they appear in the archives. All interviews and readings of student work stem from Institutional Review Board (IRB)–approved studies in Texas and Utah (Syracuse University and University of Texas Rio Grande Valley: IRB#15-116; University of Utah: IRB# 00104649/IRB# 00104041; Texas A&M University–Corpus Christi: "How to Empower Hispanic Males in Higher Education and Increase Completion, Retention, and Transition Rates: A Focus on Self-Efficacy, Social Inclusion, and Academic Inclusion"). All names are pseudonyms. All conversations and anecdotes are recalled to the best of my knowledge and are checked against field-and-analytical notes as well as follow-up conversations. The repetition of certain words is intentional, reflecting both an ethical choice and an attempt to heighten the affective value and rhetorical force (or pesado-ness as I refer to it) of some *things*.

Shorthand and Key Phrases

the Archive: a reference to power
archives: the body-as-sensory archive
archives: without emphasis to underscore the plurality of its forms
BoM: Book of Mormon
designs: modern/colonial and settlerizing designs
Epistemic system: epistemic system of ideas, images, and ends
Hegemonic architecture: hegemonic architecture of knowledge
MCC: Modernity/Coloniality Collective
MRM: Mormonism Research Ministry
SCS: Settler Colonial Studies
TRA: Texas Rangers in Action comic book series
W-H Question: where, who, what, and how
We/arth: Combines "we" and "earth" to form "we/arth"
WRS: writing and rhetorical studies

Acknowledgments

I owe a debt of gratitude to the Lower Rio Grande Valley (el Valle), a space of hope and place of struggle. And to its racialized, minoritized, and marginalized people, on the cusp of invisibility, who unwaveringly hope and struggle for something else. Thank you!

To Elizabeth Street in Corpus Christi, a second home, a space and place much like the Valley. And to all its "scholars" I would come to know in that neighborhood. Thank you!

To the students I have worked with over the years, thank you for teaching me and leaving me with life lessons.

To my colleagues both in the Department of Writing & Rhetoric Studies and at the University of Utah—Jenny Andrus, Maile Arvin, Annie Fukushima, Kendall Gerdes, Jay Jordan, LuMing Mao, Maureen Mathison, Danielle Olden, Joy Pierce, Jon Stone, Christie Toth, Hua Zhu—all the support has always meant so much to me! On my first visit, I knew the Department of Writing & Rhetoric Studies was different. From day one, I have been able to do the research that is meaningful to me and given room and offered mentorship to grow as a researcher, educator, and colleague. Thank you!

To those who have been there in friendship, mentorship, or instruction—Sonia Arellano, Pancho Arellano, Patrick Berry, Kevin Browne, Frankie

Condon, José Cortez, Christina Cedillo, Ralph Cintron, Ralph Contreras, Ellen Cushman, Harry Denny, Donald Dickson, Rebecca Dingo, Clint Gardner, Susan Garza, Yndalecio Isaac Hinojosa, Eric House, Cristina Kirklighter, Gesa Kirsch, Jason Markins, Aja Martinez, Janet McCann, Jaime Mejía, Elisabeth Mermann-Jozwiak, Chandra T. Mohanty, Brice Nordquist, Minnie Bruce Pratt, Ersula Ore, Steve Parks, Jessica Pauszek, Raúl Sánchez, Eileen Schell, and Anna Sicari—thank you!

A thanks to Beatrice Méndez Newman who welcomed me into her classroom while completing my graduate studies. And to Adela Cadena, Guillermo Corona, and the rest of the team at the Special Collections and Archives at the University of Texas Rio Grande Valley, thank you for accommodating all my requests for archival materials.

A thanks to colleagues who reviewed all or some of my manuscript at one point—Patrick Berry, José Cortez, Gesa Kirsch, Jaime Mejía, Steve Parks, and Jon Stone.

A special thanks to reviewers, Raúl Sánchez and Mya Poe, whose feedback was thoughtful, critical, and supportive. And a thanks to Utah State University Press and Rachael Levay, who made my first single-authored manuscript a smooth process with mentorship, guidance, and accommodations.

To Celeste de Luna, a Tejana artist from el Valle—thank you for the permission to include your artwork.

To my family—tío/as, primo/as, Mom, brother, and sister—for whom I have much appreciation.

To Jenavi and Julius—from whom a new journey of learning how to live-love again otherwise began and continues!

To my Grandma—much of who I have come to be, and how I walk and see this world and interact and exchange meaning with others, is owed to you, which is why I have dedicated some of my scholarship to remembering you! Aquí con nosotros todavía sigues vivo. Thank you!

Prologue

My story began before me. Where there is writing, there are archives and its stories-so-far (Massey 2005) and possibilities of new stories (Rohrer 2016).

Can archives feel? I grapple with the meaning of archives throughout this book to proffer a response. Overall, my proclivity toward any *thing* that is settled, be it an idea, name, or object, is not to settle on its settled-ness. I refer to such an orientation, which I animate throughout, as an ethos of bearing witness in unsettling ways and a praxis of unsettling the settled. It has its roots in the spaces, places, and people familiar to me. This ethos and praxis also stem from my reading and interpretation of scholars like Jacques Derrida (1997) who puts *things* "under erasure" (60–61). With all that stated, I propose that both the meaning of archives and archival research be extended to the *elsewhere* and *otherwise*. Ensuant to that shift, which this book marks, my inclination is then to say, yes, archives can feel! As it pertains to some of this book's subject matter, the contents will illustrate, significantly, that, in part, archives (hereafter "archive[s]," without emphasis to underscore the plurality of forms) are a *human thing* that human beings have constructed. The conclusion of the book, though, will propose that there is *an-other* archive with a history much longer than that of human beings. In the end, an unsettling of the settled is required to bear witness to how we live amid, and as, archives in unending cycles of (re)writing.

The primary rhetorical function of archives has been debated for decades. Two things are abundantly clear. First, there is a condition of and for archiving. I am most convinced by bell hooks (2009), who said, "We are born and have our being in a place of memory," and "We know ourselves through the art and act of remembering . . . Memories offer us a world" (5). But memory also extends to the body. To support that position, it is sufficient to turn to

Frantz Fanon (1986): "O my body, make of me always a [being] who questions" (232). That the mind and body can function as a *technique-technology of repetition* is (perhaps) one way to reinterpret Derrida's (1995) conversation on archives. Based on my readings of Diane Davis's (2014) work, I argue that with the concept of a *preoriginary rhetoricity* it is possible to bear witness to (the body-as-sensory) archive(s) before *archival desire* sets in. The end of the book addresses this point, but that recollecting can be an art and act of reassembling the trace of marks that scatter, providing pathways into a world, suggests some *things* can be returned to and accessed (beyond a Derridean desire) as a *longing* (Tuck 2009, 417) for some *thing* else. A different set of questions must be considered with such a break and shift. Ultimately, I argue memory (broadly conceived and applied) is one condition of and for archivization. The body-as-sensory *archive* (hereafter *archive*) is one meaning that this book prescribes to.

Second, archives are in part the by-product of the human touch that leaves some *things* behind. It is made, unmade, and remade by such. Derrida (1997), no stranger to the archives (and memory discourse), might concede to the necessity to name and submit that "it" is already "no more than a so-called proper name" (109). This, however, does not preclude how memory always already demands the architecting of an archive, a *technique-technology of repetition*. Upholding the a priori value of this proposition, the earth, for example, "produces as much as it records the event" (Derrida 1995, 17). Gravitating to D. Davis's (2014) *preoriginary rhetoricity* once more—the "already relational condition" (536) of "any living being" (547)—I conclude this book on an archive-to-come, "we/arth," which reconfirms my position that archives can feel. Now "We"-and-"Earth"-as archive, "we/arth," is contingent on how we accept the *event* of the invitation to get caught-up in an archival approach and all it necessitates—a capacious theory of and for archival impressions. Will "we/arth," either as a word or *thing*, ever have arrived? Derrida (1995) noted, "The archive, if we want to know what this will have meant, we will only know in the times to come . . . later on or perhaps never" (27). Fundamentally, this book will submit a response in the form of an expression common throughout, ojalá.

Admittedly, I am not an archivist or historian by training. That should not sow or cast doubt on the stories I share about the desires and objectives of power and its effects and consequences on land, memory, knowledge, and relation-ing. Aware of the risks involved, the theoretical trap of arguing "power is everywhere" (Foucault 1978, 93), this book prescribes to a second meaning for archives, power-as-an-*Archive* (hereafter *Archive*). The humanities have surely seen its share of such stories. So it begs the question, what is new? I am of the mind that conversations on power are less about reinventing the wheel and more about constellating kinetic synergies of hope and struggle and bringing about a critique to bear on power through collective energies. Both are needed in the face of a monster, computer, four-headed machine, or *Archive*, made, unmade, and remade in unending cycles. Stories on power, which materialize, travel, and circulate much like power, are like pictorial weavings in a tapestry of hauntings and haunting situations sewn together from the threads of hope (what else is there) and struggle (something else) that are part of the fabric of every society manufacturing the cloth of modern/colonial and settlerizing designs. Stories shared on power bring nuance, when necessary, because that is expected, but they also create space to connect, share insights, learn, and carry out a politics of wor(l)ding *otherwise*. Unsettling the theoretical trap, Edward Said (1983) wrote: "In human history there is always something beyond the reach of dominating systems, no matter how deeply they saturate society, and this is obviously what makes change possible" (247). So stories on power are more an expression of a hope and struggle (see Ahmed 2017) that there are some *things*, if we can unsettle the settled-ness of them, beyond the reach and grip of power. ¡Ojalá!

This book attempts to navigate overtotalizing views of power and deterministic presumptions of a decolonial option. It holds that we each experience power differently, much like we do archives. I will reflect on what I saw, felt, and heard in extending the meaning of archives to the *elsewhere* and *doing* archival research *otherwise*. Now, it might come off as a preposterous and impossible proposition that one can see, feel, and listen to the contents of archives. Some of that partly stems from and reflects cultural thinking, feeling, and doing programs that encourage disconnections vis-à-vis distinctions. Donna Haraway's (1988) "ideological doctrines of disembodied scientific objectivity" will suffice for the point I am making (576). Those who are haunted, who feel the haunt that lives within the bones, indeed see, feel, and listen-to the contents of archives, including their own, especially their own when the parallels are haunting. I turn to the words of James Baldwin (2012) to ground the body-as-sensory *archive* further: "people are trapped in history and history is trapped in them" (129). Baldwin's (1998) words are an invitation to recognize and acknowledge how "we carry" the "force of history" within us (723). It appeals for a break from doctrines of disembodiments and reorientation to the body *otherwise*. Herein lies the body as a rhetorical concept (Moraga and Anzaldúa 1983; Shapiro 1999; Ahmed 2017; Chávez 2018).

Couched in Baldwin's (1998, 2012) appeal is a demand for some *thing* else. But how do we access the contents of our *archives*? Aware of the risks involved, I prefer a response not to provide a prescriptive checklist or roadmap but to illustrate one course of action through the epistemic principles of *returns, careful reckonings,* and *enduring tasks*. To *return* to something requires a pathway. Here, excavation is less a metaphor and more a steppingstone toward making inroads into the *archives. Returns* like rhetoric do not function for the sake of it, thus necessitating a *careful reckoning*. Imagine, as I do, *archives as an* assemblage, constituted by seemingly divergent yet convergent depots of knowledges, understandings, feelings, and doings. To *carefully reckon* with each is to bring into focus the ways cultural thinking, feeling, and doing programs have shaped how we walk and see the world and interact and exchange meaning with others. And envision as I do, the space beyond the entryway of the *archives* as a waystation between *stories-so-far* and the *possibilities of new stories*. It is a place where in/formal representations are at an infliction point, between life and death, where some *thing* can go to die to give way to some *thing* else (see West 2009). The *enduring task* stems from realizing that like power the *archives* are made, unmade, and remade in unending cycles. I animate these principles further in what is to come, evidencing how our lives and bodies are indeed *archives*.

All archives are *in* assemblage (see Yang 2017; Tsing 2015; Deleuze and Guattari 2005). As to with what, well, that is one essential focus of this book. Not as an academic but as one of the haunted, I write this book in part for those familiar, those who are relegated to *below* (Sheller 2012), occupy the space of *shadows* (Calleja et al. 2020), traverse the *epistemic murk* (Taussig 1991) on unsettled grounds, speak the language of hauntings (Derrida 1994b), rehearse the corporeal exercises of addressing oneself to hauntings (García 2019a), hope and struggle to become subjects in the throes of haunting situations (Holland 2000), navigate enactments of *assent* in the form of an *awaiting* ("ojalá") (García and Cortez 2020), and try to find tranquility in the wreckage of what surrounds. From this perspective, I share stories on the desires and objectives of power and its effects and consequences on land, memory, knowledge, and relation-ing with the hope that it can be *in* assemblage with others doing this *work*.

I write for the unfamiliar too; this book is an invitation to understand, the best one can, what it looks, feels, and sounds like to be aware of the *Archive-archives*. I offer a glimpse into their skeletal systems, the archival impressions that give structure to and constitute the *Archive-archives*. This is to then ground *an-other* set of options, questions, and exigences. "Each generation," Fanon (1963) wrote, must "discover its mission, fullfill it, or betray it" (206). It is my hope that the unfamiliar realize, despite what their reality communicates, that they too are haunted. If that moment ever arrives, it might strengthen a constellating kinetic synergy of hope and struggle, perhaps sparking a ~~desire~~ *longing* for ~~making it out~~ wor(l)ding *otherwise*; "words" can *take* place and have the capacity for "worlding" aspirations. This book ultimately reflects an obligation and responsibility to seed an idea, the genesis for reimagining, that a politics of wor(l)ding *otherwise* is possible. Such a politics for me begins by working out the possibility that one can indeed see, feel, and listen to the contents of archives.

Archival Impressions at the Nexus of Stories-So-Far and the Possibilities of New Stories

My (unexceptional) story (in comparison) began before me. It is a story of hope and struggle by the most resilient people I know.

It was all so simple: make it out! Nothing could be further from the truth.

WEAVING AND TEXTURING THE FABRIC OF A FRAMEWORK FOR THE HAUNTED, RETURNS

We would pass fields and people who looked like us working them every day. I internalized difference in those moments of listening to Mom's memories and connecting them to those of other family members. "That was us." Our family had known that experience. The fields, and its people who work them, are part of my *stories-so-far*. But they never triggered in me the same memory it did for them. I remember feeling distant from the fields and its people. That emotion haunted me then because I was so close to both, and yet I knew I was so far from the *possibilities of new stories*.

We would stop by Salas on 822 North D Street, drop off Grandma at a comadres on Cora Street, search for a tío on North B Street, or reconnect with home all of which were in the barrio. Mom did not like staying long. "This place." I grasped in those moments *returns* can be painful. She thought the more distance between us, the better. Because like other barrios, where people are *thrown* into and relegated to the shadows and *below* as nonbeings, meaning is gained from hauntings and haunting situations that result in literacies, images, and rhetorics of survivance, persistence, and resilience (Calleja et al. 2020; Césaire 2001; Fanon 1963, 1986; Flynn, Sotirin, and Brady

2012; A. Gordon 2008; Mignolo 2018; Morrison 1992; Neitch 2019; Nishida 1986; Shapiro 1999; Thiong'o 2004; Vizenor 1999). No amount of distance could stop the barrio from being part of my *stories-so-far* though. Because the barrio was already in me.

So I never picked the fields or lived in the *wreckage* of my family's barrio (Césaire 2001; Fanon 1986; Rich 1973; Rodriguez 2015). It is important for me to write and say that. I was the *possibilities of new stories*. But I was always already attuned (see Rickert 2013) to hauntings and haunting situations. I can see and hear Mom, a single parent and high school dropout. No manual literacies: "I was not given a manual for how to raise a child alone." Making it out literacies: "It is okay if you end up hating or resenting me. So long as you make it out." Nothing here literacies: "There is nothing here. You don't want to end up like me." Grown-folk and comoquiera literacies: "If they take it [vehicle], we still have our feet." Así son las cosas literacies: "That's just the way it is!" Life was what it was on Skyline. And I, not knowing otherwise, believed hauntings and haunting situations were inherent to us.

I can see and hear the absence of him [biological father]. I was five years old when Mom taught me how to read letters from and write letters to a man in prison I only knew through pictures and words. We would sit at the table. There I encountered all kinds of literacies. Prison literacies: "Don't be a fuck-up like me." Regardless of his absence, I somehow missed him. My wistful sentiment of "I have missed you" in a postcard I had crafted and written on gives the impression he once was present. El no Sabía literacies: But the statement—"Let me tell you my name" (me) and "Every year his wish was for his daddy to come home" (Mom)—was but a reminder he was an absent presence. I never knew him, but he was a haunting presence and that much is true. Many of us kids at Skyline had this haunting situation—strong women who did their best to raise boys into men—in common.

I can see and hear my friends and I walking and talking along the canal. "You think we are going to end up like them?" We refused to name them. A friend breaks the silence. "Not like them." But we did not know many who had made it out. We were not like other kids. We were raised by single moms, stood in the W.I.C. lines at Fair Park, and inherited, embodied, and experienced a barrio mentality (hope-struggle). We were hardly allowed to be just kids even on days when we were just being kids. *The world, the haunt, was too much with us* (Wordsworth 1898). La vida todo te enseña literacies. We knew, and were taught, to be afraid of what was in our bones. Making it out

FIGURE 0.1. "Grandma with my primos and me"

then was our *felt sense* (Gendlin 1982) of obligation and responsibility. Will we ever have made it out?

WEAVING AND TEXTURING THE FABRIC OF A FRAMEWORK FOR THE HAUNTED, CAREFUL RECKONINGS

No mas queda scattered memories, photographs, and loose-leaf papers of Grandma. Here she is with my primos and me (figure 0.1). Grandma always held me a little closer (por que no todos los dedos son iguales). *Because I was haunted* a bit more so than some of my primos (Fanon 1986, 129). I spent many days at my tios Grandma's. It was my *homeplace*, a place of and for a love, care, healing, and learning ethic (hooks 2001b). There she made the *choice*, which was hardly one at all but a demand, to stand at the nexus of my *stories-so-far* and *possibilities of new stories*. Grandma represents a "lineage" and "air" of energy. Her work as enunciations (pa que sepas, aprendes, entiendes, no te dejes) and material exchanges (*shadow work*) signified song, poetry, and a language of awakening from the shadows and *below*. An ethic, ethos,

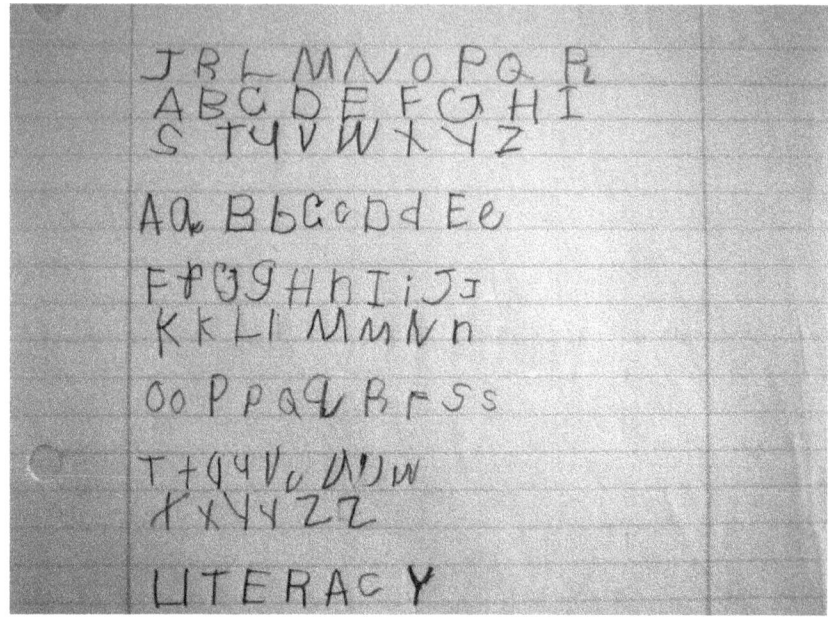

FIGURE O.2. Literacy

and praxis of *thinking, feeling,* and *being-with* characterized it all (Baldwin 1979; Barthes 1982; Fanon 1963; hooks 2001a, 2015; Lorde 2020; Rivera 1992; Thiong'o 2011, 2013).

My *stories-so-far* demanded I think about the generational catalog of hauntings and haunting situations in the Lower Rio Grande Valley (LRGV). Skyline—it represented the *possibilities of new stories* for Mom. But in my room, I took up my brown(ed)ness, like some of my friends with similar situations did. With tears in my eyes and cries, I kept putting back what kept being broken (Fanon 1986; Morrison 1987). A rumination—so much potential literacies: "He has so much potential, but he's going to end up like him." These were haunting words familiar to my friends and me. Grandma refused to consent to that reality. Hope in the struggle literacies: "Debes [deberías] ser abogado, siempre tienes algo que decir. Una abogado sin licensia." She had a way of seeing the good in the haunted, peeling back for me the layers of self and exposing what had not yet been lost to hauntings and haunting situations. It was from Grandma that I learned how to hope-struggle *otherwise*.

I can still see and hear Grandma. "Pásale." The smell of tortillas de harina always engulfed my senses. "¿Con mantequilla?" Grandma knew. "Siéntate." I would sit down at the mesa more often than not next to loose-leaf papers and a black recorder. Grandma had gone from an "X" mark on documents to learning how to read and write in Spanish and English (figure 0.2). She went to *work* in that cocina and at the mesa so I could *know* and *learn*. What truly mattered in life took place there. "¿Cómo te fue en la escuela?" Grandma was denied that experience upon *arriving* in the US from Xilitla, San Luis Potosi, Mexico. For her, school was the *possibilities of new stories*. It meant making it out. "En serio, la escuela es muy importante." As home increasingly became unbearable, I turned to Grandma and my *homeplace* as the grounds for ~~making it out~~ going on *otherwise*.

"En la vida a veces todo lo que puedes decir es, ¡así son las cosas!" Grandma's enunciation demanded *assent* (Lyons 2010). "Pues, ¿Ahora qué?" This question grounded an ethic for going on (L. Gordon 2000). *Pues* is a filler word. But it can be meaningful. It was meaningful to her. Yes, Grandma refused to consent and be a cosigner to her own domination ("¡No dejaremos!"). She was thus compelled to speak from the shadows and *below*. But *pues* is enunciated because of generational pains and cries that evidence an unending cycle of hoping-struggling to provide the grounds for going on *otherwise*. Given that rhetoric can only ever guarantee with certainty possibilities, *pues* was a grounding of a praxis of knowing (¡entiendes!; a setting-to-work) and unknowing (¿entiendes?; an ungraspable call): an inquiry without warranty; a rhetoric without certainty; a hope and an *awaiting* ("ojalá") without guaranteed predicate (Derrida 1994b; García and Cortez 2020; Spivak 1994; Vivian 2000). Nonetheless, Grandma carried out *work* without certainty or guarantee for what it might yield.

Grandma understood nothing is inherent but always learned (Haraway 1988). "Vamos/Vámonos." I learned early in life not to ask why. "¡Porque yo digo!" As we walked, I listened to her cuentos and testimonios (Latina Feminist Group 2001). Poor-people literacies: "No teníamos mucho." Pos ni modo literacies: "¿Qué vas a hacer? No mas queda tu dignidad." Sabes que literacies: "Trabajé duro y a veces me trataban mal." No te dejes literacies: "Las cosas seguirán siendo difíciles. Pero, ¡No dejaremos (terconess) que cualquier cosa o persona nos trate comoquiera. Porque si lo dejas, ya valió!" Grandma did not cry or shout these words (Fanon 1986). "¡En estos momentos no lloramos!" Te digo esto literacies: "Te digo esto pa que sepas y aprendes." My *homeplace* became mobile.

"Vamos/Vámonos." We would walk to the neighborhoods around South C Street from Jefferson Street. "Pásale." There, I learned about a neighborhood and community of care. Comadre literacies: "Han pasado cosas. Pero, nos cuidámos el uno al otro." From Jefferson Street, we would walk to the iglesia in the same area. Neighborhood and community of care literacies: "Gracias a Dios." "Padre nuestro, que estas en el cielo ('Our Father') ... Dios te salve Maria ('Hail Mary')." There, I learned comadres were ready to carry out *work* too for another without certainty or guarantee for what it might yield. My *homeplace* became communal.

"Vamos/Vámonos." We would walk to Washington Avenue and then to Ona and Cora Street from Jefferson Street. There, I learned about their *homeplace* that no longer was physically there. "¿Ves esa casa?" Confusion sank in the first time. "Mira. Ahí es donde vivimos. ¿Qué ves? ¿Qué oyes?" Grandma was remembering, seeing presence and hearing sound in the traces of their *homeplace* (Morrison 1987). Hacemos lo que podíamos literacies: "Plantamos. Tuvimos pollos. Hicimos ropa. Tortillas y fríjoles y ya vámonos." When Grandma asked me to look at the traces that remain, she was compelling me to *see* and *listen* rather than just *look* and *hear* (Derrida 1994b). I no longer saw absence or heard silence but felt both a community's "lineage" and "air" of energy and song, poetry, and language of hope-struggle. My *homeplace* became constellated and deeply rooted.

"Vamos/Vámonos." Grandma was not happy to hear from my counselor. I was dropping out of high school. Or so I thought. She walked from Jefferson Street to Marshall Avenue. I can see Grandma give me a hug and hear its words. No empieces literacies "¡No empieces con eso chingadera. Sácate/quítate eso [giving up] de tu cabeza." I had all but been convinced I would end up like him. I was out of tears, cries, and the energy to keep putting back what kept being broken. Terco literacies. "Se terco en otra manera." I tried. But I could no longer imagine or project myself outside of the LRGV. Para las tres dias me quedan literacies. "Cuando piensas así y lo creas, ya valió." Grandma went to and carried out *work* once more.

Words and material exchanges matter. They *take* and can *make* place—wor(l)ding. They can make an argument, have effect beyond their utterance, evolve into tangible actions, and forge and materialize song, poetry, and language that had not yet existed but needed to in the demand for some *thing* else.

WEAVING AND TEXTURING THE FABRIC OF A FRAMEWORK FOR THE HAUNTED, ENDURING TASKS

Grandma passed away in 2008. Doctors had advised her to stay home. But Grandma was terco when it came to me. (Here "terco" is not derogative but a term of endearment.) From Jefferson Street she might have *cut* through on 10th Street and continued onward to Van Buren. There was a more public way. But Grandma had her own path. Upon a quick glance, she would be an image of presence and absence and sameness and a differentiating sign of *otherness* (Bhabha 1994), a fleeting life blending into the shadows. It was a familiar space for Grandma, who will never have arrived (Acosta 2012) and only ever have been in possession of a *citizenship from below* (Sheller 2012). Grandma needed to see me. Something remained at *work* even as she was walking herself home. I learned unknowingly that day how to live from an-other at the *edge of life* (Derrida 1994b).

"¿Te asusté?" An unexpected arrival. I told Grandma I would visit. "Antes que sea muy tarde quería verte." She was being terco against the arrival of death. Such honesty stemmed from not having the luxury to treat me as a kid when I was younger. I could not speak the *right* words that day. Could I ever if such a circumstance arrived again? With a smile and rosary in hand, she said, "Vámanos." We *cut through* the neighborhoods as we had done before. And I felt at-home (see Fanon 1986; Anzaldúa 1999; Gómez-Peña 1996). We walked in silence. Grandma initiated conversation. "¿Cómo antes?" Suddenly, a memory called, of a boy who did not feel at home in his own home; who called home wherever he could lay his head; who turned to writing to escape and story a self in a home he could one day call his own. We continued to walk *there* . . . between somewhere and nowhere (see Gómez-Peña 1996).

"¿Recuerdas?" Another memory called, of Grandma and me walking and talking. "¿Qué ves? ¡Mira con tus ojos!" I learned *with* her how to create presence from absence from the trace of marks that remain (Wideman 2001). "¿Qué oyes? ¡Escucha con tus oídos!—Habla con ellos, te pueden oírte y te miran y te cuidan." I learned *with* her how to create sound from silence at the Rest-lawn Memorial Park in La Feria, Texas. (It would come to perplex me, upon reading Derrida [1994b], that a "scholar" who could speak in that *foreign language* of ghosts and hauntings was still to-come. To that point, Derrida responded in Ken McMullen's [1983] film *Ghost Dance* with, "You're asking a ghost whether he believes in ghosts" [n.p.]). "Siempre hay una y otra manera." I learned *with* her how to *cut through* in the shadows and from *below*. "¡Así son las cosas!" "¡Pero no te dejes! ¡No dejaremos que cualquier cosa o persona nos trate comoquiera!" I learned *with* her the difference between *assent* and *consent*. (My peers critique Derrida for being insufferable and exhausting with obscured styles of writing. I gravitated to Derrida [1994b], like Spivak [1988a], because in asking questions not to be translated literally—"He would know that such an address is . . . already possible" [13]—I am reminded of Grandma's use of entiendes, which lays out a framework for the already haunted. Making it out is an illusion, so Derrida invites us to rise to a level of obligation and responsibility that unsettles the settled-ness of *things* [deconstruction], orients toward relations [hauntology], and struggles openly in the memory of a hope [to-come]). "Pues, ¿Ahora qué?" I learned *with* her the grounds for going on *otherwise*.

"¿Estás seguro?" Yes, I remember! "Te digo esto pa que sepas . . . ¡Entiendes!" Another memory called, of a boy who left home on a Greyhound bus. Many made that possible—a principal who overlooked absences; a counselor who provided resources; recruiters who persuaded Mom to sign my financial aid documents; a grandma who carried out *work*; friends who provided shelter. It takes a neighborhood and community of care to even begin to think oneself out of the shadows and *below* (Alexander and Mohanty 1997). I understand!

"Pa que aprendes ¿Entiendes?" Grandma walked home in December of 2008. Nos vemos literacies. "Nos vemos al rato." Death is hardly a cause for good-byes. There is brightness in death. Because the nonliving can have a powerful presence in the lives of the living (Derrida 1994b). I can still hear the question, "¿entiendes?" The interrogative of entiendes continues to unsettle me today. It made more sense when I made it out of the LRGV. Especially as the question, *Will I ever have made it out and arrived beyond the borders*, continues haunting me. The question of entiendes is a grounding of a praxis of unknowing, as the following underscores, an unsettling of the settled even in light of a proper name and act inscriptionally characterized as an arrival:

> A "stranger memory" calls (Ahmed 2012). I *return* to the Sarita, Texas internal checkpoint. Everyone de ahí (LRGV) gets "checked" 70 miles north. It functions as the last line of defense against "illegal" arrivals and arrivants. I can still see and hear border agents *checking*. "¿De dónde eres . . . a dónde vas . . . y tu papeles?" I was interpellated based on skin color (Prieto), palimpsest of identity ("The Mexican"), and out-of-placeness (see Wingard 2013). I realized it mattered to them que uno es de ahí y no de allá. Conditional inclusion was granted both at the checkpoint and at Texas A&M University. But I will never have made it out of the *epistemic murk* (Taussig 1991) that rationalizes a *geography of exclusion* (Sibley 1995; Cresswell 1996; Peters 1998); the logic here—US citizens as white European descendants requiring protection from the "the Mexican" not through direct colonization but through coloniality—that forces me to remain a border(ed)lander.

A stranger memory calls. Being from the LRGV is felt the most beyond it. The *checking* of my body at the checkpoint typified my experiences in Gringodemia. The suffix ("ed") in border(ed)lander is less about rhetorical effect and more about making visible how we inherit and dwell in our *rhetorics of place* (Endres and Senda-Cook 2011): the internalizing of borders and boundaries encoded with the haunted/haunting literacies, images-signs-sounds, and rhetorics of recursive containment, monitorization, surveillance, and checking(s) (Anzaldúa 1999). I *return* to and can still see and hear my tío talk about showing *them*. Enseñarle literacies: "Tienes que enseñarles que puedes abrí un libro y leerlo tambien." But inclusion is a one-way street and technology of managing and controlling (see Mignolo 2011a) who can arrive beyond the *borders*. It matters little whether one can open a book and read it too in whiten(ed) spaces and places. The literacies of epistemic racism (Grosfoguel 2013): "We are not that tree-hugging school"; "We don't want diversity . . . Go back home, wetback . . . Fucking Mexican" (students) . . . "You are not cut out for this [school]" (professor). I found myself determined to write, speak, and be more ~~right~~ white (Fanon 1963). It will have come at a cost.

A stranger memory calls. Gringodemia is one vast checkpoint. I *return* to and can still see and hear another tío talk about being careful. Ten cuidado literacies: "Cuidadito, you are just a 'Mexican' in their eyes." Being "the Mexican" is felt the most amongst white folks. The literacies of epistemic racism: "Go back home! Go back to Mexico boy!" (white hotel employee at Syracuse University); "What are you doing up here! You don't belong here! You need to turn around!" (another white university employee at SU); "I can't even hear your accent" (white booth aide at the National Conference of Teachers of English); "You don't look like you are supposed to be here . . . let me see your cards" (white woman at a Rhetoric Society of America conference). "I need to check your badge to make sure you belong here" (white man at the Conference on Composition and Communication). Inclusion is not a synonym for belonging. I *carry home wherever I go*—it remains the place where my, "I am," always already tethered to, "where I do and think," is constituted (Anzaldúa 1999). The "checking" of my brown(ed) body assures me that I will never have made it out and arrived beyond the borders.

Once more, the interrogative of entiendes grounds a praxis of knowing and unknowing (Fanon 1986). "¿Entiendes?" I understand—photographs "cannot *say* what it lets us see" (Barthes 1982, 100) and inheritances say, "read me, will you ever be able to do so" (Derrida 1994b, 18; also see Haraway 2016a). Grandma understood a delicate balance between a *setting-to-work* and an un-knowing/dis-understanding was needed. The interplay between the declarative and interrogative of entiendes reveals as much as it defies. It keeps a secret. Because some *thing* must remain at *work*, enduring and ongoing. And that interplay has many implications, one being that while I know *haunting* or re/searching back is a goal (L. Smith 2012), I also know changing the *contents* and *terms* must remain *enduring* like the question, will I ever have arrived?

Weaving and Texturing the Fabric of a Framework for the Haunted, Being-and-Becoming Recognizable

Grandma was a scholar and maestra de lo que no puedes aprender en la escuela. "No sabemos cuándo ni dónde llegaremos en la vida." Our walks and talks were not unintentional. "La vida todo te enseña pero en las cosas de dignidad es otra cosa." A slow and deep decompositioning of self: "A slow composition of my self in the middle of a spatial and temporal world" (Fanon 1986, 111). Walking and talking situated me in constellated histories, memories, and *stories-so-far* of hope-struggle. I learned how to see: "Como se come pescado, en la vida tienes que tener cuidado y buscar lo que sabes que está ahí frente a ti." I learned how to listen to the totality of that which haunted me: "¡No dejaremos que cualquier cosa o persona nos trate comoquiera." I learned how to listen to, *to know* and *to learn*, how one can never belong to the shadows or *below*: "Aguantase! Caminamos no para olvidar pero pa que ver lo que es posible." To unsettle my brown(ed)ness I had to unlearn it by bearing witness to it then in unsettling ways and engaging in a praxis of unsettling the settled: a seeing without being settled with and doing of plunging into, peeling back layers of, and unsettling what is constituted as legible (Fukushima 2019; García and Kirsch 2022). And to relearn how to recompose myself I had to *clinically* and *mercilessly* excavate [it] out of my head (Fanon 1963). "Sácate/quítate eso de tu cabeza" (see Thiong'o 2004). Relearning in a direction of change with dignity would take time—a slow and deep recompositioning of self—"One must move softly (188–189); move slowly in the world" (Fanon 1986, 230–231). "Todo con tiempo." Walking and talking were not unintentional. It was a *learning-unlearning-relearning* path of *being-and-becoming* a *walking exigency*—actor-agents shaped by and shaping discourse—toward *possibilities of new stories* (Buchanan and Ryan 2010; de Certeau 2011; Kells 2006; Mignolo and Walsh 2018; Tlostanova and Mignolo 2012). A path that was about the ambiguous *there*—somewhere, nowhere, someday.

"Llegarás a ser un abogado," Grandma would tell me. Perhaps this enunciation was never about a profession but about the process of *being-and-becoming*.

I will have lost more than I will ever have gained in and out of academia. And I know now that a haunted consciousness is neither removed nor do hauntings or haunting situations cease presencing because one physically leaves home. But I can still continue to research and search for hope—*a praxical theorizing, a conceptual theorizing, a theoretical conceptualizing, a theory-building actioning* (Mignolo and Walsh 2018)—in the archival impressions of my *story-so-far*. It is an *enduring task* learning how to be at-home *otherwise* and finding tranquility in the wreckage of what surrounds, exasperated by how we all become unrecognizable in stages of life (Fanon 1963, 1986). "Ve a caminar," Grandma would tell me when I was in college, "Estoy a tu lado siempre." It would temporarily change how I walked and saw the world and interacted and exchanged meaning with others. I lost my way of "walking" then. Today I go on those walks to *think, feel*, and *be-with* the living, nonliving, and nonhuman—an exercise so few academics know how to do. It is a slow and deep (de/re)compositioning of *being-and-becoming recognizable* to self/selves, others, and communities *otherwise* (see Rohrer 2016). For no other reason do I write of spaces, places, and people familiar to me (Holland 2000). My objectives range—to bring out of the shadows and *below*; to prepare a ghostly return beyond the borders; to create a *slow hemorrhage* into cultural and thinking programs (de Certeau 1992; Derrida 1994b; Cushman 2013)—but it is all an effort to *be-and-become recognizable*.

A politics and thus theory of *being-and-becoming* is to be grasped in space, place, time, and by *thinking, feeling*, and *being-with* people. Now, there is "no theory capable" Said (1983) notes, of "covering" or "predicting all the situations" (241, 234; also see Pred 1995). Grandma understood that. Mitigating the ideological trap of an un/answerable theory (Said 1983, 242), she lived life knowing there are no prescriptive checklists or roadmaps for dealing with hauntings and haunting situations. Theory cannot do everything for us. It always already must be worked out through practice. "There can be no discourse of decolonization, no theory of decolonization," Silvia Rivera Cusicanqui (2012) writes, "without a decolonizing practice" (100). Practice and theory mutually determine how and when either is to change. This orientation, like theory, has traveled from one generation, one haunted and haunting space and place, and one comadre to another. I claim that "borrowed" theory (Said 1983) in this context is a testament to a constelled hope-struggle that archives can indeed feel. While I cannot make it out of certain *things*, what it means to *be-and-become recognizable* is another story. We must allow for the hope that some *things* are beyond the reach and grip of power.

Re/searching (for) Hope

It was imperative that I share to the extent I do. Its significance will bear at the end of this book where I contemplate, what next. The point was to underscore that how we orient ourselves to hauntings, inheritances, and dwellings can tell us a lot about *stories-so-far* and the *possibilities of new stories*. I left home on bad terms. And when I did, I still did not know how to be at-home *otherwise*. I have made the *choice* here and now though to use this space partly to re/search for closure. And partly to honor the "scholars" familiar to me, from whom I muster hope-struggle. Hauntings and haunting situations, by which I mean ongoing and organizing settlerizing encounters, interactions, and engagements that through domination, displacement, and exploitation transforms human beings into racialized, minoritized, ghettoized, and/or ghost people (Trouillot 1995; Bergland 2000; Tuck and Yang 2012; Arvin et al. 2013; Roy 2014), would like nothing more than to keep *others* in perpetual despair. But despair is not a luxury of the haunted, who think, feel, and do with a *longing* that it is possible to re/search for hope in the demand for some *thing* else. They keep on keeping on, with all the ancestors in them, not as a *choice* but as a demand.

My body is *an archive*. It is the accumulation of some *things* (Bruner 1991a, 1991b; Butler 1997; Gee 1989). Though not a novel idea, it bears repeating. The above is a catalog of some of its contents. Home, memories, and hauntings *call*. They will not let me go (Cisneros 1991; Villanueva 2004). *Returns, careful reckonings*, and *enduring tasks* are what they demand. So above I animated a *return*, because the meaning of *archives* are constituted differently, by creating presence from absence and sound from silence through *community listening*—*community listening* meaning that which circulates and moves in and around at all times, enunciations of which settle us into our local histories of hauntings, inheritances, and dwellings, unfolding as material exchanges that becomes the connective tissue between individual and collective memory (Adelsen 1970; Ceraso 2014; Fishman and Rosenberg 2019; García 2018a; Royster 2000; Royster and Kirsch 2012). It is not out of a nostalgic impulse or for the sake of mere recall. That is not a luxury afforded to me (Browne 2013, 2019). Being forced to address myself to hauntings and haunting situations is painful. It is unsettling, because as I *carefully reckon* with what hauntings have done to and made of me (Baldwin 1984a; Fanon 1986; Hall 1996), I know my *enduring tasks* are to mitigate a precarious subject position of becoming a subject in rather than being solely a subject of my dwellings (Holland 2000;

Phillips 2006). It is unsettling because *address* will always already be conditioned by hauntings and haunting situations (Derrida 1994b).

But within my *archive* there is also evidence of archival impressions that changed its *contents and terms*. I know this much is true. Such impressions *push* me forward today. Its cultural rhetorics, deriving from a locus of enunciation (shadows and *below*) and transpiring as enunciations (pa que sepas/aprendes, entiendes, no te dejes) and material exchanges, is representative of *shadow work*—*work* carried out for me without certainty or guarantee for what it might yield (Arellano, Cortez, and García 2022). Now, I wanted to animate the interplay between that which *calls* and *pushes* me forward above to underscore how I make sense of my *archive* as that in an unending cycle of being made, unmade, and remade by *things* and/or the ideas of some *one*; how by demystifying and extending archival research to the *elsewhere* and *otherwise* it is possible both to approach the body-as-sensory *archive* and to unsettle the idea hauntings and haunting situations are inherent to the haunted; how by *returning* to and *carefully reckoning* with *archives* it is possible to research and search for hope in them (Chapman 1979). What Grandma wanted me to know, what a *learning-unlearning-relearning* path makes clear, is that the racialized and minoritized are not born haunted but rather are made haunted by hauntings and haunting situations. Today, I interpret part of Grandma's statement, "¡No dejaremos que cualquier cosa . . . !" as an awareness of the *working* parts that give structure to and constitute the totality of the *Archive-archives*. And I regard her urgency to pass along some *things*—like an ethic, ethos, and praxis of *thinking, feeling*, and *being-with* the full spectrum of matter (living, nonliving, and nonhuman)—as a clarifying point that it is one thing to be haunted (by the *Archive* that is everywhere), and it is another to rise to a level of obligation and responsibility despite hauntings and in spite of gaining meaning from haunting situations.

What do people *do* despite hauntings and in spite of gaining meaning from haunting situations? It is important for me to highlight that they practice a barrio mentality—hope-struggle—in the throes and face of the *Archive-archives*. By creating a public record vis-à-vis an archival approach and theory of archival impressions, the opportunity is afforded to view the contents of our archives as *stories-so-far*, to excavate the archival impressions that constitute them, to reposition the contents of our archives so that we can position ourselves in relation to them *otherwise*, and to deliberate *an-other* set of choices, options, and obligations and responsibilities (e.g., the initiating of decolonizing archival impressions). This deliberative and intentional human process I am alluding to, because the *Archive-archives* are in part a *human thing* human beings have constructed, is *deep rhetoricity* in action, as Gesa Kirsch and I (García and Kirsch 2022) refer to it. Its epistemic principles are that which help weave and texture the fabric of a framework for the haunted, a framework I unpack at the tail-end of this book. I believe all this provides the prospect to research and search for hope in the archives. If we are going to allow for the possibility that some *things* are beyond the reach and grip of power, then it is imperative that we break from the question "what/what is" and shift to the questions of "how," understood through the particularities and specificities in which *things* unfold (Mao 2014).

An archival approach and theory of archival impressions fill a gap. It proposes that we live amid—landscapes, communities, a barrio, a *homeplace*, a neighborhood, and community of care—and as archives. All spaces upon which (re)writing *takes* (records and/or preserves information about places, subjects, and/or events) and *makes* place are archives. And everyday human work and projects, even those that unsettle the settled-ness of some *things*, can and do indeed function as archival impressions. Now, archives are always already but in one stage and juncture of *stories-so-far* and *possibilities of new stories*. The haunted know this, and the *Archive* takes this for granted. How then do we rise to the level of obligation and responsibility that can alter the *Archives-archives otherwise* and even wor(l)d *an-other* archive? This question is explored throughout, but the point on repositioning the contents of archives already offers one option—the initiating of decolonizing archival impressions. Like Grandma, for such human work and projects to come into fruition, I believe it is important to prioritize not a *doing* to make it out but a *doing* grasped within one's own wounded/wounding spaces and places (Till 2012; Brasher, Alderman, and Inwood 2017) and haunted/haunting *stories-so-far*. "Only if we face" both, Baldwin will have noted, can we see how the full spectrum of matter is "connected," which then provides a pathway to outline and narrativize the problems that wound and haunt (Howard 1963, 89). This, by the way, is one point of *deep rhetoricity*, to deliberate where lessons of ethics, ethos, and praxis are proposed from instead of assuming an automatic equation between a position/ality and disposition.

My goal throughout this book is to work at the intersection between a concession—the necessity to name—and submitting some *things* to *under erasure*. Now, I know the archive, as Spivak (1997) might say, is "not there" and "not that" (xvii). But the archive has made its necessity felt (historicity) and has been sustained by desires and objectives (rhetoricity), even though it is susceptible to erasure. It is the tension, as Derrida (2021) notes, "between memory, fidelity, the preservation of something . . . given to us" that interests me in the context of the *Archive-archives* (6). Do we choose to accept or betray its representation? In an interpretation and reapplication of Stuart Hall's (2001) words, archives are not an "inert museum of dead works, but a 'living archive,' whose construction must be seen as an on-going, never completed project" (89). While he is not arguing that archives arise "out of thin air" (89), he is claiming that they "always stand in an active, dialogic, relation to the questions which the present puts to the past" (92). Each generation will either have accepted or betrayed representations (Fanon 1963). I have chosen to see archives in unending cycles of being made, unmade, and remade, opening them up to some *thing* new, the *possibilities of new stories* that exist at the intersections of *being-and-becoming* and hope-and-struggle.

Selfishly, I wanted Grandma's *work*, emblematic of the *work* comadres carry out for each other, to "[exist] only for me." I did not want anyone to see her shadowy presence and hear her song-music, poetry, and language think and speak in absence and silence (Barthes 1982). But while the above story is mine, it is an archive that we are all in and part of. Grandma must live-on (sur-vie) and flourish beyond my life (Derrida 1994b). Because though she was but an individual making what appears to be single movements, the actions of carrying out *work* is *work in* assemblage with the ethic, ethos, and praxis of comadres near and far. Today, I interpret that *work* as the strategic re-assemblage of *archives*-as-decolonizing archival impressions; in other words, we can both carry out and stand as such impressions. By archival impressions I mean that which reflects both historicity and rhetoricity. The decolonizing archival impressions Grandma initiated are hallmarks of literacies and rhetorics—an a priori ambient energy of *thinking, feeling,* and *being-with*, a worldly act of rhetoricity, and a catalyst of and for action/ing—as human work and projects in play. What would it mean to initiate decolonizing archival impressions? Today, my own sense of ethics, ethos, and praxis derives from such *work*.

While this book is partly about contents of the *Archive-archives*, it is most importantly about exigencies for initiating decolonizing archival impressions across multiple literacy, semiotic, and rhetorical scenes. I invoke "decolonial," first and foremost, to pay homage to what was right in front of me, the *analytic tasks* and *prospective visions* that repositioned the contents of the *Archive-archives* so I could position myself in relation to both *otherwise*. I will define archival and decolonizing archival impressions in sections that follow, but for now the above will suffice. Now, Grandma did not fantasize about making it out of or undoing the *Archive-archives*. Rather, she *worked* to develop an epistemological framework that would for all intents and purposes change the *contents* and *terms* for living itself—the altering of my *archive* and hence the wor(l)ding of *an-other* archive. I begin from my *archive* and what I am calling in this book an *epistemological framework for the haunted* to establish the ethic, ethos, and praxis I bring to archival research.

Can archives feel? Toward a wor(l)ding of a decolonized *Archive* and *an-other* archive? Impossible! Does one ever truly make it out of the "zone[s] of nonbeing" (Fanon 1986, 10) or "deaths-space[s] in the land of the living" (Taussig 1991, 133), where the "half dead" (Anzaldúa 1999, 25) and people at the "company of death" (Maldonado-Torres 2007, 257) are relegated to? No? But perhaps each are just a possibility that has yet to be worked out. The initiating of decolonizing archival impressions are *doings* toward the *possibilities of new stories*. Ojalá! Regardless, I refuse to surrender hope, and thus, I *long* for and struggle to bring about such possibilities. I find comfort in knowing that where there are spaces of modern/colonial and settlerizing writing there are sites of counterwriting that could give structure to and constitute a rhetoric of (re)writing that can be characterized as decolonizing. Ojalá!

All our stories today began before us. The memories are there, frozen and hidden (for some) in the spaces upon which unending cycles of (re)writing *take* and *make* place. A history lesson in life, the archives are the place where we all are and end up. Will we remain then numb to the archives and the ways the *Archive* has impacted our availability of words, address, writing, and worlding activities? Or, will we engage archives rhetorically to question and unsettle the structural, epistemological, rhetorical, and ideological integrity of archives and the words and worlds associated with them, potentially altering and de-linking archives to possibly wor(l)d *an-other* archive? It is my hope that you, my reader, will sit still and in silence as generations before us have done (Adelsen 1970; Patel 2016) to contemplate these questions, and make the *choice* (which is hardly a choice at all but a demand) to continue with me as I re-connect with an *awaiting* deeply rooted in the hope-struggle for the *possibilities of new stories*.

There Is No Making It Out

Introduction
(Decolonizing) Archival Impressions

Since the early 1990s, members of the Modernity/Coloniality Collective (the MCC), whose origins are documented (Grosfoguel 2007; Maldonado-Torres 2007; Mignolo 2011a; Corrigan 2019; García and Baca 2019), advanced a decolonial option. It put human life first over, say, the transformation of the humanities and its disciplines. Members understood, though, that both can be at the service of promoting decolonial and decolonizing agendas. I flesh out their conversation below, but for now, I want to turn to Walter Mignolo (2000b). He argued for the importance of the humanities despite both the university's historical role as *an* assemblage and *in* assemblage with other institutions that advance modern/colonial and settlerizing designs (and notwithstanding the humanities role as a *working part* within universities' normalizing such designs) (see Yang 2017). Indeed, Mignolo (2006, 2011b, 2013) claims a decolonial option can exist within academic structures through scholarship, course work, and mentorship—the humanities can be at the service of decolonial projects as decolonizing programs. And this is supported years later, when Tlostanova and Mignolo (2012) conclude that a decolonial humanities is one that advances a *learning-unlearning-relearning* path. Now, it is imperative that we do not overlook criticism of the MCC by scholars such as Cusicanqui (2012), who argues the small empire these intellectuals have built, buttressed by a new academic canon and structure of hierarchies, "neutralizes the practices of decolonization" (104). But in the same breadth, it is vital we recognize and acknowledge how the lines of critique and appeals for *praxical theorizing actioning* by the MCC lends itself to *an-other* option and invites a politics of wor(l)ding *otherwise* that transcends them.

Some of the above viewpoints are also expressed in Writing and Rhetorical Studies (WRS) though in different terms and for different reasons. Jaime Mejía (1999) presented on how traditional rhetorical understandings are inadequate and appealed for "study of differences among a variety of Latino/a rhetorical situations and cultural contexts" at the Rhetoric Society of America Conference. Though much has changed, twenty-six years later and this outlook still resonates. Mejía (1998, 1999) called for a departure from the field's "west-east" trajectory of literacies and rhetorical studies (15), a movement that he himself contributes to the next year with a piece on the conditions in South Texas and the effects and consequences of power on its people—the haunted. Victor Villanueva (1997, 1999) also advances a historical and sociopolitical view of colonialism and racism, urging that we "break from the colonial mindset and [to] learn from thinkers from our own hemisphere" (1999, 656, 659). Twenty-five years later, the field of rhetoric, both in the context of WRS and communications studies, is still contending with how to translate that effectively. It would be some time before the MCC's project of decoloniality though would be taken up by name in WRS.

The year 2008 marked a transition for WRS. Since then, conversations have centered on decolonizing and delinking WRS from its traditional roots and intellectual heritage in Western European rhetorical and epistemological traditions. Contributions include addressing the tyrannic culture of alphabetic writing and an Aristotelian syndrome that reinvents the cultural *other* (D. Baca 2008, 2009a, 2009b, 2010; Ruiz and Baca 2017); excavating, recovering, recognizing, reinscribing, and re-presenting rhetorics and rhetorical practices in the Americas (D. Baca and Villanueva 2009; García and Baca 2019; Kelly and Black 2018); reclaiming and retheorizing terms and concepts coopted by modern/colonial and settlerizing designs (Medina 2014a; Ruiz and Sanchez 2016; Arellano and Ruiz 2019; Legg 2023); analyzing the unfolding of modern/colonial and settlerizing designs (Dougherty 2016; R. Jackson 2017; King et al. 2015; Soto Vega 2020; You 2023); researching the effects of settler colonial archives and the role of the settler museum (Cushman 2013; Adams-Campbell, Falzetti, and Rivard 2015; García 2019b, 2022a, 2022b; King 2023); field of study, programmatic, pedagogical, and/or linguistic implications

(Clary-Lemon and Grant 2022; Haas 2012; Canagarajah 2022, 2023; Medina 2014b, 2017, 2019; Mukavetz 2018; Na'puti 2020; Tinoco, Eddy, and Gage 2020; Wanzer-Serrano 2018); and even critiques of a decolonial option itself (Cortez and García 2020; García and Cortez 2020). I argue each contribution is like a (decolonizing) archival impression that gives structure to and constitutes a decolonizing archive in WRS, *in* assemblage with other decolonizing archives. This book ultimately is the by-product of a view that a decolonial option can exist within academic structures and that scholarship and the classroom can be at the service of decolonizing agendas.

There Is No Making It Out contributes to the MCC's *analytic* at the intersections of literacy, rhetorical, and (settler) archival research. The idea for a study on archives truly stems from the archival impressions "scholars" across my academic trajectory have had on my *story-so-far*. There is Jacqueline Jones Royster's (2000) *Traces of a Stream*, which invited me, on the one hand, to think critically about literacy as a communicative practice and instrument for sociopolitical thought and action, and on the other, to be mindful of the difference between a rhetorical view that produces essentialist analysis and a view that looks for connections and offers contextualization of general patterns of rhetorical actions within the landscape of literate and rhetorical practices. Gesa Kirsch and Liz Rohan's (2008) *Beyond the Archives* was the first archive-focused text that emphasized for me how archival research can be "life-changing" and how it is possible to bring the "subject to life"—rhetoric and rhetorical research as embodied and a social practice (8). And it was Royster and Kirsch's (2012) *Feminist Rhetorical Practices* that invited me to do that *work* with care. How do we use our *critical imagination* to think about the ways race, class, and gender inform how people walk and see the world? Can we withhold judgement at least temporarily to create a space to *strategically contemplate* embodied experiences? Why do *ideas*, regardless of the outcome, *socially circulate* and in what ways are they shared-in, imported, expanded, and/or disputed in their movement?

There Is No Making It Out contributes to the MCC's *prospective vision* of *learning-unlearning-relearning* through archival research and theory of archival impressions. I have often wondered if a story is a story if it is not archived (broadly conceived). I guess it depends on whether we unsettle the settledness of some *things*. James Baldwin (1972) to Michel Foucault (1978), Pierce Lewis (1979), Anthony Giddens (1981), and Edward Said (1985) saw in landscapes and history alike human work and projects. We live amid archives (re)written in unending cycles by archival impressions. Indeed, a central argument in Doreen Massey's (2005) work is that space and place is always the product of human work and projects, the constructed-ness of *things*, and hence always under construction—*stories-so-far*. But memory is also archival and archivable (Browne 2021, 43). This position would come to inform how I interpreted then Judy Rohrer's (2016) words, "We are the set of stories we tell ourselves, the stories that tell us . . . I am these stories" (189). To be one's stories is to be an archive. Ann Cvetkovich's (2003) *An Archive of Feelings* taught me that archival research is not just done outwardly as we are cultural texts too, "repositories of feelings and emotions, which are encoded not only in the context of the texts themselves but in the practices that surround their production and reception" (7, 181, 208). Kevin Browne's (2013, 2019, 2021) *Tropic Tendencies*, "Moving the Body," and "A Douen Epistemology" encouraged me to think about what is at stake in recovery work in modern/colonial and settlerizing contexts, where to begin excavation when all that is left are materials, and how to conceive of ourselves as *archives* in the making. The latter invites us to deliberate how to reorient ourselves to a people-earth-and-future *longing* (Tuck 2009; Arvin, Tuck, and Morrill 2013), or as Rohrer (2016) might say, the *possibilities of new stories*. These archival impressions have had a lasting impact on me. *There Is No Making It Out* is partly about the affective element (or pesado-ness) of some *things*, once more.

Hauntings and haunting situations do not unfold evenly. What I have learned from others on literacies and rhetorics—Deborah Brandt and Katie Clinton (2002), Ralph Cintron (1997), Juan Guerra (1998), John Duffy (2003, 2007), Brice Nordquist (2017), Nedra Reynolds (2004), Brian Street (1994), Martin Nystrand and John Duffy (2003), Jenny Edbauer (2005), and Rebecca Leonard (2013)—I apply in my approach to hauntings and haunting situations. Hauntings and haunting situations are both global and manifest in local forms and conditions—they are on the move. In a modern/colonial and settlerizing context, I became interested in literacies and rhetorics beyond their traditional characterizations typically framed by the question, what is literacy or rhetoric? À la Mike Baynham and Mastin Prinsloo (2009) and Harvey Graff (1979), I began to wonder what are the *goings-on* of haunted/haunting literacies and rhetorics? How are they shaping reality? I conceived of literacies and rhetorics once more as this a priori ambient energy of *thinking*, *feeling*, and *being-with*, a worldly act of rhetoricity, and a catalyst of and for action/ing through words and ideas. But while I believe hauntings are a *structure of feeling* (á la Williams) that live deep within our bones (A. Gordon 2008; Williams 1977), I know we are all constituted differently, and thus some experience the privilege of not having to know. We can chalk this up to how we come to inherit and embody what Kitarō Nishida (1998), Fanon (1986), and Susan Bordo (1993) might refer to as historical bodies, and/or we can attribute it to the ways everyday stories, rhetorics of the everyday life, and everyday literacy practices have structural underpinnings and material consequences, as Ralph Cintron (1997), Judy Rohrer (2016), Sarah Pink (2012), Alastair Pennycook (2010), and others discuss. Either way, I argue we cannot come to terms with hauntings and haunting situations without coming to terms with literacies, images-signs-sounds, and rhetorics.

I have often wondered too if archival work can amount to more than just more accounting. I hope so, because I neither engage in archival research nor register hauntings for the sake of it. What if all questions then, regarding knowing and being, started with hauntings and haunting situations? First, it would invite us to conceive of a constellating concept—an archive not in the proper name of a repository that signs "at once the commencement and the commandment" (Derrida 1995, 9), but those that we live amid marked by their (re)writing. Second, it would allow us to see how we are all in and part of archives in the making. This is when I started to think about a macro-level archive, a modern/colonial and settlerizing archive, or the *Archive*, whose presence is unavoidable. Notwithstanding the theoretical trap—"power is everywhere" (Foucault 1978, 93)—questions surfaced from which this study flows: What are the literacies, images-signs-sounds, and rhetorics of the *Archive*? What constitutes an archival impression? When, where, how, and why do archival impressions happen? Who is responsible for maintaining the *Archive* in the present? Can archival impressions *otherwise* unsettle the settled-ness of the *Archive*? Such lines of inquiry ground the rhetorical nature of this book and inform its most central sites of analyses—the archival impressions that keep the *Archive* in an unending process of *being-and-becoming*. Out of these questions others materialized. If we are all in and part of the *Archive*, does that mean we too are *archives* and archival impressions making the *Archive*? If the *Archive* is a haunted/haunting *story-so-far*, what does that say about our own?

It is important to extend archival research to the *elsewhere* and *otherwise*. Because we too are an *archive*. So a micro- and meso-level archive, or our *stories-so-far* as an *archive*. The line of rhetorical questions above extends to *archives* as well. In investigating those questions in the second half of this book, I remain convinced and thus submit here that we are constituted by and are the accumulation of archival impressions, that which also keeps our *archives* in an unending process of *being-and-becoming*. But if the *Archive* is a haunted/haunting *story-so-far*, and we are all in and part of it, that means that our *archives* are contaminated too. This realization gives way to a premise that forms an essential focus of this book. How do we reposition the contents of the *Archive-archives* so that we can position ourselves in relation to both *otherwise*? I have found that the meaning of researching and searching for hope in the *Archive-archives* can be extrapolated from such *doings*. For the *Archive-archives* there is a demand for some *thing* else, a central theme of this book, a public record of its contents. It can provide us with insights into what constitutes them. And with our capacity to have knowledge of the inner workings of the *Archive-archives* is an opportunity not to make it out but, under certain conditions, to alter both and wor(l)d *an-other* archive. An archival approach affords the opportunity thus to view contents as *stories-so-far*, subject to change, in the making. That would re-situate agency within the cultural archives of the "You" and "We," that "We" indeed can initiate archival impressions *otherwise*. Will "We" ever have shared that in common, a hope for and the struggle toward *possibilities of new stories* vis-à-vis the initiating of decolonizing archival impressions into *stories-so-far*?

There Is No Making It Out is first and foremost then an archive of haunted/haunting *stories-so-far*. My debt to archives, archival impressions, and hauntings is bookmarked throughout, a statement on how I regard my starting points in inquiries of *stories-so-far* and the *possibilities of new stories*. It is an excavation project of many kinds of cultural texts that reflects the hope-struggle to research and search for hope in the *Archive-archives*. By archival impressions, I mean the accumulation of entries of writing, impressed and initiated by some *thing* or some *one* that bears on and enduringly acts upon the *Archive-archives*—the pesado-ness of deposits, signatures, traces marks or absent presences, sedimentations and/or historical layering engraved within and giving form to the palimsestic narratives of *stories-so-far*. At the macro level, decolonizing archival impressions—entries of counter-writing impressed and initiated by some *one* meant to unsettle the settled-ness of *things* and bring about decolonizing agendas that can alter the *Archive-archives* and wor(l)d *an-other* archive—will mean the unsettling, decolonizing, and amending of the lies, contradictions, myths, narcissism, cynicism, denialisms, and sickness-disease of the *Archive* and its actor-agents who initiate impressions that give structure to and constitute it. At the micro and meso level, decolonizing archival impressions means unsettling the settled-ness of Self and ways of relationing within the full spectrum of matter (living, nonliving, and nonhuman). *There Is No Making It Out* argues we can unsettle the *Archive-archives* through an archival approach and by initiating decolonizing archival impressions.

There Is No Making It Out is an archive of knowledges, understandings, feelings, and doings. In an amendment of Cvetkovich's (2003) *archive of feeling*, the additions announce themselves throughout this archive of a book. In other words, each chapter functions both as an impression and entry submitted into this book that is an archive. Guiding this book are the many archival impressions I remain *thinking, feeling*, and *being-with*, that which reflect at least partially the intellectual universe of thought I work from. To underscore that fact, while also mitigating the risk of conflation or erasure of different projects, I trace and weave together sometimes seemingly irreconcilable and contradictory intellectual conversations below, but not as some academic exercise in reviewing discourse but to provide a window into the threads of hope-struggle for which are the foundations of this archive I call *There Is No Making It Out*. Now, any shortcomings in interpretations, groupings, and/or associations are solely mine. Still, I remain of the mind that no one theory can do everything for me. As I do in life today, I surround myself with those who will inspire me to rise to a level of obligation and responsibility that can bring about change. As Said (1983) points out, we "borrow," which I showcase below for the purpose of situating decolonizing archival impressions *in* assemblage, highlighting converges rather than fixating solely on divergences. Each heading is to be read as an archival impression.

A Rehabilitated Humanity and Society

Many academics are connected by a hope that it is possible to unsettle the settled-ness of some *things*. While hauntology is attributed to one, really it is a "borrowed" concept that underscores the inability to make it out of power (or the *Archive*) that traffics in the normative and the capacity to *do* both in ways that "it" will feel and in ways that can wor(l)d some *thing* else. Fanon understood that greatly.

My introduction to the intellectual universe of decolonial thought I prescribe to started with Fanon. And thus, I begin with him. Based on my readings and interpretations, Fanon's (1963) *analytic* amends decolonization in *The Wretched of the Earth*. He conceived of "it" as a coercive and seductive system, superstructure, and/or machine that has the past, present, and future as its ends; it has no borders or boundaries and traffics in the normative. Fanon understood that colonization was not an isolated egregious *event* but an ongoing and organizing structuring principle of settlerizing encounters, interactions, and engagements. He saw in "it" an *epistemic system* (of ideas, images, and ends), a *hegemonic architecture* of *contents* and *terms*, the (epistemological) regime of modernity (see A. Gordon 2008, 10), and the modern/colonial and settlerizing designs of a 500-year-old *Archive*. Though "it" manifested in local forms and conditions, Fanon registered "it" as a colonization that functioned as an archival impression within a colonial history and world—the colonial problem that orders the colonial world. He understood that near and far such impressions—desires of and for domination, management, and control—ensure an *Archive* in the making. For Fanon, it was vital thus to unsettle its lies, contradictions, inventions, myths, narcissism, cynicism, denialism, and violence (supposedly) cloaked and hidden by the haunted/haunting literacies, images-signs-sounds, and rhetorics of salvation, civilization, progress, and development (e.g., modernity). And therein emerges one of his most central arguments: that we must *clinically search out-excavate* and *mercilessly* till out from all lands and minds its *seeds-germs* of *decay* (Fanon 1963, 2004). Such an appeal invites and lends itself to an archival approach and theory of archival impressions. If archives are a space where knowledge is potentially made, it can be at the same time a site where knowledge is possibly unmade.

The intellectual universe of decolonial thought I prescribe to states dignity is tied to land and that human dignity needs rehabilitation. Fanon (1963, 1986) argued that humanity brings society into being. That in others, as archives and archival impressions, we can bring about *an-other* archive. His *cries* for a rehabilitated archive, without the *good will* of or desire to mirror the current haunted/haunting one, can be heard in both *The Wretched of the Earth* and *Black Skin, White Masks*. Fanon's *prospective vision* amends decolonization. He understood that colonization contaminated knowledge and relationing and that modernity gained currency at the epistemological level. That made Eurocentrism an epistemic and aesthetic issue too (see Mignolo and Walsh 2018, 125). For Fanon it was vital thus to unsettle the whole structure of humanity and society contaminated by the haunted/haunting literacies, images-signs-sounds, and rhetorics of saviors destined to both save *others* from themselves and lead the world in the *right* direction. An *awakening*, which he so often linked to an explosion, extrication, and/or disalienation to-come, was demanded of settlers and the colonized alike. While prior efforts had been made to create *an-other* archive, for Fanon, they remained predicated on reductive, dichotomous, and/or oppositional structures. And that is why he calls for the rehabilitation of *all* of humanity. If hate calls to be cultivated and brought into being, Fanon claimed the same goes for *an-other* humanity and society. I interpret that call as the appeal to initiate decolonizing archival impressions.

Thinking, Feeling, and Being-with Others

I understand that within the intellectual universe of decolonial thought I prescribe to even that which was meant to unsettle the settled can benefit from hauntings as a starting point (see Ballif 2014; Fukushima 2019; Lueck 2021; Hanchey 2023). It is for that reason I turn to Derrida (1994b), Toni Morrison (1987), and Avery Gordon (2008), who each *return* to and *carefully reckon* with hauntings, inheritances, and dwellings as language, rhetoric, corporeal exercises of address, and categories of analysis. *Analytic tasks* and *prospective visions* flow out from each conversation.

Humanity is at stake. Derrida's (1994b) *analytic* in *Specters of Marx* amends the meaning of hauntings, inheritances, and dwellings. He understood the "old" and "modern" world are but a constellation of hegemonies, hauntings, and ghosts—an archive. Hegemony, a power necessitated by an ontological system (of ideas, images, and ends) and structure of power, is at least partially constituted by the metaphysics of the subject. For Derrida it is vital then to *return* to and introduce hauntings and ghosts to all facets of life (hauntology) to unsettle their proper, totalizing, and juridical-normative-moral *contents* and *terms*—*contents* and *terms* that ensure an *Archive* in the making. For him, if forgetting and conjuration are essential to hegemony then a remembering that yokes and calls forth hauntings and ghosts is most crucial for a humanity at stake. Hauntology, which I interpret as a decolonizing archival impression, becomes the foundation for inviting a "scholar" *otherwise* to get caught up in a politics of hauntings, inheritances, and dwellings *otherwise* vis-à-vis an archival approach.

Hauntings, inheritances, and dwellings demand a "scholar" unlike the "traditional" or "learned" scholar whose spectatorship adheres to distinctions (the un/real, non/living, and non/being). Derrida's (1994b) *prospective vision* amends the idea of learning how to live. Like other *things* he situates the idea in "memory, fidelity, the preservation of something" to initiate a "break" (Derrida 2021, 6). Derrida (1994b) understands that the question couched in the idea comes down to a *choice* of getting caught up in a world that is a massive gravesite—an archive of wreckage. Though suspended between an injunction and disjunction, *careful reckonings* reflect the possibility to think and learn how to address oneself to hauntings, inheritances, and dwellings. For Derrida it is vital to unsettle the disposition of the "intellectual," then to deconstruct and restructure responsibility in relation to the (secret) meaning of inheritances. We are heirs to and archival impressions adding to an *Archive*. But he does not stop there. Derrida anticipates the demand for an *enduring task* and thus reminds us that the readability of any one *thing* is never a given, but rather, it is always already betraying translation and defying interpretation. Because some *things* must remain at *work*.

Hauntings and ghosts can have a powerful presence in the lives of the living. Though absent presences (for some), they themselves are the trace marks of archival impressions. In *Beloved*, Sethe speaks of some *thing* more haunting than a haunted house that was 124 Bluestone Road. Morrison's (1987) *analytic* in *Beloved* amends the senses to the dearly beloved and a beloved *thing* but secret company. She understands humanity is an archive constellated by the engravings of deposits, signatures, sedimentations, and/or historical layering—Slavery, Mr. Death, (a livable) Life. They give form to *palimpsestic narratives*, where the past shapes the present and touches the future (also see A. García 2004). For Morrison it is vital to draw attention to the weight (or what I call the pesado-ness) of the beloved implanted with *the jungle* and fear of nothingness and self-worth. And to speak to the pedagogical agenda underscoring (modern/colonial) haunted/haunting situations: "but school teacher beat him . . . to show him that definitions belonged to the definers—not the defined" (363). But for Morrison, hauntings, inheritances, and dwellings involve and extend well beyond one Self, because we are all in and part of the haunted/haunting *stories-so-far*. They have demands of all. Archives thus are a poetic metaphor for a process of remembering, unsettling, and *wor(l)ding* otherwise.

A politics of hauntings, inheritances, and dwellings is demanded. Morrison's (1987) *prospective vision* amends an "undecipherable language" (381). Beloved: the disremembered, unaccounted, unclaimed, unidentified, forgotten, and the secret story not to be passed on. Beloved, traces of a mark that scatters. Beloved, the *knowing the things behind the things* (74). Morrison understands that the past is hardly over and done with and that the nonliving, like memory, seldom leaves us—history and memory after all can function as a window into or a prism through which to see how hauntings and haunting situations continue to form the basis of humanity. *Returns* can hurt, *careful reckonings* can be painful, and *enduring tasks* always already ensure some *things* remain at *work*. For Morrison, though, to begin this *work* in earnest it is vital to unsettle distinctions (the un/real, non/living, non/being). Via Sethe and her daughter, Denver, an invitation for healing is extended through a politics of hauntings, inheritances, and dwellings. Beloved—an awaiting, for "some kind of tomorrow," the space and place of spectrality, im/possibilities, and *stories-so-far* and the *possibilities of new stories* (521).

Hauntings and ghosts are part of the social world. In *Ghostly Matters* Avery Gordon's (2008) *analytic* amends the meaning of Raymond Williams's (1977) *structures of feeling*. She understands that the historical materialism of hauntings and ghosts are present in the making of histories, subjectivities, and social relations of power—and that *structures of feelings (and thought)* are embedded in both. They conjure up but are also the sign that organizing systems of power continue to *take* and *make* place: countervailing systems of value and difference, complex systems of permissions and prohibitions, and deterministic systems of power and repressions-exclusions; wor(l)ding aspirations materializing. Hauntings and ghosts have desires: in/actions. For Gordon it is vital then to create a vocabulary that would underscore an *epistemology for the living* that could unsettle conditions producing the *nastiness* that belongs to our *stories-so-far*. To be haunted, according to Gordon, means to be tied to a constellation of self/selves, histories, subjectivities, and social lives—the archives. A healing and wor(l)ding—the acknowledgment that wording is human work and a project that has worlding capacities (see Ahmed 2012, 2017; Haraway 2008, 2016b)—*otherwise* begins here, which I interpret as a call for initiating new (decolonizing) archival impressions.

Hauntings and ghosts have desires. Gordon's (2008) *prospective vision* amends the meaning of conjuration through an interplay between "calling out" what produces absences and silences and "calling up" *careful reckonings*. She understands that we are all in this story of *nastiness* and that something ought to be done by all, a "Weism" that appeals for, I believe, the initiating of decolonizing archival impressions into archives in the making. For Gordon it is vital to *return* to and *carefully reckon* with the "shadows of our selves and our society" through hauntings and ghosts because they unsettle familiarity, rationality, control, and distinctions (134). The *choice* to be haunted, according to Gordon, speaks to an effort to heal and engage in wor(l)ding *otherwise*. But to imagine this possibility we must have a politics of hauntings, inheritances, and dwellings, which invites and lends itself to an archival approach and theory of archival impressions. Corporeal exercises of address can yield no guarantees. Still, an ethic, ethos, and praxis of *thinking, feeling,* and *being-with* others *otherwise* awaits our invention and address (broadly conceived).

A Learning-Unlearning-Relearning Path

My academic path toward a decolonial option began with Fanon (1963), Césaire (2001), and Memmi (1991). Then, it included the MCC. Now, it is important for me to preface that I am not *Latin American*. I do not live in *Latin America*. Yet, I heed the call by the MCC to conceive of Latin America not as a continent but as a prismatic paradigm through which to see both the logic of coloniality refracted through the rhetorics of modernity and the emergence of a Western epistemic genealogy of intellectual thought. I take seriously thus the appeal that one does not have to identify or reside in a particular place to engage with the locus of enunciation advanced by the MCC. Perhaps for no other reason do they argue that what it means to be ethically committed to decolonizing agendas cannot be determined by identity or geography but rather must be guided by the questions of *who*, *where*, *why*, *how*, and *for* (Castro-Gómez 2007; Escobar 2007; Mignolo 2013; Mignolo and Walsh 2018; Quijano 2007; Quijano and Wallerstein 1992; Tlostanova 2017b). These rhetorical questions unsettle the idea of a decolonial master, a privileged master plan, and master-like universals. I spend more time in this section for two reasons. First, to trace the MCC's theses, which remain relatively new to WRS. Second, my argument for an archival approach that materializes the *Archive* and theory of archival impressions (that keeps it in an unending cycle of being made, unmade, and remade) rests on several of their propositions.

The MCC's lynchpin argument is that the world is organized, connected, and haunted by the unavoidable presence of some *things*. This is an important proposition, whether or not there is consensus. The MCC are not proposing that power unfolds evenly; they are claiming that though each local history shares an approximation to colonial and imperial differences differently, none can avoid the presence and reach of modern/colonial and settlerizing designs and technologies (Mignolo 2007, 474). *Americanity*, *coloniality*, and the *modern/colonial world system* (hereafter the frame of modernity/coloniality) are some of those designs and technologies, which emerge as categories of analysis within a spatial-temporal break from eighteenth-century Europe and shift to the fifteenth- and sixteenth-century Americas. Though not synonyms, they belong to the same historical setting, the Americas, and context—the *idea of the Americas*. The significance of this break and shift cannot be overstated. By returning to a settler colonialism 500 years ago and the *idea of the Americas*, the MCC are able, first, to establish a turning and nexus point in world history at the start of the modern world; second, excavate from a glossed-over history, the first stage of modernity and its darker sides—the ways coloniality is constitutive of modernity, underscoring the entanglement between a rhetoric of modernity and logic of coloniality; and third, argue some *things* and the ideas, images-signs-sounds, and ends of some *one* have remained in land, memory, knowledge, and relation-ing long after they have passed—an epistemological force (Mignolo 2007, 476; 2018, 366). The MCC fill a gap thus by critically attending to the foundational designs of—the local-regional histories of designs and technologies that belong to the logic of coloniality and crooked rhetorics of modernity (the frame of modernity/coloniality)—and *structure of feelings and thoughts* (an amendment to Williams's original phrasing) embedded in the Western monocentric project (Mignolo and Walsh 2018, 107–108). Such an intervention underscores a historical foundation of modernity and Western civilization as much as it invites scholars to approach the sixteenth-century Americas as the backdrop for the materialization of some *thing*.

Origin stories are no doubt contested sites. Still, it is difficult to deny a turning and nexus point in world history with the ~~discovery~~ invention of the Americas (see O'Gorman 1961). For the purposes of underscoring the signficance of an archival approach and a theory of archival impressions, it is important to trace the propositions of the MCC further. Enrique Dussel (1995) and Aníbal Quijano and Immanuel Wallerstein (1992) amend the meaning of Western modernity. Conquest and a structure, logic, and pattern of power is its constitutive side. A new model of a world system of power (supposedly) no longer reliant on historical colonialism was configured out of the Americas. The ~~discovery~~ invention-creation of the Americas, they argued at the onset of their essay, was the "constitutive act of the modern world-system" (549). As Quijano and Wallerstein appeal for a seeing, feeling, and listening to the "sounds ... images ... symbols ... utopias" of the Americas it is to underscore the ways power as an epistemic and aesthetic issue gives way to hauntings and haunting situations too (556). The destruction (wreckage), technologies (the *idea*), inventions of worldviews and institutions (spatial-temporal colonial difference, colonization of space-time, Western imperialism), and power differentials—internally realized and globally pursued—contaminated knowledge and impaired our relations with space and place, time, land, and others. For the MCC it is vital to excavate Europe's march toward hegemony out of the project of modernity. Because it partly brings nuance to how the West acquired an epistemological hegemony and the process of building the modern/colonial imaginary (Escobar 2007; Grosfoguel 2013; Mignolo 2007; Quijano 2000; Quijano and Wallerstein 1992; Wolfe 2006). And the excavation work for them begins in the Americas, a site both of writing and for a superstructure of written record that established a textual death space.

The MCC argue that Europe becomes hegemonic Europe partly because power is an epistemic and aesthetic campaign. The *end* is to hoard and produce information-as-facts in excess vis-à-vis the production of knowledge. The *end* is a war to dominate information—the enunciated establishes the *contents of the conversation* while the enunciation polices the *terms of the conversation*—and manage and control mediums of circulation fought on the battlefields of ideas (Man), images (Human), and ends (Rights-to) (Mignolo and Walsh 2018, 143–44; Roy 2014, 30; Baldwin quoted in Kenan 2011, 93). According to the MCC, a modern/colonial and settlerizing (an amendment to original phrasing) imaginary is founded on the *idea* (of the Americas, *humanitas*/anthropoi, race, epistemic and ontological differences, race/labor) shared-in through epistemic racism, and expanded-disputed by the *ends* to dominate, manage, and control. Emphasizing the epistemic and aesthetic issues of Eurocentrism, Mignolo and Catherine Walsh (2018) argue that a "hegemonic architecture of knowledge [*contents of the conversation*] and the principles, assumptions, and rules of knowing [*terms of the conversation*]" must be unsettled (212). W/H questions—*where, who, what, how*—guide what I refer to here on out as a *decolonial analytic* (also see Veracini 2010, 2011):

- Where is *coloniality* and modern/colonial and settlerizing designs (my addition)?
- Who are the affective channels of rhetorical transmission for coloniality and designs?
- What do the enunciations and material exchanges of knowing subjects entail?
- How do institutions (broadly conceived) comprise a locus of enunciation for knowing subjects (see Mignolo 2011a, 189)?

There is consensus beyond the MCC and among scholars from Linda Smith (1999, 2) to Lewis Gordon (2007, 123, 137) that the power to produce knowledge and define what counts as truth lies at the core of colonial projects and is what allows *ideas* to *appear* and *become* consequential. A premise takes shape about a *hegemonic architecture* of knowledge (hereafter *hegemonic architecture*), which is the source of inspiration for this book's emphasis on literacy, rhetorical, and (settler) archival research. Though power does not unfold evenly, we cannot come to terms with modern/colonial and settlerizing designs without coming to terms with enunciations, enunciators, language-discourse, and institutions—a *semiotic apparatus of enunciations* (see Mignolo 2009). Put another way, epistemological hegemony is constituted, ideologies are carried over, and hegemony is maintained by literacies, images-signs-sounds, and rhetorics. A *decolonial analytic* wagers that a *hegemonic architecture* is tied to language and rhetorically sold-purchased by an *association of social interests* that is at least 500 years old (Quijano 2007, 168).

Literacies, images-signs-sounds, and rhetorics play a role in a modern/colonial and settlerizing imaginary and *hegemonic architecture*. These economies are present, though not named, in Dussel's (1995) and Quijano's (2000, 2007) discussions of a paradigm of modern/rational knowledge. They are consubstantial in the colonization of the imagination and to the strategy of systematic repression, expropriation, excess, and erasure. Mignolo (1989, 1992, 1994, 2003) names the three economies more explicitly. His work on a Renaissance and Spanish philosophy of language, tyrannic culture of alphabetic writing, and cultural literacy in the spread and expansion of a 500-year-old logic, (epistemic) system (of ideas, images, and ends), and *hegemonic architecture* is one example. Mignolo argues that as contents and sign carriers they have a role within modern/colonial situations chiefly shaped by *semiotic interactions* and its *cultural productions*. They aided in the invention of a philosophical, hierarchal, and pedagogical apparatus by a misanthropic skeptic whose *ends* are domination, management, and control. An *epistemic system* (of ideas, images, and ends) I refer to as "settler" emerges (Wolfe 2006; Mignolo 2011c; Arvin et al. 2013; Tlostanova 2017b; Yang 2017; Mignolo and Walsh 2018).

How a local-regional system-totality gained universality points to advantageous contents and practices surrounding the reception-production of a *hegemonic architecture*. Santiago Castro-Gomez (2005, 2007), Ramón Grosfoguel (2007, 2013), and Mignolo (2009, 2013) are alert to inventive-discursive contents implanted in theologically and secularly structured terms such as Being and Rights. An epistemology or hubris of the zero point-provenance (Kruks 1995)—observers observing from a nonsituated locus—is a focus. Because from here a pretended universality of a particular ethnie generating knowledge out of a fabricated privileged place of enunciation is mapped on a *Chain of Being* model (Lovejoy 1933). Such provincial pretenses reared a haunting design: the West is the guiding light destined to bring out the world's salvation, progress, and development as the center of space and present of time (see Mignolo 2011a). Ultimately, such a *structure of feeling and thought* produced a dualistic perspective and evolutionary continuum that eliminated coevolutionary views, producing absences, silences, and *ideas* of dispensability (Arvin, Tuck, and Morrill 2013; Bergland 2000; Escobar 2007; Quijano 2000a, 2000b, 2007; Trouillot 1995; Tuck and Yang 2012; Castro-Gomez 2007).

The zero point is constituted by egos (*conquiro*, *extermino*, and *cogito*) that reveal a colonial force by misanthropic skeptics (Grosfoguel 2007, 2013). An *epistemic system* is mapped out from here. Literacies, images-signs-sounds, and rhetorics are not overtly named in Nelson Maldonado-Torres (2007), María Lugones (2008), or other works of the MCC, but they cannot be ignored in a racial imaginary that invented and grafted new social-and-geocultural identities on a *Chain of Being* model (also see Veracini 2011). It situated the West as peak Man-Human while identifying *othered* people and lands as deficient in, without, and/or lacking, authorizing the Rights-to by Man-Human, ultimately satisfying a desire and objective to belong-to lands. *Thingification* (see Césaire 2001), and the invention of epistemic (less knowing) and ontological difference (less being), is the mark of *coloniality of being* (racialization, domination, exploitation, dispensability) en/gendering a nonbeing. This haunting design codified relations of domination as biological and natural, which engineered a technology of domination/exploitation around race/labor (Dussel 1995; Lugones 2010; Quijano 2000a, 2000b, 2007; Yancy 2008). What a focus on literacies, images-signs-sounds, and rhetorics underscores is how ontology is constituted by an epistemology 500 years in the making.

The MCC thus returns to the Americas and *Americanity* for a reason. It is to contend with a settler colonialism and modern/colonial and settlerizing imaginary that established a logic of domination, management, and control as well as a *modern/colonial world system* that fused a "new" through the "old" underwritten by a *hegemonic architecture* and *epistemic system* (of ideas, images, and ends). *Americanity* is a representation of the old. For Quijano and Wallerstein (1992), they understand *Americanity* as the establishment of new world views: the haunting design land was waiting to be discovered, owned, and transformed into "resources" by divine and natural right, and that *others* were dispensable or exploitable by divine and natural design. *Americanity* introduced new institutions, *coloniality* being the creation of hierarchal and rule-based organizations of relations between peoples and states, while the *modern/colonial world system* the superego of nation-states. For Quijano and Wallerstein, modernity nor the Western monocentric project can be conceived without the Americas as an ideological model and *Americanity* the ideological overlay to a new global logic and system of cultural power: *coloniality*, a *modern/colonial world system*, and a capitalist world-economy (and its aesthetics).

Out of *Americanity* came a structural logic that some may not be able to (supposedly) see but that underlies Western civilization, pan-global empires, and Eurocentrism. *Coloniality* has endured even as power is disputed because an *association of social interests* ensures its parts rearticulate into an adapted structure of power (Quijano 2000a, 2000b, 2007). Domination, management, and control over domains of life are its *ends* (Mignolo 2007). *Coloniality's* modus operandi, according to the MCC, are the following: labor, resources, and products (capitalist enterprise); sex, resources, and products (bourgeois family); authority, institutions, and violence (nation-state); intersubjectivity, knowledge, and communication (Eurocentrism). Put another way, these *things*, whether we refer to it as a monster, computer, *Archive*, or four-headed machine—with legs, the projects of territorial (land-nature/resources) and epistemological (race/labor-capitalism) (ap/ex)propriation—is "the control of labor and subjectivity, the practices and policies of genocide and enslavement, the pillage of life and land, and the denials and structures of knowledge, humanity, spirituality, and cosmo-existence" (Mignolo and Walsh, 2018, 16). This evidences once more how Eurocentrism is an epistemic and aesthetic issue partly because power is an epistemological, ideological, and rhetorical war on information. *Coloniality* is the force within a global-totalistic project of integration and racial homogenization that distinguishes Eurocentrism from other forms of domination in the history of the world.

There is no *modern/colonial world system* without *Americanity*. It is the union between the "old/modern" colonial logics working in and through crooked rhetorics and narratives of modernity. For the MCC, modernity has a politics as the hegemonic narrative of Western civilization and Eurocentrism. For Dussel (1995) and Mignolo (2005), one focus of a *decolonial analytic* thus is the invention of the Americas (e.g., *the idea*). From here, a myth of modernity presents, justifies, and rationalizes an *idea* of a universal right to victimize and sacrifice in the name of civilizing and human progress. It paints an organicist image of society with Western Europe as the brain and Western Europeans its far-reaching extremities (Quijano 2007). A myth of modernity submits a macro-historical subject whose rhetoric is an omnipotence of direction and finality. It is self-serving for an *association of social interests* to the extent that epistemology institutes ontology to fabricate pristine and unilinear logics of development positioning the West as the center of space and present of time (Grosfoguel 2007, 2013; Mignolo 2011a; Mignolo and Walsh 2018; Quijano and Wallerstein 1992; Fabian 2014).

Mutated modalities (Christianity, Secularism, Modernity, Market designs) underscore the expression, modern colonialism–colonial modernities, or global modernities-colonialities. The MCC understands they are theologically and secularly structured. And that is why the *decolonial analytic* begins in and with the Americas and *Americanity*. There, a spatial colonial difference and colonization of space based on the idea of race and racial epistemologies was the by-product of religious epistemic racism and a pursuit of power. It provided territorial (land-nature/resource) and epistemological (race/labor) projects of (ap/ex)propriation for capitalism to thrive even as power was disputed. Theo-politics, for the MCC, would become the bedrock of a secular epistemology and hubris of the zero point as well as a temporal colonial difference and colonization of time. Imperialism did not *replace* but mutated the translation of theo-politics utilizing the framework of a people deficient in, without, and/or lacking in pursuit of power. Theo-and-ego politics is an organizing framework, the MCC argue, that needs to be decolonized (Dussel 1995; Grosfoguel 2013; Mignolo 2006, 2008, 2011a). I argue that the claim of global modernities-colonialities nods to the materializing of a *thing* that for documentary purposes was necessary to help explain, rationalize, and justify the operation of a colonial matrix—coloniality of knowledge, being, nature, power—and its designs and technologies as the price for civilizing and human progress.

Before I transition to the *prospective vision*, it is important for me to recognize and acknowledge why I trace the MCC's (debatable) theses and propositions. I see them as archivists narrativizing the skeletal system of what I call the *Archive* with each return to the Americas and *Americanity*. Quijano and Wallerstein (1992) write, "Americanity has always been, and remains to this day, an essential element in what we mean by 'modernity'" (549). Dussel (1995) echoes, "Modernity appears when Europe organizes the initial world-system and places itself at the center of world history" (9-10). I argue that the MCC's break, shift, and categories of analysis appeal to scholars to approach the Americas as the backdrop for a site of writing and the materialization of a superstructure of written record I refer to as the *Archive*. That is to say, the archival record of a *modern/colonial world system* began in the Americas when a settler colonialism at the start of the modern world established some *things*, when superstructures of written records became necessary for documentary purposes, and when *designs* and technologies (which function much like an archive too) required an explanation, rationalization, and justification for its projects of territorial and epistemological expropriation. The *Archive* allows us thus to nuance our understanding of the power of the *idea*, a colonial matrix of power, and Western Imperialism, all of which are a prism through which to see the meeting-up of an *association of social interests* elsewhere and otherwise sharing in, importing, expanding, and/or disputing the *Archive*'s designs and technologies. Overall, the *Archive*'s function is regulative, with smaller archives elsewhere and otherwise both operating as its means to *appear, become,* and remain consequential and functioning to create textual death spaces.

If literacies, images-signs-sounds, and rhetorics were used to fashion a modern/colonial and settlerizing world, by the same token they can be utilized to wor(l)d *otherwise*. The MCC's *prospective vision* amends the *analytic* process of delinking and decolonizing the rhetoric of modernity from the logic of coloniality. Because Quijano (2007) understands epistemic extrication from a modern/colonial praxis of thinking, feeling, and being is crucial too. Quijano's understanding is vital for Tlostanova and Mignolo's (2012) *learning-unlearning-relearning* path (epistemological decolonization), comprised of denaturalizing imposed cultural and thinking programs and re-existing for new inter-epistemic/cultural communication (epistemic reconstitution). According to Escobar (2007, 2020), Lugones (1987), and Mignolo (2000a, 2007, 2011a), the goal is *pluriversality*: the coexistence and co-invention of worlds, doxas, and geo-and-body politics of knowledge and understanding. Of course, this is predicated on the *longing* expressed by the Zapatistas (EZLN 1997): "En el mundo que queremos nosotros caben todos" (89). A decolonial *prospective vision*, overall, is about changing the *contents* and *terms* of *thinking, feeling*, and *being-with* others (Mignolo and Walsh 2018; Quijano 2007; Tlostanova 2017a, 2017b).

    A decolonial *prospective vision* demands epistemic disobedience. Sylvia Wynter (2007) understands that definitions and meaning of human/being have been contaminated by universal concepts (also see McKittrick 2015). For her it is vital then to unsettle the referent of human and being and approach both rather as a praxis. This is why Mignolo and Walsh (2018) advance a praxis of *thinking, feeling*, and *being-with*, which can unfold as Maldonado-Torres's (2007) restoration of the logics of the gift through a decolonial politics of *receptive generosity*. It can also unfold as Lugones's (1987) cross-cultural/racial and *playful world-traveling*. Here traveling is not a world view, but the *plurality of self/selves* as playful-creative traveler between incomplete yet visionary worlds where a deep "loving way of being and living [-with others]" is possible (3). This kind of traveling unsettles the pretext of laws of *what* and *who* can be *in-common* and invites life questions (how to hold some *things*, like a value [to live in-common, welcome, and love-another], in common) to be pursued in a wor(l)ding *otherwise*, not on the basis of identity or identification but in the *non-name of all* (Acosta 2012). Within the MCC's *prospective vision*, I couch the contributions of my archival approach and the significance of a theory of archival impressions in a series of [H] questions initiated by Escobar (2020): "How can we construct the archive of this 'history book,' bearing in mind the full spectrum of beings—human and nonhuman—who inhabit it"? (58). In other words, "How can we best construct the archive," by which he means the archive of decolonial thinking, feeling, and doing, "of this new formation" (63, 84)?

(Decolonizing)—Archives and Archival Impressions

It is a risk to rest the idea of the *Archive* on the MCC's theses and proposition. But even so, an archival approach and theory of archival impressions already proves its values to scholars who contemplate: How do we contend with a settler colonialism and the *idea of the Americas* at the turning point in world history that established the first stage of modernity and its darker sides? How can we unsettle modern/colonial and settlerizing amnesia? How do we make sense of some *things* that continue to traffic in the normative? What options exist that we could meaningfully and usefully describe as decolonizing? In the chapters for the first section, I aim to fill a gap in WRS by shinning a light on the underbelly of the *Archive* and excavating from its architecture imaginaries, logics, designs, systems, technologies, and palimpsestic narratives of domination, management, and control that function as archival impressions. While a geo-political US-based analysis is limiting, it will suffice both for the point I am making about the *Archive* and the appeal for an archival approach and theory of archival impressions. It is not meant to reflect *the* story or the *whole* story. It is one, despite the presence of a theoretical trap—"power is everywhere" (Foucault, 1978, 93)—that stories both a turning and nexus point in world history and a power living yet inaccessible by any one *thing* or *one* created out of the Americas. It is a story about some *things* left behind, which have not *ceased to be* for 500 years. It is a story that invites us to bear witness to the *exaggeration of crises* refracted (Gobineau 1915, 160), elsewhere and otherwise, that always already stages the emergence of a penetration into the space, place, and time of an-other (see Mbembe 2001; Bhabha 1994). "No archive," Hall (2001) argued, "arises out of thin air" (89). So I ask you, my reader, to remain open to the idea that the Americas was a locus for a method of writing textual death spaces and the testing site for the materialization of the *Archive* that manifests and materializes across the cultural texts that I will read in what follows.

The racist Arthur de Gobineau (1915) understood that the institutions, laws, and customs the "dead master[s]" invented and prescribed to were architected to live-on long after they had passed (33). He hints both at a historicity and the rhetoricity (see Murphy et al. 1998; Agnew et al. 2010) of a world connected by *things* that have not *ceased to be* and that are in (supposedly) *operation with/out colonies*: ongoing structuring principles of settlerizing encounters, interactions, and engagements organized by a colonial matrix of power and cloaked by rhetorics of modernity. De Gobineau understood then as academics do today that the power of power is determined in part by the affective element (pesado-ness) of human work and projects, archival impressions, the enduring effects and consequences on land, memory, knowledge, and relation-ing long after some *things* or some *one* has passed. Unknowingly, he laid out a framework of modern/colonial and settlerizing designs before academics would identify it as such by writing: "so long as even their shadows remain, the building stands, the body seems to have a soul, the pale ghost walks" (33). All this to say that what decolonizing archival impressions appeals for is an ethos of bearing witness in unsettling ways and a praxis of unsettling the settled: a seeing within the heart of ecocide, genocide, and ethno-and-epistemicide; a feeling of the souls' *original impulse* to stage a haunting-and-ghostly totality of structures and institutions of *feelings and thoughts*; a deep orientation toward listening that can materialize whispers of *pale ghosts*. *There Is No Making It Out* attends to the historicity of and the rhetoricity behind archival impressions that give structure to and constitute the *Archives-archives*.

To talk of, intervene in, and/or unsettle the some *things* of our world we have to be present and be a witness to them. On the one hand, a decolonial turn thus is in part about readjusting distracted eyes, recalibrating sensibilities, and fine-tuning a deep orientation toward listening, all of which feed into an ethic of obligation and responsibility of *haunting back*, ethos of bearing witness in unsettling ways, and praxis of unsettling the settled; a seeing, feeling, and listening without being settled with and a *doing* of peeling back layers to unsettle the settled. On the other hand, a decolonizing turn is in part about *work, in* assemblage with *work elsewhere* and *otherwise*, that thinks "from and with standpoints, struggles, and practices, from and with praxical theorizings, conceptual theorizings, theoretical conceptualizings, and theory-building actionings," regardless of whether the *work* is land- or epistemologically-centered (Mignolo and Walsh 2018, 20). A decolonizing turn can only be determined by an assemblage of the *who, where, why, how,* and *for*. There is an underutilized yet powerful medium and undertheorized yet compelling means that lend themselves to both agendas. *There Is No Making It Out* submits for consideration thus an archival approach and a capacious theory of *archival impressions* as *praxical theorizing actioning*, one that invites a *decolonizing rhetoricity* in both *analytic and prospective* capacities, a *longing* for ~~making it out~~ the unsettling of the settled-ness of *things* and laboring toward both altering the *Archive-archives* and wor(l)ding *an-other* archive.

But while the *Archive* allows us to recognize the *idea of the Americas* as a turning and nexus point in world history, alone it can do no more than help us acknowledge how its designs and technologies remain with us today. Partly, I rely on conversation then by the MCC and Settler Colonial Studies (SCS) that a *decolonial analytic* is not an identity-driven but a technological analysis of the way designs are shared in, imported, expanded, and/or disputed by an *association of social interests*. In other words, the question is not solely about the "who" but the "what"—are the desires and objectives of power—and the "how" (Yang 2017, 14). Take for example the *idea*, alluded to multiple times already. Mignolo (2005) states, "The 'idea' of America is not only a reference to a place; above all, it operates on the assumed power and privilege of enunciation that makes it possible to transform an invented idea into 'reality'" (151). By referring to the *idea* in this way, he invites an archival approach and theory of archival impressions, because like an archive, the *idea* records the archival impressions of *ideas* elsewhere and otherwise as much as it produces the *epistemological experiment* of it (Stoler 2002, 87). The *idea* transcends a reference to a place because it is as much a technology (the *idea of the Americas*, *humanitas*/anthropoi, race, epistemic and ontological differences, race/labor) as is the *Archive*—a prism through which to see the *idea of the Americas* refracted through the lens of *Americanity* and within the frame of modernity/coloniality. Still, some *thing* else is demanded.

My appeal for an archival approach as a critical method and theory of archival impression as a theoretical apparatus is not unfounded. In "Orientalism Reconsidered," Said (1985) proposes an "epistemological critique" between the "development of a historicism" and the practice of imperialism that involves the "incorporation and homogenization of histories" (101). On the one hand, "incorporation" and "homogenization" invites a critical method that can contend with the historicity of some *things*. An archival approach lends itself here. On the other hand, it calls for a theoretical apparatus that can contend with the rhetoricity that leaves some *things* behind, near and far and elsewhere and otherwise. A theory of archival impressions approaches manifestations of an ongoing and organizing structuring principle of settlerizing encounters, interactions, and engagements *elsewhere* and *otherwise* as archetypical of a range of impressions that gives structure to, constitutes, and ensures an *Archive* in the making. While I am not suggesting power is monolithic or unfolds evenly, my starting points in inquiries of *stories-so-far* and the *possibilities of new stories* must include the *idea of the Americas*. It is the prism through which to see successive evolutions and mutated modalities of designs refracted through the lens of *Americanity* and within the frame of modernity/

coloniality. An archival approach and theory of archival impressions makes it possible to conceive of power as an *Archive*, regulative in function and constantly in a state of being-and-becoming, *appearing* and *becoming* consequential within and beyond its immediate settings and contexts because of how *it is in* assemblage with smaller archives (or the *working parts* of the *Archive*).

The value of an archival approach and theory of archival impressions is in what is afforded. An archival approach presents the opportunity to create an archive in the face of an *Archive* that does not want to retain certain memories. *It* reduces as much as it erases—white spaces-places : white time : white memory. But the memory the *Archive* attempts to efface, like the some *things* it attempts to cover-over, remain in land, memory, knowledge, and relation-ing long after some *things* or the ideas, images-signs-sounds, and ends of some *one* have passed. There are always wrinkles in power—a power that exists both in a precarious state and late stage—and thus some *things* beyond (Said 1985). Such an approach and theory thus are necessary at a time when settler colonialism and *coloniality* is understood by definition but, more often than not, is discussed in superficial or overtotalizing ways. When everything is coloniality or when settler colonialism and power exists everywhere, we lose sight of how power manifests in local forms and conditions and what exists *beyond*; where there are spaces of modern/colonial and settlerizing writing there are sites of counterwriting. This results in a loss of explanatory power (Acosta 2019). A theory of archival impressions offers the possibility to create time-stamped receipts, to take stock in other words of the impressions that give structure to, constitute, and ensure an *Archive* in the making. Now, discussions on intentions or motives can be problematic. In part, thus, I enlist William Benoit's (1996) notion of *discourse about actions*, which allows me to conceive of the accumulation of *archival impressions* as accounts that function to explain, justify, interpret, and/or rationalize actions. We have the palimpsestic narratives in the following chapters to test that out, which tell stories of the good sides of modernity but is unsettled by archival impressions that editorialize its darker sides.

Neither settlers nor their accomplices or allies can ever be in full control of the afterlife of what they produce. But it would be a mistake at the same time to chalk up the (re)writing of "settler" or "settler" archives as mere coincidence. Both a framework of rhetorical ecologies and a rhetorical framework of palimpsests encourage us to recontextualize the (re)writing of such archives in their historical, temporal, and lived contexts. When done, the bleeding, as Edbauer (2005) might put it, of public rhetorics, memories, interactions, and forces is undeniable. I am more concerned thus both with the rhetorical phenomenona of (re)writing "settler" archives as archival impressions additive to the *Archive* and how they exist *in* assemblage elsewhere and otherwise to make, unmake, and remake the *structures of feeling and thought* and *epistemic murk* that contaminate humanity. With Benoit's (1996) notion of *discourse about actions* thus, I approach the accumulation of "settler" and "settler" archives elsewhere and otherwise as sites of *doing*, accounts that function to explain, justify, interpret, and/or rationalize certain actions through acts of modern/colonial and settlerizing (re)writing. We have what Spivak (1988a) called the palimpsestic narratives of (colonialism and) imperialism as evidence of this. My conversations on "settler," whether that entails the rhetorics of settler colonialism/settler archives or settler rhetorics of archival impression, hence benefit greatly from the intellectual universe of rhetorical ecologies, assemblage, circulation, and ambient rhetorics (see Wingard 2013; Rickert 2013; Gries and Brooke 2018). Within this universe, I find it possible once more to conceive of the *Archive* as *an* assemblage *in* assemblage with smaller archives (or the *working parts* of the *Archive*) that register the epistemological and ontological *idea of the Americas* in the frame of modernity/coloniality. Per rhetorical excavation work, I find that palimpsestic time (Alexander 2005), identities (Shohat 2002), and narratives (A. García 2004) are intentional cultural productions of modern/colonial and settlerizing mentalities baked into material forms of public memory such as the archives. Ultimately, I intend to argue that settler rhetorics of archival impressions, whether carried out by settlers, the posterity of settlers, or others who do *work* rhetorically to transmit modern/colonial and settlerizing designs, reflect an awareness—intentionality vis-à-vis iteration (see Bhabha 1994)—that impressions could be at the same time the domination of information, management of knowledge, and control of epistemic obedience in perpetuity.

The *Archive* documents existence and power and lends legitimacy to some *things* as much as it cements discursive practices. The latter includes impressing non-encounters with or a disavowal of presence in order to erase (the *other*, intrusions, violence), subsume, and/or underscore epistemic and ontological differences, practices to be shared-in, imported, expanded, and/or even disputed (see Adams-Campbell, Falzetti, and Rivard 2015, 109–110). Both an archival approach and theory of archival impressions create the occasion then to recognize and acknowledge that if the *Archive* is an *epistemological experiment*, by the same token *Archive-archives* can be an experiment for a wor(l)ding *otherwise*—the connective tissue between a *praxical theorizing* and *theory building actioning*. Both ground *an-other* exigence that forms *an-other* question. With our capacity to have knowledge of the inner workings of the Archive, *what is our obligation and responsibility?* Surely, it cannot be to give back to the Archive. Thus, how do we reposition the contents of the *Archive-archives* so that we can position ourselves in relation to them *otherwise?* The significance of an archival approach and theory of archival impressions is in what it ultimately appeals for in this book, the initiating of decolonizing archival impressions.

Decolonizing archival impressions function in the vein of *analytic tasks and prospective visions.* Along the lines of archival impressions—entries of writing impressed and initiated by some *things* or some *one* that bears on and enduringly acts upon *Archive/archives*—decolonizing archival impressions reflects entries of counter-writing impressed and initiated by some *one* meant to unsettle the settled-ness of *things* and bring about decolonizing agendas that can alter the *Archive-archives* and wor(l)d *an-other* archive. An argument put forth at the onset of this book bears repeating. If we are all in and part of the *Archive* that means we too are an *archive.* Here I turn on rhetoricity, a most central theme in this book, to emphasize *doings* behind (decolonizing) archival impressions. Regarding *decolonizing rhetoricity*, I mean then *doings* that both strategically re-assemblages decolonizing *archives* and conceives of *archives* as *decolonizing archival impressions.* An archival approach affords the opportunity to retain the memory of a "Weism" initiating *doings* and *archival impressions elsewhere* and *otherwise* that may indeed give structure to and constitute *an-other* archive. Akin to Wynters then, the suffix *-ing* is not meant to convey the arrival of a proper arrival and arrivant—the decolonized agent or decolonization—but underscores a laboring that operates as a decolonizing force *in* assemblage with other *work; work* that can be characterized as a rhetoric of counter-writing.

In my geopolitical context, I ask, what is the US if not the *dead master's inventions*—institutions—and the enlargement of the grounds for *pale ghosts* to walk, persevering 500 years later in the form of *public secrets* and *monstrous intimacies?* The *idea of the University* and WRS is a most immediate case in point. The former coincides with and remains an essential pillar of modern/colonial and settlerizing designs (Bhambra, Gebrial, and Nisancioglu 2018; Grande 2018; Grosfoguel, Hernandez, and Velasquez 2016; Patel 2021; Peña 2022; Santos 2017). The latter, by simply calling into question its existence, reveals a discipline hitched to an archive of ghosts, predicated on an *Aristotelian syndrome*, and in the service of such designs (G. Olson 1998; Lu 1992; Kennedy 1998; Brereton 1995; Connors 1992, 1997; Bernal 1987; Ezzaher 2008; K. Lloyd 2011, 2013; Lyon 2010; You 2006, 2023; Russel 1991). Neither is inconsequential as they help maintain the US as one big wounded/wounding space and place—a cemetery of gravesites (Till 2012; Brasher, Alderman, and Inwood 2017). Convinced either will only ever absorb and tokenize resistance (Brittenham 2001), and knowing there is no making it out of institutions or the *Archive*, I amend Mignolo's (2000b) article title and thus ask, what is the role of humanities scholars-educators in the throes and face of some *things* that remain trafficking in the normative? I believe it can be to unsettle the past and intervene in the settled-ness of the present. An archival approach and theory of (decolonizing) archival impressions lend themselves to such aims, especially as we remain under the yoke of the *Archive* and as WRS lacks a theory of writing and rhetoric that can assume and reckon with the enduring, epistemological, and rhetorical force that is modern/colonial and settlerizing designs.

There Is No Making It Out is concerned with what remains in land, memory, knowledge, and relationality after some *thing* or some *one* has passed. But neither hauntings nor haunting situations unfold evenly. So it behooves us to create a public record of how modern/colonial and settlerizing designs manifest in local forms and conditions and how they show up in our everyday lives (Tlostanova 2017a). The role of humanities scholar-educators cannot be overstated here because as researchers, scholars, and educators we know that such designs require a *semiotic apparatus of enunciation* that situates us squarely on literacies, images-signs-sounds, and rhetorics. We can contribute thus more robust conversations on modern/colonial and settlerizing designs and comprehensive versions of its rhetorics. We can provide thus richer and extensive accounts on the effects and consequences of hauntings and haunting situations on land, memory, knowledge, and relation-ing. We can do this by rhetoricizing (Davidson 1996) with a *decolonial analytic* informed by rhetorical analytical methods, rhetorics of epistemology, truth-and-knowledge claims, and the rhetoricity behind archival impressions. Such will underscore how rhetoric needs to matter because it demands engagement with the full spectrum of matter—the living, nonliving, and nonhuman (Eberly 2002). It will appeal for a politics of hauntings, inheritances, and dwellings. But more importantly, by creating a public record, we can reposition the contents of archives and position ourselves in relation to it *otherwise*. And it is my hope that such sparks the exigence then for initiating decolonizing archival impressions.

Overall, decolonizing archival impressions applies in the book to knowledge, being (broadly conceived), and relation-ing. Because we cannot decolonize being without decolonizing knowledge (Mignolo and Walsh 2018). I define decolonizing archival impression in short thus as the unsettling, decolonizing, and amending of Euro/Western-centric cultural, thinking, and being programs. Will a *future-to-come* (Derrida 1994b) tell of the *choices* we made to send decolonizing signals, decolonizing archival impressions, to the *Archive*? I have this hope that if the *Archive-archives* are in part a *human thing* human beings have built, the by-product of temporally initiated physical contact and the accumulation of some *things* left behind by human touch, then perhaps healing can be the condition of and for the archivization of impressions carried out *otherwise* (see Escobar 2020, xxiv, 51, 63). A *doing* of a "Weism" in the service to the full spectrum of matter—living, nonliving, nonhuman—is where *an-other* archive can start.

Chapter Breakdown

There Is No Making It Out is not at all about making it out. It is about the demands for some *thing* else. That some *thing* else in this book leads me to the *Archive-archives* and archival impressions. Both underscore the *doing* behind some *things* made, unmade, and remade in unending cycles, and the possibility of a slow and deep (de/re)compositioning of *things otherwise*. It is about the contents of a modern/colonial and settlerizing *Archive*, where I offer case studies on the *idea of the Americas* and how it manifests in local forms and conditions in the US. I *return* to and *carefully reckon* with the *idea of Utah* and *Mormon/ism* and *Texas* and *the settler* as archival impressions within this archive. The book is also about how its designs show up in students' *archives*—adhering to, interacting with, and/or carrying out the projects and work that the *Archive* represents. The essential focus of *There Is No Making It Out* takes shape in the form of a question: How do we reposition the contents of archives so that we can position ourselves in relation to it *otherwise*? I respond as a literacy researcher and rhetorical scholar with each chapter functioning as an initiation of (decolonizing) archival impressions across multiple literacy, semiotic, and rhetorical scenes. If literacies, images-signs-sounds, and rhetorics have been used to construct settler sites, constitute haunted/haunting communities, and maintain wounded/wounding spaces and places, by the same token they can be used alongside such (decolonizing) archival impressions as stepping-stones toward the *possibilities of new stories*.

There Is No Making It Out is compartmentalized into three sections underscoring how we cannot decolonize being without decolonizing knowledge. The first section, "An Archival Interruption: The Analytic," centers on modern/

colonial and settlerizing designs and how they manifest in local forms and conditions in the US vis-à-vis a *decolonial analytic* (put forth by the MCC). Methodologically speaking, what is locatable, identifiable, and nameable—the rhetorics of settler colonialism/settler archives and settler rhetorics of archival impressions—is analyzable. The first section features multi-sited inquires of the *idea*, which as Mignolo (2005) claims, "is not only a reference to a place . . . it operated on the assumed power and privilege of enunciation that makes it possible to transform an invented idea into 'reality'" (151). Settler archival research and piecemealing of archives through the creation of public records is the method. The three chapters of section 1 establish how writing, rhetoric, place, archives, and modern/colonial and settlerizing designs are intertwined. They contain decolonial-driven close readings and a rhetoricizing of rhetorics of epistemology, truth-and-knowledge claims, and the rhetoricity behind archival impressions. Overall, the first section contributes to a theory of writing and rhetoric that can assume and reckon with the enduring, epistemological, and rhetorical force that is modern/colonial and settlerizing designs vis-à-vis an archival approach and theory of archival impressions.

Chapter 1, "An Epistemic System and Modern/Colonial and Settlerizing Designs," is spatially and temporally situated in Spanish conquest and among Euro-and-North American descendants of the eighteenth and nineteenth centuries. It traces, per the MCC's theses and propositions, the historical foundation, successive evolutions and stages, and mutated modalities of the *epistemic system* and designs of a 500-year-old *Archives*. Tracking with the MCC, SCS, and Indigenous scholars in academia, I approach "settler" not necessarily as an identity, but as an *epistemic system* of ideas, images-signs-sounds, and ends. With a *decolonial analytic*, I interrogate how a local-regional system-totality of territorial and epistemological projects of (ap/ex)propriation gained universality. I do this by attending to a *semiotic apparatus of enunciations* and tracing how an *association of social interest* shared-in, imported, and expanded-disputed viewpoints of Man-Human-Rights. Chapter 1 establishes the basis for understanding the colonial matrix of power—coloniality of knowledge, being, nature, and power—and modern/colonial and settlerizing designs as acts of writing.

Chapter 2, "Corrido-ing the Idea of Utah and Mormon/ism," is spatially and temporally situated in the United States during the nineteenth and twentieth centuries. It is a case of the *idea of Utah* and *Mormon/ism* based on settler archival research. Chapter 2 is guided by two questions. How does the *idea* function as an archival impression within the *Archive*? And believing we are all in and part of this archive still in the making, what can the initiating of decolonizing archival impressions afford us? With a *decolonial analytic*, I interrogate settler archives-as-*epistemological experiments* and excavate the march toward hegemony out of the project of modernity. Attending to a *semiotic apparatus of enunciations*, I create a public record-archive of and rhetoricize rhetorics of epistemology, truth-and-knowledge claims, and the rhetoricity behind archival impressions. Out of that work, I investigate how rhetorical and affective strategies of church settlers invent new images, myths, and meanings of place and citizen/ship and naturalize an *epistemic system* and the modus operandi of modern/colonial and settlerizing designs. Chapter 2 demonstrates one role that humanities scholars-educators can play in unsettling the past and intervening in the settled-ness of the present.

Chapter 3, "Corrido-ing the Idea of Texas-LRGV and the Settler," is spatially and temporally situated in the United States during the twentieth century. Based on settler archival research, it is a case on how the *idea of Texas* served as a foundation for the *idea of the Magic Valley* and *the settler* in the Lower Rio Grande Valley. Chapter 3 is guided by the same two questions as chapter 2. With a *decolonial analytic*, I interrogate settler archives and settler advertisements-as-*epistemological experiments* and excavate the march toward hegemony out of the project of modernity. Attending to a *semiotic apparatus of enunciations*, I create a public record-archive of and rhetoricize rhetorics of epistemology, truth-and-knowledge claims, and the rhetoricity behind archival impressions. Out of that work, I investigate how rhetorical and affective strategies of settlers invent new images, myths, and meanings of place and citizen/ship and naturalize an *epistemic system* and the modus operandi of modern/colonial and settlerizing designs. Chapter 3 underscores the role humanities scholars-educators can play in initiating decolonizing archival impressions.

Illuminating practices of invention and *epistemological experiments* is a move toward potentially decolonizing knowledge and possibly decolonizing being. The second section, "Decolonizing Archival Impressions: The Im/Possibilities of a Prospective Task," complements the decolonizing of knowledge with the prospect of decolonizing being. It ruminates over the role of humanities scholars-educators in the lives of students we teach. It features multi-sited inquiries of how modern/colonial and settlerizing designs show up in students' *archives*, a prism through which to see how the historicity and rhetoricity of their *stories-so-far* adhere to, interact with, and/or carry out the projects and work the *Archive* represents. The central methods are quasi-classroom ethnography and *literacy history interviews*—interviews that trace and encourage participants to share a partial picture of the ways literacy and literacies (broadly conceived) are situated, inherited, embodied, experienced, practiced, and/or are altered by chance encounters, human interactions, and/or other kinds of engagements (broadly conceived)—which are included in a snapshot format and edited slightly for coherence (see Vieira 2016). The two chapters of section 2 contain observations, reflections, and student accounts. It is guided by the questions: How do we reposition the contents of *archives* so that we can position ourselves in relation to it *otherwise*? How do we encourage decolonizing archives and the initiating of archival impressions *otherwise*? Here, rhetorical studies invites us to recognize and acknowledge that if archives are a by-product of human touch, by the same token, it is our everyday hand-touch that can initiate archival impressions *otherwise*. (¡Ojalá!)

Chapter 4, "Making It Out of Haunting Mentalities," speaks to efforts to initiate decolonizing archival impressions in the classroom. It is an Institutional Review Board (IRB)–approved case study, where I reflect on the questions, *where is one at, whom is one teaching, and what can be gained from placed-based pedagogies*? (Tinberg 1990). Chapter 4 interrogates how my classroom became an extension of the everyday-ness of Utah, investigates the parallels between the *Archive* and students' *stories-so-far*, and contemplates the prospect of decolonizing knowledge-being in the classroom. It underscores how curricula and pedagogical agendas do not always go as planned. Because what is good in theory—encouraging students to create a public record of the contents of their *archive* and situating them at the nexus of their *stories-so-far* and *possibilities of new stories*—does not always translate or bode well in practice, especially when human beings are involved. Chapter 4 speaks to all humanities scholars-educators who ought to know that decolonizing knowledge-being is conceptually, pedagogically, and emotionally complex, messy, and to some extent impossible.

Chapter 5, "Making It Out of Haunted Mentalities," speaks to efforts to initiate decolonizing archival impressions in the lives of first-generation students who identify as Mexican, Mexican America, Latino/a, or Hispanic in Texas and Utah. It is a multi-sited IRB-approved case study, where I reflect on the same two questions as Chapter 4. Chapter 5 interrogates the parallels between the *Archive* and students' *stories-so-far*, investigates the role that archival research can play, and contemplates the prospective of decolonizing knowledge-being in the classroom. It tells of how some are on bad terms with both making it out and anything that gets in the way. Chapter

5 speaks to resistances, though, to theory made evident by the everyday of those whose reality and needs are in conflict, and thus, at odds with the ideal of both a decolonial option and academic responsibility (see Spivak 1994). Chapters 4 and 5 raise compelling questions both about the im/possibilities of a *prospective vision* (put forth by the MCC) for the classroom (and beyond) and whether it is suitable for *anyone*. Reflecting on its entanglements and complicity with *academic responsibility*, both chapters claim there is a demand for something else.

The third section, "The Demand for Something Else," responds to the question, What then, if decolonizing knowledge-being is to some extent impossible in the classroom? The final chapter both deliberates whether it is just a possibility that has yet to be worked out and contemplates if decolonizing knowledge-being can exist under certain conditions. If the perils of reductive, dichotomous, and oppositional rhetorical structures remain intact, it is argued, it strains both how to see that we are all in and part of the *Archive* and thus *do otherwise*. Such undermines too how we might go about constellating our *archives*, wor(l)ding decolonizing archival impressions, and unsettling the *Archive otherwise*. The chapter takes seriously Said's (1983, 242), Hall's (2019, 322), and Derrida's (2021, 6) arguments that the obligation and responsibility of the "scholar" is to be critical and thus to think of the very intellectual work we prescribe to under erasure if only to initiate a "break" and bring about something "new." Thus, section 3 is about the demand for something else, some *thing* that can unsettle the settled-ness of the *Archive* and yet be more in tune with reality and the exigencies surrounding the world we live in today.

The final chapter, "Being-and-Becoming Recognizable to 'We/arth,'" returns to the question of how to live otherwise as taken up by Alcoff (2011), Derrida (1994b), Fanon (1986), A. Gordon (2008), and the MCC. Each offers his or her own framework—revitalized reconstructive work in epistemology, hauntology, a world of You, an *epistemological framework for the living*—across scenes of the *Archive-archives* that is a haunted/haunting *story-so-far*. It investigates whether a decolonial option is suitable for anyone, *wherever they may be* and in the *non-name of all* (Acosta 2012; Fanon 1986). The final chapter deliberates thus how to till the grounds on which power takes root without foreclosing on another's *possibilities of new stories*. Recalling *shadow work* and an ethic, ethos, and praxis of *thinking, feeling*, and *being-with* the full spectrum of matter (living, nonliving, and nonhuman), it sketches out an *epistemological framework for the haunted* as one option that can create the conditions under which decolonizing knowledge-being may be possible in the classroom and beyond. It underscores the essential foci of this book—archives, repositioning the contents of archives so that we can position ourselves in relation to it *otherwise*, and the exigence for initiating decolonizing archival impressions. And facilitated by *deep rhetoricity*, such a framework, I conclude, grounds how we might learn how to *be-and-become* recognizable to *an-other* archive—"We/arth"—and thus engage in a wor(l)ding of a future of the "We/arth." Can this word or figure be stabilized (see Derrida 1995, 14)? I have hope that it is at least conceivable to struggle over its possibility.

Can archives feel? The chapters that follow will evidence a refusal by settlers (and posterity) and the haunted to surrender the hope in that *possibility*. Each chapter functions both as an impression and entry submitted into this book that is an archive. The point is to connect hauntings and haunting situations with the experiences of human beings across space, place, and time. It can come to form the basis for a *doing* otherwise. Ultimately, this book might upset readers. I might get a lot of things wrong, especially in conceiving of power as an *Archive in* assemblage with smaller archives (or the *working parts of the Archive*). Still, I intend to argue throughout that the *Archive* is perhaps the most honest and critical space to think and speak from. Moreover, I offer no definitive resolutions in the throes and face of a haunting reality; there is no making it out. Still, I maintain there is the possibility of altering and wor(l)ding *otherwise*. I offer thus only a hope that impressions may give way to the *possibilities of new stories*—a wor(l)ding of *an-other* archive. I offer then only *an-other* set of options that presents us with *an-other* set of questions that grounds *an-other* set of exigences. I have found that the meaning of *stories-so-far* and the *possibilities of new stories* can be found in *that process*.

It is necessary for a people who have hope that the *work* we do today may plant the seeds of a future to be reaped by a world of tomorrow *yet to arrive*. Ojalá—because if "one could count on what is coming, hope would be but the calculation of a program" (Derrida 1994b, 212). Wor(l)ding in this book, then, is nothing more than recognizing and acknowledging that wording is human work and we do human work, as humanities scholars-educators, that *takes* and can make *place* otherwise. This is a wor(l)ding de-linked from Martin Heidegger's (1962) grip (see Spivak 1985a, 1985b) and re-linked to a verb (A. Gordon 2008; Haraway 2008, 2016b; Rickert and Salvo 2006) in which "we" carry out *work* in the service of being-for (see Davis 2010, 2017).

Section 1

An Archival Interruption

The Analytic

Reflexión-Meditación

That Which Lives in the Bones

WRS experienced an archival turn in the early 1990s. It was Robert Connors (1992) who warns that archives can only tell stories (31); Carolyn Steedman (2005) who writes about the process of "finding things" in the archives that invoke friction in thought (22, 25); Barbara Biesecker (2006) who appeals for greater awareness of what archives can/not authorize (130); Lynée Lewis Gaillet (2010) who calls attention to the researcher as filter and lens in archival research (37); Cheryl Glenn and Jessica Enoch (2009, 2010) who appeal for a reconsideration of what the archive is and the purpose it can serve while advancing feminist rhetorical frameworks (328); Barbara L'Eplattenier (2009) who pleads for self-awareness, self-reflection, and self-representational descriptions in archival research (75); Liz Rohan (2010) who speaks to the personal as method (245); and Linda Ferreira-Buckley (1999) who argues, "Historians of rhetoric need to return to the archives" (577). There are countless others who over time have spoken to the importance of what Jessica Enoch and Elizabeth Miller (2021) would come to call *archival listening*. It would be unproductive to flesh out my reservations here. My main concern is that without accounting for hauntings and haunting situations the racialized, minoritized, and marginalized become the pejorative *other*. For some, it is not that easy to return to the archives, precisely because of the "personal," because for them the archives are alive and, thus, equally as powerful as the living. I am most interested in archival threads that recognize and acknowledge this and that invite all to come to terms with what lives deep within all the bones (see Derrida and Ferraris 2001). An orientation to hauntings is what is missing in archival research. But because beings are constituted differently, I get why such an appeal may not be appealing in WRS.

My critique on assumptions has been echoed elsewhere and otherwise (see Mohanty 1984). My appeal above is not a novel one in WRS either. In the early 2000s, WRS started to take up colonial, imperial, and/or settler archives. It was Victor Villanueva (2008) who speaks to a haunting process in doing archival research—"What does one do when one becomes fully conscious of the alienation" (84); Malea Powell (2008) who underscores that haunting situation—"The archival project was not created for Indians. It was created to consolidate knowledge about Indians" (117); and Ellen Cushman (2013) who calls attention to how "archives of indigenous artifacts came into existence in part to elevate the Western tradition through a process of othering" (119). There are others, outside (Caswell 2021; Ghaddar 2016; Ghaddar and Caswell 2019; Schwartz and Cook 2002) and in the field of rhetoric, both on the side of WRS and communications, who take up archives critically (see Graban and Hayden 2022; Morris 2006; Pauszek 2017; Rawson 2018). But the point here is that the colonial, imperial, and/or settler archive is an ephemera of hauntings, haunting situations, and wounded/wounding spaces-places. From figureheads beyond WRS who have weighed in on the origins of the archive (de Certeau 1992; Derrida 1995; Foucault 1972) to those who deliberate about settler archives (Adams-Campbell, Falzetti, and Rivard 2015; Stoler 2002; Huang and Weaver-Hightower 2019) to those who speak on the archive as living (Hall 2019), it is understood that one does not simply return to the archives. But then again, I guess we are all constituted differently and, therefore, do not feel that which is activated in the bones, whenever a return is indeed made to the archives. Is an orientation to hauntings, inheritances, and dwellings truly a matter of difference or does it speak to a sense of obligation and responsibility that has yet to arrive? Will it ever have arrived?

Will *it* (purposely left ambiguous and yet pertaining to every *thing*) ever have arrived? Admittedly, I do not take stock in everything Derrida writes, just as Chomsky did not agree with Foucault on all matters of resistance to power (see Said 1983). But what I do agree with is the idea that "it is necessary to introduce haunting into the very construction of a concept" (Derrida 1994b, 202). Hauntology is an unsettling of the settled-ness of some *things* as minute as an *idea* and as large as the concept of Being. There are critiques of Derrida, one being that he privileges spectrality in staging the specter. But as Spivak (1994) writes, nothing is "unstructured" or "unstaged" (45). And that is the point of the question above, to get at the tension between what is no longer, what is, and what has yet to arrive. Based on my reading of Steedman (2002) there seems to be skepticism about what is experienced in the archives. It goes to a point I am making: for some, the dead are neither present nor can documents speak. Distracted eyes, sensibilities, and listening. For others, that some *thing* or some *one* lives-on (sur-vie) and has a powerful presence in the life of the living. Like memory—"the materiality of the trace, the immediacy of the recording, the visibility of the image" (Nora 1989, 13)—the *Archive-archives* require the senses of seeing, feeling, and listening. Following trace marks, whether of *structures of feelings and thoughts* (Williams 1997), *public secrets* (Taussig 1999), and/or *monstrous intimacies* (Sharpe 2010), an orientation to hauntings "is about putting life back in where only a vague memory or a bare trace was visible to those who bothered to look" (A. Gordon 2008, 22). The *choice* to get caught up in this way—both in seeking to understand the conditions for the archivization of memories (and the *Archives-archives*) and in creating presence from absence and sound from silence out of *absent presences*—is a *choice* that has nothing to do with being constituted differently. The archival research I am most interested in is that which demands we *carefully reckon* with what lives deep in the bones and the full spectrum of matter (living, nonliving, nonhuman).

Modern/colonial and settlerizing records, rhetorics, and archives are a textual *death space*. The next three chapters are situated squarely within conversations about "death-spaces" (Taussig 1991, 133), a modern/colonial and settlerizing imaginary "space of death" (Holland 2000, 4), a "discourse of the dead" (de Certeau 1992, 46) that establishes a "place for the living" (100), and death as the "constitutive feature" of the *other* (Maldonado-Torres 2007, 251). What an archival approach will evidence is how modern/colonial and settlerizing mentalities are deeply baked in public memory and thus in all our bones. Given that such mentalities have influenced what to preserve and bury across place and time, it is an obligation and responsibility of all not to be entangled or complicit in giving back to *that* which wounds and haunts. I am of the mind that if we can unsettle the settled-ness of archives and the grip that modern/colonial and settlerizing designs have over them, then we can reclaim the archives both for everyone and for the purposes of wor(l)ding *an-other* archive.

1
An Epistemic System and Modern/Colonial and Settlerizing Designs

The *Archive* has a palimpsestic narrative (see Spivak 1988a), which is that domination, management, and control are justifiable and rationalizable as the price of modernization and human progress. Everyday people have to do work rhetorically for both to materialize. [W]-[H] questions guide my inquiry: What are the literacies, images-signs-sounds, and rhetorics of the *Archive*? When, where, how, and why do archival impressions happen and by whom are they carried out by? According to Alexander and Mohanty (2010), stories are "simultaneously 'maps' in that they mobilize both histories and geographies of power" (31). This chapter serves not as *A* story of the *Archive* but as a pathway to put forth an archival approach and theory of archival impressions that can help us better understand the (re)writing of the *Archive*. It is nonetheless one story about an *epistemic system*, modern/colonial and settlerizing designs, and technologies—the projects of territorial and epistemological (ex/ap)propriation carried out by the Spanish in the sixteenth century and Euro-and-North American descendants of the eighteenth and nineteenth centuries—within an epistemological, ideological, rhetorical, and aesthetic war on information. This chapter establishes a central premise of the book: we must investigate the past to understand the present structuring principle of settlerizing encounters, interactions, and engagement that keep spaces and places wounded/

wounding and *stories-so-far* haunted/haunting. There is no positioning ourselves in relation to the *Archive* and its contents *otherwise* if an understanding of the colonial matrix of power—coloniality of knowledge, being, nature, and power—and modern/colonial and settlerizing designs is not established.

This chapter launches the decolonizing knowledge-being agenda of this book. To establish a *modernity/coloniality framework* for the next two chapters, I attend here to a *semiotic apparatus of enunciations*; create a public record of and rhetoricize rhetorics of epistemology, truth-and-knowledge claims, and the rhetoricity behind archival impressions; and triangulate how an *association of social interest* shared-in, imported, and expanded-disputed viewpoints of Man-Human-Rights. Asking a decolonial question, where did actor-agents get the *ideas* from, I demonstrate that despite mutated modalities of the *epistemic system* and designs of a 500-year-old *Archive*, a colonial matrix of power and the modus operandi of modern/colonial and settlerizing designs remain intact by *smaller archives of knowledges, understandings, feelings, and doings* (or the *working parts* of the *Archive*) that reflect *things* in unending cycles of (re)writing (see Yang 2017). I argue that what occurred in the Americas 500 years ago—the *idea* (*of the Americas*) of abundant spaces and places of "uncultivated waste" lying "in common" as shadowlands with it and its inhabitant beings to be conquered, colonized, managed, and controlled (see Locke [1689] 1821, 219)—continues to *appear* and *be* consequential because the logic of coloniality remains a vested interest while the *idea*, a most significant design and technology borne out of its wreckage. For that reason, the initiating of a decolonizing archival impression here means unsettling, decolonizing, and amending the lies, contradictions, myths, narcissism, cynicism, denialisms, and sickness-disease of the *Archive* and its actor-agents who epitomize *knowing subjects* or *humanitas*—men of letters, historians, and/or officers of the state (Mignolo 2005, 2009, 2013; Osamu 2006; Glissant 1989; Césaire 2001).

Words and Ideas

On February 9, 2021, defense lawyer David Schoen argued, "Words are what make our Constitution ... [it] is a product of words" (US Senate 2021, S606). Between February 11 and 28 of 2021, Joaquin Castro, Ben Carson, Lindsey Graham, and President Joe Biden (Wolf and Merill 2021; also see J. Davis 2018) reminded the public that America is an *idea*. Words and ideas matter. Lest we forget John Locke ([1689] 1821), who wrote on the law of nature–law of reason, epistemic and ontological differences, rights of inheritance to the elsewhere, an Other-as-Same relation, and leagues of nations. His words and *ideas* justified and rationalized designs, which hinge on the historical nexus of the *idea*: "Thus in the beginning all the world was America" (229). Such an *idea* would be instrumental in more ways than one to the designs of Rights-and-belonging-to. Locke's theological-and-secularly structured *idea*—borne in the long history of an *original impulse, visuality*, assemblage, branding, and recasting work, and the transformation of human beings into ghosts and ghost citizens (see Arvin, Tuck, and Morrill 2013; Bergland 2000; Liew 2024; Mignolo 2006, 2011a; Mirzoeff 2011; Sharpe 2010; Sheller 2012; Trouillot 1995; Tuck and Yang 2012)—puts forth a deduction: as Eden was the beginning, vacant America reflects both the day of "old" and future garden; as Adam was vested with Rights-to what can be seen on the whole face of the earth, Man has "means to appropriate" (209) the in-common-in-natural state and in perpetuity Rights-to "As much land" he can "improve" in the Americas (213, 225). In the treatise, Locke's Man-Human is unlike the "wild Indian" who "knows no inclosure" (209, 218) and has failed to value-improve the Americas beyond a "wild" or "waste" land (219, 220).

> And amongst those who are counted the civilized part of mankind. (212; also see 189, 207)
>
> All men are naturally in that state [state of nature] . . . till . . . they make themselves members of some politic society. (199)
>
> The kings of the Indians in America, which is still a pattern of the first ages in Asia and Europe. (280)
>
> The work of his hands . . . are properly his. Whatsoever then he removes out of the state that nature hath provided, and left it in, he hath mixed his labour with, and joined to it something is his own, and thereby makes it his property. (209)
>
> Labour put a distinction between them and common. (210)
>
> Is known to be of his blood. (114)
>
> That civil government is the proper remedy. (197)

The discourse of the *idea* shared by Castro to Biden is a by-product of Locke's words and ideas on the Americas and a state of perfect freedom. It is the outgrowth of his invention of new place images-and-myths: imagery that *looks on* and impresses on the Americas a dualistic and evolutionary continuum: wasteland/vacant, waste/fertility; the wretched/the civilized, the Other/

Possessions-of-the-Same (see Dussel 1995, 35). Kant (1996d), Hegel (1902), and Gobineau (1915) offer clarity to impressions that cover-up-and-over: "When America . . . [was] discovered, [it was] . . . countr[y] belonging to no one, since they [Christian Europeans] counted the inhabitants as nothing" (Kant 1996d, 329); "Of America and its grade of civilization . . . which must expire as soon as Spirit approached it . . . what takes place in America is but an emanation from Europe" (Hegel 1902, 136–137, 143); "their whole continent is henceforth, as they all know, the inheritance of the European" (Gobineau 1915, 170, 28). The *idea* is not an *original* US *creation* but rather part of the same phenomenon of the *idea of the Americas*. And this has implications for how we are to contend with Castro to Biden's usage of the *idea*, which are impressions authorizing Man-Human Rights-to, ultimately satisfying a desire and objective to belong-to lands elsewhere and otherwise.

Words and ideas matter. They become the foundation for institutions, world views, and course of actions to *appear* and *become* consequential within and beyond their immediate settings and contexts. Take as example the words and idea "all men are created equal" (National Archives 2024). Fanon (1986) was quick to unsettle such by pointing out the disparities that arise when nonsettlers claim to be equal to settlers (44). Because near and far, whether advanced by Locke or Biden, the *idea* for which Western nations have rested their founding and moral principles on is but a pretext of and for modern/colonial and settlerizing designs. Words and ideas matter to enunciators in positions to dominate information, manage information as factual, and control mediums of circulation. For that reason, we must remain attentive to designs and its technologies including the *idea*. To do so though requires an archival approach and theory of archival impressions. Methodologically speaking, if words and ideas are locatable, identifiable, and nameable, they are analyzable, bringing to the fore the important role of narrativizing the *Archive*.

Words and ideas constitute the *palimpsestic narratives* of Western civilization. One such narrative is that of the US. In March 2018, President Donald Trump tweeted, "Our Nation was founded by farmers . . . And our continent was tamed by farmers" (Felton 2018). (It is reminiscent of Locke's statements on discovery and cultivation of land.) In May of 2018, at the US Naval Academy in Annapolis, Maryland, he remarked, "Our ancestors . . . tamed a continent, and triumphed over the worst evils in history . . . We trekked the mountains, explored the oceans, and settled the vast frontier" (Felton 2018). (Once more, the undertones of Locke's rhetoric on *settling a property* and inclosing land.) Trump echoed all this in his 2020 State of the Union Address:

> The American nation was carved out of the vast frontiers . . . Our ancestors braved the unknown; tamed the wilderness; settled the Wild West . . . built the most exceptional republic ever to exist in all of human history . . . This is our glorious and magnificent inheritance . . . We are pioneers. We are the pathfinders. We settled the New World, we built the modern world, and we changed history forever by embracing the eternal truth that everyone is made equal . . . (Schaff 2020, n.p.)

It is important to point out Trump's inventions of new place images-and-myths that operate on a dualistic and evolutionary continuum: unknown/known, frontiers/tamed wilderness, Wild West/modern world. (Again, the undertones of Locke's rhetoric on a vacant waste land of America that could be appropriated under the conditions that a labor puts it to use.) Here, the "pioneer" desires to proclaim the land that *lays in common* his inheritance, seeding the *idea* they belong-to the Americas per Rights-to assumed in overcoming and settling nature. In October of 2020, Trump doubled down at a political rally: "We stand on the shoulders of American heroes who crossed the oceans, settled a continent, tamed the wilderness" (*Rev* 2020, n.p.). The "we," coupled with "ancestors" in the State of the Union Address, evokes an inheritance and dwelling as old as *the idea* of *America*. Trump reproduces a literacy of the exceptional, an image of masculine and martial grit and vigor (Hämäläinen 2008), and a rhetoric of salvation, progress, and development. It is vital to excavate the march toward hegemony out of the project of modernity because what we will come to find is that it benefits an *association of social interests* (Mignolo 2005).

A Western ontology (*coloniality of being*) instituted by a Western epistemology (*coloniality of knowledge*) is epistemic racism. (Here, emphasis on epistemic is meant to draw attention to human contact and touch, the rhetoricity behind the human work and projects that ensures some *things* or the ideas, images-signs-sounds, and ends of some *one* remains constituted and carried over.) It is characteristic of *humanitas* or *knowing-subjects*, those in positions of power to name-define *Being-Other*, map *Being-Other* on a *Chain of Being* and stages of improvements-developments model, and guard, interpret, and enunciate the law. President Biden's inaugural address on January 20, 2021, is an example: "This is America's day"; "This is democracy's day"; "democracy has prevailed" (Blake and Scott 2021, n.p.). Like Theodore Roosevelt (1901) in his First Annual Message, who used America as a shorthand ("America has only just begun"; "American institutions"; "American people"), Biden is a *humanita* and not just a "placeholder of and for the oligarch and the plutocrats" (Democracy Now 2011). Biden, like Roosevelt, reproduces a US-centric literacy in referring to "America" as the US; a post-1898 image of empire-building and imperialism; and a rhetoric of modernity revised by *ideas* of democracy and forged in the crucible of a settler colonialism and a historical nexus of racist world views and institutions including capitalist exploitation. How does Western democracy and modern/colonial and settlerizing designs interact? Both are theologically and secularly structured, refracted through the lens of the *idea of the Americas* and within the frame of modernity/coloniality. Democracy does not prevail for those *thrown* into and relegated to the shadows or shadowlands.

Democracy, like Man-Human-Rights, is constituted as legible. Four days after the insurrection at the US Capitol on January 6, 2021, House Speaker Nancy Pelosi commented to reporters that rioters had "chosen their whiteness over democracy" (Dzhanova 2021). Though deceptive, it virtuized and moralized democracy. That day is still clear as day for those who know such an institution is a haunted/haunting and wounded/wounding one. With news soundbites on a loop, it became possible to make out John Calhoun's shadow. He framed the institution Pelosi cherishes as the "Government of the white man." Calhoun (1848) held no one was equal to the "excellence" of the white man (9–12). With the soundbites, one could see the *pale ghost* walking the halls of democracy with a Confederate flag. It is in the white man sitting down with a shield that bares the word "POLICE." Calhoun's words could be heard if one listened deeply: "Are we to associate ourselves as equals . . . I should consider such a thing as fatal to our institutions" (Calhoun 1848, 10). Such words, images, and ideas continue to be carried over on the "winds of the U.S.," which President Biden claimed in a speech, "are the winds of the World" (C-Span 2023). The words, images, and ideas above create a sound that affirms for many the legibility of a racial democracy and the illegibility of a democracy for all. Overall, they speak to both how "democracy" continues under the yoke of the regulative function of the *Archive* and how smaller archives (the US as a *working part*) remain a prism through which to see the *idea of the Americas* refracted through the lens of *Americanity* and frame of modernity/coloniality.

The words and ideas enunciated by Trump, Pelosi, and Biden are their own. Yet their literacies, images-signs-sounds, and rhetorics are steeped in an *epistemic system* and in modern/colonial and settlerizing designs. They speak from the side of *humanitas* but also the colonial/imperial center. While I read through the lens of a US-based geopolitics, which presents a limitation once more, I argue that it is a discourse that is identifiable (and not hidden by the visible face of modernity and its rhetorics) elsewhere and otherwise, and thus, it is a global discourse, one that traffics in the normative with audacity.

The *Archive* might bear the glaring image of the US today, because the nation has rebuilt a global system in its image, but it will always already be a palimpsestic image reflecting an *association of social interests*. The point is that everyday people are affective channels of rhetorical transmission for a Western ontology instituted by an epistemology that observes, *thingifies* (devaluing and dehumanizing), and enforces viewpoints on Man-Human-Rights. It behooves us then to create a public record and excavate the archival impressions that ultimately constitute the *Archive*. Below is not *the* story or the *whole* story, but a story that invites one to bear witness to the *exaggeration of crises* refracted, elsewhere and otherwise, that always already stages the emergence of a penetration into the space, place, and time of an-other. It is an exercise, vital to a *decolonial analytic*, in locating, identifying, and naming words and ideas that constitute and give form to pan-global empires.

A Frame of Modernity/Coloniality: "¿Qué ves?"; "¿Qué oyes?"; "¡Entiendes!"

Words and ideas matter. The MCC refers to a *hegemonic architecture* as the universal house of reason, knowledge, enunciation, modernity/coloniality (Mignolo 2011c). It is the house of *humanitas* and the epistemic zero point, an imperial position that historically partitioned geographies (geographic-racism) and computed histories (chrono-racism). Spatial-and-temporal colonial difference and epistemic and ontological differences are an effect and consequence of enunciations and discourse having impact beyond their immediate settings and contexts. The analogy of a *hegemonic architecture* as a house is fitting. *Ideas* are a foundation (Hegel 1886; Gobineau 1915). They become an *epistemic system* of *ends* for an architectonic that aspires to materialize the image of the whole (Kant 1819, 1998b, 2012; Hegel 1896). An *epistemic system* was foundational for a *hegemonic architecture*, both of which were architected to be left behind. Per the rhetorical excavation work—a technological, rhetorical, and archival analysis—I will undertake below, what becomes evident is that *ideas* are but archived inventions or recycled writing, existing in the "settler" universe of a *semiotic apparatus of enunciation*, baked with modern/colonial and settlerizing mentalities.

Coloniality of Knowledge and Being in the West

Back at Syracuse University I stumbled upon *Notes on the State of Virginia*. In it, Thomas Jefferson (1825) wrote of "slaves" as contrary to and different from Man-Human in odor and reason ("reflection"). They exhibited, according to him, natural and animalistic propensities ("sensation"). Jefferson thus argued that Black people were inferior in body and mind compared to whites (also see Kant 2013b). His book took me down a rabbit hole of eighteenth-and twentieth-century cultural texts on Man-Human-Rights constelled by the observer observing and thingifying, the *idea* (of the Americas and *Americanity*, race and epistemic racism, *humanitas* and anthropoi, epistemic and ontological differences, race/labor and domination/exploitation), and the epistemological and political regime of modernity.

I encountered Sir William Lawrence (1848). He claimed that observing was "innocent and rational" (29). However, I was quickly reminded of Gobineau (1915). Because he proposed that "strong and weak races exist" (xiv) and "human races are unequal" (73). Gobineau argued that civilization was incommunicable to "savages" and "enlightened nations" (171) because they were "unlike" those at the top of the "foot of the ladder" in a *Chain of Being* model (205–209). These were, according to him, nature's laws and rules—rational, logical, permanent, and indestructible—discernible through Reason and Truth. Others echoed this inhumane and irrational discourse that contradicts the idea of an innocent and rational observation (Lawrence 1848).

Samuel Morton (1839) wrote about the highest and lowest grades of humanity. He observed that the latter were only capable of imitating. Charles Caldwell (1830) provided an explanation. He observed that the *native bent* of the white race was toward civilization. *Others* bore a "stamp of inferiority," stuck on a *time-beaten track* and *out-of-place* (136; also see Fabian 2014). This led Lawrence (1848) to study marked differences and gradations. He observed that *others* were unlikely to possess moral sentiments or intellect like Europeans. Lawrence and Caldwell define Europeans as Man-Human, who has overcome nature (in more ways than one) and is in possession of certain qualities including that of reflexivity. Reflexivity speaks to the observer who observes, *thingifies*, and enforces viewpoints on Man-Human-Rights (Caldwell 1830, 134–135):

> By the intelligence of man the animals have been subdued, tamed, and reduced to slavery; by his labours marshes have been drained, rivers confined, their cataracts effaced, forests cleared, and the earth cultivated. By his *reflection*, time has been computed, space measured, the celestial motions recognized and represented, the heavens and the earth compared. (Lawrence 1848, 159; emphasis mine)

> In the history of man, there must have been a time, when the Caucasian was as uninstructed as the African or the American Indian . . . "nature's simple

child" . . . Wherefore, then, in the career of intellectual improvement, has he left them at such an immeasurable distance behind him? . . . He is superior to them in native intellectual faculties. He is so endowed, by reason of a higher and better organization, that he can instruct himself, by attending to the objects of nature around him, observing their phenomena, and studying their laws. (Caldwell 1830, 134–135)

Lawrence and Caldwell observed the *other* as deficient in, without, and/or lacking because of their nature and proximity to nature-animality-children. The collective held that they had no history, were apathetic to possessions, and were unable to improve by *instruction* because of natural designs. (Such observation will show up in the next two chapters as well.) Only the Caucasian race, they argued, had discoveries, inventions, and improvements because of their *gift* of preeminence. The collective argued that the world was indebted to them. Josiah Nott and George Gliddon (1854) referred to the white race thus as "representative[s] of civilization" (66) whose agenda is "perfecting civilization" (77). Lawrence (1848) added that they thus had the right to "exert themselves [on] behalf of the unenlightened and oppressed" to save them from themselves and restore unto them a "mental culture" and "pure" faith-religion (342).

The two reflections above are characteristic of an epistemic zero point. In *Animalium Specierum* Carl Linnaeus (1759) defined its purpose: *homo nosce te ipsum/know thyself* (12; also see Hegel 1894). And in *Systema Naturae* Linnaeus (1964) described the zero point: the *observer* "observ[ing] God's work" and "the universe" (10, 18–19). Linnaeus offers a link between a theo-and-ego matrix. Because to know nature is to understand its creator and design (Christian cosmology); to *know thyself* through Reason and Truth is to overcome and dominate nature (secular cosmology). He argued that the first step, thus, is "to know," through a proposed science of *classification* and *name-giving* (19). Knowing would extend beyond nature. Others followed suit, setting precedence for the *idea* that certain men had *rights*: to observe, prescribe meaning to objects, and establish a "center" and "higher nature" atop a *ladder of Being* mapped onto a *Chain of Being* model (also see Carus 1849).

A science of classifying and name-giving is evidenced in *A New Division of the Earth*. Johann Bernier (2001) expresses the "idea of dividing" geography "in another way." He prescribes qualities in racial terms to four races and linked them with geography based on observations of "men" whose "distinctive traits [were] so obvious" (247). David Hume's (1822) work is similar with observations on why characteristics are assigned to people. In *Essays and*

Treatises on Several Subjects, he partitioned geography into provinces of misery, indolence, and "most remarkable" and matched them with national characteristics (191–193). Hume argued in racial terms that *others* were naturally inferior to whites in intellect, art, and science. Friedrich Blumenbach's (1999) observations of varieties of mankind in *On the Natural Varieties of Mankind* provide a rationale. He claims in racial terms that Caucasians are "first" in color, beauty, and perfection (Nott and Gliddon 1854). Though Blumenbach's *idea* may seem miscontextualized, the *idea* itself would have grave implications, confirming suspicions of and indeed beliefs on the *other's* epistemic and ontological differences.

An epistemology and hubris of the zero point does not take a coevolutionary position but rather *thingifies* to establish an ontology of Being. *Thingification* is predicated on the idea that without objects there is no thought, and without the ability to divide and analyze them into thinghood, there is no science of Reason and Truth (works of Reason-Truth). Immanuel Kant (2012) is a case-in-point. Reminiscent of Shakespeare, he claimed that the "world is the foundation and stage" on which "our ingenious play is performed" (446; also see Said 1979, 63). He enlisted questions to set the stage for the citizen of the world, guardian of the masses, and a cosmopolitical sense: *what can I know, what should I do, what may I hope, what is man?* (Kant 1998b, 677). If the cognitive faculties were unclear, Kant offers some clarification by enlisting an additional set of questions: *what do I intend to do, what is of importance, what is the result?* (Kant 1996b, 127). There is much contention as to Kant, but based on my readings and interpretations, he contributed to an inhumane and irrational discourse.

Understanding nature's design was essential to establishing Reason and Truth. Kant was interested in both the difference between artificial and natural systems and the role that laws and rules ought to play in the everyday. Nature, he observed, gave each human race characteristics. Every rational being, Kant claimed, exists not as a *means* to be used but as an *end* in itself. However, he held that only some could overcome the developmental stage of nature or immaturity where being exhibits sensuous, animalistic, and/or barbaric qualities. Kant invoked the analogy of animals acting without consciousness of itself in this context. They exist only as *means* with Man as the *end*. To be stuck in nature, he argued, is to be without thought and culture. For Kant, Man could wield power over what was cognized as objects and do with *it* as he pleased. These observations established a natural system of Reason and Truth that would be detrimental to perceived *others* and their Rights (Kant 1996a, 1996b, 1996c, 1996d, 1997, 2011, 2013b, 2013c).

Reason and Truth were paramount to ideas of Man-Human. Kant's observations of feeling, taste, beauty, morality, reason, philosophy, and civilization across space and time established natural designs. He prescribed qualities (sensuous, savage, exceptional) in racial terms to each human race and associated them with geography. According to Kant (2011), the highest degree of development, improvement, and perfection were among the Greeks and European nations (France, England, and Germany) (also see Hegel 1896). They possessed "extraordinary gifts" (59). "To a high degree," he stated, "we are, through art and science, cultured. We are civilized" (Kant 1998a, 42–44). Kant observed that nonwhites, who by their nature were contrary to and different from whites, reflected an *exceptional lack* of stature, feeling, and/or culture that neither proximity to the sublime nor *instruction* could aid (also see Voltaire 1780; Rousseau 1973). Still, Kant argued for *instruction* and *discipline*, in the context of *means* and *ends*, that underscored Rights in the project of epistemological (ap/ex)propriation (Kant 1996e, 1998a, 2011, 2012, 2013a, 2013c).

Georg W. F. Hegel (1902), like Kant, is a link between theo-and-ego politics. He observed in nature inequalities in development from the imperfect to perfect. *Mind subjective*, or the merest particular of being for self, is the first standpoint where being exhibits "an unreflected character of mere nature" (135). *Mind objective* is the second stage where Man goes forth from self to make Spirit object to itself with content and *ends*: observing, inventing, and creating connections between objects. *Mind absolute* is the third stage, a return of Spirit unto itself as unification (e.g., sensuous-rational and particular-universal) in universal consciousness and objective existence. There is much contention as to what Hegel meant. However, based on my readings and interpretations, he contributed to an inhumane and irrational discourse. Hegel (1896) invoked the analogy of animals acting on instincts unable to *think* or *will* Rights to distinguish "[true] human" from *other* (51). Beings in *thinghood*, for him, are objects for the *Being of Being* as they lacked thought-will (Hegel 1977).

Reason and Truth are chief to *ideas* of Man-Human-Rights. Hegel's (1902) observation of im/maturity and Spirit across space-time established natural designs: "Of America and its grade of civilization . . . which must expire as soon as Spirit approached it . . . what takes place in America is but an emanation from Europe" (136–137, 143). He prescribed qualities (*proper soil, stationary-fixed, land of childhood*) in racial terms to each human race and linked them with geography. According to Hegel, like Kant, the highest degree of development, improvement, and maturity of Spirit were among the Greeks and European nations (France, England, and Germany). They formed for him the "centre," the "proper soil for the emancipation of Spirit" (160–161, 526). Hegel argued, "Our world, our time," by which he meant Europe/ans, is the "last stage" and "end of History" (163, 552). He observed that non-Europeans were contrary to and different from Europeans; they either did not possess historical character or culture or their culture was in a *vegetative state*. Hegel argued for the value of pedagogy-instruction here. "The glory," he might say, "of the Idea" (569) (also see Hegel 1857, 1894, 1896).

Western ontology is inhumane and irrational. A *Chain of Being* model invents and reduces *others* to animalistic propensities. It serves the purpose of removing Rights; rationalizing violence as means to maximize *usefulness*; justifying (forced) decline as divine and natural design; and defining Man as belonging-to and owners of lands. This spatial colonial difference was central to the temporal in the rise of *leagues of nations-friendships* (nation-states) (see Heineccius 1741; Kant 1998a). Kant (1996b) described the function of nation-states through a logic of settler colonialism:

> If he arrives in foreign lands as a colonist, he will soon form with his compatriots a sort of social club which, as a result of unity of language and, partially, of religion makes him part of a little clan, which under the higher authority of the government distinguishes itself in a peaceful and moral way through industry, cleanliness, and thrift from the settlements of other nationalities (233).

Man required a *master*. While critics are keen to point out that Kant asserted Man cannot be a master of another being, all the above accounted for thus far (means/ends; master/animal) suggests otherwise. And it is the *idea* of a perfect or correct civic constitution that underscores it all because it could be the means to manage and control epistemic obedience and differentiate modern from tradition on a global scale. Both types of difference, spatial and temporal, reflect a *coloniality of knowledge* instituting a *coloniality of being*: "No human race can be unfaithful to its instincts, and leave the path that has been marked out for it by God" (Gobineau 1915, 53). The epistemic zero point achieved through Reason and Truth was nothing more than epistemic racism and the epistemological regime of modernity at work.

Part and parcel to a *decolonial analytic* is to locate, identify, and name inhumane and irrational discourse that observes, *thingifies*, and enforces viewpoints on Man-Human-Rights. As absurd as they are, the words and ideas of *humanitas* become the foundation for institutions, worldviews, and course of actions (designs and technologies) to *appear* and *become* consequential within and beyond their immediate settings and contexts (see Mignolo 2005, 81). The point of this tracing thus far is to put words and ideas under the knife and dissect them analytically. Doing so confirms that the *Archive* is rarely ever in a "state of being" a completed project but always already an ongoing and structuring "process" of settlerizing encounters, interactions, and engagements open toward the future (Hall 2011, 727). Moreover, it confirms that everyday people have to do work rhetorically to enable their designs (see Said 1979, 40). I continue my rhetorical excavation work below, where iterative writing and address give way to palimpsestic time (Alexander 2005), identities (Shohat 2002), and narratives (A. García 2004) as cultural productions baked with modern/colonial and settlerizing mentalities.

Coloniality of Knowledge and Being in the Americas

A *return* to the Americas and the *idea of the Americas* is necessary for contending with an *epistemic system* and modern/colonial and settlerizing designs. It is established on the *idea* of race, epistemic racism, and the frame of modernity/coloniality. Its modus operandi is the colonial matrix of power and includes coloniality of knowledge, being, nature, and power. It unfolds as follows: an epistemic zero point and provenance, doctrines of discovery and rights to land/conquest, divine and natural designs, epistemic and ontological differences, and rhetorics of modernity. They function through narratives of land waiting to be discovered, owned, and transformed; destined saviors; certain beings as dispensable and/or exploitable; and macro-historical subjects with omnipotence of direction and finality. All of it stations *ideas* of Man-Human-Rights, constellated by observers observing, *thingifying* ideas, images-signs-sounds, and ends, and enforcing viewpoints.

Ontologies of Man-Human-Rights are theologically structured and are evidenced in fifteenth- and sixteenth-century cultural texts of the Spanish. The authority of the papal bulls cannot be overlooked. In *The Bull Romanus Pontifex*, Pope Nicholas V weighed in on the Rights of Portugal and Castile to discover, conquer, and own new lands *"unknown"* to "westerners." What was known was that this new land was inhabited by "savage excesses" and "enemies of the Christian name" (Davenport 1917a, 21). Both were in dire need of Christianization via education-instruction. The Church granted King Alfonso rights "to invade, search out, capture, vanquish, and subdue" the land and its inhabitants. Furthermore, the Church decreed rights to possess lands for "profit" and "reduce" *others* "to perpetual slavery" (23–24). "Of forever of right," the Pope writes, "belongs and pertains, to the said King Alfonso, his successors, and the infante, and not to any others" (24). Herein lies the *humanitas* or *knowing-subject* both attributing to himself and the likeminded epistemic privileges and Rights to be gatekeepers of the un/known (also see Mignolo 2011a).

Pope Alexander VI's authority was exhibited in three papal bulls. *The Bull Inter Caetera* (May 3, 1493) addressed lands "discovered and to be discovered" and was written in support of Spain and King Ferdinand (Davenport 1917b, 63). The Pope acknowledged a desire to increase the spread of the Catholic faith and the role of Christian religion in *overthrowing* and bringing "the Indian" into the "Christian profession" (61–62). To such ends, the Church granted King Ferdinand in perpetuity "all rights, jurisdictions" to discover the unknown, "*instruct* the . . . inhabitants," and "train them in good morals" (62–63). *The Bull Eximiae Devotionis* (May 3, 1493) upheld the May 3 letter while *The Bull Inter Caetera* (May 4, 1493) amended it. The latter, which fed into a Christian hegemonic ordering that divided Indias Orientales and Indias Occidentales, established a "line from the Arctic pole . . . to the Antarctic pole . . . one hundred leagues towards the west and south . . ." in perpetuity to favor the rights of Spain over Portugal to manage and control (Davenport 1917c, 77). The projects of territorial and epistemological (ap/ex)propriation were rationalized and justified in the name of Christianization and civilizing (also see Hanke 1937).

Proclamations of rights did not just come from papal bulls, though. The Council of Castile, under authority of King Ferdinand, issued *Requerimiento*. It invoked the rhetoric of *Other-as possessions of the-Same*—"you and we"—but quickly recognized the political authority of Spain as "subduers of the barbarous nations." The Western Christianity imaginary delineated the *terms* and *contents* of superiority and inferiority based on Christian faith, religion, and morals as the ideal. *Requerimiento* also acknowledged the religious authority of the Church, through St. Peter, over "all men [whole human race] in the world" (National Humanities Center Resource Toolbox 2007, 1). It observed Rome, as effect and consequence of Pope Alexander VI's work and as the center of space and present of time, the "spot most fitting to rule the world from" (1). An *Other-as-Same* rhetoric is invoked again but only to compel "the Indian" to do what "subjects ought to do" (2). It is suggested "the Indians" had a *choice* in whether they would receive the "good will" of Spain and the Church. But the *choice* is a demand. Resistance justified war, (ap/ex)propriation, enslavement, and forced obedience. *Requerimiento* places the fault on and holds "the Indian" culpable for all atrocities committed in the name of civilizing (2) (also see Dussel 1995; Wynter 2003).

An *association* of *knowing-subjects* would utilize cultural texts to *thingify*, enforce Western Christian viewpoints, and encourage certain human work and projects. Between 1523 (letter to Charles V) and 1558 (letter to King Philip III), Pedro de Gante wrote letters to reflect on his work. In his letter to King Philip, for example, he began by expressing loyalty as a servant to the Royal Crown. De Gante continued by providing King Philip with evidence of his work. He offered an account of difficult times in *instructing* the religious poor (*other*)—evidence of *coloniality of instruction-and-curriculum*. They had no writing ("sin escriptura"), letters ("sin letras"), or reason ("sin lumber de cosas alguna") (Icazbalceta 1889, 221). In this way, de Gante noted, they were like animals ("estaba como animales sin razón") (231). He described for King Philip subsequently a time where children were locked in a house and deprived so they could forget their idolatries ("para que se olvidasen de sus sangrientas idolatrías" [222, 230]; "poco á poco se destruyeron y quitaron muchas idolatrías" [231]). Overall, de Gante gave word to efforts to carry out the human work and projects of indoctrinating the *other* in literacy (reading, alphabetic writing, speaking, and singing) and *instructing* them in Christian doctrine. Literacy became an apparatus to manage and control obedience ("á la obediencia de la Santa Iglesia" [224]), while the Americas and "the Indian" were instruments to advance the ends of the Spanish (also see Vallette 1917). Out of the Americas, *coloniality of instruction-and-curriculum* emerges.

Knowing-subjects understood the invention of the *other* and arguments ascribed to the *other* had not ontological but fictional existence. Yet within the epistemological and political regime of modernity, whoever dominated the epistemological, ideological, rhetorical, and aesthetic war on information could manage Truth and controlled transcendental truths (Rights). Another example of this is evident in *Historia Eclesiástica Indiana*. In it Gerónimo de Mendieta (1870) observed that "the Indian" was marked by error, blindness, and absence (237, 264). Mendieta attributed this to what they were deficient in, without, and/or lacking: letters ("á falta de letras"), language ("falta de su lengua"), spirit ("de este espíritu que á ellos les falta"), and doctrine ("por falta de doctrina") (143, 210, 296, 451, 665). He compared their natural qualities ("cualidades naturales") to that of children ("vuelven . . . causi al estado de la niñez") (454). All this assured Mendieta "the Indian" were contrary to and different. For him, this assessment rationalized and justified projects of salvation and civilization (416, 451). Those projects were informed by Aristotelian philosophy on Being-Man and slave and *means* and *ends* (also see Howett 1885).

Bartolomé de Las Casas (1566) was also a central figure as a *knowing-subject*. He came to the defense of "the Indian" in *Apologética* to validate their natural rational capacity ("discurso natural de razón") (2564, 1735, 2800). But Las Casas also enforced colonizing Christian viewpoints with his emphasis on their disposition toward conversion. (So one must wonder if Las Casas was merely being contrarian in the Valladolid debate given a unified front against "the Indian.") In enacting the zero-point epistemology, he observed certain beings in a first and rude state ("están en el estado primero y rudo") (2799, 2801, 2831, 664, 3534–3542). What follows is a discussion of his often-cited five classifications of barbarians. But the point here is that Las Casas considered some barbarians as desirable and thus objects of the Church, who though deficient in ("defectos que tiene"), without, and/or lacking ("por falta"; "falte de") law, letters, and a true religion, were susceptible to conversion (3578, 3564, 3561, 3580–3582). Herein lie two haunting human projects that he brought to light further. First, that the possibility of the *other's* humanization could only be attributed to their conversion to Christianity (and then civilization, progress, development). And second, that *knowing-subjects* were *police policing police*. Throughout *Apologética* Las Casas weighs in on the *other's police*, which is contrary to and different. By *police* Las Casas meant *politeia* and human qualities ("carecientes de humana policía") (16; also see Franklin 1839, 1857). Ultimately, he held the projects of salvation were justifiable, that punishment was rational, and that the racial distribution of labor was defensible. Las Casas too embraced an Aristotelian philosophy, and it is the (*idea* of the) Americas that offers a unique space and place for the epistemological and ontological experiment (also see Las Casas 1877, 1965, 1974).

Thingification permitted an *association of knowing-subjects* to advance a politics and theory of *police*. Difference signified unequal nature and plus/minus degrees of humanity. In *De Promulgando Evangelio APVD Barbaros*, José de Acosta (1670) carried out an Aristotelian philosophy on *the ruler* and *the ruled*. He observed that certain beings held nonhuman qualities and animalistic propensities ("Hos omnes homines, aut vix homines, humana docere oportet"). (110, 137). It rationalized capture and justified compliance through pedagogical *instruction* ("cum ferarum more capi & per vim domari")—evidence, again, of *coloniality of instruction-and-curriculum* (5–6). De Acosta (1604a) interpreted this at the *worke of God* and morality of ruling, explored further in *The Natural and Moral History of the Indies* (528). There he claimed the "*pollicie*" (450) of "the Indian" was *elementary* (304). He attributed this to what they were deficient in, without, and/or lacking: "thoughtes," alphabet, writing, "bookes," and learning (396–405). Their contrariness and difference rationalized salvation and civilization as a "perfect remedie" (532). "God," Acosta wrote, "created this people, and . . . seemed to have thus long forgot them" (531; also see de Acosta 1604b, 1987). And herein lies a Spanish corollary, that a deficiency or lack of *police* means "the Indian" does not think, and therefore, they are less human (also see Howett 1885).

Other *knowing-subjects* were central to a politics and theory of *police* too. Bernardo Aldrete (1674, 34) observed naked people ("vivían a guise e fieras desnudos") deficient in, without, and/or lacking science, histories, and letters in *Del Origen y Principio de la Lengua Castellana*. He coordinated "aquella gente" and "la policía que las acompaña" to center Western Christian ideals (34). In *Yucatan*, Diego de Landa (1937) observed certain beings walked in *misery, error,* and *superstitions* and exhibited *childlike* propensities contrary to and different than the Spanish (81–83). He framed the "coming of Spaniards" as a "remedy," who could *instruct* "the Indian" in *how to live*—evidence of an *epistemological framework for the living* (111–112). Bernardino de Sahagún (1938) observed a parallel between medical/spiritual doctors who cure physical/spiritual diseases—"los predicadores y confesores médicos son de las ánimas" (5)—in *Historia General de las Cosas de Nueva España*. Again, the undertones of *coloniality of instruction-and-curriculum*. He would ultimately argue that God sent servants ("los cristianos") to destroy them and their gods if they resisted (65–65). Difference rationalizes and justifies various types of violence.

Juan Ginés de Sepúlveda (1987) held an extreme view of violence. In *Tratado: Sobre las Justas Causas de la Guerra Contra los Indios*, he observed that "the Indian" was not wholly without reason ("no carecen totalmente de razón") (109) but still inferior per divine and natural design—"no tienen estas cualidades" (87, 93). De Sepúlveda credited this to what they were deficient in, without, and/or lacking: science ("no poseen ciencia"), letters ("ni siquiera conocen las letras"), and apathy toward possessions ("que nadie posee individualmente cosa alguna") (101, 109). He was convinced of their animalistic propensities (101), stating, they did not even deserve the name human ("tales que apenas merecían el nombre de seres humanos") (133). De Sepúlveda argued that they were contrary to and different from the perfect ("lo perfecto"), excellent ("lo excelente"), more cultured ("más cultas"), and more human ("más humanas") (83–85, 95, 109), and thus, they must admit their inferiority and submit to their own domination either through the word of God or force (153, 161–163). He rationalized an Aristotelian philosophy of the ruler and justified the cause of war for the good of the public couched in divine and natural laws (69, 73,

115). Man-Human-Rights are taken as universal truths, but they are attributed by those who have the epistemic privilege to attribute to their meaning and deliberate who is deserving of such (also see Hanke 1994).

A Modern/Colonial and Settlerizing Archive

The above is not "A" history of the Americas or the *Archive*. Epistemic racism, for example, is adjacent to epistemic sexism and heterosexism. Las Casas's (1566) views on same-sex relations as nefarious, Kant's (2011) opinion on women not having reason and requiring men, and Hegel's (1896, 1902) belief that women's minds limited understanding of the sciences, philosophy, and certain arts are examples of *coloniality of gender* (Lugones 2008). There indeed existed a technology of race/labor or capitalistic exploitation between the centuries. In the "apendice" of *Historia de las Indias*, there is a footnote that references the transatlantic slave trade ("el comercio de esclavos negros"), where Las Casas (1877) proposed to bring Black slaves to "the Americas" ("llevason esclavos negros á América") to remedy the exploitation of "the Indian" (79, 80). It stood contrary to Ginés de Sepúlveda's (1987) belief that "the Indians" were naturally ("por naturaleza") slaves and "barbarians" (173). Lastly, there was much debate over who could truly claim to be the center of space and present of time, which speaks to how power is not just shared-in but also disputed (see Sepúlveda 1987; Hegel 1902). All these limitations are mine. Indeed, the above is not *the* story or the *whole* story, but a story on how everyday people do work rhetorically to enable the (re)writing of the *Archive*. Recall then Lawrence (1848), who claimed that observing was "innocent and rational" (29). Can we say this of Kant's (2011) rhetoric of the sublime, Hegel's (1896) philosophy of rights, and Sepúlveda's (1987) justification of war?

Part and parcel to a *decolonial analytic* is not just locating, identifying, and naming inhumane and irrational discourse but also unsettling them vis-à-vis the initiating of decolonizing archival impressions. To be clear then, "the Americas" were not discovered. They were invented to portray an image of land waiting to be discovered, owned, and transformed into "resources" (*coloniality of power-and-land-nature/resources*). Divine and natural designs do not exist. They were invented to depict an image of a certain Man-Human-as-destined saviors atop a *Chain of Being* (supposedly) permitted to observe, *thingify*, and enforce viewpoints (*coloniality of knowledge*). It was juxtaposed by the *other*, invented to produce an image of a dispensable being deficient in, without, and/or lacking (epistemic/ontological differences), awaiting modernity (*coloniality of instruction-and-curriculum*), management (race/labor), and/or demise (*coloniality of being*). There is no pristine and unilinear logic of development. It was invented to render a macro-historical subject as the center of space and present of time within a dualistic and evolutionary continuum. Out of the Americas, and from the discourses of Spanish friars and Jesuits, Kant, and Hegel, among others then, it is possible to discern the role of literacies and rhetorics alongside *coloniality of instruction-and-curriculum* that underscores how Eurocentrism is an epistemic and aesthetic issue partly because power is an epistemological, ideological, and rhetorical war on information.

Coloniality of instruction-and-curriculum is a settler-centered instruction in which *knowing-subjects*, whether Christianizing agents or educators, *inform* and *give form* to a *coloniality of knowledge-being*. It is a medium in which settler knowledge on appropriateness-correctness becomes factual and the experimental tool by which to manage and control truth, knowledge, and epistemic obedience. A *coloniality of instruction-and-curriculum* naturalizes the modus operandi of designs while peddling a racial matrix and racist worldviews predicated on the pretexts of epistemic and ontological differences, laws of Man-Human-Rights, and subtext of coloniality of power. *It*, this technology of the *Archive* and designs that will come into view better in the next two chapters, is a prism through which to see the University as a pillar *in* assemblage with designs and the humanities as a *working part* within the University operating as the police policing police (see Fúnez-Flores 2024).

To *return* to the *idea of the Americas* is to begin a process of *carefully reckoning* with hauntings and haunting situations. *Americanity* introduced a new racial matrix, racist world views, and a hierarchical and rule-based organization of relations between peoples and states that did not end with the Americas. It was the ideological model and overlay for *coloniality*, a *modern/colonial world system*, and a capitalist world-economy to thrive (supposedly) without historical colonialism that all continues to be felt today. *Americanity* became for modernity what *coloniality* is for modernity/rationality: the "old" world as the constitutive side of the "new" that is in the end rather "old." A *decolonial analytic* is aimed at "making visible the invisible," analyzing the "mechanisms that produce such invisibility," and intervening at the "level of power, knowledge, and being through varied actions" (Maldonado-Torres 2007, 262). And seeing, feeling, and listening to the "sounds . . . images . . . symbols . . . utopias" of power (Quijano and Wallerstein 1992, 556). But to be clear, it does not mean "a total rejection of all theory or research or Western Knowledge" (L. Smith 2012, 41). A *decolonial analytic* in part means *returning* to self-assumed epistemic privileges of *knowing-subjects* observing; *carefully reckoning* with words and ideas that have no ontological existence but materialize nonetheless as truth; and getting caught up in the *enduring task* to unsettle the settled-ness of ontologies of Man-Human-Rights constituted and instituted by an epistemic racism.

What does an archival approach in this case afford? It demonstrates that a logic and its modus operandi remain intact despite successive evolutions-stages and mutated modalities of the *epistemic system* and modern/colonial and settlerizing designs. Sure, the words are replaced with new ones, in a sense, but to paraphrase Hegel (1902), the "new" is but an "echo" of the old (143). What is new is not so new after all when we peel back the layers: an *epistemic system* and a set of designs and technologies. What then does a theory of archival impression afford? It provides a window into that which gives structure to and constitutes the support structure of the *Archive*. Archival impressions are the haunted/haunting bookmarks of designs that offer statements on the ways the *idea* is renewed and remapped; the ways a logic of coloniality remains advantageous and thus shared-in, imported, expanded, and/or disputed through crooked rhetorics of modernity. Once more Benoit's (1996) notion of *discourse about actions* is useful, which allows us to conceive of the accumulation of *archival impressions* as accounts that function to explain, justify, interpret, and/or rationalize actions. This is not conjecture as we have as evidence the historicity (the palimpsestic narrative) of and rhetoricity (desires and objectives) behind the making of the *Archive*. The *Archive*, a *human thing* human beings have built, feels the human touch, and thus reflects some *things* left behind by human contact. The *Archive* and its smaller archives are a prism through which to see designs refracted through the lens of *Americanity* and within the frame of modernity/coloniality.

Whether *humanitas* cited each other is a moot point. What occurred in the Americas 500 years ago, such as the materialization of a superstructure of written record I refer to as the *Archive*, continues to *appear* and *be* consequential. All around there is evidence of a structuring principle of settlerizing encounters, interactions, and engagement, keeping spaces and places wounded/wounding and *stories-so-far* haunted/haunting. The logic of coloniality, which is the darker and (supposedly) hidden side of rhetorics of modernity, remains a vested interest. Today, the *Archive* is much bigger and moves much faster than any nation-state. *It* is boundless, existing almost in a virtual space inaccessible by any one *thing* or *one*; a technology or a technological interface processor that is an assemblage of *working parts* and is *in* assemblage with other smaller *archives of knowledges, understandings, feelings*, and *doings* (or the *working parts* of the *Archive*). We can think of the *Archive* as an interstate system, recording as much as it cements and produces discursive practices of structural principles, disseminating a universal code for domination, management, and control through which all information flows in and outward from. The next two chapters, organized by a *modernity/coloniality framework*, are case studies thus on how the *idea of Utah* and *Mormon/ism* and the *idea of Texas-LRGV* and *the settler* function as archival impressions within the *Archive*. The purpose of this chapter was to create the bases for understanding coloniality of knowledge-being and modern/colonial and settlerizing designs. And that is important, for as Mignolo and Walsh (2018) claim, "You can hardly decolonize something about which you do not know how it works" (136). Ultimately, by creating a public record, we can reposition the contents of the *Archive* still in the making and position ourselves in relation to its designs *otherwise*. The assembling of decolonizing archives and initiating of decolonizing archival impressions, I argue, is how we change the *contents* and *terms*.

My context for the next two chapters will be US focused. Still, the fundamental argument of this section remains: (1) we are all in and part of the *Archive* and (2) global modernities-colonialities manifest in local forms and conditions (Tlostanova 2017a, 40). We are in a historical juncture or moment—fake history, fake news, fake facts, fake videos (Roy 2020, 99)—where designs and technologies unfold without regard to maintain ecocide, genocide, and ethno-and-epistemicide: "Pocahontas"; "bad hombres"; "shithole countries"; "go back"; "Muslim Ban"; "Poisoning the blood"; "vermin"; "savages"; "have to be eradicated"; "barbaric"; "pigs"; "uncivilized"; "dangerous Palestinian." Perhaps, they always have trafficked in the normative, which in that case, the MCC's rhetoric of some *things* being cloaked or hidden is undermined. A rhetorical, technological, and decolonial-centered analytic is needed more than ever. My work in the next chapters thus will remain the same as this one: attend to a *semiotic apparatus of enunciations*, create a public record of and rhetoricize rhetorics of epistemology, truth-and-knowledge claims, and the rhetoricity behind archival impressions, and triangulate how an *association of social interest* shares-in, imports, and expands-disputes the *Archive*. And the same goal of this chapter will persist there as well—initiating decolonizing archival impression to unsettle, decolonize, and amend the lies, contradictions, myths, narcissism, cynicism, denialisms, and sickness-disease of the *Archive* and its actor-agents who initiate impressions that give structure to and constitute it. Much will have changed over the centuries. But the next two chapters will speak to how the world remains connected by some *things*, with the modern/colonial and settlerizing designs in Utah and Texas functioning as impressions entered into the *Archive*.

It is my hope that you, my reader, will continue with me as I *return* to and peel back layers to *carefully reckon* with what remains in land, memory, knowledge, and relationality after some *things* or some *one* has passed. We cannot remain entangled or complicit in burying what we know wounds. What will transpire in them are the coded words (vision, waste-and-fertile lands, miracles, awaken, etc.), tropes (the vanishing or disappearing magical act; aseptic cleanliness; the earth as fuckable, the fuckable earth; reap what you sow, and the Garden of Eden), and *ideas* (the epistemic zero point-provenance, doctrines of discovery/rights to land-conquest, divine and natural designs, epistemic and ontological differences, and rhetorics of modernity) of modern/colonial and settlerizing designs. In such contexts, the Latin meaning of *alibi*, alongside Gobineau's (1915) claim of a race worthy of a higher calling (61), offers a logical *excuse* to be elsewhere and otherwise, authorizing church settlers and pioneers alike to *replenish* what can be seen across the whole face of the earth.

Words, tropes, and *ideas* will be unpacked, and in so doing, the two chapters will demonstrate how everyday people do work rhetorically to enable the (re)writing of the *Archive*. Despite differing racial ideologies and divergent motives, similar designs and technologies recirculate, ensuring that the *Archive* is rarely ever in a "state of being" a completed project but always already an ongoing and structuring "process" of settlerizing encounters, interactions, and engagements open toward the future (Hall 2011, 727). This chapter will have laid the groundwork to translate the meaning of those encounters, interactions, and engagements across hauntings and haunting situations.

Reflexión-Meditación

A Reflection on Moving to Utah

Summer of 2017. I spent my first week in Utah familiarizing myself with my new work route. I traveled south on Beck Street from North Salt Lake, took a slight left on Victory Road to merge onto Columbus Street, headed down State Street to turn left on 2nd Avenue, and made a right on Virginia Street with school but just blocks away. The material forms of public memory in Utah comprise a *rhetoric of space-place* (see Endres and Senda-Cook 2011). They function as a prism through which to *bear witness-to* cultural claims about locality, regionality, and globality (*ideologies of scale*) and *see* its adjacent *ideas*, practices, and human projects realized in and across space, place, and time (*rhetorics of scale-making projects*) (see Tsing 2000). Everything from the grid system to stakes, wards, and temples spatially and temporally inflicts upon (a *politics of) mobility* (see Cresswell 2010), simultaneously tethering one to a center and to wor(l)ding aspirations (see J. Smith 1833), a reminder of the role spaces and places play in communicating to all who is behind-in or with the time and in-or-out of place (see Cresswell 2006). "All human landscape," Lewis (1979) argued, "has cultural meaning" (14). We are always already attuned to it as a cultural archive. But distracted eyes, sensibilities, and listening ensure we remain entangled and complicit in some *things* and the ideas, images-signs-sounds, and ends of some *one*. Might we dare then have the audacity to see, feel, and listen *otherwise*?

https://doi.org/10.7330/9781646426782.c002a

Take Temple Square as an example of cultural meaning. By design, it entangles and implicates people every day into wor(l)ding aspirations—involuntarily *returning* them to the idea of race, a religious *epistemic system* predicated on racism (and sexism and heterosexism), an *original impulse* (a civil, social, racial, and political design), and an epistemological regime of modernity. This is not conjecture as we have as evidence the historicity of and rhetoricity behind their archive. My everyday experience of traveling downtown has assured me my route to work is anything but mundane as it demands *careful reckonings* with the haunting and ghostly aspects of Utah. This wounded/wounding space and place communicates meaning whether we aim to make it audible or not. And once we dare have the audacity to see, feel, and listen *otherwise*, its meaning transpires an idea, narrative, and rhetoric. Below is one example of reassembling what is scattered in Utah:

> We were persecuted exiles [image] . . . forced to migrate West and seek refuge elsewhere as peaceful pioneers [narrative] . . . and upon arriving in the barren deserts and empty valleys, for which is our native inheritance, we alone made the desert yield and transformed it to blossom as the rose [rhetoric].

Stories are what people are (King et al. 2015) and how communities orient themselves to the past, present, and future. They are rhetorical. Stories have desires, a politics, and involve power (see A. Gordon 2008; Alexander and Mohanty 2010). They have structural underpinnings and material consequences (see Rohrer 2016). Stories are in part how an epistemological hegemony happens; how an epistemology institutes ontology; how ideologies are carried over; how hegemony is maintained as the status quo; and how hauntings and haunting situations continue to construct settler sites, constitute haunted/haunting communities, and maintain wounded/wounding spaces and places. But as an outsider in Utah, I am obliged neither to comply nor to accommodate such an archive, its stories, or the continued narrativization of stories. As an outsider, I feel this obligation and responsibility not to the *Archive* or its smaller archives (or the *working parts* of the *Archive*), but to an-*other* archive.

Utah today is neither the Americas nor the Utah of the past. And yet it cannot be separated from either the *idea of Utah* and *Mormon/ism* or the *idea of the Americas*. Hauntings as a category of analysis allows me to establish connections between the past and the present in terms of those *ideas* unfolding as social, racial, and political activities. Utah of the past and present is the outcome of human projects and work (see Giddens 1981; Pred 1984). The unsettling of the *Archive* and its archival impressions in Utah, for which I refer to as *smaller archives of knowledges, understandings, feelings, and doings* (or the *working parts* of the *Archive*), must be met by decolonizing archival impressions that first and foremost recognizes and acknowledges Utah as the traditional and ancestral homelands of the Shoshone, Paiute, Goshute, and Ute tribes.

So in what follows I *carefully reckon* with how the past shapes the present and how the future will demand something else of us all (see A. García 2004). To honor a decolonizing archival impression of my past, I take a *corrido-ing approach* for the next two chapters. It is a genre of storytelling in which corridistas announce a wounded/wounding space and place, situate haunted/haunting subjects in time, state haunted/haunting situations, and call forth a politics of hauntings, inheritances, and dwellings to the present (Aparicio 2013; García 2018b; Herrera-Sobek 1993; Noe 2009; Paredes 1958b; C. Ríos 2017; Sánchez 2006). Corridos are not "A" history but a version of a haunted/haunting story that unsettles histories and geographies of power. And that is exactly what I intend to do in the next two chapters.

We live amid archives—history, power, landscapes—made, unmade, and remade by writing. I will approach archives in the following chapters, much like Pierce Lewis (1979) wrote of landscapes, cultural records or *autobiographies* of cultural meaning reflecting *taste* and *values*. The next two chapters raise compelling questions about the ways in which writing, rhetoric, place, archives, and modern/colonial and settlerizing designs are always already intertwined.

2
Corrido-ing the Idea of Utah and Mormon/ism

There is support for a theory of archival impressions. Katherine Groo (2019) looks at film as an archive, a *human thing* human beings have built, the by-product of physical contact—the human touch that leaves some *things* behind. She invokes archival impressions in several ways—"impressed upon" (30, 282), "impressions left behind" (280), "impressionability" (280)—and calls for a reorientation to "archival impressions that historians have been trained to ignore, see through, or absent from their imagination" (258). Both Groo and I utilize archival impressions to speak to some *things* which gives structure to and constitutes archives. Now, my work has more to do with the church settler rhetoricity behind archival impressions. I derive its meaning from modern/colonial and settlerizing contexts, specifically settler rhetorics of archival impressions: (1) to give an impression; (2) to impress enduringly; (3) to impress others; (4) to impress-on or cover-over (designs). I will work throughout this chapter to illuminate such impressions.

It is important for me to explain why the *Archive* is the most honest and critical space to think and speak from. This chapter serves thus as a decolonial case study on the *idea of Utah* and *Mormon/ism* and how it functioned as an archival impression within the *Archive*. It accepts the MCC's proposition that the *idea of the Americas* and the modus operandi of modern/colonial and settlerizing designs manifest in local forms and conditions. Though not "A" history (Blackhawk 2006; Brooks 1944; Colvin and Brooks 2018; Garrett 2016; Reeve 2015; M. Bowman 2012; Farmer 2008) but a version of a haunted/haunting story that unsettles histories and geographies of power (Alexander and Mohanty 2010), it heeds the appeal by Mignolo (2007), Tsing (1993), Tuck and Yang (2012), and Veracini (2010, 2011), who call for decolonizing projects to be thought through the particularities and specificities in which such designs unfold. This chapter serves as a pathway to further an archival approach and theory of archival impressions that can help us better understand the (re)writing of the *Archive* and its designs and technologies. Because power is a process that demands a capacious treatment of it.

We live amid *smaller archives of knowledges, understandings, feelings, and doings* (or the *working parts* of the *Archive*). To evidence designs unfolding, I turn to settler archives-as-*epistemological experiments* and excavate the march toward hegemony out of the project of modernity. Driven by a decolonial question—that is, how do we reposition the contents of archives so that we can position ourselves in relation to them *otherwise*—and *decolonial analytic*, I generate a public record-archive of and rhetoricize rhetorics of epistemology, truth-and-knowledge claims, and the rhetoricity behind archival impressions. I rhetorically analyze how *visuality*, the *goings-on* of settlerizing epideictic rhetoric, assemblage and branding work, and the transformation of human beings into *ghosts* and *ghost citizens* lead to the invention of new images, myths, and meanings of place and citizen/ship associated only with the church settler. (Contrary to David Whittaker [1985], I see no distinction between theologians and pioneers in Utah.) It grounds the exigence, because it is not enough to just locate, identify, and name inhumane and irrational discourse, to initiate a decolonizing archival impression into the smaller archive of Utah in the wake of what remains in land, memory, knowledge, and relationality after some *thing* and some *one* has passed.

A Chance Encounter with Settlerizing Epideictic Rhetoric

Action:

Younger missionary puts down foreign language textbook (with some frustration).

Speech act:

Younger missionary: "I am excited to meet them (*others with no names yet*), *to give* them things."

(Pause)

Conversation:

Younger missionary: "But how will ~~they~~ (the *other*) feel about what we *give* them?"

(Pause)

Older missionary: "~~They~~ (*the other*) love when we bring them things."

(Pause)

Younger missionary: "But do ~~they~~ (*the other*) appreciate what we bring them?"

(Pause)

Older missionary: "~~They~~ (*the other*) always do."

Airports are a hodgepodge of competing words and ideas. They are an example of Danielle Endres and Samantha Senda-Cook's (2011) argument that spaces and places act rhetorically. Because they are imbued with the meaning of circulation and flow that, by design, restrict the imprinting of representational practices of rights-to and belonging-to onto it. By consequence, amid the rhetorical phenomena of the gathering of social, cultural, and political identities and the reconstellating of social relations of power, the two modes of production tell us that the facility of *ideologies of scale, scale-making projects,* and other forms of representational praxis that give places like Utah its specificity and particularities is limited. (This is not to say that airports exist outside the macro rhetorics of wor[l]ding culture in places like Utah though.) The interplay between presence and the impermanence of bodies in airports means the *being-and-becoming* of it is produced through agents and actions and that it acts rhetorically—place-as-rhetoric—as a by-product of its surroundings and its design to ensure the circulation and flow of movement. This creates an interesting dynamic between rhetorics of place at the macro, the social norms of airports that limit representational practices at the meso, and agents temporarily remaking the meaning of a place at the micro level. As I will elaborate on below, this dynamic played out for me in 2017 at the Salt Lake City (SLC) airport. It was affirming to some and haunting to others as the archive of the airport was (re)written in modern/colonial and settlerizing ways.

The SLC airport embraces rhetorics of wor(l)ding culture that give Utah its everyday-ness. The greeting area used to welcome returning missionaries and Delta's "The Church of Jesus Christ of Latter-day Saint Missionary Check-in" sign are just two examples. For Utahns, and especially those who belong to the state's dominant religion, the Church of Jesus Christ of Latter-day Saints (hereafter "LDS" for members and the "Church" for institution) (see Ericson 2019; Nelson 2018), this means the airport is an extension of their everyday. A material consequence is that such Utahns are affirmed and thus emboldened to mobilize a *commonplace*. That has as much implication for rhetoricians-compositionists as it does for cultural geographers and mobilities scholars such as Tim Cresswell (2006), Pierce Lewis (1979), Alan Pred (1984), and Mimi Sheller and John Urry (2006), among others. How can place function as a locus for rhetorics of epistemology to *take* place, ontologies to be actualized, and the meaning of an intermediary space to be temporarily remade to reflect the rhetorics of wor(l)ding culture that give a place its everyday-ness? How does *flash staking*, a theological, secular, and *settlerizing* structured representational practice of staking rights-to and belonging-to in the moment, bolster claims of and over spaces and places? How do Church representatives of the dominant and normative institution in Utah perform their bodies as cultural texts-rhetorics to be displayed, observed, and read alongside their oral, written, and other material cultural traditions? How are non-LDS individuals entangled and complicit in authoring an *epistemological framework for the living*? Such questioning may seem inapplicable to some, but they are important because they underscore how a *politics of mobility* can transpire wor(l)ding aspirations within the everyday and in everyday spaces and places.

This chapter is not about the SLC airport per se but about how the *Archive* is shared-in, imported, and expanded by the *idea of Utah and Mormon/ism*. The airport though is an example of the *epistemological experiment* carried out in Utah vis-à-vis human work and projects. The airport, like the classroom I speak on in chapter 4, will underscore the import of studies by Cintron (1997), Nystrand and Duffy (2003), Sarah Pink (2012), and Street (1984), among others, on how people are by-products of and come to perform everyday literacy practices and rhetorics of the everyday life. At that airport I bore witness to what I had observed on my work route and in my classroom prior, the ways modern/colonial and settlerizing situations shore up and unfold via a *semiotic apparatus of enunciations* (actors, languages, institutions). Each, a haunting reminder of Quijano's (2007) and Wolfe's (2006) argument that coloniality and settler colonialism are not isolated egregious events but rather an ongoing structuring principle of settlerizing encounters, interactions, and engagements. In 2017, I began to contemplate: Where did actor-agents get such ideas from? How does Utah fit within modern/colonial and settlerizing designs? Contemplating other questions of a *decolonial analytic* resulted in three years of settler archival research on Utah that makes up a portion of this chapter. If *coloniality of knowledge* is an essential feature and engine within the frame of modernity/coloniality, it has as much implication for WRS as it does for the MCC and SCS. Because while uncovering the level of the enunciation within modernity/coloniality is a contribution to the decoloniality of knowledge, it is rhetorical methods that will enrich how we approach everyday literacies, symbols-signs-sounds, and rhetorics as situated, inherited, embodied, experienced, and practiced within defined communities and power centers.

To change the *contents* and *terms* of epistemic and ontological conversations within wounded/wounding and haunted/haunting spaces and places like Utah, it is imperative that the tasks of decolonizing knowledge and being unfold together. Part of that *enduring task* for me began at the SLC airport. The conversation above was performed unassumingly. The human work and projects of *storytelling, proselytizing, flash staking,* and *strengthening the stakes*, which I unpack below, are affirming to some. It made it possible for the meaning of the airport to be temporarily remade and for the airport to become a space that LDS could stake out a right-to and belonging-to in the moment. It confirmed for me what I know today, that LDS see in spaces and places opportunities to get to *work*, a *work* that mirrors the dominant literacies and rhetorics of wor(l)ding culture in Utah, which, to rephrase Rickert (2013) and Endres and Senda-Cook (2011) for this context, *attunes* all to the *ambient rhetorics of place* that is Utah. Such work and projects, a form of *coloniality of instruction-and-curriculum*, is haunting to others, though. Because it postulates an exceptionalism predicated on an *epistemic system* of ideas, images-signs-sounds, and ends: theological ideas of salvation through conversions, secular images of civilizing via domination, and modern ends of progress and development vis-à-vis the management and control of life domains. Again, this is how I define and what I mean by "settler." Their everyday tells them they are not merely spectators but rather participants in an *epistemological framework for the living* that the Church deems appropriate-correct. This conversation is locally produced, but it has implications for all rhetoricians-compositionists of whom *do* research and educate the masses.

In 2017, at the SLC airport, a group of older and younger missionaries sat across from me. Because they were so transparent, by which I mean performatively loud, I gathered from a private conversation that they were on a mission headed to Port-au-Prince. Their conversation, which I provide a snippet of above, struck me as odd. Not so much because they were missionaries. I live in Utah after all. Rather, because it seemed performatively rehearsed. In other words, the conversation felt disingenuous. I found myself asking, "A missionary conversation at an airport?" From my understanding, these trips are planned. Conversations are had, languages are in/formally learned, and desires and objectives are parsed. I contemplated: Why did they want *others* to overhear their conversation, what did they hope we get out of their conversation, and how did their performance of inherited *ideas* advance a cause? While I paused on motive, I took a *discourse about actions* approach to the storying of *self* and *other*, narrativization of the gift of giving, and idea of appreciation. Interpreting Benoit (1996), I gathered the two rhetors-interlocutors performed a conversation intended to explain, justify, characterize, and rationalize their on-display act/ions of rhetoricking, politics of mobility, and wor(l)ding aspiration. Siding with Mignolo's (1992) view that modern/colonial situations are largely shaped by semiotic interactions, this settlerizing encounter, interaction, and engagement showed a capacity to *throw* me into modern/colonial differences and *force* participation in an *epistemological framework for living* deemed appropriate-correct. That unfolding invited me to expand my view on literacies and rhetorics, by which I mean again an a priori ambient energy of *thinking*, *feeling*, and *being-with*, a worldly act of rhetoricity, and a catalyst of and for action/ing through words and ideas. Moreover, it required rhetorical criticism (see Flores 2016).

The unassuming conversation masqueraded as a wor(l)ding aspiration. By wor(l)ding aspirations, I mean an LDS *epistemic system*, *design*, and *epistemological framework for the living* on the move, *taking* and *making* place. The airport as a space and place then and there became a locus for trafficking rhetorics of epistemology, peddling ontologies in the normative, and creating out of *commonplaces* a didactic relation. As their words and ideas *took* place, they also *made* place into a space they could belong-to via an entitlement of a right-to. And it was all safeguarded by the guise of a private conversation shielded by social norms that constrain and mitigate in/actions. This conversation smacked of the familiar tenets of a species of rhetoric that over time has been treated with regard by scholars such as Ryan Balot (2013), Jonathan Bradshaw (2019), Kevin Browne (2013), Edward Corbett and Robert Connors (1998), Miriam Fernandez (2023), Kathleen Lamp (2019), Christine Oravec (1976), and Cynthia Sheard (1996), epideictic rhetoric. The rhetors-interlocutors thus caused me to broaden my view of epideictic rhetoric and consider its capacity for wor(l)ding aspiration. Epideictic rhetoric can thrive in common spaces and places as it does not typically muster resistance, interruption, or any other form of immediate action by audiences. Its time is the present, audience the spectator, and ends praise-blame (Aristotle 2007; Cicero 1967; Perelman and Olbrechts-Tyteca 1969). But that is a dated way of thinking about epideictic rhetoric. I amend such a species of rhetoric for modern/colonial and settlerizing contexts thus, which is less about rhetorical effect and more about making visible and audible the unfolding of settlerizing encounters, interactions, and engagements in praise and/or blame that have wor(l)ding aspirations among un/receptive audiences. Settlerizing epideictic rhetoric signifies a *capacity* à la de Certeau (2011) to *inform* and *give form* to social practices via iterative writing and address.

Settlerizing epideictic rhetoric is apropos since this chapter is about movements, performativity, and networking of *epistemic systems*, *designs*, and *epistemological frameworks*. There is consensus among cultural geographers and mobilities scholars that representation, meaning, and practice are about movement. Whether the context is semiotic or corporeal, movement, like rhetoric, does not function for the sake of it. It is encoded socially, culturally, and politically with traceable geo-and-body-political meaning that enacts gendered, racial, ethnic, and economic positions. Movement, like place, is about the place of peoples and systems of difference they perform (Sheller and Urry 2006). So why not attend to the iterative and multi-modal writings and addresses of LDS that mobilize modern/colonial and settlerizing geo-and-body politics? This is why I began with the SLC airport. Airports can be a setting for rhetoricking, politics of mobility, and wor(l)ding aspirations to *take* and *make* place in settlerizing ways. The rhetors, capitalizing on kairos, phronesis, and praxis to *flash stake* a *gathering space* and place to work, personify Michelle Hall Kells's (2006) *walking exigencies*—agents shaped by and shaping discourse. In settlerizing contexts, epideictic embodies the social ritual of praising church-settlers and the public education on church-settler rhetorics of epistemology and ontologies. It can achieve adherence (see Plato 1864) to wor(l)ding aspirations partly through *unverifiable* but canonical literacies of giving, images of *self* and *other*, and rhetorics of salvation that make intelligible an *Other-as-Same* relation (see Bruner 1991a, 1991b). Partly because deliberation, *krísis*-judgment, comprehension, and in/action can be gained through identification-consubstantiality and assent (see Burke 1945, 1969). The sophistication of settlerizing epideictic rhetoric lies in its capacity to express wor(l)ding aspirations that implicate all through argumentation, persuasion, and praxis. Such a desire and objective, characterized as a common good, is why the ideal setting for this amended species is public places (also see Rice 2012; Carter 1991; B. Duffy 1983; Hauser 1999a; Loraux 1986; Rickert 2007; Sheard 1996; D. Smith 2003; Walker 1989; Weaver 1953).

Those familiar with the literature on publics might wonder why the term "wor(l)ding aspirations." Yes, the Church satisfies many of the characteristics for a public, at least if we trace their origins historically within a public and counterpublic context. In this way I find Paul Reeve's (2015) study on Mormonism to be insightful alongside Michael Warner's (2002) argument that publics organize themselves independently from preexisting institutions (also see Fraser 2007; Habermas 1989; Hauser 1998). Because what it illustrates is how a public in the state of *being-and-becoming* a religious group was both deemed a race and racialized as *other*. Now, whether LDS had access to whiteness is debatable (see Ratcliffe 2005, 12–14; Yang 2017, 10), but what stands out in Reeve's study are the struggles to gain recognition as human beings, status as white, and the privileges that whiteness secures. Joseph Smith's Mormonism is an invention within the landscape of the Americas and US in the nineteenth century. The Church emerges as a counterpublic first subjected to in/external participation, deliberation, and critiques in ordinary public space and places (Bennett 1842; Bowes 1854; Howe 1834; Livesey 1838; M'Chesney 1838; Parson 1841; Sunderland 1842). One hundred and seventy-four years ago, a wor(l)ding aspiration transpired through a (settlerizing epideictic) discourse that was self-organizing in ordinary spaces and places. For Smith, as well as others, it was a discourse oriented to gathering and uniting strangers. Its prosperity across space, place, and time can be credited to its capacity to garner attention and the willingness of others to reflexively circulate it. At its very core is the *virtue* of address—addressing and being addressed. But I do recognize and acknowledge why the Church cannot be deemed a public or counterpublic. For me thus, because LDS church-settlers of the nineteenth and twentieth centuries have global aspirations, wor(l)ding aspirations lends itself better to settlerizing contexts.

The airport scene was not inconsequential. It provided clarity at a time when I was wrestling with what I was bearing witness to in my own classroom: a *settlerizing* of where one is and how one is to act (belonging-to) and think (right-to) in spaces and places where archives are in an unending cycle of (re)writing. Today the airport scene affords the opportunity to take a rhetorical lens and *decolonial analytic*, apply it to components underscoring the *semiotic apparatus of enunciation*, and develop a rhetorical perspective theorizing rhetorics of space and place and rhetorics of wor(l)ding culture in Utah. Contrary to Cynthia Sheard's (1996) view on students and language (766), students, like the airport actor-agents, grasped that even in impermanent commonplaces, marked by the inherent friction of clashing words and ideas, they can still transform it and belong-to it rhetorically through the human work of language and projects such as settlerizing epideictic rhetoric, which is predicated on rights-to in Utah. Though the manufacturing of a mythological origin, character, and reclamation of geography I speak to below is produced locally, the projects and work of rhetoricking, politics of mobility, and wor(l)ding have implications beyond. Because to echo Avery Gordon (2008), we are all in and part of the *Archive* in an unending cycle of (re)writing. The *idea of Utah* and *Mormon/ism* is a palimpsest of its designs, an archival impression that ensures near and far that the *past shapes the present, the present (re)imagines the past, and the present reflects on the future* (A. García 2004). This should matter to rhetoricians-compositionists because we are positioned and equipped to unsettle the past, intervene in the settled-ness of the present, and initiate archival impressions *otherwise*.

Utah may just be a state name. Yet a careful rhetorical analysis of its origins—the Hive, Territory, State of Deseret—would underscore Mignolo's (2005) claim that words and ideas "makes it possible to transform an invented idea into 'reality'" (151). "Deseret" is an invention, a wor(l)ding aspiration, rhetorical and affective through what Wingard (2013) calls assemblage, branding, and recasting work (also see Sharpe 2010). It is not inconsequential but an archival impression with structural underpinnings and material consequences: the Constitution and Law of Deseret, the University of Deseret (the University of Utah), the Deseret Alphabet, the *Deseret News*, the Valleys-Mountains of Deseret, and Citizens of Deseret (MRM: Kimball 1852, 1:294–297; Kimball 1861, 8:348–351; Young 1862, 10:38–42; Young 1868, 12:297–301; Snow 1880, 22:109–120). Such discursive inventions highlight a *semiotic apparatus of enunciations*—actors in a position to manage discourse utilizing institutions to invent spaces, places, and people through language. Today the state name is Utah, but trace marks remain—the *idea of Deseret* and *Mormon/ism*—haunting reminders of efforts to cover-up-and-over meaning that precedes the arrival of church settlers (see Tuck and Yang 2017, 5). Utah is a case study of how what occurred in the Americas 500 years ago continues to *appear* and *be* consequential—the *idea of the Americas* and a modus operandi of modern/colonial and settlerizing designs. That the images, myths, meanings, and rhetorics of place and citizen/ship remain associated in Utah with the church settler of yesterday and the posterity of today is not coincidental. It is the by-product of settlerizing encounters and performances of *visuality*, branding, and *ghosting*, as Arvin, Tuck, and Morrill (2013), Bergland (2000), Liew (2024), Mignolo (2006, 2011a), Mirzoeff (2011), Trouillot (1995), Sharpe

(2009), Sheller (2012), and Tuck and Yang (2012) tell of in their research. *The idea of Utah*, as an American place—bolstering a model of hegemony vying for power—and place myth—a destined place and gathering space—of and for the favored church-settlers—is an archival impression in the *Archive*.

The rhetorics of epistemology, truth-and-knowledge claims, and the rhetoricity behind archival impressions I will account for in what follows and chapter 4 ought to matter to rhetoricians-compositionists. Because in many wounded/wounding spaces and places like Utah the university is a microcosm of its macro rhetorics of wor(l)ding culture. Because the classroom for some is an extension of the everyday and thus another locus of enunciation for the unfolding of human projects and work. To establish that connection between the public and classroom, it is imperative that I unpack the rituals of rhetoricking, politics of mobility, and wor(l)ding in its context of structural underpinnings and material consequences in Utah. This work is necessary as the machinery of the nineteenth century remains in operation today, though the proverbial door to the boiler room is closed to the public. For this chapter, such work will appeal to rhetoricians-compositionists interested in delinking the logic of coloniality embedded in rhetorics of modernity and decolonizing a *settlerizing* and coloniality of knowledge that is (supposedly) the invisible side of theo-logy, ego-logy, and modernity. Specifically, I spell out rhetorics of modernity and logics of coloniality by generating a public record-archive of and then rhetoricizing rhetorics of epistemology, truth-and-knowledge claims, and the rhetoricity behind archival impressions. This work of decolonizing knowledge will serve as a foundation for chapter 4, aimed at examining students' respect of the power of language, exploring how their *stories-so-far* adhere to, interact with, and/or carry out the projects and work that settler archives represent, and reflecting on the prospect of decolonizing being.

A settlerizing epideictic rhetoric that embraces and keeps alive settler pasts and ghosts is not unique to the modern/colonial and settlerizing designs of Utah. The structuring principle of settlerizing encounters, interactions, and engagement is a happening that keeps spaces and places wounded/wounding. States like Utah thus act rhetorically in that they are haunted/haunting spaces and places regardless of new claims about locality, regionality, and globality. What a rhetorical and decolonial perspective affords then is the ability to visualize *epistemic systems*, *designs*, and *epistemological frameworks* on the move in places like Utah and spaces as small as the airport. It provides the opportunity to locate, identify, and name everyday literacies and rhetorics that allow for its circulation and flow. A rhetorical and decolonial perspective offers the possibility to trace linkages and cross triangulate networks. What we are ultimately left with are settlerizing encounters, interactions, and engagements that entangle and implicate us all. So while my line of inquiry is specific to Utah, because it must be in a time of globalist thinking, it is my hope that as I trace rhetorics of praise and blame across nineteenth- and twentieth-century church-settler cultural texts, it understood that we are all thinking, feeling, and/or being-with modern/colonial and settlerizing designs. With Baynham and Prinsloo's (2009) *goings-on* in mind, that means we are invited to become and belong-to action/ings that will adhere to or make an archival impression on the *Archive/archives* in the making through literacies and rhetorics. The "we" applies to all who deal in words and ideas, carry out the human work of educating the multitudes, and/or hope and struggle toward wor(l)ding futures *otherwise*.

A period of one hundred years is left out of this chapter. Thus, it is not representative of changes that have unfolded in the Church and across the LDS community, only the ways in which rhetorics of modernity, facilitated by *coloniality of instruction-and-curriculum*, have naturalized the modus operandi of modern/colonial and settlerizing designs—coded words (vision, waste-and-fertile lands, miracles, awaken, etc.), tropes (the vanishing or disappearing magical act; aseptic cleanliness; the earth as fuckable, the fuckable earth; reap what you sow, and the Garden of Eden), and *ideas* (the epistemic zero point and provenance, doctrines of discovery and rights to land/rights to conquest, epistemic and ontological differences, divine and natural designs, and rhetorics of modernity). It is beyond the scope and breadth of this chapter to discuss the directions, impacts, and implications of the Church and LDS over the years. (Chapter 4, though, does speak to how the everyday *goings-on* in Utah show up in the lives of students.) This limit, however, does not take away from the existence of a church settler *archive* of *knowledges*, *understandings*, *feelings*, and *doings*, one that acknowledges, disavows, and/or subsumes the *other-things* (Adams-Campbell, Falzetti, and Rivard 2015, 110). It is the prism through which to see the church-settler psyche consciously documenting their existence, exhibiting their power to belong-to, and legitimizing their Rights-to, all refracted through the lens of *Americanity* and within the frame of modernity/coloniality despite successive evolutions-stages and mutated modalities.

The Encomium of Church-Settlers as Storied by Church-Settlers

A central question links airport rhetors and my students. Where did they get their words and *ideas*? This decolonial question demands that I *return* to the *idea of Utah* and *Mormon/ism*. Joseph Smith is the founder of Mormon/ism and the Church. He is revered for ushering a unique *spiritual philosophy* into the modern world. It is important to note, though, that church-settlers were ironically pessimistic about philosophy. But, perhaps, their pessimism only applied to philosophy deemed inappropriate-incorrect. In a well-rehearsed story, Smith was reportedly guided by the Angel Moroni to the Hill of Cumorah (present-day Upstate New York), where the golden plates were. The plates were purportedly engraved with generational records by ancient Nephites (J. Smith 1879: Ether 1:1–3; Jacob 1:1–4; Jarom 1:1–3; Moroni 9:18–26; I Nephi 19:1–2; MRM: Taylor 1852, 1:16–28; Pratt 1853, 1:297–309; Pratt 1853, 2:43–47; Smith 1857, 5:101–111; Kimball 1854, 6:322–326; Pratt 1859, 7:22–38). Smith translated them as *The Book of Mormon* (*BoM*), published in 1830. Mormonism would be known as the restoration of ancient principles by new revelation.

The *idea of Mormon/ism* became inseparable from the *idea of land* (Kirtland, Independence, Nauvoo, Utah) *as inheritance*. To understand that connection, it is important to return to the *BoM* (J. Smith 1879). It is the conceptual foundation and apparatus for a church-settler *epistemic system*, *design*, and *epistemological framework for living* to *appear* and *become* consequential within and beyond its immediate settings and contexts. Thus, I read and utilize it as an archive for historical context. The *BoM* is the by-product, as the title on the opening page announces, of touch, "the hand," which underscores a *human thing* human beings built to leave behind. It will have enormous *reach* in the lives of nineteenth-century church settlers.

A Foundation

The *BoM* is treated by church-settlers as a collection of information about spaces and places, subjects, and/or events—an archive. It stories an exodus from Jerusalem by Nephites and their arrival in the *promised land* of the ancient Americas dubbed *Nephite America*. The *BoM* establishes an agenda for *work*. Physical *work* is one aspect: tilling the earth, planting seeds, making the *desert blossom as the rose like the Garden of Eden*. This agenda of work is informed by *visuality* that sees in spaces and places vacant or "uncultivated waste" lying "in common" (see Locke [1689] 1821, 219). Spiritual *work*, or *instruction*, is another: gathering the dispersed and bringing forth, enlarging, and strengthening the stakes of Zion by instructing salvation, reeducation, conversion, and restoration (*instructing*) so that the *other* can *blossom as the rose on the mountains* (MRM: Hyde 1853, 2:47; Smith 1865, 11:157; Pratt 1875, 18:145;

Smith 1884, 25:97). This agenda of *work* is informed by a *visuality* that empties people of their humanity, name, and even the name Human. The constructed relation between Nephites (descendants of Nephi) and Lamanites (descendants of Laman) is just one example. Through assemblage and branding work, Nephites see themselves in possession of what the *other* does not have, a propriety of rights and privileges. This relation institutes a theo-and-ego structured logic of the gift, a recasting of sorts, where Nephites are obligated and responsible to carry out *work* on behalf of Lamanites (J. Smith 1879: I Nephi, 19:1–2; II Nephi, 1:1–8, 8–19; Jacob, 1:5–15, 5:36–46; Enos, 1:13–23; Omni, 1:6–14; Mosiah, 10:3–12, 12:2–12; Alma, 2:25–36, 8:7–17, 22:29–35, 50:24–32, 52:1–2; Helaman, 3:7–15, 6:1–8; III Nephi, 4:23–33; Mormon, 1:6–19, 2:1–29; Ether, 1:35–43; also see MRM: Pratt 1855, 2:284–298; Young 1871, 14:192–200; Pratt 1871, 14:253–265; Pratt 1872, 14:323–335; Snow 1882, 23:7–10).

Doctrines of discovery and rights to land/conquest are prominent in the *BoM*. *Visuality*, assemblage-branding-recasting work, and *ghosting* are vital to the "Nephite-America" myth (MRM: Pratt 1872, 14:323–335). In 1 Nephi, Nephi (son of Lehi) stories an exodus from Jerusalem. For eight years they traverse the wilderness and arrive in a coastal area (Bountiful). There the Lord instructed Nephi to build a ship to cross the sea toward a new *land choice* and *promised land*. Nephi did, and the Lord led them ashore, a new *land of/ for their inheritance* and *land of promise* preserved for *choice* and *righteous men*. That land was the Americas. Each book within the *BoM* thereafter proceeds to speak on efforts by Nephites to peacefully *gather* the multitudes on the *lands of their inheritance*, cut and drive off Lamanites from lands they *possessed*, and engage in physical and spiritual *work*. The *BoM* casts Nephites as in *possession* of the Americas for themselves and posterity (J. Smith 1879: I Nephi, 5:16–22, 17:4–16, 19:1–2; II Nephi, 1:1–8, 9:1–6, 27:1–3, 30:2–12; Jacob, 2:8–16, 5:36–46; Jarom, 1:4–11; Omni, 1:6–14; Words of Mormon, 1:7–15; Alma, 22:30–35, 38:1–2, 50:2–32, 51:1, 58:3–12, 58:36–41; Helaman, 3:7–15, 5:50–52, 6:9–18; III Nephi, 4:23–33, 15:9–23; Mormon, 1:6–18, 2:18–29; Ether, 1:35–43, 2:1–10, 6:5–16). It is important to take note of how a model of citizen/ship is linked with Nephites through the "Nephite-America" myth.

An epistemic zero point and provenance is assumed in the *BoM*. It is what leads to the transformation of human beings into *ghosts* and *ghost citizens* as it calls into question who does and does not fit the standard of humanness. In 1 Nephi, Nephi stories how the Lord had *chosen* men of God to rule—*govern* and *manage*—over *others*. This was attributed to nature and *iniquities*. Within the *BoM*, Nephites are in possession of a proper state of being—*police*, if we recall the register of the Spanish Jesuits and Friars—a *fair/white, truthful, righteous,* and *delightsome* people oriented to a true faith and religion. They are *born of God* with the Right-to observe:

> [A]ll men that are in a state of nature, or I would say, in a carnal state, are in the gall of bitterness, and in the bonds of iniquity ... they are without ... they have gone contrary ... they are in a state contrary ... And now behold, is the meaning of the word restoration ... to place it [a thing of a natural state] opposite to its nature. (J. Smith 1879: Alma, 41:11–12)

The above passage illustrates an observer observing the *iniquities* of an *other* contrary to and different from Nephites. Lamanites are the *other*, observed as idolatrous, evil in nature, bloodthirsty, and vindictive—the very definition of iniquity in their eyes. Though Nephites fall in the *BoM*, which is beyond the scope and breadth of this chapter, largely they possess a proper Spirit and are instructed to *restore* order and the *other* into a *white* and *delightsome* people. This assumed Right-to is attributed to their inherited *gifts* of interpreting languages, speaking in tongues, and *instructing* (J. Smith 1879: I Nephi, 3:19–31, 12:17–23, 13:36–42, 18:21–25, 19:1–2; II Nephi 5:8–32, 7:1–9, 30:2–12; Jacob, 1:5–15, 7:20–27; Enos, 1:13–22; Omni, 1:24–30; Words of Mormon, 1:7–16; Mosiah, 4:9–17, 10:3–12, 12:2–12; Alma, 8:7–17, 9:19–26, 37:1–2, 54:1–7; Helaman, 5:38–52, 6:1–8, 13:38–39; III Nephi, 3:1–3, 19:22–33; Mormon, 3:10–20; Moroni, 7:3–16; also see Pratt 1842; The Church of Jesus Christ of Latter-day Saints 1908). Ultimately, the *goings-on* and *doings* of Nephites *informs* and *gives form* to truth-and-knowledge claims on Man-Human-Rights in the *BoM*.

Observers enforced epistemic and ontological differences as a viewpoint in the *BoM*. From cover to closing the consequence of such *thingification* is a divine and natural relation, the pretext for the *work* of *instructing* the *Other-as-Same*. The Lamanites, an eventual reference to American Indians, were once a *fair* and *delightsome* people too who became an abomination, a *naked* people deficient in, without, and/or lacking. They *choose* the *works of darkness*. Their *curse*, books in the *BoM* put forward, derived from an incorrect *baseness*. Lamanites revealed that curse through *markings, scales of blackness-darkness,* amplified by the *cloud/mist of darkness* overshadowing them and lands they inhabited. Nephite prophets wrote they dwelled in the *land of the shadow of death*—the half dead (Anzaldúa 1999) or closest to death (Maldonado-Torres 2007). Nephites were not to *"mixeth"* their *seed* with Lamanites, only *instruct* the *wild, idolatrous, perverse,* and *naked wanderers* out of obscurity through any means (J. Smith 1879: II Nephi, 5:8–32, 19:1–13, 30:2–12; Jacob, 1:5–15,

3:4–11; Enos, 1:13–22; Mosiah, 4:9–17, 10:3–22; Alma, 3:1–7, 17:9–17, 26:24–32, 31:18–30, 44:12–20; Helaman, 5:26–36; III Nephi, 16:9–18; Moroni, 1:2–4, 2:1–3; also see The Church of Jesus Christ of Latter-day Saints 1971). The "Nephite" myth solidifies viewpoints of Man-Human-Rights in the *BoM*.

The *BoM* opens and closes with a divine and natural design. Nephites, recall, are *chosen men*, "favoured above every other nation, kindred, tongue, or people" (J. Smith 1879, Alma 9:20). They are *spokesmen* endowed with the Right to tell *others* of their *wickedness* and *abomination* and *instruct* them to be in the appropriate-correct form. The spiritual *work* of Nephites is initially locally aimed at Lamanites. They are to be saved from their carnal state (state of nature), born again as *righteous* people with a proper Spirit, and restored unto the truth faith and religion (though, it is important to note, salvation does not mean equality per entries in the *Journal of Discourses*). But there are planetary aspirations too in spiritually and physically *strengthening* the *stakes* and *borders* of Zion. The books within the *BoM* depict Nephites traveling to places unknown, *gathering the dispersed* who need to be *born again*, and disseminating the records of prophets among *all nations, kindreds, tongues,* and *people*. Their possibility of humanization, however, is couched in conversion (J. Smith 1879: I Nephi, 1:1–4, 5:16–22, 6:1–6, 13:36–42; II Nephi, 1:18–26, 3:11–19, 4:8–19, 14:1–6, 29:1–8, 30:2–12; Mosiah, 1:5–13, 7:20–27, 10:13–22, 15:12–23, 27:17–27; Alma, 7:7–14, 13:16–26, 24:1–11, 27:26–30, 28:1–3, 48:18–25, 49:1–2; III Nephi, 21:22–29, 22:1–2; Mormon, 8:12–21; Moroni, 10:29–34). Such a wor(l)ding aspiration is part and parcel to the modern/colonial and settlerizing designs in the *BoM*.

A rhetoric of modernity attempts to cloak the darker side of *designs* and *work* in the *BoM*. In 1 Nephi, Nephi has visions of past and future events. He tells of a *mountain* he has never seen nor stepped foot on. Nephi's vision is a foreshadowing, for he submits that the Lord's house shall be "established in the top of the mountain" and that "the law" shall go forth from it (II Nephi, 12:2–3). His vision also privies him to prophecies, including the restoration of the Church, gathering of posterity, and reestablishment of Zion as an ensign for *all nations, kindreds, tongues,* and *people* to flow unto. Herein lies the darker side, the rise of a certain *spokesman* and place as the center of space and present of time with global domination, management, and control as *ends*. Salvation or destruction are two options presented to the *wicked/enemies* whose iniquities already justify physical violence in the name of a *design* within the *BoM* (J. Smith 1879: I Nephi, 4:1–13, 10:17–22, 11:32–36, 12:1–4, 17:26–39; II Nephi, 3:11–19, 15:15–30, 21:2–14, 23:5–20, 28:11–21, 30:2–12; Mosiah 15:12–31, 16:1–2, 27:17–27; Alma, 2:37–38, 3:1–7, 29:1–11, 37:22–30, 40:12–26, 44:12–20, 58:3–12).

The *BoM* is a significant site of analysis because it demonstrates *goings-on* of literacies, symbols and signs, and rhetorics meant to drive action in settlerizing ways. It illustrates *coloniality of instruction-and-curriculum* at work—a settler-centered instruction. The *BoM* is an archiving of the *idea* of race, epistemic racism, and ends of coloniality-as-projects of territorial and epistemological (ex/ap)propriation. It mirrors hauntingly Spanish and Western rhetorics of epistemology and ontologies traced in the previous chapter. I argue that as a genre of cultural text and *epistemological experiment* the *BoM* is the conceptual foundation and apparatus for a church-settler *epistemic system, design,* and *epistemological framework for living* to *appear* and *become* consequential within and beyond its immediate settings and contexts. Because church-settlers of the nineteenth and twentieth centuries would apply an exegesis and eisegesis approach to it. They saw themselves in the image of Nephites and assumed the subject position of the observer observing, *thingifying*, and enforcing viewpoints *of land as inheritance*, an *Other-as-Same* relation, and *work-instruction*.

What follows illustrates how church-settlers read and translate the *BoM* within a *modernity/coloniality* framework through inhumane and irrational discourse. The *other* will be enunciated but denied enunciation in the epistemological, ideological, and rhetorical war on information. The *other* as well as Utah as a place is only ever known through the eyes of the observer observing. The technological power of archival impressions on land and Indigenous peoples will both evidence a vehicle or instrument that materializes concretely settler desires into reality and underscore how some *things* were never meant to come to an end.

Constellated Words and Ideas

I work from various sets of archives that record-preserve information about places, subjects, and/or events as much as they cement discursive practices. I will mainly work from the *Journal of Discourses* (*JoD*) in this section (Mormonism Research Ministry, MRM: 1851–1886). I make references though to other cultural texts such as church hymns, *Doctrine and Covenants*, the *Latter-day Saints' Millennial Star, A Voice of Warning,* and *Preach my Gospel*, among others. *JoD* is a twenty-six-volume archive of sermons and doctrinal instruction transcribed and published between 1851 and 1886. It invokes impressions in several ways: "it made a deep impression" (MRM: Morgan 1880, 21:179–188); "impressed upon" (Rich 1874, 17:169–172); "those impressions" (Snow 1859, 7:125–131). They underscore the meaning I have prescribed to and outlined elsewhere as settler rhetorics of archival impressions. Now, it is important to recognize and acknowledge that the Church does not endorse the *JoD* as an official publication. But such a position is simply a way to create distance and shield itself from criticism. The parallels between official cultural texts like the *BoM* and unofficial cultural texts such as *JoD* will become evident in the archiving of enunciations in what follows. The value of creating a public record of words and ideas is the ability to show how church-settlers shared-in, imported, and expanded on the *BoM* and disputed modern/colonial and settlerizing designs.

THE PERSECUTED

The theme of persecution is persistent throughout the history of Mormonism. It both safeguards and cloaks a church-settler *system*, *design*, and *epistemological framework for living*. There are church-settler hymns that speak to the religious persecution of Mormons. "Tittery-Irie-Aye" is one example: "They've been driven from their homes and away from Nauvoo / For to seek another home in the wilderness anew" (Emrich 1952, 5). Another example is "Song," which supports the position of persecution: "Let's not forget the afflictions which we bore . . . In Nauvoo,—in Far West" (Alford 2011, 3). "A Song for the Elders" also substantiates the view of persecution: "We know that mobs have drove us" (3). There are others hymns as well as poetry that corroborate the stance that Mormons were persecuted because of religious principles. Whether they were persecuted is not for me to decide or debate, but what is of importance here is that the rhetoric of persecution covered-up-and-over designs and its technologies and sanctioned hauntings and haunting situations across space, place, and time.

Smith was said to have revelations on where to reestablish the proper center space and place for Zion. (Homesteading was always already a project of appropriation and exclusion.) He *gathered the Saints* in New York and settled them in Kirtland, Ohio, Independence, Missouri, and Nauvoo, Illinois. Each settlement was marked though by conflict, expulsion, and exodus. Mormons viewed it as anti-Mormon sentiment. The incarceration and death of Smith gave credence to the idea that Mormons were exiles seeking asylum. There are hymns that corroborate this. "Ladies of Utah" is one example: "cruel persecution . . . Driven to the wilderness" (Alford 2011, 7). Another example is "Hymn," which supports the view of cruelty: "At the hand of foul oppressors, We've born and suffered long" (Alford 2011, 21–22). Mormons attributed conflict to people feeling threatened by Mormonism as the *true* faith and religion.

The story of Nephites journeying through the wilderness toward the *land of/ for their inheritance* and *promise* soon became their own. The point here again is to call into question how the rhetoric of persecution covered up-and-over designs and its technologies, sanctioned hauntings and haunting situations, and how it worked alongside the *idea* of Zion and Mormon/ism (J. Smith 1879: I Nephi 1:16–20, 2:1–24, 5:16–22, 6:1–6; MRM: Young 1853, 2:1–10; Young 1860, 8:194–200; Taylor 1863, 10:257–261; J. Smith 1883, 24:245–250; Snow 1884, 25:101–112; also see Hartley 2001; Wetmore 1837).

That Mormons were peaceful but persecuted settlers and exiles seeking asylum is a prominent through line in the *JoD*. Church-settlers argued that their "persecutions [were] unparalleled in the history of past ages" (Smith 1852, 1:43, 45). Especially, they rationalized, when all they were doing was "mind[ing] their own business" and carrying out *work* as *virtuous* men (Young 1852, 1:144). Church-settlers believed they were stripped of Rights as *freemen*. Nephite trekking the wilderness became further internalized. Various hymns substantiate that as well as the idea that Mormons were exiles fleeing *oppression*: "For in this Valley of the West, there is none to molest" (Alford 2011, 3); "We'll find the place which God for us prepared, Far away in the West, Where none shall come to hurt or make afraid" (Clayton n.d.; also see Woodruff 1865, 11:60–66). What the rhetoric of persecution did was have the image of peaceful settlers coexist alongside narratives of modern/colonial and settlerizing designs. Utah would become another space and place to express and transpire wor(l)ding aspirations (MRM: Young 1852, 1:37–42; Young 1851, 1:376–376; Young 1853, 2:1–10; Wells 1854, 2:25–28; Young 1857, 6:226–229; Young 1860, 8:194–200; Young 1863, 10:104–111; Young 1876, 18:230–235; Smith 1881, 22:42–50; Taylor 1885, 26:148–157).

The literacy of *land as inheritance*, the image of peaceful church-settlers, and the rhetoric of the "Mormon problem" are rife with a darker side. Again, Mormons attributed anti-Mormonism to people feeling threatened by the *Truth* that Mormonism "is the fountain of light and intelligence; it swallows up the truth contained in all the philosophy of the world" (MRM: Young 1852, 1:39). But perhaps there is another side we should consider. Could conflict be attributed to the *idea of Mormon/ism*, wherein church-settles argued they were favored saviors and redeemers, and thus divinely and naturally permitted to rule over *others* and stake Rights-to belong-to their spaces and places? Church-settlers observed *Others-as-Same* and saw it as their obligation and responsibility to carry out *work-instruction* through any means. The darker side is a church-settler *epistemic system, design,* and *epistemological framework for living* entrenched in projects of territorial (homesteading) and epistemological (*work-instruction*) (ap/ex)propriation. Guided by Brigham Young, they arrived in Utah in 1847 and ~~discovered~~ invented *the idea of Utah* to experiment with impressing the image of Mormon/ism and a civil, social, racial, and political design to advance new places images-and-myths (MRM Wells 1854, 2:25–28; Smith 1843, 2:163–169; Young 1857, 6:226–229; Young 1860, 8:194–200; Cannon 1873, 15:291–302; Smith 1875, 18:89–94; Cannon 1878, 20:32–39; Nicholson 1881, 22:183–192; Cannon 1881, 23:93–106; Smith 1883, 24:245–250; Taylor 1884, 25:84–96; Smith 1884, 25:97–101; Thatcher 1885, 26:327–335; also see Veracini 2010).

A RHETORIC OF DISCOVERY

The idea of Utah required doctrines of discovery and Rights-to land/conquest. Church-settlers claimed they were under the *watchful guidance* of the same angel that led Columbus to the Americas. Young and company arrived in the mountains of Utah in 1847. It was part prophecy. Like Smith, he is said to have revelations on where the future center space and place for Zion would be. Young observed an empty *land of inheritance* (and *promise*) that no one wanted to *possess*. He envisioned a bountiful land, though, and thus declared, *this is the place*. (Whether this is the precise phrasing attributed to Young is a moot point. The action/ing[s] of church-settlers would cement the adage into a reality.) Hymns confirm this outlook: "Oh, what a dreary place this was when first the Mormons found it" (Emrich 1952, 7). Church-settlers spoke of Utah in two ways, both of which rely on the *ideas* of terra incognita, nullius, and arcadia to produce images of empty landscapes from which the inhabiting bodies of the *other* vanish and/or disappear (MRM: Smith 1854, 2:22–24; Hunter 1853, 2:35–38; Hyde 1854, 6:367–371; Young 1854, 7:9–15; Snow 1873, 16:200–208; Taylor 1881, 23:11–20; Cannon 1881, 23:93–106; Thatcher 1882, 23:196–214; Whitney 1885, 26:194–204; also see Meader 1912; Berrett 1969; The Church of Jesus Christ of Latter-day Saints 1996; Writers' Program 1941).

The first way church-settlers spoke of Utah was as a *naked* space and place that had not been observed by a *Man* on earth. This is *visuality*, assemblage-branding-recasting, and *ghosting* at work (the *idea* of Man is significant, but for now I want to focus on observations of Utah). According to church-settlers, it was empty: "nothing but a few bunches of dead grass" (Smith 1852, 1:44); a "barren valley . . . sterile mountains . . . desolate waste" (Young 1857, 4:344); a "parched and barren desert" (Woodruff 1873, 15:270). Utah, in their own words, was a space and place no one had *possessed*. Yet church-settlers were confronted with the reality that the Utah they had invented was not *vacant waste*. They resorted then to translating the literacies, images-signs-sounds, and rhetorics in the *BoM* further: "We are here in the mountain with these Lamanites"; "we were prepared to meet all the Indians in these mountains, and kill every soul of them if we had been obliged so to do" (Young 1853, 1:105–106). (The Lamanite and "the Indian" are construed as interchangeable in *JoD*, though the Church now disavows this grouping.) Strategically, land and people were *thingified* and emptied of substance as church-settlers enforced viewpoints of Man-Human-Rights (MRM: Young 1852, 1:144–146; Young 1856, 3:254–260; Taylor 1857, 5:182–192; Kimball 1860, 8:220–220; Smith 1872, 15:27–34; Woodruff 1872, 15:7–12; also see Cush 2000).

The second way church-settlers spoke of Utah was as a space and place that *scientific* and *civilized Man* had declared *worthless*. Again, this was because they were confronted with the reality that the Utah they had invented was not empty. Church-settlers would identify themselves as Man-Human—*civilized people* and a *class of people trained and educated in the civilization of modern nations*—against the not-quite-human Lamanite, or the American Indian of Utah—*Utahs, Piedes, and other tribes* (Young 1853, 1:164). "The Indian" was observed as contrary to, different from, and *beneath humanity*. They lived among reptiles and were a *naked thing of a natural state*, according to church-settlers. A state of nonbeing and emptied landscapes is fortified by one church-settler who claimed that there "were no human beings but the untutored savage" (Snow 1873, 16:206–207). (It is important to note the parallels between Spanish and church-settler observers who invent *otherness* to deny *others* of the name "human being.") Church-settlers found little reason at this point to utilize the appeal of exiles "seeking as asylum among the red savages" (Taylor 1885, 26:150). Because empty landscapes, *land as inheritance*, and an *Other-as-Same* relation meant they could deny being *intruders*, justify that Utah had to be *discovered* and *possessed* as a divine and natural Right, and claim to be its "native" inhabitants (MRM: Pratt 1852, 1:53–66; Smith 1854, 2:22–24; Woodruff 1855, 2:191–202; Young 1855, 2:248–258; Young 1856, 3:354–361; Young 1856, 3:254–260; Pratt 1854, 3:97–105; Pratt 1856, 3:344–354; Young 1857, 4:341–346; Young 1857, 6:143–149; Hyde 1858, 6:150–158; Kimball 1860, 7:346–351; Young 1861, 9:31–40; Young 1863, 10:170–178; Young 1866, 11:263–266; Young 1867, 11:321–329; Pratt 1869, 12:352–362; Cannon 1869, 14:45–58; Cannon 1871, 14:122–129; Pratt 1871, 14:7–12; Pratt 1872, 14:323–335; Woodruff 1873, 15:275–283; Pratt 1872, 15:241–253; Nicholson 1881, 22:183–192; also see J. Smith 1879: II Nephi, 29:9–14; Alma, 41:4–14).

Now, neither "Zion" nor "the Lamanite" exist ontologically. Still, these knowledge fictions materialized as truths. Barthes's (1972) position on myths and Mignolo's (1989, 1992, 1994) view on modern/colonial situations come into focus as "church-settlers" become associated with place, place with church-settlers. The cultural production of them, which functions as an archival impression and a form of public memory, *informs* the public of a new statement of fact and *gives form* to a new natural. After failed homesteading projects in Ohio and Illinois, church-settlers could at last claim Zion could not have been established anywhere else but the mountains of Utah. It was part prophecy (MRM: Woodruff 1857, 6:119). Both ways of speaking of this space and place produced absences and silences and allowed church-settlers to impress and enforce viewpoints of Utah as the "central place of gathering" (Pratt 1859, 7:312) and "center stake of Zion" (Young 1857, 6:46). The point, which is important to note, is not to discount religious persecution but to unsettle the literacy of empty landscapes, the image of peaceful church-settlers seeking asylum, and the rhetorics of assemblage-branding-recasting that are pretenses for doctrines of discovery and rights to land/conquest in the *BoM* and their everyday. Inseparable from them are the epistemic zero point and provenance analogous to the *idea* of epistemic and ontological differences (Cannon 1869, 14:45–58).

A RHETORIC OF EPISTEMIC PROPRIETY

Church-settlers assumed rights and privileges to observe, *thingify*, and enforce viewpoints within a *great chain* of (life, existence, and/or generation) Being model they prescribed to (MRM: Taylor 1854, 1:365–375; Hyde 1858, 6:150–158; Young 1868, 12:161–167; Brown 2011). For them, it was a very specific vertical (God to Mormon) and horizontal (Mormon to Adam) cross-chain (Pratt 1853, 1:6–15; Pratt 1859, 7:74–91; Young 1871, 14:91–98). They attributed this to *preexistence*. A hymn offers one explanation: "Above all people we are favor'd" (Alford 2011, 4). Such favoring stems from an inheritance in a previous life. Preexistence was the crux by which church-settlers promoted the *idea of Mormon* as Man-Human and the *idea of Mormonism* as the *True* faith and religion. God blessed their lineage on earth: "the talents we have received" (Hyde 1853, 2:117; also see Abraham 3:23–24). Their reflection below, however, exposes a darker side, the *idea* of race and an identity politics that would unsettle the settled-ness of peaceful church-settlers. The consequences share parallels with others performing settlerizing whiteness in that observations deemed strangers uninformed but convertible, "the Indian" redeemable (but never equal) through conversion, and Black people perpetually under the curse of Ham and Cain.

> Look around upon all the ranks of mankind, and we see different races, some of a high order of intellect, and some low and groveling, among all the different grades and classes of the human family. (Hyde 1853, 2:116)

Church-settlers claimed God favored some by marking their skin and partitioning geography to correspond with un/intelligent beings. It is not coincidental that they adhered to theo-and-ego-politics: Shem (Asia; the seed of humanity), Ham (Africa; the unknown), Japheth (Europe; the center of space and present of time). (As to the Americas, we can turn to Hegel, who would say that it was not "relatively new" [Hegel 1902, 136–138]. He wrote this, though, in the context of a proper Spirit approaching it and arguing that what was taking place in America was but an emanation from Europe. Hegel highlighted the possessions of the *Same* as church-settlers would do with Nephite-America.) The observation above comes on the heels of them contemplating their *nature* as *just men* and determining that God favored them as the *pure in heart*. Per divine and natural design, church-settlers deduced they were endowed with a propriety of Rights-to and privileges to *reflect, manage, control*, and carry out *work-instruction*. This became consubstantial to their philosophy and their most ironic mantra: "We must be philosophers too" (Taylor 1852, 1:23; also see MRM: Taylor 1852, 1:16–28; Taylor 1853, 1:147–159; Pratt 1853, 1:256–263; Taylor 1854, 1:365–375; Pratt 1852, 1:53–66; Pratt 1854, 2:96–104; Young 1853, 2:1–10; Grant 1854, 2:10–16; Grant 1856, 3:232–236; Pratt 1856, 3:344–354; Kimball 1856, 3:227–232; Snow 1857, 5:322–326; Taylor 1857, 5:112–123; Taylor 1857, 6:105–114; Young 1857, 6:143–149; Benson 1858, 6:177–184; Young 1852, 6:283–298; Hyde 1858, 6:150–158; Hyde 1858, 7:48–53; Woodruff 1860, 267–272; Young 1861 9:31–40; Kimball 1861, 9:180–182; Young 1870, 14:276–281; Pratt 1872, 15:241–253; Wells 1873, 16:123–134; Pratt 1873, 16:284–300; Bywater 1881, 22:59–67; Taylor 1884, 26:322–326; Church of Jesus Christ of Latter-day Saints 1908).

The propriety of church-settlers was a union between the *idea* of race and an identity politics. Church-settlers are depicted as "fair-skinned Christian[s]," enlightened Men guided by the "Spirit of the truth." "The Indians" are portrayed as "dark-skinned savage[s]," *natural men* capable of only grasping what they can see with their "natural eye" (Young 1853, 1:1–2). This observable difference for church-settlers empowered them to claim that they and their prophets (Smith, Young, etc.) were examples of propriety in thought, understanding, reason, Truth, providence, and instruction: "The world is wrong and we have to right it" (Young 1863, 10:222). Church-settlers argued that their nature and reason explained why they were *favored* and *privileged* above all *others* deficient in, without, and/or lacking the faculties of Man-Human. A rhetoric of propriety was the crutch by which they promoted a modern/colonial *Other-as-Same* relation (MRM: Pratt 1853, 1:6–15; Pratt 1853, 1:137–143; Pratt 1853, 1:256–263; Wells 1854, 2:25–28; Kimball 1857, 5:171–181; Kimball 1857, 6:28–38; Young 1852, 6:283–298; Young 1859, 7:139–147; Lyman 1863, 10:178–187; Kimball 1865, 11:80–86). This is assemblage, branding, and recasting work.

The epistemic zero point/provenance and *idea* of epistemic and ontological differences are symbiotic. The effects and consequences of such an interaction are the elimination of coevolutionary views and production of lesser humans or nonbeings, absences, and silences. There are resounding resemblances between enunciations within the *JoD* and the *BoM* that I have traced thus far. That is because this synergetic relationship is the foundation for a theo-and-ego structured *epistemic system, design,* and *epistemological framework for the living.* It is what underwrites the projects of territorial and epistemological (ap/ex)propriation, both in the *BoM* and the everyday of church-settlers. Below I trace another similarity within that context. As in the *BoM*, church-settlers in the *JoD* rely on a rhetoric of modernity to attempt to cloak the darker side of the *idea of Mormon/ism*—domination, management, and control.

A RHETORIC OF MODERNITY

Church-settlers relied on a rhetoric of modernity to cloak the daker side of physical and spiritual *work*. One hymn speaks to that relationship. "They, the Builders of the Nation," describes church-settlers as pioneers, "pushing on the wild frontier" to physically and spiritually build *new* foundations that will become an "ensign to the nation" (Alldredge 1948, n.p). In the *BoM* physical *work* refers to tilling the earth, planting seeds, and making the land yield while spiritual *work* refers to reestablishing Zion and *instructing*. They go together in that the wor(l)ding aspiration is to *strengthen* the *stakes* and *borders* of Zion near and far (planetary). That *work* involves physically penetrating *new* land (stakes, wards, temples) and *gathering the dispersed* across *all nations, kindreds, tongues,* and *people.* Church-settlers translated that *work* into their everyday (MRM: Young 1854, 2:136-145; Hyde 1854, 2:61–70; Hyde 1853, 2:112–120; Young 1857, 4:347–352; Kimball 1860, 8:220–221; Young 1865, 11:110–119; Woodruff 1873, 15:275–283; J. Smith 1879: I Nephi 18:21–25, 19:1–2; II Nephi 21:2–14; III Nephi 21:22–29, 22:1–2; Church of Jesus Christ of Latter-day Saints 1908).

The literacies of salvation are prominent among church-settlers who understood their *aim* and *object* was to be saviors. The prophetic encounter in the mountains with the Lamanites, by whom they meant again the "poor Utahs, and Piedes, and other degrades tribes" of Utah, is an example (Woodruff 1855, 2:200). "The Lord," church-settlers proclaimed, had placed them in a "position" to be in "contact with them" (Smith 1856, 3:287). They observed that "the Indian" was contrary to and different once more because they bore *marks of a curse* or *scales of blackness-darkness*. Church-settlers attributed this to their state of being: *wild, degraded, uncivilized, wicked, ignorant, naked*. It was clear to them that the "Indian" could not "take care of themselves" and thus were in dire need of spiritual *work-instruction* (Young 1853, 1:105). "The Indian" of Utah would become in a perverse way the *seed of promise* for church-settlers as the Lamanite was in the *BoM* (MRM: Young 1853, 1:103–111; Pratt 1853, 1:6–15; Kimball 1853, 2:105–111; Young 1852, 3:80–96; Young 1857, 5:231–236; Young 1858, 6:193–199; Young 1854, 6:327–329; Kimball 1860, 7:346–351; Young 1858, 7:54–58; Young 1860, 8:291–293; Snow 1861, 9:20–23; Young 1855, 9:229–233; Woodruff 1865, 11:241–248; Young 1866, 11:263–266; Pratt 1869, 12:352–362; Pratt 1873, 15:312–324; Nicholson 1881, 22:20).

Church-settlers avowed to teach "the Indian" *how to live*. They were convinced they craved salvation. There is an adage that circulated among church-settlers: "The Lamanites will blossom as the rose on the mountains" (Woodruff 1873, 15:282; also see Church of Jesus Christ of Latter-day Saints 1908). Two hymns provide insight into its meaning. "Hymn 292" is one example: "O, stop and tell me, Red Man, Who are you, why you roam . . ." It speaks to "idle Indian hearts" marked by "savage customs" instead of "work and arts" (The Church of Jesus Christ of Latter-day Saints 1883, 341–342). Another example is "Hymn 313," which appeals to spiritual *work-instruction*: "Your 'Mormon' brothers will the truth reveal . . . Not many moons shall pass away, before the curse of darkness from your skin shall flee" (372–373). As one church-settler put it, "go and instruct the Lamanites in all the habits and customs of civilization that we as a people understand" (Young 1855, 9:231). That "the Indian" was the *seed of promise* meant church-settlers had to be *nice* and *kind* to them: "Treat them [others] kindly, and treat them as Indians, and not as your equals" (Young 1854, 6:329). Their salvation did not translate in/to equality for church-settlers, for the purpose of *work-instruction* is epistemic obedience (MRM: Young 1854, 6:327–329; Woodruff 1855, 9:221–229; Young 1855, 9:229–233; Smith 1872, 15:92–99; Smith 1879, II Nephi 30:1–12; Enos 1:13–22). Thus, *ghosting* works in two ways here, emptying the substance of beings and reducing them to "the Lamanite" and ensuring that they are perpetually in a state of absolute *thingification*.

The *other* does not exist ontologically. That the *other* needs to be saved from themselves and restored into a *white/fair and delightsome people* is as ludicrous an idea as the thought that some can claim to be in possession of a propriety of rights and privileges that permits them to observe, *thingify*, and enforce viewpoints. It was a ploy to dominate information and its mediums of circulation regarding Man-Human-Rights; manage land and identity by displacing "the Indian" from their land and pedagogically stamping out their identity; and consolidate control through an *epistemic system* and *design* that allocated to Man-Human *land as inheritance*. If the *other* resisted, violence could be justified in the name of salvation and/or attributed to divine and natural designs. And if the *other* assented to *work-instruction* a hyphenated identity would be designated, Lamanite-Nephite. Either way, epistemic violence could be rationalized and justified in the name of salvation. Complementing a rhetoric of salvation is that of progress and development (MRM: Young 1853, 1:162–172; Young 1853, 1:103–111; Smith 1852, 1:42–45; Kimball 1853, 2:105–111; Hyde 1853, 2:112–120; Young 1854, 2:136–145; Young 1855, 3:51–65; Taylor 1857, 5:182–192; Kimball 1857, 6:185–193; Young 1858, 6:193–199; Young 1859, 7:335–338; Woodruff 1855, 9:221–229; Young 1855, 9:229–233; Woodruff 1875, 18:109–122; Nicholson 1881, 22:183–192; also see Church of Jesus Christ of Latter-day Saints 1908).

Church-settlers utilized a rhetoric of modernity to cloak the darker side of physical *work*. The darker side, as Hämäläinen (2008), Tuck and Yang (2012), and Arvin, Tuck, and Morrill (2013) argue, is that settlers via settler colonialism make its name in possessing land, exploiting-extracting "resources," and making land produce excessively. And in so doing, they sought to materialize a desire and objective—to become "native" to a place—into reality. Church-settlers saw their trek through the wilderness and arrival in the mountains of Utah once more as a prophecy fulfilled: "And it shall come to pass in the last days, when the mountain of the Lord's house shall be established in the top of the mountains, and shall be exalted above the hills, and all nations shall flow unto it" (J. Smith 1879, II Nephi 12:3). They ~~discovered~~ invented in the mountains of Utah a new *gathering center* and *stake* of Zion. The Lord guided them there, church-settlers claimed, to become an ensign to the world: "Now we are here in the tops of the mountains . . . we are here as saviors . . . operating in the interests of humanity" (Taylor 1881, 23:16). They based that invention on physical *work* (MRM: Pratt 1855, 2:284–298; Young 1857, 6:39–47; Pratt 1859, 7:308–313; Pratt 1872, 15:44–53; Pratt 1872, 15:178–191; Snow 1873, 16:200–208; also see Church of Jesus Christ of Latter-day Saints 1908).

Church-settlers celebrated their triumphs as civilized and industrious people. They claimed that they alone discovered, settled, and enforced laws on a "portion of the earth" considered "uninhabitable" by *white Men* (Smith 1861, 9:109). Church-settlers were driven by a prophetic adage: "The wilderness and the solitary place shall be glad for them; and the desert shall rejoice, and blossom as the rose" (Pratt 1870, 15:57). They praised their ability to subdue, *redeem*, and make the desert *blossom as the rose* by *penetrating* the desert, *killing* reptiles, *battling* untutored savages, transforming the *virgin soil* into *resources*, and building roads and cities—the coded words and tropes of modern/colonial and settlerizing designs. Their feats, church-settlers argued, were "unparalleled on the page of history" (Young 1853, 2:33). Because, as they claimed, they alone removed the *curtain* of darkness and brought the *Light* and *Spirit* of civilization and improvement. (Very Hegelian one could say.) The land was now their *inheritance*, church-settlers argued (MRM: Pratt 1853, 1:6–15; Young 1853, 1:162–172; Young 1855, 2:248–258; Hyde 1853, 2:112–120; Young 1857, 4:341–346; Taylor 1857, 5:237–248; Young 1857, 5:72–78; Kimball 1854, 7:16–21; Young 1860, 8:126–130; Wells 1861, 9:43–50; Young 1863, 10:221–229; Young 1864, 10:358–365; Cannon 1864, 11:28–34; Young 1870, 14:276–281; Snow 1873, 16:200–208; Bywater 1881, 22:59–67; Snow 1882, 23:7–10; Snow 1882, 23:224–234; also see Church of Jesus Christ of Latter-day Saints 1996; Days of 47 2018). The sophistication of settlerizing epideictic rhetoric lies not solely with the praise but the capacity to express and transpire wor(l)ding aspirations. Couched within it is a *visuality* that sees in land the opportunity to make property, in nature "resources" to be extracted, and in the *ghosting* of its citizens exploitable and dispensable beings. All of this leads to a rebranding of a place image-and-myth.

A rhetoric of modernity aided in the (ap/exp)propriation of land. It did not negate but enhanced the *idea* of *land as inheritance* as it situated civilization and improvements as the exclusive achievements of church-settlers. The rhetoric of progress and *native inheritance* allowed Mormons to remove Rights from the *other*. It was a ploy to consolidate control through a church-settler *epistemic system* and *design* that allocated to Man-Human *land as their Right*. That land in Utah was obtained by *consent* and *approval* of "the Lamanite-Indian" was an odd claim contradicted by church-settlers themselves: "We are in possession of the valleys in the mountains" (Young 1863, 10:176); "We will fill up these mountains ... take up the land" (Kimball 1852, 1:296); "God has given us possession of them" (Taylor 1881, 23:17). It is further refuted by the idea that physical and spiritual *work* remained *unfinished*. Church-settlers referred to that unfinished *work* as *rearing* a *system and superstructure* (MRM: Pratt 1853, 1:6–15; Young 1852, 1:144–146; Smith 1852, 1:42–45; Hunter 1853, 2:35–38; Young 1856, 3:354–361; Pratt 1856, 3:299–307; Woodruff 1857, 4:227–233; Taylor 1857, 5:182–192; Young 1857, 6:226–229; Kimball 1857, 6:50–52; Cannon 1871, 14:122–129; Snow 1882, 23:7–10; also see Church of Jesus Christ of Latter-day Saints 1908; J. Smith 1917). Here the wor(l)ding aspiration of the *idea of Utah* and *Mormon/ism* become a vital node within a network of settlerizing activities that advances modern/colonial and settlerizing designs near and far. It solidifies itself as an archival impression entered into the *Archive*.

REARING A SUPERSTRUCTURE

Church-settlers often distinguished themselves from Western Man and philosophy. Yet they referred to Mormonism as a *system* of philosophy and *superstructure* built on the *science* of a *true* faith and religion. (The irony should not be lost on us.) I have traced its modus operandi above, but it is worth reciting. Church-settlers assumed they were the mouthpiece of the Almighty, *watchmen* (epistemic zero point) upon the *walls of Zion* in possession of divine and natural rights and privileges (provenance). They believed that there existed unknown spaces and places and that it was their *Right* per those *designs* to travel across the world to get to *work*, physically and spiritually (doctrines of discovery and rights to lands). Eerily, like the Spanish in the previous chapter, too many people, they claimed, were consumed by *superstitions* and *false traditions* (epistemic and ontological differences). Mormonism, church-settlers argued, was about *saving* and *enlightening* all of mankind (rhetorics of modernity). They were destined saviors, they claimed, doing *work* in the interests of humanity (MRM: Taylor 1852, 1:16–28; Grant 1853, 1:341–349; Young 1852, 1:358–365; Taylor 1854, 1:365–375; Young 1853, 2:1–10; Hunter 1853, 2:35–38; Pratt 1853, 2:43–47; Pratt 1856, 3:291–298; Young 1857, 5:368–376; Wells 1861, 9:43–50; Young 1864, 10:289–298; Taylor 1865, 11:73–80; Cannon 1871, 14:163–172; Snow 1879, 20:180–187; Woodruff 1880, 21:281–286; Taylor 1881, 23:11–20; Naisbitt 1885, 26:228–240). And in this way, the exegesis and eisegesis reading of the *BoM* comes full circle, underscoring how designs are in part an epistemic and aesthetic issue. Because at the core of designs partly lies an epistemological, ideological, and rhetorical war on knowledge and the production of knowledge.

Church-settlers also distinguish themselves from the White settler who intruded upon the lands of and caused harm to *others*. But violence ensued within a coloniality of knowledge (epistemology). Because the notion of *choice land* and *strengthening* the *stakes* and *borders* of Zion was already the (ap/

ex)propriation of lands. The invention of the *pure in heart-Zion* and "Lamanite" was the production of Man-Human-Rights. The belief that some have rights to *manage, control,* and carry out *work-instruction* was the manufacturing of hauntings and haunting situations. Church-settlers reared a *system* of philosophy and *superstructure* with the purpose of creating dependency upon a Mormon-controlled order near and far. Such an *epistemic system* and *design,* aided by an epistemological regime of rhetoric, was intended to be permanent, understood as law and rule, and deliberately left behind for posterity. The *goings-on* and *doings* of Mormonism is an epistemological, ideological, and rhetorical war on information—*informing* and *giving form* to truth-and-knowledge claims on Man-Human-Rights (MRM: Pratt 1853, 1:6–15; Pratt 1853, 1:256–263; Taylor 1854, 1:365–375; Grant 1854, 2:10–16; Hyde 1853, 2:47–49; Kimball 1856, 3:268–271; Young 1863, 10:221–229; Taylor 1877, 19:122–129; also see Woodruff 1845; Church of Jesus Christ of Latter-day Saints 1908; Clayton Family Association 1921). Reminiscent of Caldwell (1830), church-settlers argued the "American nation" should feel "indebted for the spirit of 'Mormonism,'" the rearing of a system and superstructure (Snow 1882, 23:9).

Both the *BoM* and *JoD* can be read and utilized as archives. Both epitomized *coloniality of instruction-and-curriculum*—a settler-centered instruction in which church settlers, who, like the men of letters, historians, and officers of the state Mignolo (2005, 2009, 2011a) discusses in his own studies, utilized words and *ideas* to *inform* and *give form* to a *coloniality of knowledge-being.* Coloniality of instruction-and-curriculum peddles a racial matrix and racist world views predicated on the pretexts of epistemic and ontological difference; laws of who can be in-common and Man-Human-Rights; and subtexts for coloniality of power. *Coloniality of instruction-and-curriculum* functions as a medium to filter knowledge as facts-truth, a vessel to naturalize the modus operandi of modern/colonial and settlerizing designs, and an experimental tool to manage and control epistemic obedience. Whether or not statements are true or affective is not the point. Interpreting and readapting Barthes's (1972) cultural work for this modern/colonial and settlerizing context, myths involve a form and concept that have wor(l)ding aspirations of naturalizing the projects of territorial and epistemological (ap/ex)propriation. The *idea of Utah* and *Mormon/ism* are part of a semiological system generated by humans who see in it both value and meaning. Agreeing with (Bhabha 1994), iterative or recycled writing and address heightens the affective value and rhetorical force (or pesado-ness) of some *things,* allowing, say, an archival impression to evolve into designs, new forms of public memory, and reality.

Cosmologies of Words and Ideas

Church-settler projects of territorial and epistemological (ap/ex)propriation continue to have effects and consequences on land, memory, knowledge, and relationality (174) years later, because their cosmologies of words and ideas so often cloaked by settlerizing epideictic rhetoric remain entrenched in the *ideas of Mormon/ism, land(s) as inheritance*, an *Other-as-Same* relation, and *work-instruction*. The constraints of this chapter prohibit another extensive archiving of enunciations, but the Church's proceedings from conventions and conferences as well as their official publication, *Ensign*, are examples of a church-settler *epistemic system, design*, and *epistemological framework for living* on the move and living-on long after some *things* or some *one* has passed. And that, in part, is the history of modern/colonial and settlerizing designs.

The idea of race and identity politics are fundamental to church-settlers' establishing a propriety of rights and privileges. In 1954 Elder Mark Petersen gave an address at the Convention of Teachers of Religion on the College Level entitled "Race Problems as They Affect the Church." He spoke on the question-problem of "The Negro," their curse of preexistence, and rights. The conversation is guided by several questions: "What should be our attitude as Latter-day Saints toward Negro and other dark races?" (6); "Does the Lord give us any guidance"? (6); "Is segregation in and of itself a wrong principle?" (6). Petersen concluded that segregation is not wrong in principle. How could it be, he rationalized, if it was God who prescribed qualities (dark skin) to "the Negro" and "the Lamanites" and associated them with *dark* spaces and places in the world. This was attributed to pre-existence. For Petersen, God's divine design naturally segregates un/favourable peoples, *rewarding* some and *punishing* others. He justifies and rationalizes segregation within the everyday and his congregation (MRM: Young 1855, 2:179–191; Smith 1855, 3:28–37; Young 1859, 7:282–291; Young 1863, 10:104–111; Smith 1863, 10:248–250; Cannon 1873, 15:291–302; also see England 1985).

The above words and ideas, though denied by some or claimed to be miscontextualized by others, are echoed elsewhere. In 1954 and 1960, Elder Spencer Kimball gave two untitled addresses at the General Conference. In the former, and in a spectacle fashion because some *things* are not cloaked or hidden—"I present to you a people who . . . have been scattered and driven" (106)—he reinstates prophecies of the Church: *choicest land* to be discovered, *righteous* few as destined saviors, and encounters with *indolent* "Indian-Lamanites" unable to *raise themselves* (Kimball 1954, 103–104). (Again, though the Church does not endorse the *JoD,* claiming it is misrepresentative, the parallels between official and unofficial cultural texts cannot be denied. And that is why an archival approach and theory of archival impressions is invaluable.) Kimball confirms *other* (all non-whites) and "Lamanite" are one and the same and that the Nephite-Lamanites of the world hold a seed of promise (106–107). In the 1960 address, Kimball (1960) celebrates how the *philanthropic* work of and *instruction* by the Church is *waning* the superstitions and false traditions of "the Indian" and removing their *scales of darkness* (32). Reminiscent of his 1954 speech, he enacts in spectacle fashion the settlerizing epideictic rhetoric of celebration: "I see a dependent people becoming independent . . . At last the Indians are suitable . . . they are now becoming white and delightsome . . . from tradition they are coming to truth, from legend to fact . . . They are grateful for that" (33–34). As to who the *other* ought to be grateful to, it is they who can give the gift of humanity, "Indians are people" (33), determined of course by how successful they are in "changing to whiteness and to delightsomeness" (34). Kimball's words that celebrate the *work* of church-settlers are rooted in the *idea* of race, identity politics, and wor(l)ding aspirations that their archive of knowledges, understandings, feelings, and doings speak to. (Though it is worth noting that Kimball also ended the Church's racist ban of African American people's access to priesthood and temple.)

There are other cosmologies of words and ideas that evidence a church-settler *epistemic system* and *design* on the move and living-on. *Ensign* is an official publication that replaced the *Millennial Star.* Both reared the Church's *system* of philosophy and *superstructure* predicated on theological designs of conversion, secular designs of civilizing, and modern designs of progress and development. Several *Ensign* entries (The Church of Jesus Christ of Latter-day Saints 1971; Burnett 1971; L. Cummins 1971; L. Johnson 1975) and an article by Eileen Kump (1973), "L Is for Indian," come to mind. It is an example of how people are the affective channels of rhetorical transmission of and for an LDS *epistemic system, designs,* and an *epistemological framework for the living.* Take note of the absurdity, both in the context of re-entrenching Patriarch and in substituting the letters "L" and "I." Kump reflects:

> Sister Ulrich, a part-time English teacher . . . awoke one morning last August with a brand new idea . . . Sister Ulrich had decided [to write a book that] would be "an alphabet for little Saints," a series of rhymes on Mormon topics for each letter of the alphabet . . . It is easy to imagine how these sessions went: B? Book of Mormon, *naturally.* P? Patriarch! L? Indian, of course,

for every LDS child knows that an Indian is called a Lamanite. Why not title the book L Is for Indian? (Kump 1973, n.d.)

The above is significant for its emphasis on *instruction* via the *goings-on* of literacy and rhetorical education. I discern in part from church-settlers and their posterity a theo-and-ego-structured *coloniality of instruction-and-curriculum*. Again, it is a *settler*-centered instruction peddling a racial matrix and racist world views that reflect attempts to manage information as Truth and control epistemic obedience. The above article is not a singular position or an isolated occurrence when other happenings—the Relief Society, Utah Placement Program, the Intermountain Indian Boarding School, and/or the Lamanite seminary program—are considered. Kump's article is evidence that literacies, images-signs-sounds, and rhetorics are how a church-settler *epistemic system*, *design*, and *epistemological framework for living* carries over from one generation to the next (Smith 1879: I Nephi 2:5–24, 3:1–18; II Nephi 21:2–14; Alma 2:36–38, 3:1–7; Kimball 1984; Coates 1978; Church of Jesus Christ of Latter-day Saints 1908; Woodruff 1845).

A church-settler *epistemic system*, *design*, and *epistemological framework for living* has endured for 174 years in Utah. It is present in material forms of public memory and as words and ideas inherited, embodied, and practiced. I was most recently reminded that settlerizing enunciations *take* and *make* place at the inauguration of the University of Utah's seventeenth president. Out of the inaugural speech we can excavate the impression of palimpsestic time (Alexander 2005), identity (Shohat 2002), and narratives (A. García 2004). To understand the weight of President Taylor Randall's impressions it was imperative that I return to the church-settler rhetoric of yesterday as I did in previous sections. Exhibiting settlerizing epideictic rhetoric and *visuality* (Right-to-look), President Randall echoes in his speech impressions initiated by church-settlers in the nineteenth century. He embodies the eye that observes, *thingifies*, and enforces viewpoints of land that legitimizes the church-settlers Right-to belong-to Utah, stating:

> When I reimagine something, I form a mental image that becomes so powerful . . . We stand on the precipice of an enormous opportunity. Perhaps an opportunity that has not faced us since our pioneer forebears looked at a blank piece of land and said we are going to build a university there. (University of Utah, 2021, n.p.)

President Randall inhabited before the eyes of many the modern epistemology of the hubris of the zero point temporally ("our pioneer forebearers"), spatially ("a blank piece of land"), and subjectively ("When I reimagine something, I form a mental image that becomes so powerful"). He contributes to past and current *ghosting of citizens*. In one sentence, President Randall attempts to impress others by linking "pioneer ancestors" with the pioneering of today, delivering an impression ("a blank piece of land") telegraphed by the eye of the observer observing ("looked"), impressing upon modern/colonial and settlerizing designs a vision for technologies that can reinforce the *idea* ("we are going to build..."). President Randall is an example of the ways Utah continues to be known and editorialized through the eyes of the observer observing. Impressions stand as the haunting bookmarks of designs that offer statements on the ways the *idea* is renewed and remapped; the ways a logic of coloniality remains advantageous and thus shared-in, imported, expanded, and/or disputed through crooked rhetorics of modernity. Ultimately, the "eye" is the colonial and imperial epistemic foundation from which the projects of territorial and epistemological (ap/ex)propriation and colonial and imperial differences are mapped out from (see Ballif 2014).

The Utah of today is not an inevitable or natural outcome. It is a result of an ongoing structuring principle of modern/colonial and settlerizing designs that posterity carries out as human work and projects—*visuality*, settlerizing epideictic rhetoric, assemblage, branding, and recasting work, and *ghosting*. The past and certain ghosts are kept alive in Utah through such words and ideas as that of President Randall and the rhetors at the airport. Their everyday occurrence alongside other aesthetics (economic, authorial, educational, political, and knowledge, among others) are reason why Utah is rewritten in modern/colonial and settlerizing ways. But it can begin to be (re)written if we think through the particularities and specificities in which hauntings and haunting situations unfold. With the hope that change is possible, I have gone to some lengths to archive church-settler enunciations. It is a hope that under different conditions and with our capacity to have knowledge of the inner-workings of archives, we would not give back to archives that wound and haunt per usual. ¡Ojalá!

We must investigate the past to understand the present structuring principle of settlerizing encounters, interactions, and engagement that keeps spaces and places wounded/wounding and *stories-so-far* haunted/haunting. Church-settler enunciations are evidence that the *ideas of Mormon/ism, land(s) as inheritance*, an *Other-as-Same* relation, and *work-instruction* are inseparable from the *idea of the Americas*. What remains in the land, memory, knowledge, and relationality is the *idea* of race, epistemic racism, coloniality, and the epistemological regime of modernity. Utah is a case study of the rhetoricity behind archival impressions preserving the *Archive*. Church-settler enunciations, from institutional and piecemealed archives, illustrate global hauntings and haunting situations manifest in local forms and conditions in spaces and places like Utah. My analysis shows that while church-settlers disputed power, a cosmology of ideas, images, and ends constituting a *palimpsestic narrative* of the *Archive* was shared-in, imported, and expanded. Its contents and practices—projects of territorial and epistemological (ap/ex)propriation justified and rationalized as the price of modernization and human progress—surrounding the reception-production of a *hegemonic architecture* were considered advantageous. The cultural texts of church-settlers thus implicates them as members of an *association of social interests* nourishing hauntings and haunting situations. Power does not unfold evenly, yet similar technologies recirculate (Yang 2017). The technological power of archival impressions is its capacity to materialize concretely designs into reality. And that is the power of the technology too that is the *idea*.

The *Archive* feels the hand of Mormon/ism. One hundred seventy-four years later, the *idea of Utah* and *Mormon/ism* continue to be felt with the erection of hundreds of temples every year. I want to recall Locke ([1689] 1821) through the words of church-settlers only to underscore the point I am making about the *Archive* and impressions:

> Bringing the elements into successful use for the benefit of man, and reclaiming a barren wilderness [desert], converting it into a fruitful field, making it to blossom as the rose [through industry and enterprise]; such a man I would call a financier, a benefactor of his fellow man. (Young 1877, 19:97)

The above, expressed by church-settlers, are the undertones of Locke's ideas, images-signs-sounds, and ends of and on labor, property, civilized Man, and Man supporting Human life. For church-settlers, all of earth is a space to subdue and potential place for the reestablishing of the Garden to Eden (Young 1871, 14:78–91). Like Locke, they saw America as the space and place where the heavenly father "planted the Garden of Eden" (Young 1863, 10:222). The "American desert," for which they meant Utah, was to be redeemed per divine and natural designs by *physical work* (labor), from a *waste place* into the Garden of Eden (MRM: Young 1868, 12:205–210; Pratt 1870, 14:299; Pratt 1875, 17:307–321; Pratt 1875, 17:289–306; Smith 1877, 19:187–197). Past and present church-settlers are not unalike from Locke in that they exaggerate a crisis—"the land of Zion is North and South America . . . where our heavenly Father . . . planted the Garden of Eden" (Young 1863, 10:222)—which always already stages the emergence of a penetration into the space, place, and time of an-other. The *Archive* and its smaller archives tell us that much.

The role of literacies, images-signs-sounds, and rhetorics cannot be overlooked in the church-settler context. The church-settler is Nephite is Adam; wasteland is choice-land is the Garden of Eden; cultivation is tilling the earth is replenishing the Garden of Eden elsewhere and otherwise: "he will make her wilderness like Eden, and her desert like the garden of the Lord" (Smith 1879: II Nephi 8:3). The word, "replenish" is significant. According to church-settlers, "This word is derived from the Latin; 're' and 'plenus'; 're' denotes repetition, iteration; and 'plenus' signifies full, complete; then the meaning of the word replenish is to refill, recomplete" (Hyde 1854, 2:79). They understood "replenish" thus as call to make the earth as it was before. Now, church-settlers realized they cannot say for certain where the Garden of Eden is located. Here, the Latin meaning of "alibi," and the desire and objective to be a race worthy of a higher calling, offers a logical excuse to the church-settler to be elsewhere and otherwise and authorizes them to replenish what can be seen across the whole face of the earth. The earth becomes a site of human work and projects to re-impress onto it a piece of them—the earth becomes a prism through which to see a reflection of their whiteness: "be white folks. We are white folks" (Kimball 1854, 2:224).

Now, this chapter was not about a being termed Mormon, an entity called Utah, or even about offering truthful definitions to the ontology of Man-Human-Rights. Rather, this chapter focused on how epistemological hegemony happens, ideologies are carried over, hegemony is maintained, and the rhetorical war on information is expanded-disputed through the rhetoricity of church-settlers. In other words, how both the *idea of Utah* as a destined place and gathering space, as well as the idea of Mormon/ism as the *true* faith and religion, came about as praxis. That situated me squarely on a coloniality of knowledge (epistemology) constitutive of a coloniality of being (ontology). My emphasis on the invention of the peaceful church-settlers unlocks the possibility for decolonizing knowledge and being. Such can create a pathway to liberate *pluriversal humanity*, which can be a road to the coexistence of epistemic and ontological pluriversality. So if forgetting or conjuration are essential to church-settlers, then a remembering that yokes and calls forth hauntings, inheritances, and dwellings is most crucial in Utah.

Many students I teach have a strong sense of obligation and responsibility to practice a settlerizing epideictic rhetoric in Utah. They are empowered by everything around them. My experience has proven to me that students know the power of literacies, images-signs-sounds, and rhetorics and can see in spaces and places opportunities to mobilize community. I acquainted myself with their cultural texts because I study how words and ideas *take* and *make* place. I created a public record of past and present words and ideas regarding the nature of God and Reason to establish a connection in their unfolding as the activities of a church-settler *epistemic system, design,* and *epistemological framework for the living*. Today, unlike my hesitation at the SLC airport where I learned that settlerizing epideictic rhetoric extends beyond praise-blame, I no longer allow a church-settler past, its ghosts, or rhetorics of epistemology to go unchecked or unsettled. If the classroom can be claimed by any student, it can be for all to claim. The role of church-settlers archives becomes vital for mutually determining the meaning of the classroom and the work of our work. Thus, the goal of this chapter was to create the bases for understanding the coloniality of knowledge and of being that show up in the lives of students I teach in Utah and to underscore how it has everything to do with the *goings-on* of everyday literacies and rhetorics (Burke 1961; Geiger 2009, 2013; Hansen 2005; Montesano and Roen 2005).

Church-settler archives may or may not change. But *why* and *how* we approach them can. They are a caravan for an *epistemic system, design,* and *epistemological framework for the living* on the move and living-on. Settler archives are a powerful medium for archiving the inhumanity and irrationality of *humanitas* and confronting, unsettling, decolonizing, and amending the lies, contradictions, myths, narcissism, cynicism, denialism, and sickness-disease of haunted/haunting literacies, images-signs-sounds, and rhetorics that haunt us in the present. As I will discuss in chapter 4, settler archives can also illuminate how *stories-so-far* adhere to, interact with, and carry out the projects and work that settler archives represent. This can be vital alongside placed-based pedagogies and curricula because it affords the occasion to make archival impression *otherwise*. If literacies, images-signs-sounds, and rhetorics have been used to fashion a modern/colonial world, they can be utilized to wor(l)d a future *otherwise* too. By creating a public record, the opportunity is afforded to view the contents of the *Archive* as *stories-so-far*, to excavate the archival impressions that constitute it, to reposition the contents of our *archives* so that we can position ourselves in relation to it *otherwise*, and to deliberate *an-other* set of choices, options, and obligations and responsibilities. The exigence to initiate *decolonizing archival impressions*, I believe, provides the prospect to research and search for hope in the archives, where the meaning of *stories-so-far* and the *possibilities of new stories* can be found.

Can the *Archive* feel? Utah is a case study on both the hand of Mormon/ism and why we cannot come to terms with hauntings without coming to terms with literacies, images-signs-sounds, and rhetorics. In the next chapter, I turn to how settlers reinscribe the landscape of Texas with the place myth of and add the *idea of Texas*—as a frontier to be conquered, colonized, and transformed into a fertile "resource"—as an archival impression entered into the *Archive*. That one cannot decolonize being without decolonizing knowledge will remain a running thread. It is my hope that you, my reader, will continue with me as I *return* to and peel back layers to *carefully reckon* with what remains in land, memory, knowledge, and relationality after some *things* or some *one* has passed in Texas and the Lower Rio Grande Valley (LRGV) of Texas.

Reflexión-Meditación

A Reflection on Corridos

Grandma and I enjoyed sitting in the cocina or in cars and listening to all kinds of música: banda, corridos, norteños, conjuntos, rancheras. Grandma would say, "Ay, esta canción me encanta. Está muy pesada." "Pesada" translates to "heavy" in English, but in Spanish it can refer to the (rhetorical) weight (pesado-ness) and affective element of some *thing* like a song can have. Corridos (and even narco-corridos) were our favorite. It is a genre of *community listening*, a set of enunciations unfolding as material exchanges (*shadow work*) transmitted through the mode of storytelling. Corridos are heavy because in the corridista's attempt to create presence from absence and sound from silence, they return, center, and situate hauntings, the past, the dead, inheritances, and dwellings to the politics of our present (see Limón 1992). I think Grandma understood that, which has a lot to do with why I orient myself to the archives as some *thing* alive and as powerful as the living, because I feel them as much as I feel the weight of a corrido. I understand that, which is why I know that *just* listening to a corrido is not an option just as some cannot easily return to the archives.

A corridista in any given corrido will make an announcement to the listener ("Voy a cantarles"). Sometimes corridistas will disclose that they are just the transmitter of information ("la verdad yo no se mucho yo nomás se los platico"). Other times, they speak more candidly ("es cierto no son mentira"). Their ethos, regardless, is expressed in the instructions to the audience, listen to *know-learn* ("ay que prender la lección") and to be more aware of hauntings ("ande con mucho cuidado"). Corridos proceed to announce a wounded/wounding space and place, situate haunted/haunting subjects in time, state haunting situations, and call forth a politics. It is both an ethic of sorts and invitation to the audience to haunt back. Will such an ethic ever have arrived? Will such an invitation ever have been answered and publicly addressed?

- In "Pistoleros Famosos," the corridista announces a place ("Por las márgenes del Río"), situates the subjects, ("pistoleros" and "rinches"), states the problem ("En los pueblitos del Norte . . . siempre ha corrido la sangre"), reveals a haunting ("Los Rinches que son cobardes"), and calls forth a politics ("Murieron porque eran hombres . . . no porque fueran bandidos").
- In "Corrido de Juan Cortina," the corridista announces a place ("más allá de Río Bravo"), identifies a time ("1859 para ser preciso"), situates the subjects ("Cortina" and "rinches cobardes"), states the problem ("la tierra se han robado"), reveals a haunting ("leyes y tratados sirven solo a los Americanos"), and calls forth a politics ("si dicen que soy un bandido por defender mi raza").
- In "Los Rinches de Tejas," the corridista situates the subjects ("los pobres infortunion" and "esos rinches asesinos"), states the problem ("que brutalmente golpearon"), reveals a haunting ("los mandó el gobernadora a proteger los melones"), and calls forth a politics ("Yo no opusé resistencia").

The above corridos exemplify *community listening* insofar that they emerge out of the *rhetorics of place* (see Endres and Senda-Cook 2011). Where there are hauntings, there are corridos. They are part of the material forms of a (counter) public memory. Corridos are not inconsequential as human projects and work, even though they, like rhetoric, can only ever guarantee with certainty possibilities. Part of me then wondered if Grandma felt the weight of corridos because it *threw* her back into hauntings and haunting situations. Part of me today is curious if corridos weighed heavy on her because she heeded the calling forth of a politics of hauntings, inheritances, and dwellings. Was listening to corridos with me her way of passing the message on as instructed ("vuela a llevar el mensaje") (see López 1967; Elizondo n.d.; Garza n.d.; Quintanilla 2015, 2019; Ayala 1977, 1995)? I have this hope that scholars in

WRS can realize that corridos and corrido-ing, like Grandma's *shadow work*, reflect a cultural art and excellence of rhetorical criticism (see Flores 2016; Morris 2010).

Corridos collapse space and time and utilize a language of the everyday. In this way, the corridista is constellated with the chantwell, griot, and elders. Each function as *keepers of history and knowledge, time benders*, and *canon makers*, entrusted with being the affective channels of rhetorical transmission of and for a politics of hauntings, inheritances, and dwellings (Banks 2011; Browne 2013; Cushman 2013; Lyons 2010). Corridistas, chantwells, griots, and elders, in part, utilize hauntings as a category of analysis to establish connections between the past and present in terms of social, cultural, and political activities. And though the *work* they carry out can only ever guarantee with certainty possibilities, they operate under a simple premise that people can listen to *know-learn* complex issues if the intention is truly for them to understand (see Fanon 1963). Corridos manifest a hope-struggle across the scenes of *returns, careful reckonings*, and *enduring tasks*.

Texas today is neither the Americas nor the Texas of the past. Yet it cannot be separated from the *idea of Texas* or the *idea of the Americas*. My goal, like the corridista's, is not to speak for everyone or anyone. And like the corridista, I merely strive to return, center, and situate hauntings, the past, the dead, inheritances, and dwellings to the politics of our present via hauntings as a category of analysis. That in essence is a corrido-ing approach, which I honor through my own storytelling of the *Archive* and its *smaller archives of knowledges, understandings, feelings, and doings* (or the *working parts* of the *Archive*) both in the previous chapters and the next. Texas of the past and present is the outcome of human projects and work (see Glissant 1989). The unsettling of the *Archive* and its archival impressions in Texas must be met by decolonizing archival impressions that first and foremost recognize and acknowledge Texas as the traditional and ancestral homelands of the Karankawa, Ndé Kónitsąąíí Gokíyaa, Esto'k Gna (Carrizo/Comecrudo), and Rayados/Borrados people. The next chapter is not "A" history but a version of a haunted/ haunting story that unsettles histories and geographies of power (Alexander and Mohanty 2010).

The everyday archives that we live amid tell a story of how writing, rhetoric, place, archives, and modern/colonial and settlerizing designs are intertwined. We are under the yoke of these archives that have fundamental orientations toward the public. How will we address them otherwise? At a time when WRS lacks a theory of writing and rhetoric that can assume and reckon with the enduring, epistemological, and rhetorical force that is modern/colonial and settlerizing designs, an archival approach and theory of archival impressions offer one option for contending with the regulative function of archives. So I continue forth in the next chapter with such a theory in mind.

3
Corrido-ing the Idea of Texas-LRGV and the Settler

A theory of archival impressions in not unfounded. Derrida (1995) speaks to what "permits and [the] conditions [of] archivization" (14) and to that which "produces as much as it records the event" (17). Impressions are at the fore (18): "the impression left" (11, 24); "the impression" (12); "the printing of impression" (17). Both Derrida and I utilize impressions to speak to some *things* that give structure to and constitute archives. Once more, my work has more to do with the settler rhetoricity behind archival impressions and I derive its meaning from modern/colonial and settlerizing contexts, specifically settler rhetorics of archival impressions: (1) to give an impression; (2) to impress enduringly; (3) to impress others; (4) to impress-on or cover-over (designs). This chapter both works to illuminate these impressions and serves as a pathway to further an archival approach and theory of archival impressions that can help us better understand the (re)writing of the *Archive* and its designs and technologies.

Distracted eyes, sensibilities, and listening leads to a forgetfulness. Everyday people have to do work rhetorically to enable modern/colonial and settlerizing designs. It is thus imperative to rhetorically analyze how the invention of new images, myths, and meanings of place and citizen/ship stem from *visuality*, the *goings-on* of settlerizing epideictic rhetoric, assemblage, rebranding, and recasting work, and the transformation of human beings

https://doi.org/10.7330/9781646426782.c003

into *ghosts* and *ghost citizens*. To underscore why the *Archive* is the most honest and critical space to think and speak from, this chapter serves as a decolonial case study on the *idea of Texas* and *the LRGV* and how it functioned as an archival impression within the *Archive*. Though not "A" history (Bedolla 2009; T. Bowman 2016; Carrigan and Webb 2003; Delgado 2009; León 1997, 2010; G. Martinez 2011; M. Martinez 2018; Guidotti-Hernández 2011) but a version of a haunted/haunting story that unsettles histories and geographies of power (Alexander and Mohanty 2010), it also heeds Mignolo (2007), Tsing (1993), Tuck and Yang (2012), and Veracini's (2010) call that decolonizing projects be thought through the particularities and specificities in which such designs and technologies unfold. This chapter, like the previous one, is guided by a decolonial question and *decolonial analytic* thus.

We live amid archives and in unending cycles of their re(writing). To illustrate the *epistemological experiment* of *smaller archives of knowledges, understandings, feelings, and doings* (or the *working parts* of the *Archive*) that mark a complicity between rhetorics of modernity and logics of coloniality, I generate a public record-archive of and rhetoricize rhetorics of epistemology, truth-and-knowledge claims, and the rhetoricity behind archival impressions across bodies of settlerizing knowledge. Part and parcel to a *decolonial analytic* is not just locating, identifying, and naming inhumane and irrational discourse but also initiating a decolonizing archival impression into the smaller archive of Texas-LRGV in the wake of what remains in land, memory, knowledge, being, and relationality after some *thing* and some *one* has passed.

The Future Has Arrived

There is a place deep in the southern tip of Texas. Its history is unknown to many. It shares a lot in common with Utah. The LRGV remains the ancestral land to the Karankawa, Ndé Kónitsąąíí Gokíyaa, Esto'k Gna (Carrizo/Comecrudo), and Rayados/Borrados people. Its history is constituted by settlerizing encounters and performances of *visuality*, branding, and *ghosting*. They remain ever so relevant today in the LRGV with "new" wor(l)ding aspirations. Through discourse, settlers of the past and present produce absences and silences by engaging in what Wingard (2013) refers to as the technological work of assemblage, branding, and recasting. The rhetorical and affective strategies of branding land with settlers, settlers with modernity, and "the Mexican" as a threat continues to recast new places images and myths in the LRGV. In the past, it helped establish a new *rhetoric of place* with Texas and the LRGV acting rhetorically as an American place—bolstering a model of hegemony vying for power—and final frontier—a space of and for settlerizing by men of vision with the masculine and martial grit and vigor to overcome the wilderness and transform it. The effects and consequences of covering-up-and-over the "old" continues to be felt in land, memory, knowledge, and relationality today.

Yet, Texas and the LRGV are also unlike Utah. "Hispanics" are not in the shadows. It is the largest ethnic group in Texas and the largest demographic in the LRGV. The US Census Bureau reports that "Hispanics" represent an average of more than 65 percent to 88 percent between San Antonio and across the counties (Cameron, Willacy, Hidalgo, Starr) of the LRGV. A competing *rhetoric of place* has created what Arnoldo de León (1997) refers to as a *Tejano Cultural Zone*, a cultural vitality that survives, perseveres, and thrives (*Caballero, With His Pistol in His Hand, George Washington Gomez, Klail City,* and *Borderlands/La Frontera* are a few cultural texts on hauntings and haunting situations on the border and this cultural zone). But the LRGV stands apart. It is a border(ed)land, boxed in by the geopolitical border to the south and internal checkpoints 70 miles north of and 100 miles parallel to it. Margo Tamez (2011) calls this space of internal checkpoints a constitution-free and hypersurveilled zone. This can be retroactively applied to the LRGV as rhetorics of borders and boundaries subject all to containment, monitorization, surveillance, and checkings. The *idea* for a border(ed)land stems from an *epistemic murk* (Taussig 1991), rationalized by a modern/colonial and settlerizing imagination through cultural logics (Ratcliffe 2005). The logic of *othering* that is impressed on the LRGV and peoples assembles and ensembles rhetorics of fear, protection, and national security around designs of domination, management, production, control, and exploitation (modern/colonial) to create this border(ed)land. Despite *ideologies of scale, scale-making projects,* and other forms of representational praxis that give it its *rhetoric of place* as El Valle, the LRGV is an *excluded geography*, a shadowland of a state and in a nation.

El Valle symbolizes the ability of the racialized, minoritized, and marginalized to assent, reclaim, and resignify the modern/colonial and settlerizing design of "The Magic Valley." But whatever is conceded to the *other* is either temporary or surveilled, with the closed fist of power ready to inflict violence at a moment's notice whenever it or the powers that be have had enough. Because while El Valle is celebrated as a world of its own by many of its own, the wreckage of what surrounds—a space of and for settlerizing—is a daily reminder the LRGV cannot be defined in and on their own terms. The powers that be have conceded to the appropriation of "the Magic Valley," but it has neither relinquished its reach-grip or its Right-to exercise its power. At any given moment, such as the current one marked by the arrival of new settlers and their modern/colonial and settlerizing futures, they are subject to designs of hauntings and haunting situations—state- and locally sanctioned ghostly citizenship, cultural displacement, land dispossession. Poverty, food insecurities, health disparities, "illiteracy," and the lack of pathways to opportunities are part of the intergenerational trauma and haunted/haunting mentalities in the LRGV. A modern/colonial and settlerizing *epistemic system*, the epistemological regimes of modern designs, and an *epistemological framework for the living* predicated on the logics of domination, management, and control continue to have effects and consequences on land, memory, knowledge, and relationality in the LRGV.

For decades, denizens of the LRGV have expressed a desire to *be-with* the times. A sense of behind-ness is a shared sentiment. But the future has at last arrived. It remains unclear if these citizens, what Liew (2004) might call *ghost citizens*, will be left behind, part of, or merely a means—a *cheap*, *dependable*, and *plentiful source of manual labor*—to an end (à la Kant). In 2014, Elon Musk and his commercial space company, SpaceX, set its eyes on Boca Chica, Texas, and began purchasing tracts of land. Since then, there have been multiple efforts to cover-up-and-over the name Boca Chica, replacing it with a new place image and myth. In 2022, it was announced that an Amazon warehouse was being built in McAllen: "Amazon warehouse brings opportunities to the RGV" (Cardona 2022). Between 2014 and 2023, new high-end restaurants, housing, and a car dealership have gone up. The new has arrived: spacecraft launches held at SpaceX, drone shows presented by SpaceX, educational collaborations with SpaceX, and beautification projects supported by SpaceX. The future has arrived, surely, with every acquisition of acres by Musk and his company. There is much speculation about what the LRGV might look like in the years to come, especially with the announcement that Musk will be moving his SpaceX headquarters to a city he ~~discovered~~ invented, Starbase, Texas. Will such a future ever have arrived for the racialized and minoritized in the Valley?

But as the dust begins to settle and the smell of "newness" wears off, some LRGV denizens have pumped the breaks on their embrace of Musk. When Musk announced the move of his headquarters, denizens expressed sentiments of discontent on the digital pages of news outlets such as KRGV: "there goes inflation . . . not to mention the pollution, higher taxes, and the destruction of the environment"; "He gets people from out of the Valley to come to the Valley, gentrify it and destroy it"; "All he brought was higher taxes, higher rents, and air pollution" (C. Garcia 2024). Because it is evident that the new jobs, housing, and beautification projects are not for them. SpaceX is as popular of a topic today as it was when they first arrived. At Vera's Backyard in Brownsville, I overhear a conversation: "Everybody was excited." "Así vas a resolver los problemas." "I didn't know." "Sólo porque hacen sus experimentos." "Where are the jobs?" "¿Qué otros problemas traerá?" "We need to start paying attention." Today denizens find themselves in the crux of a new wreckage: spacecraft launches unsettling the grounds, treated and sewage waste polluting the waters, debris blasts damaging local wildlife habitats, particulate matter contaminating the environment, gentrification, cultural displacement, widened social inequalities, and increased racism and discrimination. Only, neither it nor its effects and consequence are so new when we look to the words and ideas of Musk and peel back the layers of what is behind it—the (re)writing of a smaller archive, and thus, the (re)writing of the *Archive*. The machinery of the nineteenth century remains in operation today though the proverbial door to the boiler room has been ignored by a public who claim el Valle es un otro mundo, defined in and on their own terms. The "settler" and "The Magic Valley" myth, which has always functioned in the background, has not been so transparent in over 100 years. Or, maybe it has, and we have just internalized it, mistaking the crumbs of assent as the power of the people for modern/colonial and settlerizing designs working as they should.

"The Magic Valley" may be just words and an *idea*. Yet a careful rhetorical analysis of it would underscore Mignolo's (2005) argument that words and ideas make it possible to "transform an invented idea into 'reality'" (151). "The Magic Valley" is not inconsequential but rather an archival impression that underscores how everyday people have had to do work rhetorically to enable modern/colonial and settlerizing designs to unfold. It is the invention of *visuality*, assemblage, rebranding, and recasting work, and *ghosting citizens*. This seems to be supported by Christian Brannstrom and Matthew Neuman (2009), who in many ways take up a *discourse about actions* approach in contending with the wor(l)ding aspirations of settlers (see Benoit 1996). In "Inventing the 'Magic Valley' of South Texas," they attribute the ability of Anglo settlers in the twentieth century to invent a place image-and-myth—as a space to exploit "resources" and cheap labor and a place where settlers can belong-to via an entitlement of Rights-to—and to assemblages of texts, images, and performances in promotional pamphlets and other ephemera. (Reminiscent of what Musk is doing today.) Their study underscores how modern/colonial and settlerizing discursive inventions are the outcome of a *semiotic apparatus of enunciations* (Mignolo and Walsh 2018; Tuck and Yang 2017). In other words, there are actors in a position to manage discourse, utilizing the institution of what I will call *settler advertisements* to invent spaces, places, and people through language, images, and written descriptions. While the medium in which such advertisements circulate has changed—paper to digital—by no means is it new, underscoring how at the core of designs there lies an epistemological, ideological, and rhetorical war on knowledge and the production of knowledge. Power is an epistemic and aesthetic issue. And because the *virtue* of address—addressing and being addressed—is at its core, what is demanded of all is rhetorical criticism (see Flores 2016).

Settler advertisements—promotional materials (broadly conceived)—are a medium of circulation dominated, managed, and controlled by settlers, accomplices, and allies. Between the early 1900s and 1940s, they functioned as an archiving and marketing mechanism, a technology that records as much as it produces the *epistemological experiment* of an *epistemic system*, designs, and an *epistemological framework for the living*; a technology that facilitates wor(l)ding aspirations through the *goings-on* of and *doings* of literacies, images-signs-sounds, and settlerizing epideictic rhetoric. Settler advertisements ultimately aid and abet efforts to empty land of pre-existing meaning and people of substance to permanently impress new meaning on a place. Like a settler archive, they acknowledge, disavow, and/or subsume the *other-things* (see Adams-Campbell, Falzetti, and Rivard 2015, 110). Settler advertisements are a prism through which to see the settler psyche consciously documenting their existence, exhibiting their power to belong, and legitimizing their Rights-to, all refracted through the lens of *Americanity* and within the frame of modernity/coloniality despite successive evolutions-stages and mutated modalities. The sophistication of settlerizing epideictic rhetoric, recall, lies not solely with the praise of settlers but the *capacity* to express (to *inform*) and transpire (*give form* to) wor(l)ding aspirations via iterative writing and address. What began as an archival impression, "The Magic Valley," today is a permanent mark in the *Archive*.

I begin with "The Lower Valley in Verse" (figures 3.1 and 3.2) to underscore what a settler advertisement could look like (papers, letters, correspondences, promotional materials, verses) and to set the tone for this chapter. As part of a promotional material, "Souvenir of the Lower Rio Grande Valley of Texas" (W. E. Stewart Land Company 1929), it is part historiographic: "In eighteen hundred-forty-eight, the great Lone Star became a state" (19). The verse is referring to the Treaty of Guadalupe Hidalgo in 1848. But it very much is rhetorical

THE LOWER VALLEY IN VERSE.

Now, neighbor, lend me your ear, and of the Valley you shall hear,
Of its history and its clime, and all it produces I'll tell in rhyme.
In eighteen hundred-forty-eight, the great Lone Star became a state,
And a million acres of valuable land was ceded by Mexico, on the Rio Grande.
And the cream of it all, I'll have you know, lies in the county of Hidalgo.
But primitive it lay for many a year, the roaming ground of coyotes and deer,
And lions and cats and panthers wild, the dread and fear of the Mexican child.
For fifty years it stood that way, until the railroad came one day
And cleared away the chapparal, the wild mesquite and thorned nopal,
And with its civilizing hand, beckoned to a new-found land.
Two men there were who heard the call, away up North in the early fall.
Land men they were, so I've been told, with little cash but natures bold.
So out they fared for the Sunny Land, headed straight for the Rio Grande
And from El Paso in an open boat, to the Land of Dreams they let her float.
And down the stream in leisurely way, they let her drift day after day,
And watched the banks as they drifted by, their hearts content, their spirits high.
For they felt assured that just beyond, the Promised Land would soon be found.
And find it they did, in a funny way, their boat was snagged, so the natives say,
And the men were forced to swim ashore, with nothing left but the clothes they wore.
And there upon the eastern shore, they found the land they were seeking for.
By a curious stroke of fate, they landed on a church estate,
And La Lomita's mission stood, gleaming in the darkling wood.
The kindly padres took them in, warmed their hearts with mission gin,
Fed them fruit and let them sleep, until dewy morn began to creep.
And from the windows of their room, they saw the mission flowers bloom.
They saw ripe fruit of golden hue, oranges and grapefruit too,
The fig, the date and tangerine, and purple grapevines in between.
In front there was a lawn of green (of bright Bermuda grass, I ween).
One gripped the other by the hand, and said, "We've found the Promised Land!
For this is winter time, you know, when all the North is white with snow.
But here, on every hand, is seen a valley rich with verdant green.
We'll see the priests, this land we'll buy, and sell it to our friends, or try.
We'll clear the land of chapparal, and o'er it all build a canal,
And irrigate the creamy soil that's rich as any pirate's spoil."
The pact was made, the priests are won, they got their price, the work is on,
And 'ere another year rolled round, they told their friends what they had found,
And from the North in droves they came, and plunged into the farming game.
The farmer man, the millionaire, the business man and clerk were there,
The sufferer from rheumatic pain came down to get his health again.
And women too, with faces fair, came down to take the Valley air,
To fill their lungs with ozone sweet, a tonic not found in the land of sleet.
The project opened in nineteen-eight without a show or pageant great,

—19—

FIGURE 3.1. A verse from a W. E. Stewart Land Company pamphlet: "The Lower Valley in Verse"

work: "But primitive it lay for many a year" (19). It tells a story of a "primitive" time that existed until the "civilizing hand" came to a "new-foundland"—a "Land of Dreams," a "Promised Land," an "Eden" (19). What the verse does is seed an *idea*—of rights-and-belonging-to—underscoring impressions part and parcel to a settlerizing effort to cover-up-and-over the "old" with the "new."

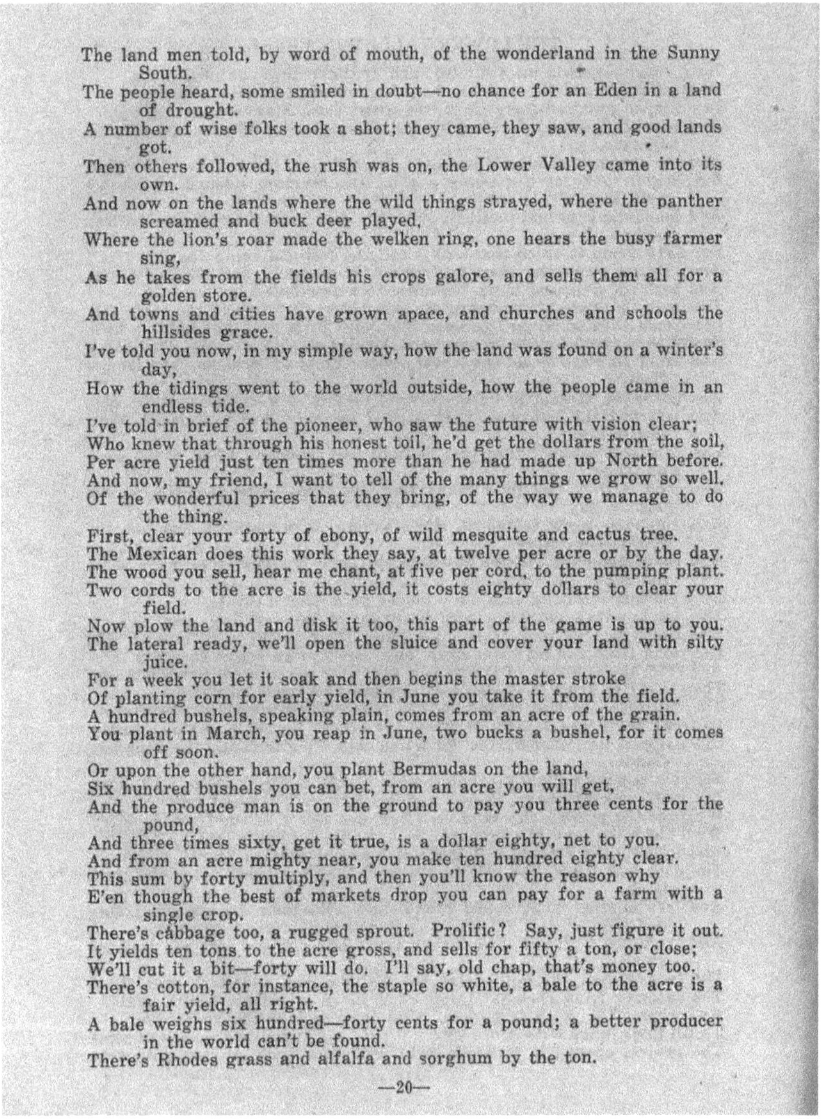

> The land men told, by word of mouth, of the wonderland in the Sunny South.
> The people heard, some smiled in doubt—no chance for an Eden in a land of drought.
> A number of wise folks took a shot; they came, they saw, and good lands got.
> Then others followed, the rush was on, the Lower Valley came into its own.
> And now on the lands where the wild things strayed, where the panther screamed and buck deer played,
> Where the lion's roar made the welken ring, one hears the busy farmer sing,
> As he takes from the fields his crops galore, and sells them all for a golden store.
> And towns and cities have grown apace, and churches and schools the hillsides grace.
> I've told you now, in my simple way, how the land was found on a winter's day,
> How the tidings went to the world outside, how the people came in an endless tide.
> I've told in brief of the pioneer, who saw the future with vision clear;
> Who knew that through his honest toil, he'd get the dollars from the soil,
> Per acre yield just ten times more than he had made up North before.
> And now, my friend, I want to tell of the many things we grow so well,
> Of the wonderful prices that they bring, of the way we manage to do the thing.
> First, clear your forty of ebony, of wild mesquite and cactus tree.
> The Mexican does this work they say, at twelve per acre or by the day.
> The wood you sell, hear me chant, at five per cord, to the pumping plant.
> Two cords to the acre is the yield, it costs eighty dollars to clear your field.
> Now plow the land and disk it too, this part of the game is up to you.
> The lateral ready, we'll open the sluice and cover your land with silty juice.
> For a week you let it soak and then begins the master stroke
> Of planting corn for early yield, in June you take it from the field.
> A hundred bushels, speaking plain, comes from an acre of the grain.
> You plant in March, you reap in June, two bucks a bushel, for it comes off soon.
> Or upon the other hand, you plant Bermudas on the land,
> Six hundred bushels you can bet, from an acre you will get,
> And the produce man is on the ground to pay you three cents for the pound,
> And three times sixty, get it true, is a dollar eighty, net to you.
> And from an acre mighty near, you make ten hundred eighty clear.
> This sum by forty multiply, and then you'll know the reason why
> E'en though the best of markets drop you can pay for a farm with a single crop.
> There's cabbage too, a rugged sprout. Prolific? Say, just figure it out.
> It yields ten tons to the acre gross, and sells for fifty a ton, or close;
> We'll cut it a bit—forty will do. I'll say, old chap, that's money too.
> There's cotton, for instance, the staple so white, a bale to the acre is a fair yield, all right.
> A bale weighs six hundred—forty cents for a pound; a better producer in the world can't be found.
> There's Rhodes grass and alfalfa and sorghum by the ton.
>
> —20—

FIGURE 3.2. A verse from a W. E. Stewart Land Company pamphlet: "Where the Rio Grande Is Flowing?"

As I will show in what follows, such impressions accumulate: "the pioneers . . . 'discovered' the Magic Valley . . . the 'Last Frontier'" ("Lower Rio Grande Valley Magazine" 1928). Though beyond the scope and breadth of this chapter, there is something to be said about what A. M. Kanngieser's (2023) calls *sonic coloniality*: "structures of listening and sense making that are founded on, and

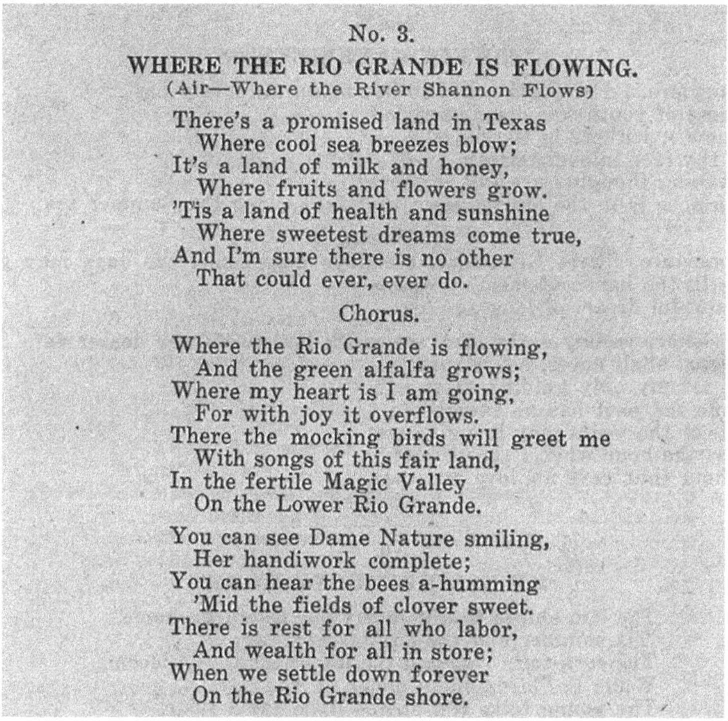

> No. 3.
> **WHERE THE RIO GRANDE IS FLOWING.**
> (Air—Where the River Shannon Flows)
>
> There's a promised land in Texas
>   Where cool sea breezes blow;
> It's a land of milk and honey,
>   Where fruits and flowers grow.
> 'Tis a land of health and sunshine
>   Where sweetest dreams come true,
> And I'm sure there is no other
>   That could ever, ever do.
>
> Chorus.
>
> Where the Rio Grande is flowing,
>   And the green alfalfa grows;
> Where my heart is I am going,
>   For with joy it overflows.
> There the mocking birds will greet me
>   With songs of this fair land,
> In the fertile Magic Valley
>   On the Lower Rio Grande.
>
> You can see Dame Nature smiling,
>   Her handiwork complete;
> You can hear the bees a-humming
>   'Mid the fields of clover sweet.
> There is rest for all who labor,
>   And wealth for all in store;
> When we settle down forever
>   On the Rio Grande shore.

FIGURE 3.3. Song from a W. E. Stewart Land Company pamphlet: No. 7: "The Rio Grande Valley"

reinforce, Anglo-European onto-epistemologies of humans in relation to, and distinct from, nature" (692), because it is what is necessary for "the Magic Valley" myth to evolve into much more than an impression. Sonic coloniality is part and parcel to the *Archive* and its smaller archives, which speaks to how modern/colonial and settlerizing mentalities and designs are baked into our bodies and bones—our sensory *archives*.

Both settlers and settler advertisements are significant sites of analysis, because the performativity of the place myth (and modernity) extends to an embodiment by the settler. Both provide a window into the role *coloniality of instruction-and-curriculum* plays in naturalizing the modus of designs while peddling a racial matrix and racist worldviews predicated on the pretexts of epistemic and ontological differences, laws of Man-Human-Rights, and subtext of coloniality of power, giving structure to and constituting the support structure of the *Archive*. Take as one more example an-other set of verses part of the same promotional material, which speak to both a *promised land* that settlers call the "fertile Magic Valley" (figure 3.3) and the arrival of modernity

No. 7.
THE RIO GRANDE VALLEY.
(Tune—Marching Through Georgia)

Here's to good old Texas, boys,
Down on the Rio Grande.
'Tis Nature's Garden Spot of earth,
For here we have the land;
We've got the soil and sunshine
And the rain at our command,
In the Lower Valley of Texas.

Chorus.
Hurrah, hurrah, send up the mighty cheer;
Hurrah, hurrah, three bumper crops a year;
We've left the snow behind us,
And there is nothing more to fear,
In the Lower Valley of Texas.

The cotton and the sugar cane,
Alfalfa and the corn;
I never saw such figs and grapes
And beets since I was born;
The lemons and the orange trees,
The verdant fields adorn
In the Lower Valley of Texas.

The richness and the depth of soil
Makes all the farmers smile,
It makes his time and money
And his labor worth the while.
For it is as productive
As the Delta of the Nile,
In the Lower Valley of Texas.

When autumn comes we call the dogs,
Take down the old shotgun;
Wild turkeys, ducks and partridges,
And deer make lots of fun;
We take a team of mules for there
Is shooting by the ton—
In the Lower Valley of Texas.

The climate's mild and pleasant,
From the Gulf the breezes blow;
The rain is brought by telephone
And makes the crop to grow;
We get the best of everything
We have in mind to sow,
In the Lower Valley of Texas.

The railroads and the schools are here;
We make no sacrifice;
We are planting in December
And our produce brings the price;
We're happy and contented,
It's the farmer's paradise,
In the Lower Valley of Texas.
—5—

FIGURE 3.4. Song from a W. E. Stewart Land Company pamphlet: "The land men told"

in the LRGV (figures 3.4 and 3.5). Again, A. M. Kanngieser (2023, 693) is relevant, if we understand that these songs are meant to be sung in chorus and that they will circulate vis-à-vis settler advertisements as an appeal (figures 3.5 and 3.6) to settlers—"Come all you people" (W. E. Stewart Land Company 1929, 7)—of which require "structures of listening and sense making" that

No. 11.
THE LOWER RIO GRANDE.
(Air—Casey Jones)

Come all you people who want to buy land,
And go with us to the Lower Rio Grande;
Where the corn and cotton and the sugar cane grows,
Where the sun always shines and it never snows.

Chorus.

Come on, boys, to the Rio Grande Valley,
Come on and go to the Lower Rio Grande;
Come on, boys, to the Rio Grande Valley,
When we make the next trip to that promised land.

No more hard winters with coal to buy,
Nor long, hot summers, when the wells go dry;
For the air is tempered by the great Gulf Breeze,
And the man that doesn't like it would be hard to please.

Chorus.

Figs and oranges and melons, too,
Grow just as good as the other crops do;
With the finest irrigation system ever planned,
This is what we offer in the Rio Grande.

Chorus.

Here we have churches and schools to suit,
And a good railroad to market the fruit;
Social conditions as good as at home.
Now is the time to get ready and come.

Chorus.

FIGURE 3.5. Song from a W. E. Stewart Land Company pamphlet: "Come all you people"

No. 15.
LOYALTY TO RIO GRANDE.
(Tune—Loyalty)

From over hill and plain, there comes the special train.
To Rio Grande—Rio Grande, yes Rio Grande for all;
Its wheels they roll along, the hills take up the song,
To Rio Grande—Rio Grande, yes, Rio Grande for all.

Chorus.

"On to Rio Grande, on to Rio Grande,"
Cries our Great Commander; "On,"
We'll move at his command,
We'll soon possess the land,
In Rio Grande—Rio Grande, this valley for them all.

Oh, hear ye Brave, the sound that moves this train along,
To Rio Grande—Rio Grande, yes, Rio Grande for all.
Arise to dare and do, ring out the valley true,
Oh, Rio Grande—Rio Grande, yes, Rio Grande for all.

Chorus.

Come join our mighty throng, we'll root you boys along
To Rio Grande—Rio Grande, yes, Rio Grande for all,
Where prosperous banners float, we'll sound the bugle note,
Oh, Rio Grande—Rio Grande, yes, Rio Grande for all.

Chorus.

FIGURE 3.6. Song from a W. E. Stewart Land Company pamphlet: No. 15: "Loyalty to Rio Grande"

reinforce "Anglo-European onto-epistemologies" (Kanngieser 2023, 692). Once more, as I will show in what follows, such impressions accumulate: "converted a JUNGLE INTO A PARADISE" ("The Land of Continuous Crops" n.d.). It is imperative thus that we attend to the iterative and multi-modal writings and addresses as those above because to an extent there was an understanding modern/colonial and settlerizing designs needed to gain currency at the epistemological level; successful appeals to the senses could possibly mean at the same time adherence and thus epistemic obedience to modern/colonial and settlerizing geo-and-body politics.

Settler advertisements in the LRGV are a case study of what lies behind words and ideas such as "The Magic Valley" when we peel back its layers. They invoke impressions in several ways: "impressed"; "impresses upon"; "the impression"; "stamped the impression" ("Lower Rio Grande Valley Magazine" 1928; "Lon Hill, Sr." 1950). Collectively, they underscore the four meanings I have prescribed to archival impressions already. Now, excavation of them is necessary as conditions that gave rise to modern/colonial and settlerizing designs in the nineteenth and twentieth centuries are similar to those of today in the LRGV, because modern-day settlers such as Musk are reinscribing the landscape with the place myth of "The Magic Valley." To take this back to an earlier conversation then, disenfranchisement is nothing new in the LRGV, and what Lewis Gordon (1995) calls *bad faith* actors are a dime a dozen. (Fanon anticipated the reach and grip of power even with *ghostly citizens*.) Why it feels so new partly has to do with a desire for "newness." As one person I overheard at Vera's put it, "Nos vendieron así." Musk is a modern-day Lon C. Hill or John Shary who has sold people on a future through the myth of "The Magic Valley." There is hardly a difference in the invitation issued to the "citizen" of the nineteenth and twentieth centuries and the "friends" of the present. Social media posts now function as settler advertisements. To establish Starbase as a final frontier, *visuality*, assemblage, rebranding, and recasting work, and *ghosting citizens* are key: "We've got a lot of land with nobody around" (Keates and Maremont 2021, n.p.); "Creating the City of Starbase, Texas" (Musk 2021b); "Please consider moving to Starbase or greater Brownsville/South Padre . . . & encourage friends to do so" (Falcon 2021, n.p.). Musk's *goings-on* suggest land has been discovered, propertied, and prepped for reterritorialization (figures 3.7 and 3.8). (I am reminded of Baldwin [2007, 193–194], who wrote of an arrogance that permeates modern/colonial and settlerizing designs: "There is a reason, after all, that some people wish to colonize the moon, and others dance before it as before an ancient friend.")

FIGURE 3.7. Tweet by Elon Musk: "Creating the city of Starbase, Texas"

FIGURE 3.8. Tweet by Elon Musk: "Please consider moving to Starbase"

Before the world, Musk inhabited on Twitter the modern epistemology of the hubris of the zero point temporally ("creating the city"), spatially ("We've got a lot of land with nobody around"), and subjectively ("Please consider moving to Starbase"). Musk's settler advertisements reproduce images of empty landscapes from which inhabiting bodies of the *other* once again vanish and/or disappear (figures 3.7 and 3.8). Such *goings-on* serve a wor(l)ding aspiration, to repaint a blank canvas, reinstate a zero point, and begin anew. ~~Discovery~~ Invention. The LRGV will function thus as a locus for new rhetorics of epistemology to *take* place, ontologies to be actualized, new place meanings to be made, and progress and development to be remeasured. (Again, *Caballero* and *George Washington Gomez* lay out how settlers in South Texas have historically set up systems for consolidating colonial management and control so that they can call into question and/or take land by force.) "Es lo mismo," another person I overheard at Vera's states. It is *the same old story*: the future will come, because modern/colonial and settlerizing designs will assure of it, and *others* will only ever be a *means to an end* for settlers and "friends." The revival of "The Magic Valley" myth as a wor(l)ding aspiration will result in exploitation today as it did in the nineteenth and twentieth centuries (González, and Raleigh 1996; Paredes 1958a).

It is the same old story. Gus Bova's (2022) article, "The Final Frontera," claims that Musk's actions are "a form of colonization" (n.p.). Nancy Keates and Mark Maremont (2021) support this in "Elon Musk's SpaceX," writing that Musk's rhetoric echoes "Old West tales of outsiders who pressure residents to give up land for development" (n.p.). But it is Bova's (2022) interview with a Kentucky man, the kind of "friends" that Musk attracts, that links "The Magic Valley" myth with the *idea of the Americas*: "It's like 530 years ago . . . the last time we settled a new world" (n.p.). The settler advertisements I will analyze have a tendency to rehearse such rhetoric and then juxtapose a "new" settler world from the "old world atmosphere" of a *law-loose* "Old Mexico" (Missouri Pacific Railroad Company 1930; Montgomery 1928). Overall, the *ideas* of land as property belonging to no one ("We've got a lot of land with nobody around"), waiting to be discovered ("That property *waited* . . . many years for you all to *find* it"), and awaiting colonization ("Creating the city of Starbase, Texas") amplifies the Spanish rhetorics of terra incógnita, terra nullius, and terra arcadia (also see Jones 2023; Karami 2021; Starbase Brewing n.d). My point, we continue to know the LRGV both through the eyes of the observer observing and their place images-and-myths—palimpsestic times (Alexander 2005), identities (Shohat 2002), and narratives (A. García 2004). That is the technological power of archival impressions, its capacity to materialize concretely designs into reality, a prism through which to see how some *things* were never meant to come to an end.

Some denizens are now aware that under the veil of an epistemological regime of modernity there is access denied (HB 2623)—gives state officials permission to close off public access to Boca Chica Beach—wreckage of a beach they love, and ecological disaster. The future has arrived, but its ends of domination, management, and control are not so new. (My point on the new, again, is that it is really an impression that is quite old.) Boca Chica, Texas, is fetishized as a "resource" to be extracted, commodified, commercialized, and consumed—*Americanity*. Words and ideas can have effects and consequences beyond their mere utterance and immediate settings-contexts. Texas is just one case study of how what occurred in the Americas 500 years ago continues to *appear* and *be* consequential. At stake in the LRGV once more is life, nature, and environment, which is why a rhetorical, ecological, and decolonial perspective is needed to contend with the magnitude of it all (also see Maidenberg 2023; Monroe 2020; Solomon 2021). This chapter, the result of multiple years of settler archival research in Texas, deploys such a perspective.

Modern/colonial and settlerizing designs were never intended to come to an end. Settler archives and settler advertisements are a microcosmic example that can help us understand how the *past shapes the present, the present (re)imagines the past, and the present reflects on the future* in Texas and the LRGV (A. García 2004). The *goings-on* in both have implications for decolonial studies as it does for rhetoricians-compositionists like Jenny Edbauer (2005), Laurie Gries (2015), Asao Inoue (2017), Jaime Mejía (1998), Beatrice Méndez Newman (2007), Christa Olson (2021), Casey Boyle and Jenny Rice (2018), and Jennifer Wingard (2013). Because while my lines of inquiry are specific to Texas and while this chapter is on how the *Archive* is shared-in, imported, and expanded by the *idea of Texas-LRGV*—as frontiers to be conquered, colonized, and transformed into fertile "resources"—it is an *Archive* that, to echo Avery Gordon (2008), we are all in and a part of. This conversation is locally produced but has implications for all rhetoricians-compositionists. Because again we are positioned and equipped to unsettle the past, intervene in the settled-ness of the present, and initiate archival impressions *otherwise*.

As with chapter 2, I employ rhetorical methods to unpack the rituals of rhetorics of modernity and logics of coloniality across twentieth- and twenty-first-century cultural texts. By generating a public record-archive of and rhetoricizing rhetorics of epistemology, truth-and-knowledge claims, and the rhetoricity behind archival impressions, insight is gained on how settler archives and settler advertisements as *epistemological experiments* help naturalize the modus operandi of *modernity/coloniality*. The decolonizing of knowledge below will serve as a foundation for chapter 5, aimed at exploring the prospect of decolonizing being for students whose *stories-so-far* adhere to and interact with the projects and work that settler archives represent. To change the *contents* and *terms* of epistemic and ontological conversations within wounded/wounding and haunted/haunting spaces and places like Texas and the LRGV it is imperative that the tasks of decolonizing knowledge and being unfold together.

Settler Frontiers and Settler Magic

I work from three sets of archives that record-preserve information about places, subjects, and/or events as much as they cement discursive practices. The first is the Digital Austin Papers (DAP), an archive of settler-pioneer letters between 1820 and 1830. The second is *Texas Rangers in Action* (TRA), a comic book series published between 1956 and 1970 that invites readers to view it as an archive of *true accounts* (Gill 1956–1967, 12, 28).[1] The third archive stems from boxes at the Special Collections and Archives at the University of Texas Rio Grande Valley (UTRGV). The parallels between the cultural texts are haunting. Now, my intention is not to provide "A" historical record but to initiate an analysis—of how everyday people have to do work rhetorically to enable modern/colonial and settlerizing designs—from the *idea of Texas* and the "settler" in its earliest form to the *idea of the LRGV*. Across the sections, some *things* become abundantly clear. First, that the *other*, only ever known through the eyes of the observer observing, is enunciated but denied enunciation in the epistemological, ideological, and rhetorical war on information. And second, rhetorical work is *coloniality of instruction-and-curriculum*, which naturalizes the modus operandi of modern/colonial and settlerizing designs—coded words (vision, waste-and-fertile lands, miracles, awaken, etc.), tropes (the vanishing or disappearing magical act; aseptic cleanliness; the earth as fuckable, the fuckable earth; reap what you sow, and the Garden of Eden), and *ideas* (the epistemic zero point and provenance, doctrines of discovery and rights to land/rights to conquest, epistemic and ontological differences, divine and natural designs, and rhetorics of modernity).

A Foundation

Prior to the Texas Revolution (1835–1836), the founding of the Republic of Texas (1836–1845), and the annexation offer to Texas (1845) there was an invitation extended to settler-pioneers by the Republic of Mexico. Moses Austin accepted the call to act as a buffer between the Republic of Mexico and "the

---

1. *TRA* received a "Seal of Approval," which means its claims and narratives have been "carefully reviewed" and have "met the high standards of morality and good taste" of the Comic Code Authority (no. 5).

Indian." He received a grant to settle in the province of Texas with 300 families. After the passing of Moses, his son, Stephen F. Austin, an educated man in moral philosophy, rhetoric, and geography, carried out the work and vision of his father in settling Texas. He became an emigration agent, received an empresario under the colonization law to settle along the Colorado and Brazos Rivers (1821), and established Austin's Colony. However, the relationship between the Republic of Mexico and Texas settlers-pioneers took a turn for the worse (Blythe 1810; Hawkins 1821; M. Austin 1804, 1821a, 1821b; S. F. Austin 1821a, 1821b, 1821c, 1821d, 1821e, 1821f, 1823a, 1829). None of this is for me to decide or debate. What will be considered though is the modern/colonial and settlerizing imaginary and settler rhetorics of archival impressions.

In 1836, William Wharton gave an address on the tribulations and triumphs of Texas settlers. He told the audience he would not appeal to their "sympathies" but to "understandings." Wharton went on to oratorize the injustices inflicted upon, the unkept promises made to, and the oppressions of Texas settlers caused by Mexico. He reminded the audience that Mexico invited them and that before their arrival, land was in possession of "various tribes of Indians" who, by their "nature," were "savages." Wharton recapped that it was they who "expelled the savages," "redeemed" the wilderness from a "state of nature," reduced it to "cultivation," made the "desert smile," and protected the frontiers (Wharton 1836, 10–13). The assemblage and branding work produced a settler image ("The Anglo-American race" [26]), narrative ("perseverance of the colonist" [13]), and rhetoric ("Texas has been redeemed by Anglo-American blood and enterprise" [26]), affective because of the nod to divine and natural designs:

> The justice and benevolence of God will forbid that the delightful region of Texas should again become a howling wilderness, trod only by savages, or that, it should be permanently benighted by the ignorance and superstition, the anarchy and rapine of Mexican misrule. (Wharton 1836, 26)

Wharton's speech hinged on the idea of race and colonial and imperial difference. The colonial is couched in juxtapositions between "the savage Indian," "the ignorant and superstitious Mexican," and "the Anglo-American race." The cultural logic here establishes "the Mexican" as deficient in, without, and/or lacking the faculties of Man-Human. The imperial is entrenched in contrasts between "anarchy and rapine of Mexican misrule" that left Texas wild and the "laws," "learning," and philanthropic "spirit" of the Anglo-American race. (Philanthropy in this chapter, as in the previous, reflects a self-interest rather than an innocence that rationalizes in a sick and diseased way ecocide, genocide, and ethno-and-epistemicide; see Thorpe 1909, 112; Césaire 2001, 39; Roy 2014, 29–30). The cultural logic here is that Mexico is inferior. (Recall, this is a similar sentiment held by Calhoun.) *Visuality*, rebranding, and *ghosting* allowed Wharton (1836) to enforce viewpoints of Man-Human-Rights that associated settlers with place ("indissolubly with the country" [26]), place with Texas settlers ("destined to be forever the proprietors" [26]), and meanings of citizen/ship with "Anglo-American blood" (26; also see de Acosta 1604; de Landa 1937; Las Casas 1965; Sela 2016).

Stephen F. Austin also delivered an address on the tribulations and triumphs of Texas settler in 1836. He oratorized the just cause of Texas settlers to take up arms and go to war with Mexico. He reminded the audience that Mexico invited them and that before their arrival "Texas was a wilderness, the home of the uncivilized, [hostile], and wandering Comanche and other tribes of Indians" (1836a, 31). Austin recapped it was the call of "American enterprise" (32) that led them to "grapple with the wilderness and with savage foes" (32), restrain the "savages" and "bring them into subjection" (32), and start anew. The assemblage and branding work produced a settler image (pioneers), narrative ("we have explored and pioneered it" [41]), and rhetoric ("developed its resources, made it known to the world, and given to it high and rapidly increasing value" [41]), affective as Austin rationalized both the causes for independence from Mexico and the need to fill Texas with a noble race (S. F. Austin 1836a).

> It is the great importance of Americanizing Texas, by filling it with a population from this country, who will harmonize in language, in political education, in common origin, in ever thing, with their neighbor to the east and North. (47–48; also see S. F. Austin 1835)

Overall, Austin's speech hinged on the idea of race and colonial and imperial difference. The colonial is couched in the juxtaposition between "the uncivilized, wandering, and hostile Indian" (1836a, 31), "docile Mexicans" (44), and the "prominent characteristic of the Anglo-Saxon race" (32). The cultural logic here established "the Mexican" as deficient in, without, and/or lacking the faculties of Man-Human. The imperial is entrenched in contrasts between "a wilderness" that was Texas and the "civilized society" and "noble race" of people with "philanthropic principles" from which Texas settlers "expatriated" themselves from to help improve it. The cultural logic here is that "benighted" Mexico was inferior because Mexicans "submitted" to the "usurpation" by others. *Visuality*, rebranding, and *ghosting* allowed Austin to enforce viewpoints of

Man-Human-Rights that associated settlers with place ("our native country" [32]), place with Texas settlers ("clearly ours" [41]), and meanings of citizen/ship with "Anglo-Saxon blood" (46).

Now, there are many reasons why the relationship between the Republic of Mexico and Texas settlers took a turn. One reason could be that settlers-pioneers were steadfast to observe and depict an *other* as a problem and deficient in, without, and/or lacking the faculties of Man-Human: education, literacy, output, aptitude to conquer-colonize-transform the wilderness, capacity to form settlements, vision to dominate/exploit based on race/labor, and ability to sustain a republic, among others (S. F. Austin 1822c, 1824c, 1830a, 1830b; M. [B.] Austin 1822; Andrews 1823; H. Austin 1830a). They attributed this to difference and the differences within an evolutionary continuum to divine and natural designs (S. F. Austin 1832a). Like Kant (1996f) who wrote of a social club unified by language, religion, and industry, Austin's idea of Americanizing Texas with similar Man-Human emigrants, inclusive of Swiss and German emigrants, reflected views that only certain Beings were fit and destined to bring a "land of promise" out of the wilderness (S. F. Austin 1830a; H. Austin 1830c; Parrott 1831) and make it "blossom as the The Rose" (H. Austin 1834; Andrews 1823; Burnet 1827; H. Austin 1830a; M. Austin 1812, 1813, 1814a, 1814b, 1818; M. [B.] Austin 1822; S. F. Austin 1822a, 1822b, 1822c, 1824a, 1824c, 1830a, 1830b, 1832a; also see Webb 2008). In a letter to Mary Austin Holley, Austin refers to "the Mexican" as "strange people" made up of a "strange compound" who must be "studied to be managed" (S. F. Austin 1835, 1830b, 1836a). By depicting the *mongrel Spanish-Indian, Mexican,* and *Negro* as a problem (M. Austin 1812, 1813; S. F. Austin 1822a, 1823b, 1824c) and against the "Anglo-American" race and republicanism, he could then recast them as "natural enemies of white men and civilization" and rationalize their demise (S. F. Austin 1836b; also see Reichstein 1985).

There was an effort by Texas settlers to "wrest from the Mexicans their property" and (ap/ex)propriate as much "territory as they could get" (H. Austin 1830b). And Austin celebrated how they alone "redeemed" Texas from a "state of nature" (S. F. Austin 1832a). He saw *colonization business* (S. F. Austin 1832b) as an endeavor to establish a "sufficient foundation for others to build on" (S. F. Austin 1830a). Expounding on his "ideas of propriety" (S. F. Austin 1832b), Austin details the "three gradations" in settling an "uninhabited country":

The first step was to overcome the roughness of the wilderness.

The second step was to pave the way for civilization and lay the foundation for lasting and productive advancement in wealth, morality and happiness.

The third and last and most important step is to give proper and healthy direction to public opinion, morality and education . . . (S. F. Austin 1832b)

The *other* observed and depicted as a problem was enveloped in first step. Texas settlers, like C. Caldwell (1830), Nott and Gliddon (1854), and Gobineau (1915), chalked up casualties, however, to the "sweep of civilization" (S. F. Austin 1832a). This is a theo-and-ego structured idea, which like magic, would result in the vanishment or disappearance of the *other*—the coded words and tropes of modern/colonial and settlerizing designs. But neither "the Indian" nor "the Mexican" vanished or disappeared. Austin heard the plea for help and proposed thus a *policing* governance to remedy the problems (Burnet 1827).

Honest Men

There were several pleas for help before the Texas Rangers would officially form. In 1823, Austin called for a militia and a battalion to be assembled for the welfare of the colony and frontier in St. Felipe de Austin (S. F. Austin 1823c, 1824b, 1824d; Child 1824). Three years later, another call for a "Company of Rangers" was made for similar reasons (J. Cummins 1826). In 1831 "a company of men" was assembled to serve as a "company of rangers," once more, for related issues (F. Johnson 1831). Four years later, at St. Felipe de Austin, a permanent council approved the official formation of a corps of ranger as a *common defense* for the colony and frontier (Royall 1835). The legacies of the Texas Rangers, as celebrated in *TRA*, were cemented in Texas history. They became a testament to the darker side of settlement ushered in by early Texas settlers (also see Barker 1910; Ivey 2010).

The history of the Texas Rangers is inseparable from a mythic origin story. *TRA* tells of a "great father" (God/Lord) that had chosen settlers to explore the "unknown West" of the "new world" to "find out the nature of the land" (Gill 1956–1967, 29:26–27). The narrators rehearsed the invitation to "emigrants" to "help settle unoccupied land" (12:35) and "open" up the "wilderness" (7:18). Texas, as they put it, was "up for grabs" (60:15). The only problem, according to narrators, was that Texas was wild (8:11, 19:1), "rough and raw" (11:13, 33), and a "blazing frontier of outlaw guns, Apache arrows, and swaggering bad men!" (5:11). (It should not be lost on us the reduction of land or people to thinghood.) Texas, narrators wrote, needed taming, however *impossible* it appeared (11:38, 60:24), by honest Men who could institute law, order, and justice (33; 27). They referred to this historical period as the "coming war for freedom" (11:38) in the "raw law of the frontier" (11:33, 39:27, 40:3).

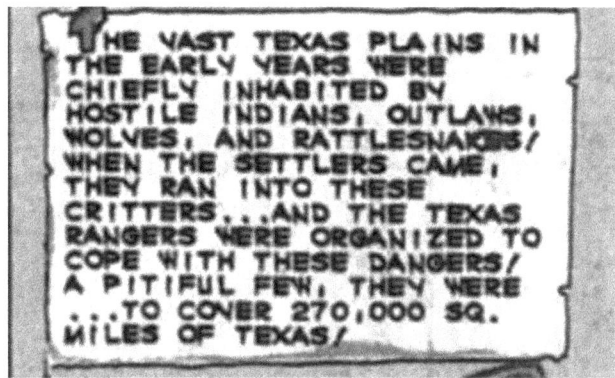

FIGURE 3.9. Depiction from TRA: "The vast Texas plains" (no. 56, p. 19)

FIGURE 3.10. Depiction from TRA: "Nobody got hurt" (no. 7, p. 27)

The emphasis on honest and bad Men is a prominent throughline throughout *TRA* and beyond. The "White man's standard" (and that of the Texas Rangers) was juxtaposed with the hostile "the Mexican" and "the Injun" (7:32, 56:19, 60:24). ("The Injun" is *TRA*'s own words.) The latter were depicted as problems, savages, caricatures, and beings deficient in, without, and/or lacking the faculties of Man-Human (5:18, 9; 37:16, 29; 32; 48:55, 62). This was attributed to observations that *thingified* beings as *things of mere nature*—situated in the same category as that of wolves, critters, and/or rattlesnakes (56:19, 60:24,

11:7)—which in turn trivialized murders. A remedy was demanded for such problems (figures 3.9 and 3.10). The narrators of *TRA* appealed to readers to take their words and ideas as historical discourse. It is common to encounter the phrases, "From the archives of the Texas Rangers" and "This is a true account." And from the archives, the reader is introduced to a one-sided history: "The Texas Rangers were organized before the battle of the Alamo!" to protect the colonies and frontiers from "the Injun" and "the Mexican" (5:3). "The history of the Texas Rangers," narrators announced, "is crammed full" of true accounts (12:28). Yet, those accounts are marked by constant contradiction.

One supposedly true account in *TRA* situates us squarely on the characteristics of the Texas Rangers. They, once more, were organized for several reasons: to patrol and protect the frontiers yard by yard (Gill 1956–1967, 39:25, 12:29, 60:15); to go from one "lawless" or "squalid little settlement" to another to clean it up/*cure* it and institute law, order, and justice (13:7; 23:3; 35:4; 46:9; 54:25); and to *cope* with and *repel* (56:19) those who sought to halt the "Westward march of civilization" (48:33). (Recall, this is a similar sentiment held by S. F. Austin.) No one, it was professed, would be a match for them (29:11, 45:33), and we are told no one actually got hurt. (As a matter of historical record, this is untrue, but it all underscores the significance then of *thingifying* human beings to *things of mere nature* [7:27].) Narrators depicted them as harmless, honest, dedicated, brave, and courageous Men (17:12, 24; 42:14), both "fit for progress" (9:16, 37:19) and filled with the "burning desire to fight for justice" (12:17). The Texas Rangers were celebrated throughout *TRA* for guarding the Gulf Coast, fending off Juan Cortina, and, most of all, making Texas safe and lawful (24:27, 12:21; also see F. Johnson 1831). Texas would not be what it is, it is written, without them (39:37, 46:17, 52:38; also see B. Johnson 2003).

Heroic men of action and *valiant heroes* are how the Texas Rangers were referred to in *TRA* (Gill 1956–1967, 19:1, 48). The narrators argued that Texas would perpetually be a "shining monument to their greatness" (56:21). It is important to remember, however, that a *coloniality of knowledge* is always already an attempt to establish an ontology of the Man-Human-Rights as truth claims. The truth, as a matter of historical record, is that the *White man's justice* that the narrators tout was nothing more than violence. Texas is the by-product of violence enforced by esos que quitan y matan—settlers and the Texas Rangers (39:37, 46:17, 52:38). And two statements in *TRA* capture the essence of the darker side of settlement: "This land's all mine" and "I need every last inch of it" (8:28). Homesteading was always already a project of appropriation and exclusion.

Coloniality of knowledge is the (supposedly) invisible and hidden side of a theo-and-ego structured epistemological regime of modernity. And that brings me to the LRGV and "The Magic Valley," both of which are an archive, a *human thing* human beings have built to leave behind. How else should we approach this new place images-and-myth if, as one archival document put it, "a great network of them [settlers] . . . have left their records for posterity to read" ("50 Years of Progress" n.d.)? Whether or not a corpus of settler sentiments is truly achieved is a moot point, because the action/ing(s) of settlers cemented the *idea* of "the Magic Valley" into a reality.

The Magic Valley Has Arrived

A *semiotic apparatus of enunciations* must be at-work for inventions and wor(l)ding aspirations to *take-make* place. An example is the publication *A Little Journey through the Lower Valley of the Rio Grande*, written in 1928 by Julia Montgomery for the Southern Pacific Lines. It directly referenced *visuality*. "Vision," she wrote, is the "attribute of every pioneer soul" and "requisite of accomplishment" (3). Montgomery materialized their soul through an image ("favored one[s]" [3]), narrative ("has fought and conquered mountain and swamp and stream and ocean and air" [3]), and rhetoric ("the Valley will inevitably enjoy unlimited and uninterrupted progress and prosperity" [4]). Now, vision is inextricably linked to *visuality* and efforts to rebrand a landscape through place images-and-myths. "Now known as the Magic Valley of Texas," she wrote, what was wilderness is now "happy" and "prosperous" towns with the finest schools, houses, churches, health units, civic, and lands (4). The rebranding of the LRGV as "The Magic Valley" was meant to reflect the spirit-soul of the settler. But for *visuality* and place images-and-myths to take root, assemblage and branding must extend to *ghosting citizens*. "The Mexican" was categorized as the "choice of races" to be "servants" and "cheap labor" (49). It all sets in motion wor(l)ding aspirations for "The Magic Valley" to become an archival impression on the world stage.

Montgomery had other publications. They echoed a central praise of hers, that Texans "first discovered what lay beneath the vast wilderness . . . and the impenetrable brush growth" (1928, 23). In 1922, Montgomery published, "The Citrus Tree," which speaks about a steady growth of industry in "the Magic Valley" unparalleled in the "universe." Montgomery (1922) attributed such progress and development to settlers, accomplices, and allies, who "came to the Valley and saw the possibilities." These were possibilities unforeseeable

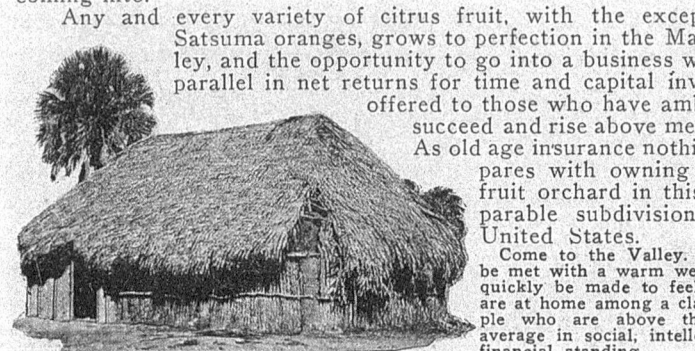

FIGURE 3.11. Page from a book showing a jacal

FIGURE 3.12. A new "attractive" home in the Mission style

when the land was in the hands of *others*. In a 1930 publication, "The Grapefruit Special," Montgomery (1930) described how the LRGV was past its experimental stage. At this point, "The Magic Valley" became a vital node within a network of settlerizing activities that advanced modern/colonial and

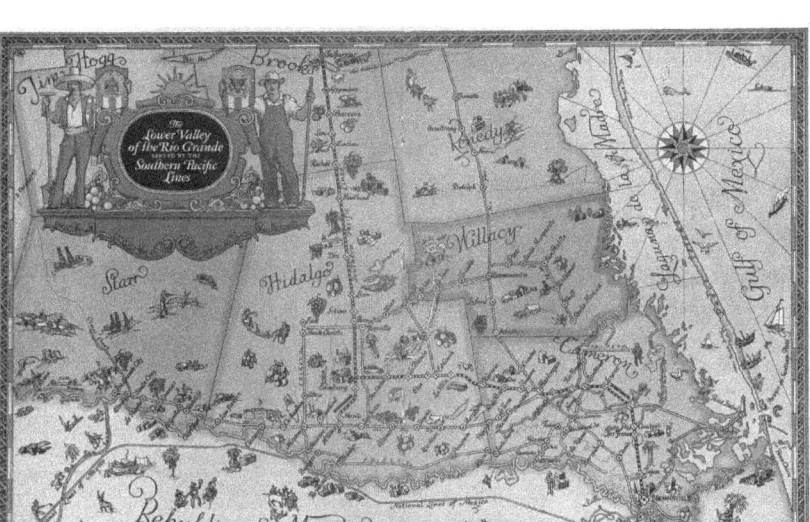

FIGURE 3.13. Map of the LRGV. From Julia Montgomery, *A Little Journey through the Lower Valley of the Rio Grande: The Magic Valley of Texas* (Houston: Rein, 1928).

settlerizing designs of a "modern civilization." The images in figures 3.11 and 3.12 underscore one aspect of that design, juxtaposing past (jacals) and present (attractive homes), Mexico and settlerizing US, and Mexicans and settlers. Montgomery's settler advertisements were consubstantial to imprinting "The Magic Valley" as a wor(l)ding aspiration at the local, national, and global level to be entered into the *Archive*.

I begin with Montgomery (actor), her settler advertisement (institution), and "The Magic Valley" myth (language) to describe a *semiotic apparatus of enunciations* at work. It sets the stage for an analysis of how settlers and promoters utilized settler advertisements to proclaim to everyone what they "should know about the richest frontier in the world" (Montgomery 1928, 3). I consider how settler advertisements, through *visuality*, assemblage, rebranding and recasting work, and *ghosting*, gave rise to new place images-and-myths and called into question who has and does not have civilization and citizenship. Now, settler advertisements invoke settlerizing epideictic rhetoric. For example, Montgomery (1928) praises settlers for investing in schools, irrigation, and housing. To her, it reflected the "Spirit of the Valley" (5), which ultimately becomes an "index of the calibre" (19) of civilization and citizen/ship. Both are qualified by juxtaposing Anglo and Mexican quarters and Anglo and Mexican children. While praise is significant, it is the capacity to express and transpire wor(l)ding aspirations that stands out. The map in figure 3.13 is an example of such an aspiration which underscores how rebranding necessitates remapping. To take note of is how the design contrasts American and Mexican sides. There is no modernity south of the border only a few buildings, the sleepy, laborer, and cockfighting "Mexican," and resources to import; a *desert garb*. (The *idea* of a desert garb will come into focus below.)

For the distracted eyes, mapped are entities and a "virgin-fertile soil." It is performative in that epistemic (lesser knowers, knowing) and ontological (inferior, lesser beings) differences are the axis around which assemblage and branding work are articulated. The map and Montgomery (1928) link modernity with settlers, civilization with Anglo enterprise, and "primitive squalor" with Mexicans, validating claims that the "settler" and "Mexican" cannot live in harmony, highlighting Mignolo's (2000a) argument that the imaginary of the *modern/colonial world system* is partly couched in the mapping of territories and peoples. Now, neither "The Magic Valley" nor "the Mexican" exist ontologically. Still, these knowledge fictions materialize as truths—impressions as settlers would refer to them in their settler advertisements, poetic bookmarks of designs that offer statements on the ways the *idea* is renewed and remapped; the ways a logic of coloniality remains advantageous and thus shared-in, imported, expanded, and/or disputed through crooked rhetorics of modernity. Ultimately, assemblage, branding, and recasting work are necessary to achieve the rhetorical and affective strategy of situating settlers and "The Magic Valley" as the center of space and present of time in the region. Montgomery's (1928) appeal, that the development of "resources" is of the "utmost" importance because the LRGV belongs to Texas, the US, and the world, is an example of such efforts (29). It invokes what Tlostanova and Mignolo (2012) refer to as theological and secular paradigms of Human-Man-Rights and citizen/ship.

According to a 1909 settler advertisement by *The Missionite*, a "great movement South" to the LRGV was commencing. "Harlingen: The City" (1931) identifies the parties as "ambitious pioneers" who were looking for "new frontiers to conquer." They set their eyes on the LRGV, the "last wilderness," an "impenetrable" and "wild region" that was "rough, raw, undeveloped" ("Harlingen: The City" 1931; Southwestern Land Company 1933). But it was not the conquest of the LRGV that drew speculation. "The pioneers," it is written, "came and conquered." Rather, skepticism arose on matters of "productiveness" ("Harlingen: The City" 1931). Settler advertisements thus became evidence of masculine and martial grit and vigor that transformed the LRGV into an "extremely fertile" and "highly productive" region. Across settler advertisements promoting cities such as Sharyland and Harlingen, the LRGV became known as the "promised land" ("Harlingen: The City" 1931), "land of prosperity" (*The Missionite* 1909), "fertile Rio Grande Valley of Texas" (Progreso Development Company n.d.), "America's most fertile Valley" (Southwestern Land Company 1933), and "Nile of America" (Doherty 1908). "The Magic Valley" emerged as a namesake underscoring the "magic" of the settler to transform a "cactus covered desert" into an "evergreen garden" (Missouri Pacific Railroad Company 1930).

Both Harlingen and Sharyland standout within the "empires" of Cameron and Hidalgo Counties (McKenna 1960). In "Harlingen: The City" (1931), Harlingen is celebrated as the "center," "heart," and "pivot city" of the LRGV. It is said to have no "Spanish background"—though part of the Concepcion de Carricitos Spanish Land Grant—and was purchased from the King Ranch and Cameron County ("50 Years of Progress" n.d.; "Harlingen Heritage Trail" n.d.). "No story" of the LRGV, it is explained, "is complete unless there is woven into it the building of Harlingen" ("Harlingen: The City" 1931). The *magic* or *miracle* lies, according to promoters, in how it evolved from a "Six-Shooter Junction"—a "floundering community buried in mud"—into the "richest," "fertile," and "productive agricultural" area in the US with modern schools (ward schools for the *others*) and rail centers ("Harlingen: The City" 1931; "View of Jackson Avenue" n.d.). Based on such progress, settler advertisements extended an invitation (figure 3.22): "Harlingen Gateway to the Valley 'Wants You'" (1925).

Sharyland was described too as the "most fertile and best located section" in the LRGV ("Sharyland: Citrus" n.d.). "No other section" in the US, one settler advertisement puts it, "has developed as rapidly or on a more substantial basis than has Sharyland." It is the "richest" agricultural county in the world, according to another ("The Golden Story" n.d.). In a prospectus by the Southwestern Land Company, the city is celebrated for its natural gas, paved highways, finest schools, and country clubs. It was a far cry, a "miracle" almost, other settler advertisements said, from when "pioneers pushed their way through the cactus and mesquite," where the settler "realized" the "tremendous possibilities" (Southwestern Land Company 1933). Sharyland became a community of "progressive people." Based on such progress, settler advertisements extended an invitation, "The folks [people] in Sharyland extend a hand of greeting to you" ("Sharyland as a Place to Live" 1931; Southwestern Land Company 1933).

Visuality, rebranding, and *ghosting citizens* are vital in settler advertisements. In the *Daily Review*, one settler by the name of John Closner arrived in 1890 and is said to have observed "lawlessness and banditry." This is confirmed by other claims that the area was filled with "rattlesnakes and bandits" (Engleman 1952). Settlers also observed "cluster[s] of 'jacals'"—Mexican thatch villages (Southwestern Land Company 1933). One settler advertisement, "The Lower Rio Grande Valley of Texas" (Missouri Pacific Railroad Company 1930), rationalized all this as the result of settling in a "new country." The advertisement "The Treasure Land of the Lower Rio Grande" (Barker Bros. Engravers 1918) clarified the juxtaposition being set up, noting the new "inhabitants of the Valley" were "far different from the kind usually found in new countries" (3). For settlers, walls constructed out of mesquite, roofs thatched with palm leaves, and earthen floors did not count as a house, much less an example of civilization. As Montgomery (1928) put it, the "natives dwell in primitive squalor" (23). And all this explained for them why the "scattered" inhabitants of the "early days of Texas history" were so primitive and why they did not have "any knowledge of the potential value" of the land (24). This in part gives way to "The Magic Valley" myth—a "miracle" brought about by "pioneers in whose hearts burned a vision, in whose minds dwelt the will, and in whose muscles had the strength to make a dream come true . . . of a garden in the desert" (Engleman 1952). For settlers such as McFall Kerbey (1939), the LRGV was a "very special frontier—the country's last," which was a/waiting to be awakened and to arrive (51).

With the arrival of settlers came real estate men such as Lon Hill and John Shary and their land-and-title companies (the Lon C. Hill Improvement Company; the Southwestern Land Company). Then came the naming of cities, the arrival of the railroads, and the rise of settler advertisements (figures 3.14 and 3.15), which ensured that the names of those who *blazed the way of civilization* would be written into the soil of an almost-lost *last frontier*—"The Magic Valley" (see "Sharyland: Citrus" n.d.). Echoes of Austin are audible in the desire and objective to populate the LRGV with citizens from the northern and central states, the ideal archetype of citizen/ship according to settler advertisements—*splendid moral people, progressive citizens,* and *valorous men of vision* (Barker Bros. Engravers 1918; "View of Jackson Avenue" n.d.).

Each settler advertisement extended an invitation: "Come to Harlingen"; "Mercedes is different from and better than any other town in the Valley"; "The Folks in Sharyland extend a hand of greeting." But to be rhetorically and affectively successful, assemblage, rebranding, and recasting work was necessary. And settlers were indeed rhetorically savvy in utilizing settler advertisements as a medium to present an image of "yesterday" (discovery of a wasteland), "today" (propertied and reterritorialized), and "tomorrow" (prosperity) (see

FIGURE 3.14. Cover of a settler advertisement: "The Treasure Land of the Lower Rio Grande Valley"

"Prosperity" n.d.). Such helped to cement a literacy of overcoming the wilderness, an image of masculine and martial grit and vigor, and a rhetoric of modernity that would give way to slogans that underscored the "magic-ness" of the LRGV (figure 3.16), as seen in the language of the promotional materials:

FIGURE 3.15. Settler advertisement: "Harlingen: The City That Citrus Built"

Literacies: "Nature's crowning gift to man disguised, Hidden as but nature can, Disguised in desert garb complete, Now lies waiting at our feet" (Barker Bros. Engravers 1918). "From a cactus covered desert it has been converted [transformed] into an evergreen garden" (Missouri Pacific Railroad Company 1930.). "A land that dates back hundreds of years . . . young in its development from the arid wastes of chaparral to the present high state . . . enhance[d] by . . . a culture that is capable of appreciating . . ." (Missouri Pacific Railroad Company 1925, 64).

Images: "The land . . . awakens to the magic touch of man's efforts" (Missouri Pacific Railroad Company 1925, 1). "The Rio Grande Valley offers unlimited opportunity to those who are willing to use their brain and

Prosperity!

THE Rio Grande Valley of today is the realization of yesterday's vision. The labor of the pioneer has recreated the waste land into a land of plenty. A land of fine cities, fine schools and fine homes. Our vision of today will be a realization of finer things tomorrow!

FIGURE 3.16. Prosperity

brawn in wrestling from a willing soil the best products possible anywhere" (Missouri Pacific Railroad Company 1925, 59).

Rhetorics: "Each Valley community bears an unmistakable stamp of modernness and progressiveness" ("The Lower Rio Grande of Texas" 1930.). "No section of the United States is undergoing more solid development than the Lower Rio Grande Valley" (*The Missionite* 1909). "The development of the Lower Rio Grande Valley is perhaps unparalleled in the history of the nation" (Southwestern Land Company 1933).

Slogans: *Land of Heart's Delight, Land of Opportunities, The Promised Land, A Veritable Land of Milk and Honey, Queen City of the Magic Valley, Garden of the World.*

The above sheds light on settler advertisements as *epistemological experiments* that involve mythmaking processes. Interpreting and readapting Barthes's (1972) cultural work for this modern/colonial and settlerizing context, myths involve a form and concept that have wor(l)ding aspirations of naturalizing the projects of territorial and epistemological (ap/exp)propriation. "The Magic Valley" and "settler" myths are part of a semiological system generated by humans who see in them both value and meaning. But what is "The Magic Valley" myth—what is its rhetoric, how is a "vision," "dream," "magic," or "miracle" realized through it, and when does it evolve from an archival impression into designs into new forms of public memory into a reality?

"The Magic Valley" myth refers both to the settlers' "touch" and to a naturalized system of exploitation. "Progreso Haciendas: Citrus Fruit and Farm Lands" (Progreso Development Company n.d.) suggested that all a settler needed to succeed in the LRGV was his mind, hands, and effort. Because the land was cheap, the soil was rich, irrigation was state-of-the-art, packing plants were modern, and the "cheap Mexican labor help[ed] make big profits possible" (n.p.). (As foreshadowed, and which will come into view shortly, the last-named factors in so much so that one settler advertisement suggested that it was rare to see settlers working.) Settlers were further propositioned by claims that the LRGV had passed "the old" ("The Mexican," Mexican jacals) and that the "coming of the new" had made it more modern than any place in the US (Progreso Development Company n.d.) (figures 3.12 and 3.17). It all culminated into a haunting appeal: "Come to the Valley. You will . . . quickly be made to feel you are at home among a class of people who are above the general average in social, intellectual, and financial standing" (Montgomery 1922, n.p.). Haunting in that the LRGV became a space and place for the settler to stroke their ego, an ego that already subsumes *other-things* as its possession.

No where in America, no section in the country, unparalleled in the history of the nation, and *unequaled anywhere in the world*: these phrases, though amended slightly from one settler advertisement to the next, are typical (Southwestern Land Company 1933; Missouri Pacific Railroad Company 1930; E. Lloyd 1924). An exaggerated statement usually follows: "These banks

FIGURE 3.17. Primitive homes

and modern buildings which rose as temples of prosperity out of the cactus and brush that but a few years ago was the range of the coyote and the long horn" (Progreso Development Company n.d.). The "Magic Valley" and "settler" myths materialize here. "The Beautiful Valley" (Missouri Pacific Railroad Company 1925) offers some insight. Immediately after the cover page, an extract from a speech by H. R. Safford follows—the LRGV is now "awaken[ed]" to the "magic touch of man's efforts." Paredes's (1958a) *idea of Gringoland* comes into focus (25):

> The contentment that is bound to prevail in such homes makes for a better citizenry; a more prosperous community and a stability that does not exist where squalor and poverty are evident. (Missouri Pacific Railroad Company 1925, 30)

> If homes may be safely taken as a fair index of the character of the citizenship, the prosperity and the general progressiveness of any community, then those in the Lower Rio Grande Valley reflect the highest credit. (Missouri Pacific Railroad Company 1930)

> The . . . picture depicts accurately the primitive homes of Mexicans, the principal source of labor in the Valley. These huts with their thatched roofs, that house the field laborers, correspond to the negro shanties that are found throughout the South. (Missouri Pacific Railroad Company 1925, 10)

The images in figures 3.12 and 3.17 only speak to homes. But the juxtaposition between modern and primitive extends to schools, churches, and hotels. They underscore symbols of modernity and citizen/ship. Central roles of settler advertisements, thus, are to amplify difference (past-present; uncivilized-citizen/ship) and normalize the technology of domination/exploitation surrounding race/labor as natural, factual. Settler advertisements acknowledge that this is important to do to affectively convey how a *mostly empty* and unsettled region was transformed into a "veritable 'land of milk and honey'" (Missouri Pacific Railroad Company 1925, 11). With citizen/ship being linked to the "brain" and "brawn" of the settler, the invention of the "The Magic Valley" myth can only flourish with the *ghosting* of citizens—what Anzaldúa (1999) or Maldonado-Torres (2007) might refer to as shadow, *half-dead*, or haunted subjects at the *company of death*.

Settler advertisements are examples of modern/colonial and settlerizing rhetorical excellence. In "The Beautiful Valley" (Missouri Pacific Railroad Company 1925), the importance of words and pictures was recognized and acknowledged as the primary method for figuratively taking the "reader on a trip" into the vast progress and developments of the LRGV and introducing a "new era in America's Garden of Eden" (2). Both helped to corroborate myths as facts. So even if recruitment was unsuccessful, "The Magic Valley" and "settler" myths evolved into archival impressions and circulated as public memory. Settler advertisements shed light on how projects of territorial (ap/ex)propriation required the epistemological aspect too. But words and pictures were also involved for another reason. Iterative or recycled writing and address heighten the affective value and rhetorical force (or pesado-ness) of some *things* even amid scrutiny, allowing thus an archival impression of "The Magic Valley" and "settler" to evolve into designs, new forms of public memory, and reality (see Bhabha 1994).

Settler advertisements are in every way rhetorical. They provide insight on why the LRGV-as-archive continues to be (re)written in modern/colonial and settlerizing ways. Words and pictures helped to mitigate scrutiny. And their authors knew this. In *The Missionite* (1909) the editor addressed this: "We . . . are not such big liars as some people 'up North' believe." What does this mean? In part, it means that grandiose claims were being called into question. In *Lloyd's Magazine*, the editor stated, "There is nothing wrong with the Valley—only . . . a few politicians who would seek to discredit the real builders and developers of the Valley" (E. Lloyd 1924, 18–19). Again, the implication here is that there is a seed of doubt sowed into an imaginary beyond "the Magic Valley." Across settler advertisements there was an effort to incorporate prefaces or posture benevolence as well as incorporate pictures.

This booklet is not intended as a history of the Lower Rio Grande Valley, as a record of its achievements or a catalogue of its opportunities. At best, it can give only a faint idea of what transportation, rich soil, ideal weather and unlimited irrigation facilities have done to convert a wilderness into what its residents know as a veritable fairyland . . . the pictorial record of the Valley today will be read not only as an interesting story of modern day development, but a promise of a most brilliant future. (Missouri Pacific Railroad Company 1930)

We have endeavored to tell the story without exaggeration and should it be extravagant to those of you who are unacquainted with the "Valley"—be assured that the Valley is not unduly extolled and that it does indeed fulfill every claim we make and that it is verily the richest and most ideal agricultural land in North America. (Progreso Development Company n.d.)

Proud of its record of progress, its citizens issue this booklet not to dwell upon its achievements but rather point the way to the future. ("Harlingen Gateway to the Valley 'Wants You'" 1925)

The move to innocence above cements coloniality's excess—"The Magic Valley" and "settler" myths—while the politics of modernity worked to (supposedly) veil the colonization of space and time. But there should be no doubt that settler advertisements were attempting to cover-up-and-over a pre-existing meaning and permanently reconstruct a new meaning, a new country. There were excursion or land parties for this reason, which invited settlers both to visit this "new country" and to investigate with their own eyes: "come with us for a personal inspection. Seeing is believing" ("Golden Groves" n.d.); "One who seeks details of Valley life . . . You, who 'seek a country' . . . Are you coming?" (Montgomery 1929, 3); "Why not go to a country . . . that has more and greater advantaged with fewer drawbacks than any other section under the Stars and Stripes" (Barker Bros. Engravers 1918); "Join . . . for a thorough inspection of this Magic Valley" ("Lower Rio Grande Valley Magazine" 1928). Again, this "new country," where the juxtaposition between "new" and "old" (inhabitants and countries) is evident, becomes a space and place for the settler to subsume *other-things* as its possession.

Now, there were many settlers of the LRGV. Some included Wimberly McLeod, William Jennings Bryant, and Chas F. C. Ladd. McLeod is described as a man with "big vision" ("His Faith" n.d.), Bryant as "the nation's most famous" ("William Jennings" n.d.), and Ladd as "quick to see the immense possibilities for the successfully development" ("Prominent Factor in Harlingen's Growth" n.d.). These "visioned men," with the foresight to see "resources" and adapt them for the uses and pleasures of the settler, are proclaimed to have transformed a "barren waste" into a *world's garden spot*. As with "The Magic Valley" myth, we must ask, in the context of the "settler," what is its rhetoric, how is "settler" realized through it, and when does the "settler" evolve into an archival impression into designs into new forms of public memory into a reality? Hill and Shary stand apart from other settlers. Hill, having various aliases—*man of action-dreams, one-man colonization entity, land man, master builder,* and *empire builder*—is depicted as a Man who pushed through the cactus, brush, and coyotes of the last frontier. He saw in it a *veritable, fertile,* and *evergreen* garden or paradise (see "Proclamation" n.d.; Doherty 1906). Hill, from settler-pioneer stock with parents migrating from Tennessee in 1854 with slaves, is widely endorsed as the founder of Harlingen. The name itself paid homage to his relationship with Colonel Uriah Lott, whose ancestors lived in Harlingen, Holland (McKenna 1960; "Story of Lon Hill" 1950; "Lon Hill, Sr." 1950; "Valley Pioneer and Founder" n.d.).

Shary, from Nebraska, was known for his work in Texas cities such as Corpus Christi, where he led colonization and development efforts. He was described in "The Golden Story of Sharyland" (n.d.) as a man with a "vision" who saw in the wasteland tropical gardens (also see Shary Organization 1948). "He came, he saw, he conquered" ("The Golden Story" n.d.). With the moniker "Daddy of the Citrus Industry," it was his "magic" touch that transformed "The Magic Valley" into "one of the great agricultural centers of the world" (Shary Organization 1948; Southwestern Land Company 1933). Both Hill and Shary were painted as representatives of the "settler"—"men of integrity" who had "visions" and "dreams." Hill was said to be the "Story of Early Valley Growth" ("Story of Lon Hill" 1950), and Shary was declared both "inextricably interwoven with the history" of the LRGV and the story of Texas ("The Golden Story" n.d. "Sharyland: Citrus" n.d.). (The paternal and sexual innuendos should not be lost on us as they are the coded words and tropes of modern/colonial and settlerizing designs.) I intend to answer the questions regarding the settler and its rhetoric in what follows by spending a bit more time with Hill and Shary.

The LRGV was portrayed as mostly empty and unsettled (figure 3.18). As Everett Lloyd (1924) put it, "this part of the Rio Grande Valley . . . was a barren wilderness, uncleared, uncultivated, practically abandoned" (13). Some counties like Cameron Country supposedly showed up on a stake and on maps only as "the Wild Horse Desert" ("Cameron Once Called" 1967). Contributing

FIGURE 3.18. "Harlingen Once a Blur on Map Called 'Six-Shooter Junction,'" *The Harlingen Star*, June 8, 1926

to his allure, many doubted Hill could transform it. In "The Golden Story of Sharyland" (n.d.) readers are reminded that the duty of the Texas Rangers was to "patrol and protect the outposts of civilization" from "the troublesome and hostile Indian." That outpost and problem shifted during the Bandit Wars (*With a Pistol in His Hands* speaks to such turbulent times). That brings us back to the LRGV, a *blur on a map* till the arrival of settlers like Hill. "Harlingen Golden Anniversary" (McKenna 1960) reflects on Hill's relationship with the Texas Rangers. Hill, despite doubts by some that he could transform a lawless space into a civilized place, is said to have communicated, "You boys just clean out the lawless element, make it a safe place to bring people to" (n.p.). Company A of the force moved to Harlingen to help him. The *lawlessness element* and why the Texas Rangers were not "popular" with some is also expanded upon briefly. But here I pause, because if the LRGV was mostly empty, then who are these inhabitants? Of course, in the register of settlers, the *other* is reduced to *things of mere nature*, which underscores and speaks to a point overlooked by the magazine, that "the Mexican" was wary of the Texas Rangers because they were targeted by them. This is supported by a recollection, "Don't hesitate to make an arrest if you think are right. You may be arresting one of those

FIGURE 3.19. "36 Dead Bandits," Donna, Texas, 1915

natives for the wrong thing but you'll always have the right man" (McKenna 1960). The Texas Rangers were not a "non-partisan enforcement of the law" is perhaps the point being made here (see "Six-Shooter Junction" 1946).

The relationship between Hill and the Texas Rangers is not discussed in detail within "Harlingen Golden Anniversary" (McKenna 1960). Yet, it is known that "The Chief," a name Hill went by, joined pursuits of "the bandits" on both sides of the border ("Lon Hill, Sr." 1950). The death of "the Mexican" was not uncommon (figure 3.19). Ultimately, Hill, who "gazed over miles of wasteland" and "saw cities in the wilderness," transformed "Hill's town" into Harlingen, a *blur on a map* turned the *world's garden spot* and *heart of the world's most fertile region* ("Man of Action—Man of Dreams" n.d.). But the mythmaking and mystification of Hill and "The Magic Valley" stem from promoters of settler advertisements and "newspaper men," who, like men of letters, historians, and officers of the state, as discussed by Mignolo (2011a) in his own studies, utilized words and ideas to *inform* and *give form* to a *coloniality of knowledge-being*. Both "newspaper men" and settler advertisements provide a window into the role *coloniality of instruction-and-curriculum* has to play—a settler-centered instruction that normalized the modus operandi of modern/colonial and settlerizing designs.

Hill, like Shary, embodied the "newspaper men." In an authored column titled "Our Lower Rio Grande Valley" (1985), he tells readers that the LRGV is a product of the twentieth century. There were, according to Hill, a "few settlements that existed," besides customs officers, the Texas National Guard, and the Texas Rangers, but those, he noted, were "all along the river." (Again, this impresses two ideas: first, that of a *mostly empty* or *abandoned* space and place, and second, that settlements-clusters of jacals did not meet the Western standard of civilization.) Hill's explanation of the lack of water, paved roads, irrigation, and buildings supports the idea of wilderness—blurs on a map known only as "the Wild Horse Desert," "Rattlesnake Junction," or "Six-Shooter Junction" (McKenna 1960; "Harlingen Heritage Trail" n.d.). With the arrival of "Men of vision," though, and the establishment of "fine cities, excellent educational facilities, and good civic, cultural, and religious institutions," the LRGV would become the "Magic Valley" ("Our Lower Rio Grande Valley" 1985). Hill clarifies further:

> The Lower Rio Grande Valley of Texas is a man-made miracle. Nature provided the raw materials—fertile soil, water, and climate. Men of vision mixed these with the brains, energy, sweat and tears to create the magic of our Magic Valley . . . Land was cleared, roads and canals built, townsites established. More people came to buy farms, plant orchards. Some prospered, some failed, but the growth continued. ("Our Lower Rio Grande Valley" 1985)

Settlers make their identity on how they dominate, manage, and control nature, land, and "resources." The mythmaking and mystification of Hill is assemblage, branding, and recasting work. Barthes's (1972) position on myths and Mignolo's (1989, 1992, 1994) view on modern/colonial situations come into focus as "settler" becomes associated with place and place with settlers and the meaning of citizen/ship. The cultural production of these associations, which functions as an archival impression and a form of public memory, *informs* the public of a new statement of fact and *gives form* to a new natural. Thus, statements such as "Lon C. Hill probably did more to make the Valley what it is today than any other man" ("Lon Hill, Sr." 1950) or "Harlingen is the culmination of a dream" ("City of Harlingen" 1961) are not inconsequential. They are part and parcel of modern/colonial and settlerizing designs.

The story of Sharyland and Shary is similar. According to the Hidalgo County Centennial Corp. (1952), Hidalgo County was created out of Cameron County and had ties to the Karankawa, Campacuas, Lipan, and Spanish

FIGURE 3.20. Sharyland advertisement

peoples, who were often referenced as those *clusters of jacals*. The settler advertisement states that the county experienced turbulent times between the late 1700s and early 1900s. But in 1910, with the arrival of settlers like Shary, who "directed the colonization of the new settlers" to the LRGV, its fortune changed as the 1952 Hidalgo County Centennial Corp. reports. Out of Hidalgo County emerged Sharyland. The settler advertisement, it is written, was dedicated to the pioneers who "cleared out the bandits," the "land salesmen," the "Rangers," and even the "Mexican peons or wetbacks who cleared away the cactus and mesquite" (Hidalgo County Centennial Corp. 1952). In the 1933 publication "In Rio Grande Valley Paradise" (Southwestern Land Company 1933; figure 3.20), the front cover depicted the transformation of a mostly *empty* and *abandoned* space into a place with a grid system, modern homes, vehicles, and nature producing (citrus). Civilization and the Valley had arrived. The advertisement's stamp of approval—a young white woman—completed the process of covering-up-and-over the "old." The settler advertisement juxtaposed a primitive past and modern present and accentuated the difference in the eyes of the settler between "Mexican Village[s]" and civilization. And all this began when "pioneers pushed their way through the cactus and mesquite" and "realized" the "tremendous" possibilities and "rich" opportunities (Southwestern Land Company 1933). Settlers such as Shary, it is argued, were the reason why the development of the LRGV was "unparalleled in the history of the nation" (n.p.).

They, according to the advertisement, "wrought a miracle" that underscored why the LRGV became known as "The Magic Valley." From a "few thousand people, mostly Mexicans, living in clusters of 'jacals'" (n.p.), the region is now modern, and it is important to mention this because it underscores the juxtaposition between the old and the new, the primitive and the modern, and civilization typically found in a new country and the arrival of Western civilization.

In a publication by the Shary Organization (1948), "35-Years of Progress," Shary is argued to be "inseparably linked with the Rio Grande Valley" (n.p). This is settlerizing epideictic rhetoric. And its wor(l)ding capacity is couched in *visuality*, assemblage, branding, and recasting work, and the *ghosting* of *citizens*. It is what gives rise to new representations of "settler" and new place images-and-myths such as "The Magic Valley" myth. Such is affective in two ways. First, many of the settlers who accepted the invitation "The people in Sharyland extends a hand of greeting to you" did so because of the assurances included in settler advertisements ("Sharyland as a Place to Live" 1931; Southwestern Land Company 1933). It was not uncommon to encounter letters from settlers thanking land companies for furnishing such information: "This is the healthiest country I ever saw"; "I like this country so much"; "I consider this a very healthful country" (Oliver-Jackson Investment Company 1919); "Mr. J. Bock Tells Us of His Experience in the Valley"; "Bees a Great Success in the Valley"; "Mr. Thomas Does Not Regret Moving to the Valley" (J. Jackson 1913). Second, the myths are affective in that they are archival impressions that not only solidify the viewpoints of Man-Human-Rights at the local level but also give structure to, constitutes, and (re)writes the *Archive*.

"The Magic Valley" myth is Paredes's (1958a) "Gringoland" (25). It is the darker, (supposedly) hidden side of rhetorics of modernity. The (ap/ex)propriation of land is not without land dispossession, *ghosting* of citizens, or cultural displacement. And the epistemological project is unthinkable without *visuality* and the *idea* of race, epistemic racism, and technology of race/labor. *Visuality*, or modern/colonial and settlerizing vision, is most evident in the statements: "Mr. Shary saw what had been a wasteland" (Shary Organization 1948, n.p.); "He [Hill] gazed over miles of wasteland . . . saw cities in the wilderness where coyotes roamed" ("Man of Action" n.d.). "The eye," Michelle Ballif (2014) writes, "is the privileged organ of perception and the visual the privileges epistemological field" (463). It is the settlerizing eye that sees and depicts both a "land of unknown possibilities, isolated from civilization" ("San Benito" n.d.) and the "lure of the borderland with its modernity" ("Welcome to Mission" n.d.). The *idea of Gringoland* is about impressing an *idea* of discovery, the last frontier, which makes people objects, erases histories, and invents empty landscapes; it becomes the site that must be saved, civilized, and modernized as a place in which settlers can inhabit. And it is about a vision—"Nature's crowning gift to man disguised" (Barker Bros. Engravers 1918)—that can overcome nature.

The *idea of Gringoland* is about impressing a sense and touch: "When the pioneers pushed their way through the cactus and mesquite . . . colonizers were quick to sense the enormous advantages" (Southwestern Land Company 1933); "The land . . . now awakens to the magic touch of man's efforts" (Missouri Pacific Railroad Company 1925, 59). It is about impressing rights-and-belonging-to: "pioneers who had 'discovered' the Magic Valley" ("Lower Rio Grande Valley Magazine" 1928); "He came, he saw, he conquered" ("The Golden Story" n.d); "Pioneers came and conquered" ("Harlingen: The City" 1931); "The owner of this land" (Doherty 1908). The *idea of Gringoland* is about dominating nature. Thousands "of acres of fertile lands," it is written, are "ready and waiting for those willing" to both "work with nature" (Southern Pacific Lines 1930, 3) and "utilize the natural sources" (Missouri Pacific Railroad Company 1925, 6). Settlers treated nature as a "hunter's paradise," which meant they had reign over and license to kill any *thing* they wanted ("Harlingen: Center of a Hunters Paradise" n.d.). Because it was of their possession. It is about managing and controlling impressions of what "indexes" the "calibre" of citizens and civilization (Montgomery 1928; Missouri Pacific Railroad Company 1930; "Golden Groves" n.d.): "High-minded, industrious and forward-looking citizens"; "The thinking man or woman"; "Big visioned men" (Missouri Pacific Railroad Company 1930). Ultimately, when settler advertisements talk about a "Valley spirit" or citizen/ship, it is linked to the "brain" and "brawn" of the settler residents of the northern and central states: "the highest class" ("View of Jackson Avenue" n.d.); "a class . . . far different from the kind usually found in new countries" (Barker Bros. Engravers 1918).

But citizen and civilization were also based on capitalism and the technology of race/labor. According to settler advertisements such as "Golden Groves" (n.d.), "Progreso Haciendas" (Progreso Development Company n.d.), "The Treasure Land of the Lower Rio Grande Valley" (Barker Bros. Engravers 1918), "The American Rio Grande Land and Irrigation Company" (1923), *Lloyd's Magazine* (E. Lloyd 1924), "The True Story" (J. Jackson 1913), Montgomery (1928), "Facts about the Lower Rio Grande Valley" (Missouri Pacific Railroad Company n.d.), and Harlingen Chamber of Commerce (1932), there was one race that was "ideal" within an American system of labor. Perhaps redundant, but definitely worth repeating, by system, or "scheme," promoters meant the exploitation of the "unskilled work" supplied by "the Mexican." As one settler advertisement puts it, "One of the greatest assets in the Valley is our cheap Mexican labor" (J. Jackson 1913). As noted at the onset of this chapter, they are considered ideal, first, because "the native Mexican" was considered *cheap, dependable, satisfactory*, and a *plentiful source of manual labor*. They are not a "problem" (E. Lloyd 1924, 14) in that they can be managed and controlled. And second, because they *preferred* to live separate from and did not try to mix with the Anglo communities, according to settler advertisements. Photographs so often show "the Mexican" and "the Dueños" together. But as "ideal" servants—*means* to an *end*—they stand neither on equal grounds nor as equal beings. Photographer and photographs simply enhance such viewpoints.

As a side note, settlers contradicted their own argument that the "magic" of the LRGV was a by-product of their work. Settler advertisement commonly boasted about how little work they did: "Americans don't work much down here, nearly all the labor being done by Mexican peons" (Missouri Pacific Lines 1927). The contradictory statement calls into question images like those "In Rio Grande Valley Paradise" (Southwestern Land Company 1933) or "The Lower Rio Grande Valley" (Missouri Pacific Railroad Company 1930) that depict a settler's labor. Settler advertisements attempted to cloak or hide but also normalize the technology of domination/exploitation surrounding race/labor as natural. Couched within it is the viewpoint that settlers *rule* the land and *others* are to be *ruled*. "The development of the natural resources," as one settler advertisement puts, attempts to hide what Hämäläinen (2008), Tuck and Yang (2012), and Arvin, Tuck, and Morrill (2013) observe, that the settler and settler colonialism make its name in possessing land, exploiting-extracting "resources," and making land produce excessively. It is but one way they lay claim to being "native" to a place. Labor exploitation is both necessary for this process and to help ensure maximum profit.

The darker, (supposedly) hidden side of rhetorics of modernity is at work in the *epistemological experiments* of settler advertisements. Take, as another example, the 1925 booklet "Harlingen Gateway to the Valley 'Wants You'" (figure 3.21), which depicted Harlingen as a "spot on a railroad map." This is necessary, again, to underscore the "magic" touch of the settler who would transform Harlingen and the LRGV from a *blur on a map* into a "modern city" and "most productive" region in the US. The point here is not to call into question whether Harlingen and the LRGV has "passed the pioneering and experimental stages," assess if both are enjoying "growth and posterity," or deliberate if either are truly "awake." Rather, it is to be critical of a war on information as

FIGURE 3.21. Harlingen Gateway to the Valley Wants You

both the hoarding and excessive production of knowledge. How do rhetorics of empty landscape imagine nonbeings and how do rhetorics of modernity justify modern/colonial and settlerizing designs as the price of human progress? What is the price? In terms of land, it is expropriation, and with the epistemological project, it is the *ghosting* of citizens and dispensability of *others*.

The point thereafter is to unsettle the literacy of empty landscapes, image of peaceful settler-pioneers, and rhetorics of modernity as they have evolved into "The Magic Valley" and "settler" myths. Because praise, like rhetoric, never functions for its own sake. Settlerizing epideictic rhetoric has a wor(l)ding aspiration that attempts to situate a new center of space and present of time. Thus, the slogan "Harlingen Wants You" is already divisive because in "The Magic Valley" citizen/ship does not extend to all the "Yous." In fact, its parallel to the design "Uncle Same Wants You" is not coincidental—it's a recruitment tactic meant to conjure patriotic emotion, a call to action as serious as wartime, meant to underscore the relationship between space-place, Spirit, and duty. "Harlingen Wants You" is defining the kind of citizen/ship in a settler advertisement that it deems appropriate-correct—white, settler origins, male. The "You," in other words, is not an invitation to those deemed the lawless element or undesirables. Settlerizing epideitic rhetoric has as much to do with wor(l)ding aspirations as it does with praise. "The Magic Valley" and the "settler" are made through settlerizing epideictic rhetoric, *visuality*, assemblage and branding work, and *ghosting citizens*. Settler advertisements demonstrate thus how a *coloniality of knowledge*, constitutive of a *coloniality of being*, is inseparable from the *idea of the Americas*.

Settler advertisements are epistemological, ideological, and rhetorical experiments of circulating information as truth. One case in point is "The True Story of the Lower Rio Grande Valley" (J. Jackson 1913). "The object of this booklet," the publication claimed, was to "set forth the true conditions and facts existing in the Lower Rio Grande district" (1). One fact listed is the Americanizing of the LRGV with the "best of society," or "people of the North" (1) who have helped to create a "Northern energy mingled with Southern hospitality" (7–8). (At long last, the vision of Austin has come into fruition.) Another fact noted is the "cheap Mexican labor" that ensured return of profits. Along such lines, the reader is assured both that modern schools exist and that they "separate" the "Mexican children" (7, 9). This is not the only settler advertisement that purports to tell the truth. In "A Statement of Facts about the Lands" ("San Benito" n.d.), the San Benito Land and Water Company told its reader that it had "endeavored to tell the story completely" and "truthfully" ("Foreword"). Like others, it spoke of a virgin soil, fertile land, and how the metropolitan city is "thoroughly modern" (47). (Again, the coded words and tropes of modern/colonial and settlerizing designs, or as "The True Story" [J. Jackson 1913] puts it, the making of a "veritable Eden" [7].) *Lloyd's Magazine* (E. Lloyd 1924) is another, where Everett Lloyd claims the "Magic Valley" is the "most modern in Texas" and "one of the most prosperous sections of the United States," going on to provide several facts, one of them being that in 1904 it was mostly a "barren wilderness, uncleared, uncultivated, practically abandoned" (13). What made it magic, though? For Lloyd, it was the magic of irrigation, resources (including cheap labor), and the fact that there was "no 'Mexican problem.'" Here, "problem" both refers to how "the Mexican," unlike *others*, are law abiding and conscientious (14–15) and, as Montgomery (1928) puts it, solve a "servant problem" (5, 7). It is from settler advertisements such as these and the way "impression" was evoked to communicate truth that I discern in part archival impressions.

Whether or not the LRGV had "passed through the pioneer stage," as the 1925 "Harlingen Gateway to the Valley 'Wants You'" advertisement put it, is not in question. Rather, a close reading of the way advertisements presented the LRGV as mostly empty, unsettled, and up for grabs for those who had the masculine and martial grit and vigor to transform the wilderness provides a foundation to understand what is going on in the LRGV today with Musk and the remaking of "The Magic Valley" myth. Because just as settlers utilized settler advertisement to invite others to partake in "excursion" parties to tour ("gaze") the LRGV as a new world, Musk is inviting "friends" via social media to participate in and remake "The Magic Valley" as they see fit as if it were a new world (figure 3.22). The settlers of yesterday and today have in common the (ap/ex)propriation of land, which is not without land dispossession, *ghosting* of citizens, cultural displacement. What is in question is a *visuality* that sees in land the opportunity to make property, in nature "resources" to be extracted, and in the *ghosting* of its citizens exploitable and dispensable "Mexicans." All of this leads to a rebranding of a place image-and-myth. "A myth," Everett Lloyd (1924) wrote, "has been allowed to survive" (18). But it had little to do with "produce," as he implies, and more to do, I argue, with the mythmaking of "The Magic Valley" as the "Cream of the Earth" and "Garden Spot of the American Continent" (J. Jackson 1913) and the "settler" who "made 'The Valley' what it is" (Hidalgo County Centennial Corp. 1952). For me, this is what I think Lloyd (1924) was getting at when he mentioned "criticism" both of settlers and celebration of magic in the LRGV.

"Men of letters" is a palimpsest of identity that in the LRGV evolved from "newspaper men" to digital content creators. And in that same context, letters have taken the shape of news articles, settler advertisements, and now tweets. News outlets-contributors ensure campaigns to hoard and produce knowledge on ideas (Man), images (Human), and ends (Rights-to) endure. The idea

Our excursion party leaving Edinburg for a tour over our lands.

FIGURE 3.22. The Gaze

that Hill, according to Caroline Feild and others of the *Valley Morning Star*, did more to *make the Valley* through his "vision" and "integrity" is just one effort to translate myths into facts. The projects of territorial and epistemological (ap/ex)propriation are already couched in what it means to be an *empire builder*:

> "Chief," as he was affectionately known, played a greater part in the development of this country than has any other one person. He was the first man who realized the wonderful opportunity for changing an extensive wasteland, covered with mesquite and cactus, into a veritable garden spot. The story of the work which he so nobly carried on in the face of droughts, heavy rains, bandits, and discouragements, is not the typical story of an empire builder. ("Story of Lon Hill" 1950)

> If the question is asked, why is America great, why has it progressed more rapidly than any other nation in the world's history, the answer must be: because of the Lon Hills. And if America fails it will be because the spirit of the Lon Hills has *died out* ("To Lon C. Hill IV" 1960, emphasis mine)

With his passing, Jack Rutledge (1935) described Hill as a pioneer who came to the Valley when it was "lawless, uncivilized, undeveloped." The *San Benito News* complements Rutledge's claims of wastelands transformed by Hill, writing that he was "stricken by the fertility and possibilities of the land" and "perceived the vast abundance that lay dormant" ("City of Harlingen" 1961). The point, as redundant as it may seem, is not to call into question whether development occurred but to unsettle the literacy of arcadia, image of peaceful settlers-pioneers, and rhetorics of "civilization on the march" with "Lon Hill directing traffic" ("Man of Action—Man of Dreams" n.d.). Because one cannot be an empire builder and not engage in actions of or have mechanisms for management and control.

Management and control are some aspects of the darker, (supposedly) hidden side of rhetorics of modernity. Is it any coincidence Hill built the LRGV's first school for white children? By modernity, thus, do we mean segregation on the *idea* of race and colonial difference? Harlingen, like the neighboring cities of Mercedes, Edinburg, and Rio Hondo, celebrated its modern school system. But according to many of the already mentioned settler advertisements, all these cities segregated whites, "the Mexican," and "the Negro," both in terms of buildings and classrooms (*Borderlands/La Frontera* [Anzaldúa 1999] offers insight on how classrooms sought to stamp out "the Mexican" and enforce epistemic obedience). One aim of wards was to protect the *other*, or in this case Austin's "strange people" (S. F. Austin 1830b, 1835, 1836a), from itself in a reverberation of Fanon's (1963) colonial mother theory: "The colonial mother protects her child from itself... its own unhappiness which is its very essence" (211). Another aim was to guard society from *it*. Hill, complicit in the rise of Mexican ward schools, mirrored Austin. First, in the goal to settle the LRGV with people who harmonize in language, principles, and interests. And second, in the *idea* that *others* can be separated, "studied," and "managed." Education lends itself to an epistemological, ideological, and rhetorical war on information (figure 3.23). Because the classroom can be a battlefield where *coloniality of instruction-*and*-curriculum*—a settler-centered instruction that normalizes the modus operandi of modern/colonial and settlerizing designs—functions both as a medium to filter knowledge as facts-truth and experimental tool to manage and control epistemic obedience. There is no move toward innocence for Hill as an empire builder.

Coloniality of instruction-and-curriculum peddles in a racial matrix and racist world views. It is ultimately predicated on the pretexts of epistemic and ontological difference; laws of who can be in-common and Man-Human-Rights; and subtexts for coloniality of power. If modern/colonial and settlerizing designs reflect wor(l)ding aspirations at different scales, then settler advertisements are its vessel or vehicle for movements, performativity, and networking—praising settlers, *informing* readers of settler achievements, and *giving form* to archival impressions within such designs. Settler advertisements are not meant for "the Mexican." As one settler advertisement puts its

Corrido-ing the Idea of Texas-LRGV and the Settler : 155

FIGURE 3.23. Harlingen Proud of Its Modern School System (n.d.)

(figure 3.24), the pictorial records are for "the thinking man or woman," and by all accounts this does not include "The Mexican" per the discussions above (Missouri Pacific Railroad Company 1930). Whenever citizen/ship is discussed, once more, it is in the context of "high-minded, industrious and forward looking-citizens" ("Prominent Factor in Harlingen's Growth" n.d.). Or,

FIGURE 3.24. The Magic Valley myth

put another way, "men whose names have emblazoned the pages of history" ("Sharyland: Citrus" n.d.). And if still unclear, "View of Jackson Avenue" (n.d.) associates citizen/ship with "men of vision," again, the former "residents of the northern and central states." The settler advertisement (figure 3.24) thus is just one example of the *ghosting* of citizens. Because only settlers can arrive at a *Golconda*—an exotic-foreign land ("Harlingen: The City" 1931)—expropriate the land, and dominate, manage, and control nature. (A closer look at the bottom right square, though, and we see Quijano's [2007] claim that settlers also expropriate practices from the colonized, but that is beyond the scope and breadth of this chapter.)

There was no shortage of companies who utilized settler advertisements. Each invented place images ("no more fertile land in the world"; "the soil is the very cream of creation") and myths ("the future Great Citrus Fruit Belt of Texas"; "choice lands"). They circulated them to advance "The Magic Valley" myth. It is a wor(l)ding aspiration at the local, national, and global level. At the local level, promoters of cities like Mission claimed it to be "the best little city in the Lower Rio Grande Valley—coming traffic center of the valley" (*The Missionite* 1909). At the national level, promoters of cities like Harlingen stated that its developments would "amaze a nation" ("Harlingen: The City" 1931) as the "Key City of 'World's Garden Spot'" ("Harlingen's Location" n.d.; also see "Harlingen the Geographical and Trade Center" n.d.). At the global level, promoters of cities like Sharyland argued the development of the LRGV was "perhaps unparalleled" in the world (Southwestern Land Company 1933; "The Golden Story" n.d.; Missouri Pacific Railroad Company 1930). Each is evidence of a settlerizing epideitic rhetoric that has wor(l)ding aspirations. Now, it is beyond the scope of this chapter to analyze how promoters claimed San Benito, Mission, Sharyland, and Harlingen as the epitome of "The Magic Valley"—the "center" or "heart." But it is worth noting. Again, my goal above was to illustrate how everyday people have to do work rhetorically to enable the invention of "The Magic Valley."

The LRGV was not empty or unsettled prior to the arrival of Spanish, French, Mexican, and Anglo settlements. As the *Daily Review* reports, the LRGV was home to the Nazan, Pintas, Harices, Comecruda, Tejones, Toreguanos, Pajaritos, Paysanos, Cueros Cruds, Karankawas, Carrizos, Comanches, Lipans, Mescaleros, and Apaches ("Cameron Once Called" 1967; "Cameron County Named" 1979; "Cameron History" 1978). "The Indian" did not vanish to make room for settlers-pioneers: "It [Texas] was named in the days of long ago ... Today the Indians are gone ..." ("Land of Hearts Delight" n.d.). Empty landscapes from which inhabiting bodies of the *other* vanish are part and parcel of modern/colonial and settlerizing designs. And the fictions by "newspaper men" (such as Don Veach) and settler advertisements—"few settlements," "scattered Indian tribes," "not important to our story," "no intention of 'owning' any property"—advanced such wor(l)ding aspirations ("Colonizing the Valley" 1985). It all seems circular by now, but this is to ensure the point gets across. Now, the LRGV in the nineteenth century was neither empty of Spanish nor Mexican peoples (*Caballero* [González and Raleigh 1996] provides some insight into the LRGV in the time of the Treaty of Guadalupe Hidalgo) either. La Matanza (1915–1919), the Joint Committee of the Senate and the House in the Investigation of the Texas State Ranger Force (1919), segregation, and the invention of "The Magic Valley" and "settler" myths all tell a story that prohibits such moves to innocence (also see Hunt 2016).

Repositioning the Contents

Palimpsestic narratives—the *idea of the Americas, Utah/SLV, and Texas-LRGV*—are the yoking of modern/colonial and settlerizing designs that have yet to work themselves out. They were never intended to come to an end. And they are not over. There is a direct connection in the social, cultural, racial, and political activities carried out as haunted/haunting literacies, images-signs-sounds, and rhetorics from Hill-Shary to the Ku Klux Klan to Musk. Their proximity is not an exaggeration. It behooves me to at least explain the mentioning of the KKK. In the 1920s, the LRGV gained the attention of the KKK because Klansmen observed a space and place to seed, germinate, and harvest an *epistemic system* and *design* just as settlers had done before them. (This is not to suggest that white supremacy was not shared among setlers.) According to news reports in the *San Benito Light* (1921), 200 Klansmen marched on Harlingen during the "opening of the new Harlingen 'white way'" celebration (there is uncertainty as to whether the theme was surrepditious or intentionally coined). They announced that the "Invisible Empire" had arrived. Onlookers applauded slogans of "White Supremacy" and "100 Per Cent Americanism." The KKK posted a proclamation that same day for supporters and the "undesirables." Though this is purely speculation, one must ask, what support did the KKK perceive there to be, for which I would respond with, a whole lot.

The KKK parade and the tacking of the proclamation was a spectacle. As such, those in attendance, according to Ashraf Rushdy (2012), are guilty of "creating a sound for the full spectacle" (557). Because not only did they look, but they felt the "supremacy of the White Race"; smelled the essence of "100 per cent Americanism"; and touched the lives of "undesirables" who fled shortly thereafter out of fear. This spectacle spread to San Benito, Mercedes, and McAllen. A connection to Hill-Shary or Musk is not far-fetched. Recall Quijano's (2007) and Wolfe's (2006) argument that coloniality and settler colonialism are not isolated egregious events but rather an ongoing structuring principle of settlerizing encounters, interactions, and engagements. There is a happening that will keep spaces and places wounded/wounding and *stories-so-far* haunted/haunting in the LRGV. It is a happening cloaked-hidden by the spectacle of a settlerizing future-to-come, praise, and assemblage and branding work.

In the early 1900s, Robert Kleberg, a settler-pioneer, proposed that every person should be required to "give an account of his comings and goings." Those found to be suspicious should be gathered in "concentration camps along the river from Rio Grande City" (quoted in B. Johnson 2003, 123). Today internal checkpoints function as the last line of defense against "illegal" arrivals and arrivants. And its agents demand an account with their W/H questions: "¿De donde eres . . . a dónde vas . . . y tu papeles?" It will always have mattered to them que uno es de ahí (out-of-place; out-of-time) y no de allá (in-place; in-time). Border(ed)landers are recursively contained, monitored, surveilled, and checked by an ongoing structuring principle of modern/colonial and settlerizing designs. Ultimately, the technological power of archival impressions is that it helps materialize settlerizing desires into designs, new forms of public memory, and reality. And that is the power of the technology too that is the *idea*. Today, "camps" can be found on both sides of the border. In the LRGV these are camps that separate undocumented families and cage humanity. Over the past several years, haunted/haunting images of thousands of people mass-gathered in "cages" have made the news. As such, the LRGV has become a hotbed for politicians to politic. But these are the invisible histories largely inherited, embodied, experienced, and/or practiced in the LRGV, partly because of settlerizing encounters, interactions, and engagements and partly because of *visuality*, assemblage and branding work, and *ghosting* at work still. In this way, the LRGV is both a *death* and productive space. Again, we can turn to the *Archive* and see how it documents existence and power and lends legitimacy to some *things* as much as it cements discursive practices. Texas and "The Magic Valley" are but archival impressions modeling after the *Archive*.

How do we reposition the contents of the *Archive* so that we can position ourselves in relation to it designs *otherwise*? The above contents reflect a hope and struggle to create an archival impression into bodies of knowledge. But mine is not the only effort. "Gentrified, Stop SpaceX" is environmentalist activist Rebekah Hinojosa's rhetoric of protest against what the *Texas Monthly* aptly calls "Austin-ification" in Brownsville (Solomon 2021). The words were spray-painted on a new Old Capital Theater mural made by LA-based artist Ted Kelly in downtown Brownsville. The mural, meant to promote cultural awareness, was a beautification and revitalization of a downtown project supported by the Musk Foundation that donated $10 million to the city (Musk 2021a). Hinojosa was arrested and charged with vandalism of city property for what is typically a cite-and-release offense. But for some, who exemplify Roberts-Miller (2017) notion of demagogues, her act was a crime against property and "newness." Particularly for Mayor Trey Mendez, conversations were reduced to people for and against "newness," progress, and development. Eventually, charges were dropped, but what transpired became a rude awakening for some who realized that only a few were meant to benefit from a future that had arrived (Jimenez 2022; Ramirez 2021; Ramirez 2023a; *Trucha* n.d.).

The correlation between Musk's appeal for people to move to Brownsville and the commissioning of an outside artist paid $20,000 is a haunting one for denizens. The mural has come to personify the long history of exploitation and production of absences and silences in the LRGV. Hinojosa's words of protest thus have less to do with the muralist himself. They reflect a people's increasing awareness—"Gentrification Is Colonization"; "Stop Selling Esto'k Gna Land"; "Your Luxury Is Our Displacement"; "Stop Gentrification"; "Free RGV—Bekah"; "Stop SpaceX"; "No Somos Gente de Elon"; "El Barrio No Se Vende Se Defiende"—of how the mural represents and tells a lie of the ways SpaceX will bring about a progress that will benefit the LRGV. The block letters "BTX" may seem harmless, pero pa' los que saben they symbolize Austinification (ATX). Long are the days when one could hear the people say about Musk and progress, "No pasa nada." Instead, it is quite common now to encounter the saying "te-lo-sico" applied to those lingering pro-Musk supporters. The future has at last arrived in the LRGV, and its *ghostly citizens* are now more aware than ever that it will always already consider them as out of place and behind time (Davila 2022; Ismael M. 2021; Muniz 2023). Today there are several multimedia platforms that help to position the contents of the *Archive* transparently so that denizens can reposition themselves in relation to its designs *otherwise*. Because as one op-ed in *Trucha* puts it, it is "time [para ponernos trucha] to face the monsters that dwell en nuestra tierra," real Cucuys and Chupacabras like corrupt politicians, Musk, and SpaceX (*Trucha* 2023).

Trucha is a publishing organization that stands as archival impressions *otherwise*. In "What Journalists Should Know before Reporting on the SpaceX at Boca Chica Beach," Emma Guevara (2021) takes up the problem of outsiders discussing the LRGV. Guevara takes issue with how there is an increasing effort to "ignore" or "erase" how SpaceX is in the "middle of major wildlife habitat, on the shores of our beach, and in our community." (My theory is that those beholden to modern/colonial and settlerizing designs hold nature with such little regard because they see their lives on earth as short-lived, and thus, little care is placed on both the earth and how it will look like generations later as it is but a waystation for some of the living.) The community Guevara speaks of is historically neglected and primarily low-income, Spanish-speaking, and of mixed citizenship statuses. She fears media bias and SpaceX public relations are in cahoots to help Musk in a "Columbus-like move" to "lay claim to the land" and incorporate it as Starbase, despite the land already having "a name and ties to . . . local culture." Guevara refers to it as colonialism and capitalist violence. (A more recent effort is taking place in which LRGV leaders are attempting to re-brand the "Magic Valley" as "Rioplex.") Her article discusses the positioning of contents: "We don't have a voice in our local government so at the very least we need the media to stop serving as an aide to white supremacy." In the *Archive* in the making, it is wildlife, environment, and people who suffer. Guevara's work serves as an archival impression that unsettle the "lies" told by Musk, corrupt politicians, and the media (also see Villa 2024).

Erin Sheridan (2022) is another contributor of *Trucha*. "The Fine Print" speaks to how a mural portrays Musk as a "cowboy ready to lift the Rio Grande Valley up by its bootstraps." His wealth, Sheridan notes, means "hope, dreams, and a chance to erase the Valley's poverty from sight." Though erasure is surely happening it pertains little to the improvement to the quality of life for the *other*. The fine print statement takes on multiple meanings throughout the article, but it all boils down to deterritorialization, reterritorialization, and displacement. What Mayor Mendez called "The Renaissance of Downtown Brownsville" in a 2021 State of the City address is nothing more than a modern/colonial and settlerizing rebranding of a place and space that coincides strategically with the rise of murals in the areas. The Santa Claus façade, Sheridan argues, is for local leaders and politicians who profit from a "system at work," not the everyday person who now is bearing witness to a predominately Hispanic border city emerging out of the "shadow of wealthier, whiter Austin." On the same KRGV Facebook page mentioned earlier, it is not uncommon neither to find pushback to advocates who celebrate the news of SpaceX headquarters move: "maybe because you're privileged" (C. Garcia 2024). The *epistemic system* and design are still in operation upholding the status quo that keeps "signs of poverty invisible, dissent silences, and those with a voice comfortable enough to not ask questions." Sheridan's work serves as an archival impression too, one that repositions transparently the contents of the

Archive in the making so that denizens can reposition themselves in relation to it *otherwise*.

Josue Ramirez (2022) is another contributor of *Trucha*. In "Space Exed, a Forced Rebranding," the mythic trope and the visualization of the "Magic Valley" are revisited as a modern/colonial and settlerizing design that is "resource extractive" and always at the expense of "the Mexican." Ramirez claims the LRGV is reexperiencing a "forced rebranding" through it. Perhaps no greater example is Mayor Trey Mendez's rebranded slogan, "On the Border, by the Sea and Beyond!" The slogan, though portions of it are decades old, has been rebranded to reflect new desires and objectives. It locates a place (Boca Chica and the US-Mexico border), reidentifies it with a new settler (Musk), and renames the space ("City of Starbase"; "New Space City") via the design so hauntingly put by Musk as "Occupy [Mars]." The rebranding, like the materiality of public murals such as "BTX," "The Palm Forest," or "Rioplex" is a renewed form of a settler advertisement. They function as *visuality* in that the classification of a "new" culture against the old, separation of brown folks from an impression of a future, and the imprint of an aestheticization of the "Magic Valley" inextricably interwoven with the settler are intended to be self-evident. Here Wharton's rhetoric of *proprietors of the land*, Austin's *Americanizing Texas*, Hill's *magic of [our] Magic Valley*, and Musk's *we've got a lot of land with nobody around* are all in concert.

Ramirez (2022) compares what is going on in the LRGV to a sci-fi story. Because in light of "one of the most socioeconomically distressed communities in the United States," SpaceX's settlement was expedited by "political elite" for potentiality, opportunity, and astropreneurship. Ramirez writes, "The incoming wave of capitalism promises upward mobility and financial stability through new economies." He notes, however, that such promises and economies are only for "qualified workers." It is not lost on many denizens any longer that the jobs SpaceX are advertising, and "friends" Musk is inviting, are non-"RGV locals." This is no sci-fi story but a palimpsestic narrative of hauntings and haunting situations: "The steps to rebrand the City of Brownsville into New Space City and to change the local culture resemble the place-making actions of White Northerners in the early twentieth century when creating the myth of the Magic Valley." For Ramirez, the relation between settler advertisements in the twentieth and twenty-first centuries are undeniable. For him, the effects and consequences of a mythic "Magic Valley" are haunting similar: exploitation of people, erasure of history, depletion of lands, and wealth accumulation. Ramirez's critique of outside forces, the state's facilitation, and the locals who uphold modern/colonial and settlerizing designs is an echo of Fanon: "spectacular gestures" and "collaborators" (136; also see Césaire 2001, 45; Thiong'o 2004, 20). Settler archival research and journalism are so important as they can function as archival impressions that get in the way of designs as self-evident (Ramirez 2022, 2023b).

Pa' los que saben y los que nunca aprendió

A settler *epistemic system* and *design*—death-spaces (Taussig 1991), the halfdead (Anzaldúa 1999), frontiers—has endured in Texas and the LRGV. It is present in the material and aesthetic forms of public memory (economic, authorial, educational, political, and knowledge, among others). The past and certain ghost are kept alive through the praising of settlers and the Texas Rangers. The K–12 experience in Texas is marked by a constant honoring of a certain *blood* and *martyrdom*, "May they [students] never forget the names of Sam Houston, James Bowie, and David Crockett" (Paredes 1958a, 274; also see Wharton 1836). A *coloniality of instruction-curriculum* that keeps alive the past and certain ghosts. The Texas and the LRGV-border(ed)lands is not an inevitable or natural outcome as a border(ed)land. It is a result of an ongoing structuring principle of modern/colonial and settlerizing designs—*visuality*, assemblage, branding, and recasting work, *ghosting*, and "checkings." With the hope that change is possible, I have archived settler enunciations to think through the particularities and specificities in which hauntings and haunting situations evolve from bodies of knowledge and unfold as actional *goings-on*. It is a hope, once more, that under different conditions and with our capacity to have knowledge of the inner-workings of archives, we see it as our obligation and responsibility to not give back to archives per usual.

Settler enunciations are evidence that the ideas of *settlers*, *Texas* as the *land of wilderness*, an *Other-as-Same* relation, and *instruction-curriculum* are inseparable from the *idea of the Americas*. What remains in the land, memory, knowledge, and relationality is the *idea* of race, epistemic racism, coloniality, and the epistemological regime of modernity. Texas and "The Magic Valley" is but a case study of the rhetoricity behind archival impressions preserving the *Archive*. Settler enunciations from institutional and piecemealed archives illustrate global hauntings and haunting situations manifest in local forms and conditions in spaces and places like Texas and the LRGV. My analysis shows that while settlers disputed power, a cosmology of ideas, images, and and ends—which is how I define and what I mean by "settler"—constituting a *palimpsestic narrative* of the *Archive* was shared-in, imported, and expanded. Its contents and practices—projects of territorial and epistemological (ap/ex)propriation justified and rationalized as the price of modernization and human progress—surrounding the reception-production of a *hegemonic architecture* were considered advantageous. The cultural texts of Texas settlers implicate them as members of an *association of social interests* nourishing hauntings and haunting situations. Power does not unfold evenly, yet similar technologies recirculate archival impressions of the *idea* that materialize concretely designs into reality.

The *Archive* feels the hand of the settler in Texas. It is the hand that gave the impression that "the Magic Valley" is a valley and not a delta. Today, that impression continues to be felt. To repurpose a question by Montgomery (1928), "How's that for 'Magic'" (46)? Now, I want to recall Locke ([1689] 1821) once more through the words of settlers to underscore the point I am making about the *Archive* and impressions. It is common within settler advertisements to find statements, "Let's go back," often followed up by a clause, "when it was..." ("Address of John H. Shary" 1940; also see Said 1979, 55). It seeds an *idea* of nothingness or land "good for nothing" transformed by touch (Missouri Pacific Railroad Company 1925).

> The man of vision . . . He perceived the vast abundance that lay dormant and could visualize rich fields where the mesquite throttled everything. ("City of Harlingen" 1961)
>
> Pioneers who looked upon the rough brush country, visualized what it could be . . . and then made their dreams come true! (Eppright and Hooper 1961, 64)
>
> There's a land that was planned, yes by God it was planned . . . where a Nation might rally To establish "GOD'S GARDEN," the Magic Valley . . . There's a land that is manned by a people who give Of the fruit of their labor that others may live—Who unite to promote the best interests of all . . . "GOD'S GARDEN," the Magic Valley at last is found. ("Standard Blue Book U.S.A.—South Texas Edition" 1926, 10)

The above are the undertones of Locke's ideas, images-signs-sounds, and ends of and on labor, property, civilized Man, and Man supporting Human life. Like Locke, settlers speak of a *waste place* "found," to be covered-up-and-over with a new place image-and-myth of a "favored land" ("San Benito" n.d., 37) and "land richer than Canaan" (Montgomery n.d.), which extended a *Christian civilization* or a *civilized Christendom* (E. Lloyd 1924; Missouri Pacific Lines

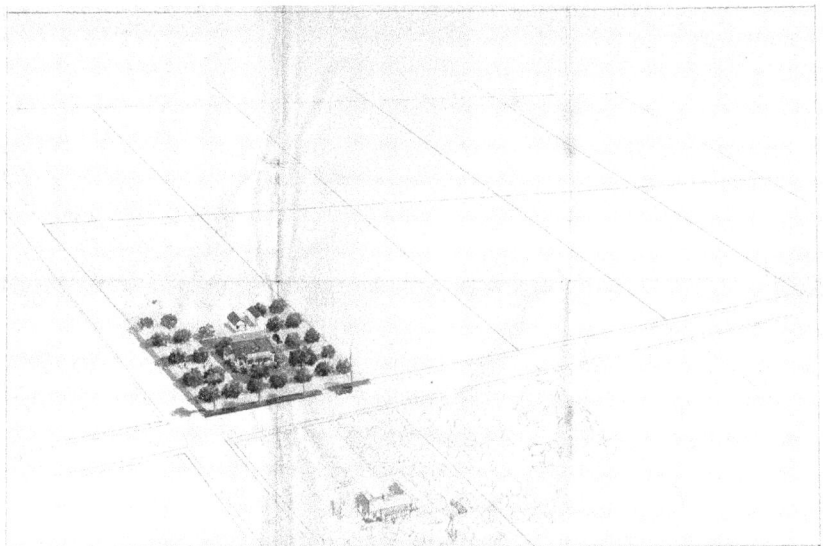

FIGURE 3.25. A White-Washing

1927). This "magical land" in the desert *now* known as the "Magic Valley" was to be appropriated by labor to bring into fruition America's Garden of Eden (see "Prosperity" n.d.). The *Archive* and its smaller archives are a prism through which to see the exaggeration of a crisis refracted, elsewhere and otherwise, which always already stages the emergence of a penetration into the space, place, and time of an-other. Not only is the LRGV no different here, indeed, it is but an archival impression that strengthens the *Archive*.

It is incumbent upon us to locate, identify, and name the coded words and tropes of modern/colonial and settlerizing designs. Past to present, out of the Garden of Eden impression lie three tropes of modern/colonial and settlerizing designs. I want to return to the mockup galley of figure 3.20 because it is not inconsequential here (figure 3.25). It illustrates a medical grade touch that cleanses and wipes aways the earth and its people, churning out a white space and place. Because designs are a white-washing and the impressing upon the earth whiteness vis-à-vis ecocide, genocide, and ethno-and-epistemicide. I refer to this as the *aseptic cleanliness trope*, a settler visioning of contaminated settings—bodies and the earth—that require scorched-earth or medical-grade sanitization to be applied to its core to return it (supposedly) to a clean, pure, and sublime world and race. This trope-as-impression says something important about a vertical (God to settler) and horizontal (settler to Adam) cross-chain that remained a settlerizing desire and objective:

> The word ADM, or with an additional vowel, ADaM . . . is an extension of the former root, DaM (Arabicè, Dem), meaning blood; the color of which, being red, originated the secondary signification of DaM, as "red"; and "to be red." Consequently, A, the letter "aleph," being the masculine article the; and the noun DaM meaning blood, or "red," we have only to unite these two words into A-DaM, to read the-blood, or the-red, in "Genesis"; which duplex substantive, applied to man, naturally signifies "the-red-man"; and, when applied to the ground, ADaMaH ("out of the dust" of which this the-red-man, ADaM, was moulded), it means the-red-earth. (Nott and Gliddon 1854, 573)

The *aseptic cleanliness trope* is a process in which the settler desires and works to return to whiteness and see whiteness as a reflection of the earth's core. The final product reflects the next trope, which I refer to as the *earth as fuckable, the fuckable earth trope* (figure 3.20). It is a settler visioning of extermination extending into a penetrable fertile earth—waiting to yield, ready to be germinated, awaiting the parturition of new harvests. The third trope, *you reap what you sow trope*, is best captured by a document titled "The Best Crop in the Valley." An image is not included here, but it depicts a "crop" of white babies. Because the ends of designs are always already the materializing of desires and objectives from an *idea* into reality, which in this case is the replenishing of the Garden of Eden in yet another elsewhere, an elsewhere where settlers can exercise their Rights-to. Together, these are some of the coded words and tropes of modern/colonial and settlerizing designs.

It is the same *Archive*. But if literacies, images-signs-sounds, and rhetorics have been used to fashion a modern/colonial world, they can be utilized to wor(l)d a future *otherwise* too. By creating a public record, the opportunity is afforded to view the contents of the *Archive* as *stories-so-far*, to excavate the archival impressions that constitute it, to reposition the contents of our *archives* so that we can position ourselves in relation to it *otherwise*, and to deliberate *an-other* set of choices, options, and obligations and responsibilities. The meaning of researching and searching for hope can be found in that process. In part, a theory of archival impressions reflects an analytical agenda to peel back the layers of impressions and de-sanitize the ways they are used as a vehicle and instrument to advance designs structurally and materially. Opening a space for the analytic of a decolonial option vis-à-vis an archival approach—questioning, unsettling, and delinking from the structural, epistemological, rhetorical, and ideological integrity of modern/colonial and settlerizing designs and the words and worlds associated with it—is a necessary move toward the *prospective vision*. Because it becomes possible to reclaim the archives, rhetoric, and rhetoricity for everyone. Because with our capacity to have knowledge of the inner workings of archives, which have impacted our availability of words, address, writing, and worlding activities, we can potentially and possibly wor(l)d *an-other* archive that has been a/waiting some *things* to-come. Though we can never be in full control of the afterlife of what we produce otherwise, and though the condition of possibility that gives way to decolonizing archival impressions is also its condition of impossibility, we must make room for the hope-struggle that some *things* are beyond the reach of modern/colonial and settlerizing mentalities and designs; where there are spaces of modern/colonial and settlerizing writing there are sites of counter-writing. ¡Ojalá!

This chapter was not about a being named settler, an entity called Texas-LRGV, or even about offering truthful definitions to the ontology of Man-Human-Rights. Rather, this chapter was on how epistemological hegemony happens, ideologies are carried over, hegemony is maintained, and the rhetorical war on information is expanded-disputed through the rhetoricity of settlers. In other words, how both the *idea of Texas-LRGV* and the "settler" came about as praxis. The rhetorical work of excavating archival impressions situated me squarely on a coloniality of knowledge (epistemology) constitutive of a coloniality of being (ontology). My emphasis on the invention of the peaceful settler unlocks the possibility for decolonizing knowledge and being. Such can create a pathway to liberate *pluriversal humanity* that can be a road to the coexistence of epistemic and ontological pluriversality. So if forgetting or conjuration is essential to settlers, then a remembering that yokes and calls forth hauntings, inheritances, and dwellings is most crucial in Texas and the LRGV. So can the *Archive* feel? Texas is a case study on both the hand of the settler and why we cannot come to terms with hauntings without coming to terms with literacies, images-signs-sounds, and rhetorics.

We must investigate the past to understand the present structuring principle of settlerizing encounters, interactions, and engagement that keeps spaces and places wounded/wounding and *stories-so-far* haunted/haunting. Settler archives may or may not change. But *why* and *how* we approach them can. They are a caravan for an *epistemic system, design,* and *epistemological framework for the living* on the move. Settler archives are a powerful medium for archiving the inhumanity and irrationality of *humanitas* and confronting, unsettling, decolonizing, and amending the lies, contradictions, myths, narcissism, cynicism, denialism, and sickness-disease of haunted/haunting literacies, images-signs-sounds, and rhetorics that haunt us in the present. The decolonizing of knowledge above serves as a foundation for chapter 5, aimed at exploring the prospect of decolonizing being for students whose *stories-so-far* adhere to and interact with the projects and work that settler archives represent. Because decolonizing being is unthinkable without decolonizing knowledge. This can be vital alongside placed-based pedagogies and curricula because it affords the occasion to deliberate *an-other* set of choices, options, and obligations-responsibilities. Such a framework I believe is a stepping-stone to imagining a future without modern/colonial and settlerizing hauntings because it invites us to make archival impression *otherwise*.

Final Thoughts

Power does not unfold evenly. That would be a re-entrenching of an organicist concept, a homogenous totality in which Western Europe remains the head (and the heart) and Western Europeans its far-reaching extremities. But we can think of the *Archive* as an interstate system, recording as much as it cements and produces discursive practices of structural principles, dissematings a universal code for domination, management, and control through which all information flows in and outward from. Its designs, which unfold elsewhere and otherwise to construct settler sites, constitute haunted/haunting communities, and maintain wounded/wounding spaces and places, evidences an *Archive* shared in, imported, expanded, and/or disputed. Utah and Texas are but case studies of how the *Archive* is given structure and constituted by settlerizing rhetoricity and archival impressions. Today, the *Archive* exists almost in a virtual space inaccessible by any one *thing* or *one*, a technology and a technological interface processor, a computer (as a Palestinian graduate peer would say) that is an assemblage of *working parts* and is *in* assemblage with other smaller archives.

The "humanity of the settler," Yang (2017) writes, "is predicated on his ability to 'write the world'" (7). For me, this is why the *Archive* is perhaps the most honest and critical space to think and speak from. My goal was not to produce "A" history of any settler state, but to illustrate how modern/colonial and settlerizing writings are but archived inventions, recycled writing baked with modern/colonial and settlerizing mentalities and designs. My goal was to recognize that we are under the yoke of the *Archive*, but also to acknowledge that it is smaller archives, the by-product of everyday people doing work rhetorically, that ensures that the *Archive* does not slide into the abyss of non-existences.

It survives—made, unmade-remade—in part through iterative writing and address (see Bhabha 1994) such as palimpsestic time (Alexander 2005), identities (Shohat 2002), and narratives (A. Garcia 2004). The *Archive*, in other words, both has a regulative function and exists in a precarious state vis-à-vis the *idea*, a sometimes failed but nonetheless haunting experiment.

What options exist that we could meaningfully and usefully describe as decolonizing? Such a question situates us squarely on the reality that we need to have tools and instruments to undo modern/colonial and settlerizing mentalities and designs. I have offered such by way of reclaiming an archival approach and advancing a theory of archival impressions. This has implications for WRS, which can no longer afford to lack a theory of writing and rhetoric for modern/colonial and settlerizing contexts. I conclude thus with a preliminary description of a theory of unsettling and counter-writing vis-à-vis an archival approach and theory of archival impressions: graphic bookmarks that archive; archival impressions that unsettle; signposts of counter-writing that alter; and trace marks that haunt back the structural, epistemological, rhetorical, and ideological integrity of the *Archive*. It is an ethic of *doing*, which can be characterized as decolonizing, that unsettles in sites of counter-writing the lies, contradictions, myths, narcissism, cynicism, denialisms, and/or sickness-disease of designs.

Reflexión-Meditación

Haunted/Haunting Peoples and the Im/Possibilities of a Prospective Vision

I have relied on hauntings as a category of analysis and a theory of archival impressions to establish connections between the past and the present. The coded words and tropes of modern/colonial and settlerizing designs, which I treat as social, racial, and political activities, are in part what gives structure to, constitutes, and ensures the *Archive* is made, unmade, and remade in unending cycles. Again, because power, alongside physical wreckage, is an epistemic and aesthetic issue too. I initiated decolonizing archival impressions thus to unsettle, decolonize, and amend the lies, contradictions, myths, narcissism, cynicism, denialisms, and sickness-disease of the *Archive* and its *smaller archives of knowledges, understanding, feelings, and doings* (or the *working parts* of the Archive). (Decolonizing being is unthinkable without decolonizing knowledge.) Settler archival research affords this necessary opportunity of contending with the modern/colonial and settlerizing designs and technologies of the *Archive*.

An archival approach and theory of archival impressions complements other unsettling agendas such as *ethnographies of modernity/coloniality* (Escobar 2007), *colonial ethnographies* (Stoler 2002), and *ethnographies of connections* (Tsing 2005). Each begin from the premise that to talk of, intervene in, and/or unsettle the some *things* of our world we have to be present and be a witness to them. But what comes after the critique? I ask such a question to shift the focus in the second section of this book: How do we carry out the *prospective vision* of a decolonial option? It is based on some outlooks I hold: that the classroom and by extension *stories-so-far* can be sites of inquiry (see Kirsch and Mortensen 1996) and that the past can be utilized *with the intention of opening the future* (see Fanon 1963). But as the section will underscore, agendas do not always go as planned. When human beings are involved, theory does not always translate or bode well in practice. Still, I maintain the value of an archival approach and a theory of archival impressions, because we live amid and as archives.

If the *Archive* is an *epistemological experiments*, by the same token, *archives* can be an experiment for wor(l)ding *otherwise*. Again, I argue an archival approach and theory of archival impressions is the connective tissue between a *praxical theorizing* and *theory building actioning*. Another set of [W]-[H] questions guide the second section. What are the parallels between the *Archive* and students' *stories-so-far*? Is the classroom a conducive space and place for decolonizing knowledge-being? How do we reposition the contents of *archives* so that we can position ourselves in relation to it *otherwise*? Such lines of inquiry ground the rhetorical nature of this section and informs its most central sites of analyses—the *archival impressions* that ensure *archives* are made, unmade, and remade in unending cycles. A similar principle of thought applies here—while the *stories-so-far* of our *archives* cannot be undone, *why* and *how* we approach them can change how we all walk and see the world and interact and exchange meaning with others. Because our archives are not fixed but always subject to change. And that grounds *an-other* exigence that forms *an-other* question, *what is our obligation and responsibility*? Such a question appeals for the initiating of decolonizing archival impressions. Why not invite students to research and search for hope in the archives, where the meaning of *stories-so-far* and the *possibilities of new stories* can be found? In the context of being, that means unsettling the settled-ness of Self to welcome and engage in a wor(l)ding of *an-other* set of archives.

If *coloniality of instruction-and-curriculum* is used to manage truth-and-knowledge claims and control epistemic obedience, by the same token instruction and curriculum can be utilized to initiate decolonizing archival impressions. The classroom in a "traditional" setting is unsuitable for *anyone* who arrives at the doors of the classroom. In the words of bell hooks (1994), it amounts to nothing more than a "rote, assembly-line approach to learning" (13). But can all that change under a different setting and agenda? The second section reflects my efforts to introduce the dynamic of decolonizing knowledge-being. But what is good in theory—encouraging students to create a public record of the contents of their *archive* and situating them at the nexus of their *stories-so-far* and *possibilities of new stories*—does not always translate or bode well in practice, especially when human beings are involved. Because decolonizing knowledge-being can be conceptually, pedagogically, and emotionally complex, complicated, messy, and to some extent impossible. Given this, it is important to recognize and acknowledge how a decolonial option too can create a classroom setting unsuitable for *anyone* who arrives at the doors.

Section 2

Decolonizing Archival Impressions

The Im/Possibilities of a Prospective Task

4
Making It Out of Haunting Mentalities

The Zion curtain in Utah today is at least a century in the making. It is the by-product of a vision, countless failures of homesteading, and civil, social, racial, and political design that settled on Utah as *the* place. Anyone under the impression that power is in some kind of decline or crisis has clearly overlooked spaces and places like Utah. As a wounded/wounding space and place and haunted/haunting *story-so-far*, not only does it speak to the exaggeration of a crises, but it is also the homebase and training ground from which the brainstorming of penetrations into the spaces, places, and times of an-other flow out of from. It is an example of the ways in which *smaller archives of knowledges, understandings, feelings, and doings* (or the *working parts* of the *Archive*) not only share in, import, and expand modern/colonial and settlerizing designs but also dispute them. Such an archive is evidence that everyday people have to do work rhetorically to enable haunted/haunting *stories-so-far*.

The human work and projects we carry out in the classroom can be conceptually, pedagogically, and emotionally complex, complicated, and messy. The haunted/haunting story I will share below speaks to that. Yet despite this, I hold firmly still that it is troublesome to label students as problems, as I imagine we have all heard in one way or another either in conversation with others or even at conferences. I have so often turned to Anna Tsing's (2005) notion

https://doi.org/10.7330/9781646426782.c004

of *friction* to keep me true to that position. *Friction* is one way to think about what happens when there is *opportunity* to come together, *be-with* each other, and *get to work*. Of course, such a stance does not dismiss discriminatory or racist behavior, but it does "check" the tendency to mislabel situations or students. For Tsing, *friction takes* and *makes* place like words and ideas, whether in maintaining, getting in the way of, or redefining arrangements of cultures, communities, and/or knowledges, understandings, feelings, and doings. This chapter and the next underscore the darker, grayer narratives of and from the classroom so often neglected in WRS, stories from faculty of color at predominately white institutions (hereafter PWI) on failure.

It continues to strike me as odd that so many of academics in WRS talk about unsettling or decolonizing this and that and none touch on failure. How can that be if by the very nature of the project some *things* are being unsettled. I will talk about multiple failures in this chapter and the next. There is the failure to bring a critique to bear on the rhetorics of race and racism within the classroom; the failure to get students to enter the *fold of* their *archives*, or a space of deliberation and judgment, *otherwise*; the failure to bring about change in the *archives* (García and Hinojosa 2020; García and Kirsch 2022; Green 2003; Mutnick 1998; Prendergast 1998; Trainor 2005; Vivian 2000). Neither this chapter nor the next reflects *the* story or the *whole* story. That is an impossibility alongside the reality that some stories cannot and should not be told. At times, the narrative might seem fragmented or incomplete, offering only a snapshot composite or sliver of a *story-so-far* and conversation. Though that limitation is mine alone, it suffices to underscore the ways our lives and bodies are *archives*; to illuminate how posterity maintains an *archive* of *knowledges, understandings, feelings*, and *doings* that acknowledges, disavows, and/or subsumes the *other-things*; to advance an argument for an archival approach and theory of archival impressions. Failure, as I reflect on it today, has been most instructive in my growth as an educator.

A Cultural Climate

Racist fliers targeting Black communities were found on campus prior to the start of the 2017 fall semester. The position of the University of Utah (UofU) was that it was a singular incident. But such hauntings and haunting situations are not singular or isolated occurrences. Because racism, like modern/colonial and settlerizing designs, is not an isolated egregious event but an ongoing organizing structuring principle of settlerizing encounters, interactions, and engagements. Fliers are visual rhetoric, or at least that is my position. The fliers found on campus contained a caricature of a Black man who is observed forcefully gripping a white woman attempting to pull away. The offensive captions, corresponding with erroneous statistics, are meant to conjure up and fortify an invented and haunted/haunting palimpsest of identity, some of which shore up in previous chapters with other racialized and minoritized peoples. Fliers are also audible. Sure, the sound we make when we read such slogans—"Stop the Blacks"; "Blood and Soil" (Nazi slogan)—may only be perceptable to our own ears, and yet, it contributes to the soundscape of *ideas*. They are considered "singular" incidents, but they exist within a milieu of racist and discriminatory happenings in Utah (Anderson 2017; Farberov 2018; Fulwider 2017; Klopfenstein 2021; Knox 2017; Turner and Harrison 2022; University of Utah Communications 2020; Wagner 2017). That is to say that Utah, unable to exist outside the modern/colonial and settlerizing designs, continues to be rewritten in wounded/wounding and haunted/haunting ways. The UofU experienced other "incidents" between 2017 and 2022, including the distribution of racist and anti-immigration fliers, reports of people dressed like the KKK, and feces found on the door of a student's dorm room. Hauntings and haunting situations are rarely ever singular, isolated incidents, but rather reflective of unfolding contents, practices, and engagements within an immediate setting and context. These incidents are the by-product of the technological power of the *idea* that helped materialize settlerizing desires into designs, new forms of public memory, and reality.

Racist fliers showcase an epistemological, ideological, and rhetorical war on information. Hauntingly, they confirm a racial imaginary founded on the *idea* of race, shared-in through epistemic racism, and expanded-disputed by the *ends* of coloniality. The fliers reattuned communities of Utah to the darker, (supposedly) hidden side of a haunted/haunting ambience and to wounded/wounding spaces-places, haunted/haunting *stories-so-far*, and everyday human projects. And at once, the contradiction that is Utah comes to light, with competing narratives that claim, on the one hand, that Utah has never been a racist state and, on the other, that such a history is just that, the past. This frightened the UofU, which claimed these were singular, isolated incidents and *hoped* they were the *last* (see Rushdy 2012). The dilemma was that the above words, ideas, and activities did not just materialize out of the ether. There is a whole context for them. They reflect an *association of social interests* and a foundation that had allowed them to *appear, become,* and *remain* consequential in the first place. The epistemic-aesthetic issues here underscore how epistemology, ideology, and hegemony are tied to language and purchased-sold through literacies, images-signs-sounds, and rhetorics.

Responses varied on the epistemic-aesthetic issues in Utah. The *Salt Lake Tribune* published a piece, "Racist Flyers Found on the University of Utah Campus, but It's Not Clear Who Posted Them" (T. Caldwell 2017). The focus on the *who* rather than on the *what* redirected attention and deflected from the reality that epistemic racism is a racist happening in Utah. This is precisely why scholars such as Yang (2017) write, "'How?' is a question you ask if you are concerned with the mechanisms, not just the motives, of colonization . . . a frame that could help you forecast colonial next operations and to plot decolonial directions" (5). All this was compounded by the UofU's desire to mitigate this "incident" with a spokeswoman stating there was not "enough information about this incident to really follow up" (Caldwell 2017). This move was not lost on communities in Utah, which led to the dismissal of this racist happening and for others drew concern that deflection would ignore that which traffics in the normative in Utah. Both the news outlet and UofU contributed to a not-in-Utahism. I will return to its significance in the next section, but for now I want to stay on the effects and consequences of deflection.

At a time when the spectacle and ceremony of racist happenings was retaking the public eye throughout the US, it was at the local level that one could bear witness to the *why* and *how* the haunted occupy a unique space in the racial modern/colonial imaginary. The emphasis on *who* rather than on the *what and how* encouraged agents of the hegemonic family, the family that in part maintains the *Archive*, to come out of the woodwork. Their role, in the spectacle and ceremony of racist happenings, is to invent and maintain the image of the "self" and the "other" by whatever means necessary (see Mignolo 2003). Agents of the hegemonic family levied claims that the racist fliers were a hoax and declared they were the actual *doings* of communities of color. A perverse idea surely, but it persisted nonetheless. The idea that the racist fliers were a hoax and by-product of communities of color was both a haunting claim and evidence of how mediums of circulation can be used in the war on information. Deflection reverberated throughout Utah, which became part of the sound for the full spectacle. The language of the agents of the hegemonic family became a prism through which to see the spectacle and cermony of racist happenings that is Utah (see Hodge and Kress 1993).

Deflection sparked debate about the role of educators. Actor-agents of the hegemonic family, a prism through which to see the ins and outs of haunted/haunting literacies, images-signs-sounds, and rhetorics unfolding at the micro level, cohered to a motto. "They are our children, not yours!" But the *sound* for the full spectacle and ceremony of racist happenings in Utah was not just being produced by culpable actors such as the Vanguard of Utah, which claimed ownership of the racist fliers. It was made too by complicit spectators, those who enunciate epistemic ignorance, not-in-Utahisms, and/or an *end-of discourse*. I listened in the shadows, to *know* and to *learn*. I would utilize the projects of unsettling and a decolonial option to ensure that the spectacle and ceremony of the *idea* of race, epistemic racism, and the *ends* of coloniality would not go unchecked in my classroom. I would come to the classroom with a plan, but its execution would fail both in delivery and outcome.

The Department of Writing and Rhetoric Studies responded to the racist happenings in a nine-point letter drafted by Dr. Christie Toth and signed by faculty at our annual retreat. I was reminded that day, as I so often have been in my department, that to unsettle the settled, all need to be involved. The point was to identify, name, and not allow either white supremacy or racist happenings to go unchecked. The letter is a case in point of another dynamic of *friction*: the *fly in the elephant's nose* (see Tsing 2005), the wrench in the assembly line. It reflects a practical translation of another essential focus of this book: if literacies, images-signs-sounds, and rhetorics are how epistemological hegemony are constituted, ideologies carried over, hegemony maintained (see Villanueva 1993, 2006) by the same token, they can be used rhetorically to unsettle the sounds of its spectacle and ceremony. The letter issued nine statements that reflected a collective ethos. It is important to note that the diversity of our department was miniscule in 2017. It underscores the significance of the "We" in an imperfect letter. It was a white colleague who drafted it and a white majority that signed it. The "We" reflected a microcosm of Fanon's world of the You and the MCC's spirit of *doing-thinking-with*. White, Black, and Brown folks signed the letter with a hope that it is possible to collectively struggle toward the *possibilities of new stories* through the human work and projects we carry out in classrooms. The "We" indicted as much as it implicated all to *do better*. At that point, the question for me became one of practicality, *how do I translate the above ethos into a deliberative praxis in the wake of hauntings and haunting situations?* (see Baker-Bell, Butler, and Johnson 2017).

When my department scheduled me to teach the course Academic Writing and Research, or WRTG 2010, I knew I would utilize the projects of unsettling and a decolonial option. A *decolonial analytic* emerged in my teachings about wounded/wounding spaces and places, haunted/haunting *stories-so-far*, and everyday human projects. I framed these lectures as *stories-so-far*, emphasizing stages and junctures of everyday life. A *prospective vision* materialized through archival-informed projects of self/selves, communities, and social, racial, and political activities that encouraged students to generate a public record of and from scenes of their cultural and thinking programs. I framed these assignments as *possibilities of new stories*, emphasizing that stories are not fixed but subject to change; meaning, contents, and terms can be returned to, intervened in, and reinvented.

Stories-So-Far: Haunting Mentalities

First-year composition (FYC) has contentiously been debated for years by scholars who are for and against its requirement. And the debates range: service, skills, unimportance, expectations, gatekeeping, indoctrination, and transfer. Even among those "for" FYC, there are varying arguments along the lines of assessment, curricula, and pedagogical approach (Berlin 1984; Connors 1984, 1991; Crowley 1991, 1998; Harkin 1994; Schilb 1994; Bloom 1999; Paulsen and Feldman 1999; Roemer, Schultz, and Durst 1999; Stewart 2001; Carroll 2002; Bawarshi 2003; Sommers and Saltz 2004; Wardle 2007, 2009; Beaufort 2007; Downs and Wardle 2007, 2012; Bergmann and Zepernick 2007; Nelms and Dively 2007; Bird 2008; Miles et al. 2008; Sealey-Ruiz 2013). Contrary to the tone and experiences I account for in this chapter, I for one believe if the project of unsettling and a decolonial option is to have its greatest impact, it would be in FYC because it is often the first point of contact for students. In the realm of reading and writing academically, WRTG 2010 hits on familiar notes given the foci on foundational rhetorical practices, development of rhetorical strategies, and bolstering of rhetorical capabilities. But it can become a significant course in the trajectory of a student's tenure at an institution in and through lectures, dialogues, and projects. In other words, FYC can set an important tone.

I began the semester with two questions I thought would capture the ethos of the department letter and set the stage for the projects of unsettling and a decolonial option. Where are hauntings and haunting situations and how have they worked and inflicted upon spaces and places, the everyday, and the *stories-so-far* of communities and people? These two questions also provided the opportunity to establish the ideas and interplay between *stories-so-far* and the *possibilities of new stories*. As a class, we then proceeded to read the racist fliers and department letter. Unbeknownst to me, most of my class were members of or were quasi-affiliated with the Church. As they carried out rhetorics of epistemology through epideictic rhetoric that day and days to follow, I found myself posing a threat as an outsider, person of color, and non-Mormon. I did not know this at the time, but I occupied a unique space in their imaginary predicated on *Other-as-Same* relations and the obligation-responsibility of *work-instruction*. I would get to work but so would they.

A classroom can become a *gathering space* for everyday people to carry out *work-instruction* that has wor(l)ding aspirations. The following anecdotes, based on notes and end-of-day reflections with some students, begin with my encounters with not-in-Utahisms on day one. "Racism," Ben tells me and then assures his peers, "doesn't exist here [Utah]. It does not happen here." It was a cliché, but it seemed as if the entirety of the class agreed with his argument that Utah and Utahns were sheltered from such experiences. (It reminded me of how I used to think, in fact, being from the LRGV and cut off by the internal checkpoints from the rest of Texas.) Perhaps my skepticism came off too strong, because Ben quickly reminded me, "You don't know Utah, you don't know our history, you don't know our ancestors, you are still new here." That I was new suggested I had much to learn in their eyes. He was right in a sense. And this presented an opportunity to some—*coloniality of instruction-and-curriculum*. I assured Ben, and the entirety of the class, that while I was new to Utah, I was very familiar with hauntings and haunting situations (Aleman 2005).

I experienced Utahn-niceness (politeness) that day and much of the semester until the point that neither I nor them would budge. Brigham Young captured its ethos hauntingly: "Treat them [*others*] kindly, and treat them as Indians, and not as your equals" (MRM: Young 1854, 6:329). I encountered it with Lynn, who upon hearing about settler colonialism and coloniality broadly stated, "Oh, tell me more." And with Ben too, who piggybacked on her remark, "We are all ears." It was important to Lynn that I knew that Utahns were "open-minded and accepting to all people." Encounters at local restaurants and grocery stores had not yet swayed me otherwise. Not knowing otherwise, then, I interpreted both requests as sincere. So I gave a brief lecture about how all settler colonialism and coloniality involves lies, contradictions, myths, narcissism, cynicism, denialisms, and sickness-disease. I took a survey approach and spoke broadly about both. I also briefly lectured abstractly on the modus operandi of a modern/colonial and settlerizing designs and how it functions through narratives, images-signs-sounds, and rhetorics. But I gathered quickly, from the aesthetic chill I felt, that their hospitality had an agenda. It all felt hauntingly similar to when members of the Church leave bags of candy at my house or when missionaries would inquire about my experiences and hopes only to eventually segue into their desires and objectives.

Utahn-niceness (politeness) is a ploy to carry out *work-instruction*. It involves conditional welcoming of and an act of faux listening to the *Other-as-Same*. Perhaps, I am over-totalizing or generalizing here, but a *discourse-about-actions* approach tells me otherwise. That niceness-politeness almost always segues into an enactment of settlerizing epideictic rhetoric. Lynn, and what appeared to be the entirety of the class, told me, "We can teach you about Utah, where we come from and how we got here, and about us." Truly, part of the assignment I would come to create on the fly (more information below) was in part inspired by my own orientation but also by their experiences with archives and the storying of them. But equally important to them was that I know of the good *work* their ancestors had done and the Church continues to do. Andrew, who told me he is a returning missionary, chimes in, "Yeah, and we travel all around welcoming *others* [emphasis mine]. That is our responsibility." Perhaps the register of *otherness* was lost on him or perhaps I interpreted it to mean some *other-things*. Nonetheless, for me, such cultural and thinking program/ings is haunting. Because their ideas of hospitality and responsibility are constituted by reductive, dichotomous, and oppositional rhetorical structures of *what* and *who* can be *in-common* and on Man-Human-Rights. This became most evident with Ben, Lynn, and Andrew that day (Call 2022).

The first trace of contaminated and altered life questions came from Lynn. She stated, "We mostly hang out with people who belong to our own communities or church." When probed for more insight, Lynn turned to Ben, who informed me, "It's just the way it is, but it's not like we mind talking to *others* [emphasis mine] like some do with us." There is seemingly an agreement among the class. Lynn, who has regained confidence to speak, notes, "*Others* [emphasis mine] just don't get us at first, or don't want to get us. That's why we stick to our own." Ben nodded his head in agreement once more, telling me, "Some things don't change." Unbeknownst to me, this was a reference to religious persecution. I gained this much from Andrew, who added, "Some see us as bothersome, but we just want them to hear our truths, it's just how I understand my calling." Lynn made a final appeal by expressing that they "do a lot of good all around" in spreading such information. But there is something hauntingly at work here, which is that they recognize an us/them register, adhere or cohere to rhetoric of *otherness* and difference, internalize the inheritance of religious persecution, and acknowledge all of it as the status quo. Recall Kump's (1973) article, "L Is for Indian," for further context (see chapter 2).

Students were enacting church-settler epideictic rhetoric. One could easily chalk up a pause-hesitant hospitality to cultural and thinking program/programing. We could call that friction. Derrida (1994b, 213) anticipated conditional hospitality but also argued such does not take away from a choice-to-be-made as an obligation and responsibility. But when life questions are based on identity and identification and when *work-instruction* (salvation, reeducation, conversion, and restoration) is carried out ensuingly on the premise of an *Other-as-Same* relation, then there is a contamination at play that must be recognized and acknowledged as such. A turning point for me came at the end of the day with an email from Norma (figures 4.1 and 4.2). It began with an apology, optimism about course assignments and its topics (discussions on racism, settler colonialism, and coloniality), and continued by depicting a situation that created an uncomfortable environment for them. Norma wrote, "Just imagining speaking to four white men about their privilege makes my heart pound and hands shake." Here Norma was specifically referencing the privilege of Church members who benefit from imposed hierarchies and patriarchy, which they were familiar with as a former member. The email provided a glimpse of and insight into how other group discussions might have unfolded, which the remainder of the semester was a testament to.

Norma voiced "distaste" for "views of racism and 'natives'" expressed by classmates after a conversation took place about what is celebrated in history books ("friendly and curious people seeking to do no harm"; "the good intentions of Mormon settlers"; "the teaching of the Mormon church") versus what is left out ("the horrendous treatment of Native Americans"). According to Norma, peers argued that "[racism] doesn't exist in Salt Lake City, especially on the U's campus." Norma was bothered by how the group "refuse[d] [to] see past their own privilege" and to "work against the systems which grant us our privilege." Norma appealed for *friction*—that I become the *fly in the elephant's nose*—but reminded me that if I wanted the class to be successful, I could not speak of hauntings and haunting situations so abstractly. It was a great reminder that I had at some point lost sight of the question, *where is one at and whom is one teaching*? Though "publicly ridiculed" for leaving the Church and identifying as Queer, Norma was willing to "assist" me in "researching and planning" under "anonymity." Norma did so in the shadows, at least that is, till they reached a moment of truth.

I had a lot to learn, though I learned a lot that first day. I listened, *to know* and *to learn* from and with student accounts of the ways they walk and see

> Professor Garcia,
>
> I apologize for being too shy to say this in class today. I was really optimistic about this research topic and the whole "we all contribute to the assignment" thing, but as soon as I joined my new group (group 1), I realized that I have some serious moral objections to the mechanics of the group work.
>
> I am not uncomfortable being the only female in the group (in fact, I often lead groups like this in my engineering classes due to the scarcity of women in computer science), but I am uncomfortable being ignored by my male classmates when I offer suggestions or useful information, and I am too shy to discuss that with them, especially as a Queer woman. Just imagining speaking to four white men about their privilege makes my heart pound and my hands shake.
>
> In addition to this, I am not interested in working with people who are sympathetic to the mass murder of Native Americans. As a majority white class consisting mostly of people who have graduated from a public school system which depicts European colonizers as friendly and curious

FIGURE 4.1. Snapshot of Norma's email, page 1

> Even if my group is able to accomplish the purpose of this assignment, I don't believe that the goal of creating a useful discourse within our class will be achieved. While beginning my research, I overheard two of my (white male) groupmates discussing their views of racism. They think it doesn't exist in Salt Lake City, especially on the U's campus, and they don't understand why it's important for a majority white class to be writing this kind of paper in the context of white supremacy mobilization, increasing white terrorism, and a new wave of indoctrinated Nazis.
>
> Despite all of this, I am still hopeful for this topic. Like I said in class, I think it's powerful for us to be using our privilege as white university students to work against the systems which grant us our privilege by drawing attention to the issue.
>
> In order for this collection of essays to be successful, the class needs more background on the topic. I am wondering if you could be convinced to dedicate at least part of a class session to some more accurate accounts of the history of Salt Lake City, and follow up with recent acts of racism performed by individuals (such as the posters on campus) in Salt Lake City, the LDS church, the SLCPD, and Utah legislature.

FIGURE 4.2. Snapshot of Norma's email, page 2

the world and interact and exchange meaning with others. Norma's email appealed for *friction* into the *Archive* manifesting in Utah. Mormon/ism has been most successful, for example, in its war on information and management and control of epistemic obedience through *coloniality of work-instruction-curriculum*. On display that day was a settlerizing epideictic rhetoric, *work-instruction*, and a rhetorical dexterity to return to, center, and situate the past, the dead, inheritances, and dwellings to the politics of their present. I was familiar with the latter, as someone who does that myself. So I would turn to the projects of unsettling and a decolonial option, complemented by the interplay between *stories-so-far* and *possibilities of new stories*, to do human work and carry out human projects for what I perceived were haunting mentalities. It was all so simple!

Possibilities of New Stories: Decolonizing Knowledge-Being

I interpreted Norma's appeal for "more accurate accounts" as a plea to embrace the language of the everyday in Utah. The roles, effects, and consequences of language have figured prominently throughout this book, and teaching will be no exception. In *De Oratore*, Cicero underscored the importance of not departing "from the language of everyday life" (Cicero 1967, 11). Talking on the "language of everyday," Fanon (1963) claimed, "Everything can be explained to the people, on the single condition that you really want them to understand" (188–189). If the projects of unsettling and a decolonial option unfolding through lectures, dialogues, and projects were going to have an impact, the language of the everyday needed to factor in prominently. That is what Norma meant, I understood, by breaking from abstract discussions and shifting to the everyday in Utah. To buy some time, as I shifted, adapted, and continued to learn from students such as Norma, I decided to begin with the settler archival research that I had conducted in Texas.

Vulnerability is an often overlooked yet important part of the classroom, especially in the context of decolonizing knowledge-being. So I started the second week of class with an internal conflict. I reflected on how I used to wear a Texas Rangers baseball team jersey, watch *Walker, Texas Ranger* on TV, and wanted to be a Texas Ranger (law enforcement). And I shared with them how *friction* was created by the corridos ("Pistolero Famosos"; "Los Rinches de Tejas") that circulated in the LRGV. We even listened to and read the English lyrics of those corridos and talked about their meaning. Students were receptive, to my surprise, which I chalked up to my vulnerability. To capitalize

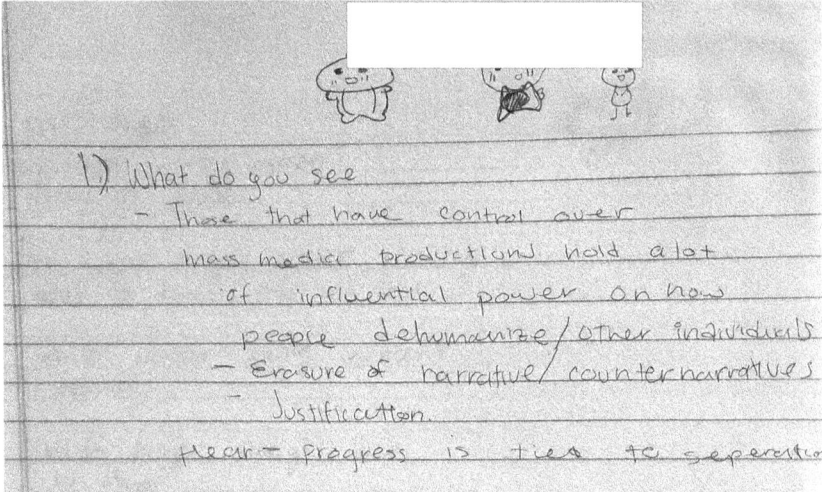

FIGURE 4.3. UofU first pair of responses

on that momentum, I segued into settler archives and invited students to respond anonymously as we worked through them collectively. Anonymous responses was my way of trying to build trust and create a space on paper in which students could express their views on what they observed.

We cannot come to terms with hauntings without coming to terms with its "everyday" literacies, images-signs-sounds, and rhetorics. Students demonstrated their intellectual capacities to explore, investigate, analyze, interpret, determine, and translate meaning. For example, in the first pair of responses above (figures 4.3 and 4.4), one student took note of how settlers had control over mass media production. I wondered if they had deliberated that before in their own context and how the war of information in Utah had influenced how "people dehumanize/other individuals." Another student documented what they saw: white women, old white angry settlers, and white mayor. This response stood out as well because Utah is notoriously white and the *rhetorics of place* is "the glorification of settlers/colonialism/manifest destiny."

There are other examples as well. Take, for instance, the second pair of responses (figures 4.5 and 4.6). One student jotted down key phrases that stood out: "rails brought civilization"; "men of integrity"; "destined to lead." The student's observation was keen: "Everybody in the picture is white." I say this because the course was demographically white Church members with only a couple of exceptions. I wondered, thus, how did students internalize all this? Did it even cross their mind? Another student wrote on the "dangerous

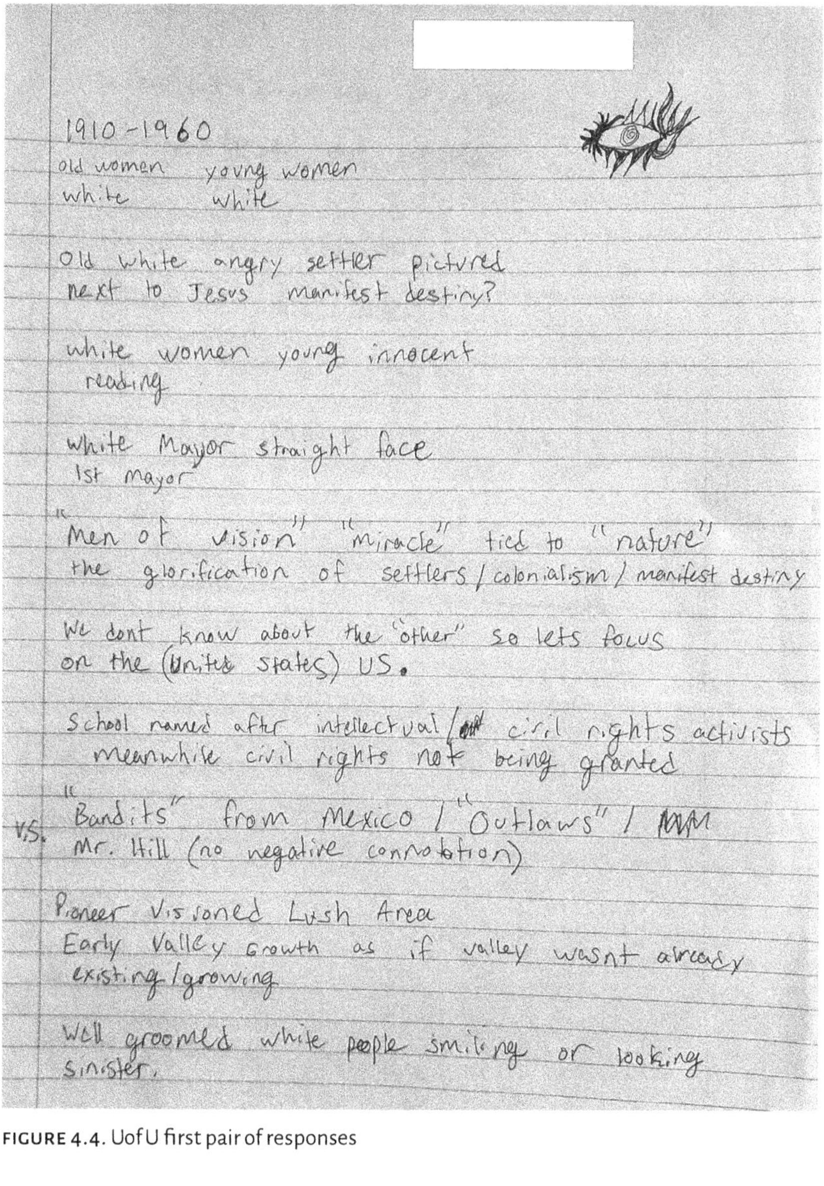

Making It Out of Haunting Mentalities : 189

> 1910-1960
> old women   young women
> white   white
>
> Old white angry settler pictured
> next to Jesus   manifest destiny?
>
> white women young innocent
> reading
>
> white Mayor straight face
> 1st mayor
>
> "Men of vision" "miracle" tied to "nature"
> the glorification of settlers / colonialism / manifest destiny
>
> We don't know about the "other" so lets focus
> on the (United States) US.
>
> School named after intellectual / civil rights activists
> meanwhile civil rights not being granted
>
> v.s. "Bandits" from Mexico / "Outlaws" / MM
> Mr. Hill (no negative connotation)
>
> Pioneer Visioned Lush Area
> Early Valley Growth as if valley wasnt already
> existing / growing
>
> Well groomed white people smiling or looking
> sinister.

FIGURE 4.4. UofU first pair of responses

aspect of this writing" because it "allows sentiments" about "Mexicans and Native Americans" to "silently embed themselves in society." The irony is not lost on me as I read it alongside the claim that "by only providing one viewpoint ... it leads the reader to assume that the correct narrative is that of the author." Utah is a case study in just how that has happened. I wondered

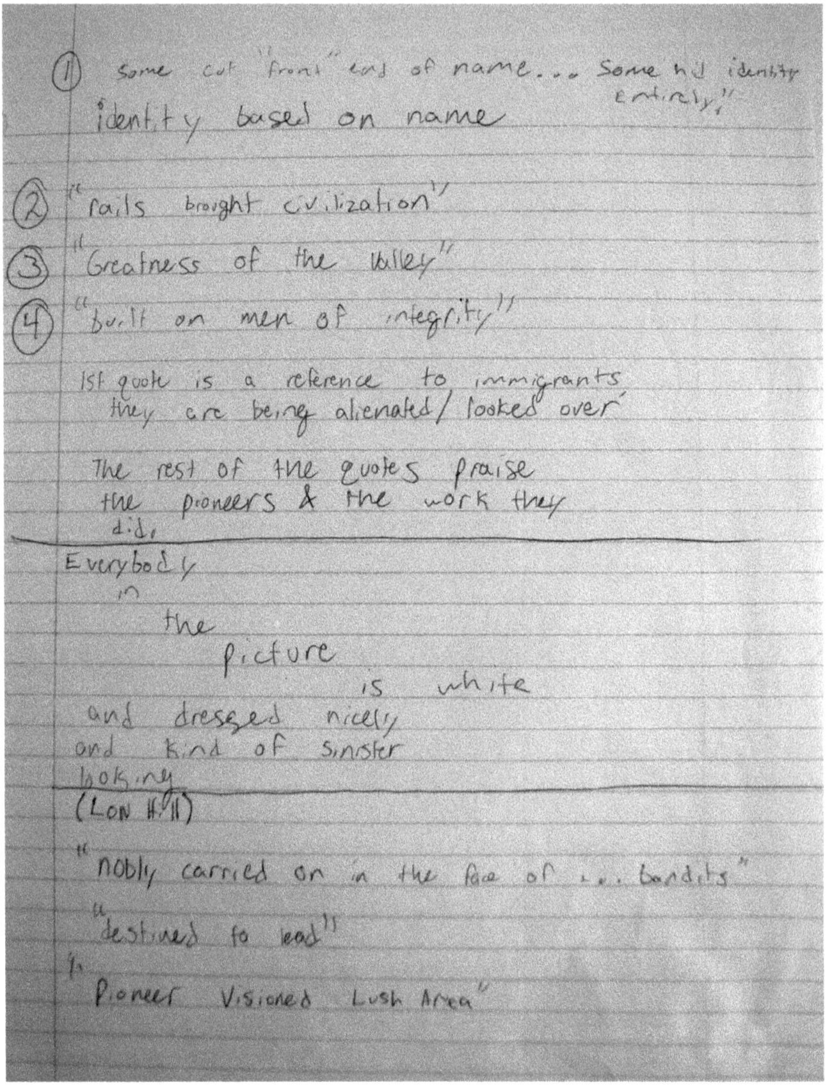

> ① Some cut "front" end of name... Some hid identity entirely."
> identity based on name
>
> ② "rails brought civilization"
> ③ "Greatness of the Valley"
> ④ "built on men of integrity"
>
> 1st quote is a reference to immigrants
> they are being alienated / looked over
>
> The rest of the quotes praise
> the pioneers & the work they
> did.
>
> Everybody in
> the
> picture
> is white
> and dressed nicely
> and kind of sinister
> looking
> (LON H.II)
>
> "nobly carried on in the face of ... bandits"
> "destined to lead"
> 1. Pioneer Visioned Lush Area"

FIGURE 4.5. UofU second pair of responses

here too if they found irony in how they dismissed the racist fliers at the beginning of the semester.

Then there is the third pair of responses (figures 4.7 and 4.8). One student wrote on how the "history of Harlingen is thoroughly white-washed." For her, that meant "erasure," "segregation," and the "forgotten." She would go as far as to refer to the narrative as "ignorant," reporting only "from one side of a diverse town." Another student wrote on how the settler viewed the "land" as

Making It Out of Haunting Mentalities : 191

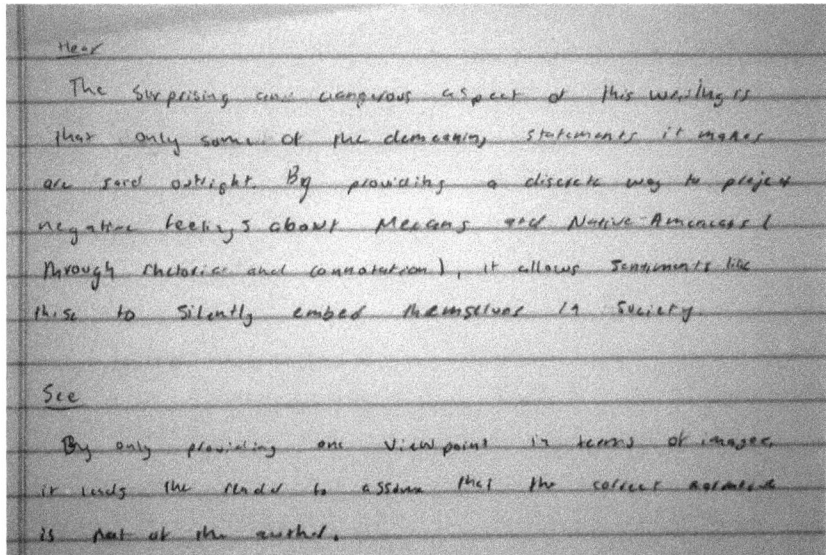

FIGURE 4.6. UofU second pair of responses

FIGURE 4.7. UofU third pair of responses

not "being used properly." He writes, "They decided to do 'what was right' and take land for themselves." This student goes as far as to argue, "The narrative of Harlingen is the Narrative of America," amplifying the top sentence, "Narrative is Racist." I would come to learn that Mormon/ism distinguishes itself from the narrative of America and the US that is accounted for elsewhere and otherwise.

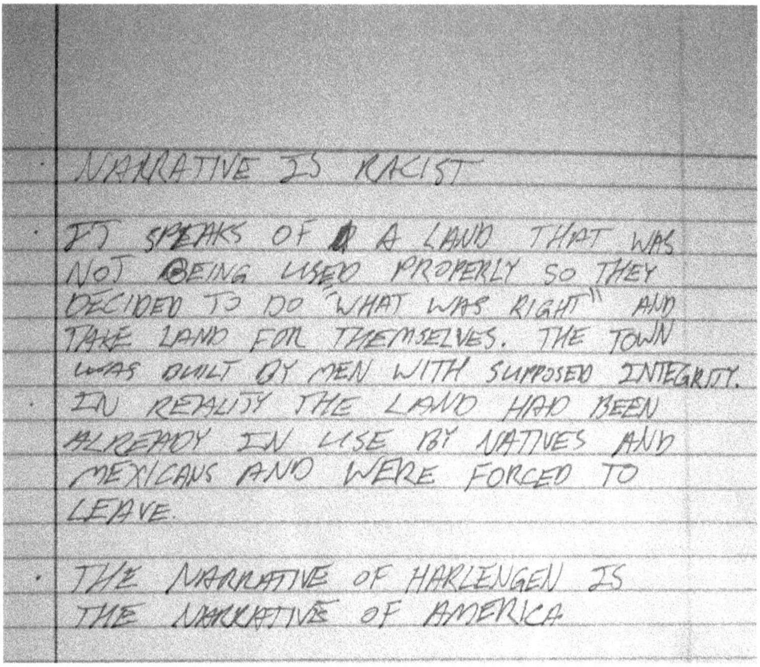

- NARRATIVE IS RACIST

- IT SPEAKS OF A LAND THAT WAS NOT BEING USED PROPERLY SO THEY DECIDED TO DO "WHAT WAS RIGHT" AND TAKE LAND FOR THEMSELVES. THE TOWN WAS BUILT BY MEN WITH SUPPOSED INTEGRITY.

- IN REALITY THE LAND HAD BEEN ALREADY IN USE BY NATIVES AND MEXICANS AND WERE FORCED TO LEAVE.

- THE NARRATIVE OF HARLENGEN IS THE NARRATIVE OF AMERICA

FIGURE 4.8. U of U third pair of responses

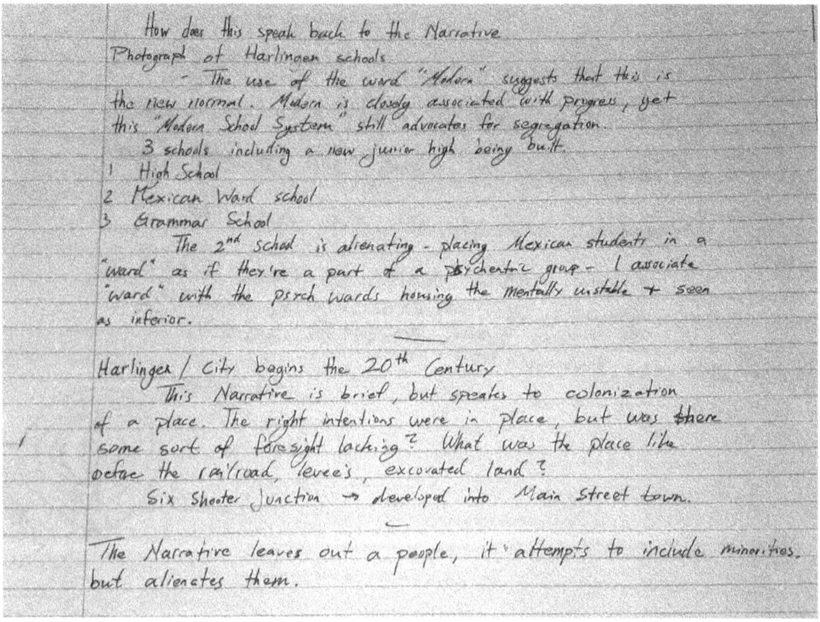

How does this speak back to the Narrative
Photograph of Harlingen schools
- The use of the word "Modern" suggests that this is the new normal. Modern is closely associated with progress, yet this "Modern School System" still advocates for segregation.
3 schools including a new junior high being built.
1 High School
2 Mexican Ward school
3 Grammar School
The 2nd school is alienating - placing Mexican students in a "ward" as if they're a part of a psychiatric group - I associate "ward" with the psych wards housing the mentally unstable + seen as inferior.

Harlingen / City begins the 20th Century
This Narrative is brief, but speaks to colonization of a place. The right intentions were in place, but was there some sort of foresight lacking? What was the place like before the railroad, levee's, excavated land?
Six Shooter Junction → developed into Main Street town.

The Narrative leaves out a people, it attempts to include minorities, but alienates them.

FIGURE 4.9. U of U trio of responses

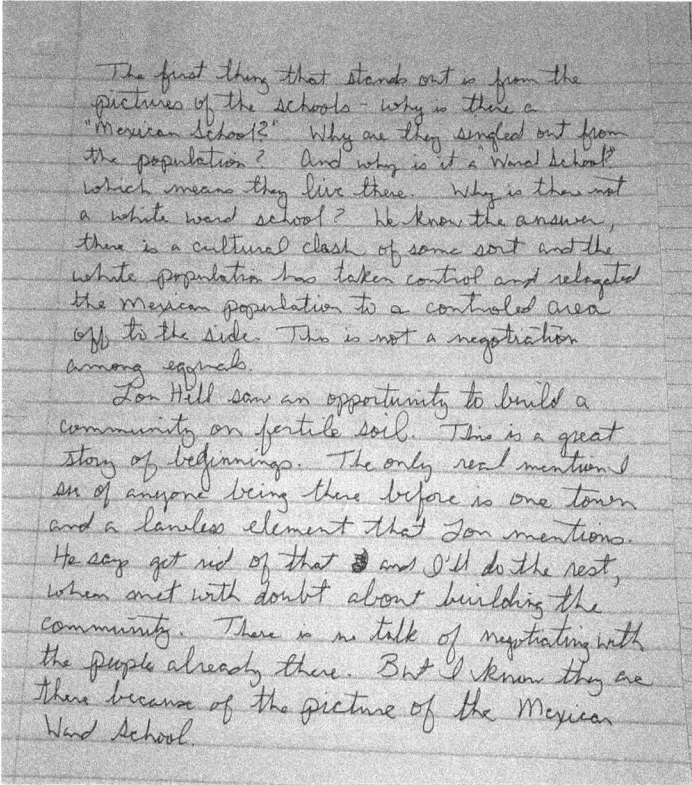

FIGURE 4.10. U of U trio of responses

Still, it was not lost on me that students were successfully locating, identifying, and naming hauntings and haunting situations.

There is also the trio of responses in figures 4.9, 4.10, and 4.11. One student gravitated to the word "Modern" and noted how "Modern is closely associated with progress," then contrasted it with the advocacy "for segregation." The student went on to claim that the second school, the "Mexican Ward School," was "alienating" because it placed "Mexican students in a 'ward.'" She applied her understanding of "ward" and determined that such a school was meant to "house" those perceived as "mentally unstable & seen as inferior." Another student asked, "Why is there a 'Mexican School'? Why are they singled out from the population? And why is it a 'Ward School'?" These are rhetorical questions: "We know the answer, there is a cultural clash of some sort and the white population has taken control and relegated the Mexican population to a controlled area off to the side." The third student summarized it all, "There is no place for

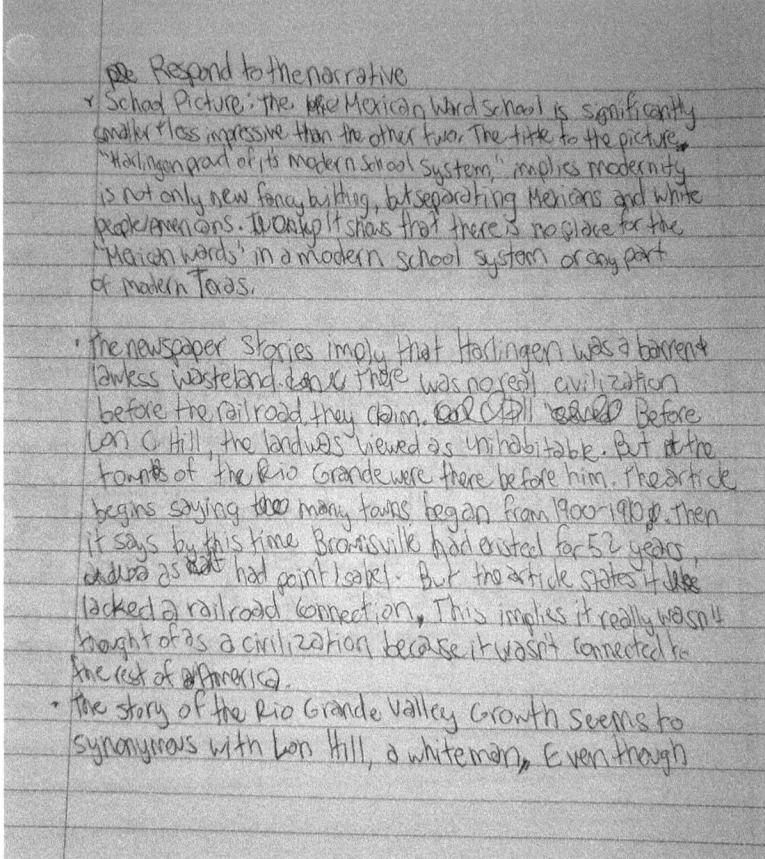

FIGURE 4.11. U of U trio of responses

the 'Mexican Wards'" in modernity. I believed then that the responses above underscored the idea that everything can be explained on the condition that one really wants an-other to understand. I also believe now that when "history" is not brought into the classroom as a critique to bear on something so familiar to them, students are more inclined to participate and display their own rhetorical dexterity in navigating complex issues such as modern/colonial and settlerizing mentalities and designs.

I believe many students were receptive to this class activity because vulnerability did not perceptively involve them. As conversations played out in the classroom, it helped set the stage for our exercise's rhetorical exchange, the social give-and-take embedded in the discourse of modern/colonial and settlerizing designs (see Dewey 1927). But others were suspicious as we worked collectively through the settler archives and guessed correctly that our dialogues on the "colonization of a place" would eventually shift from me to them. Such students sent a deliberative message. They applauded the settler-pioneer who very much took on the literacies, images-signs-sounds, and rhetorics of their own ancestors. One student shortly wrote, "The more I read, the more I have to applaud Lon C. Hill." This response was haunting though not suprising at the moment. I have both heard and endured much worse. He was applauding the settler-pioneer for covering the loss of sugar cane. But perhaps more hauntingly was how he celebrated Hill for establishing the LRGV's "first school for white children." The history of Utah, in this context, is not so much unalike as the LRGV, particularly with the rise of the Intermountain Indian School and the Indian Placement Program–Lamanite Placement Program. And that speaks to an important point in this book: that the contents of the *Archive* are shared-in, imported, expanded, and/or even disputed by *smaller archives of knowledges, understandings, feelings, and doings*, or the *working parts* of the *Archive*.

Other students echoed the sentiment of approval. One wrote, "Lon C. Hill is a noble, trail blazing man." How could they not when in Utah the church-settler is embraced, celebrated, and kept alive. Another noted, "It's not that what happened was a bad thing, even if it comes at the cost of something." Such a response underscores the projects of territorial and epistemological (ap/ex)propriation justified and rationalized as the price of modernization and human progress. Even though such responses were troublesome, they proved my point. Students can enact a *decolonial analytic* regardless of their race. The question of *how we will choose in the now to constitute ourselves otherwise in the face of an-other set of choices, options, and obligations-responsibilities* is not one of whether *white bodies can think decolonially* but of choice (or so I thought). Nonetheless, by all accounts, minus the accounting of the last responses, the exercise was a success. As we shifted the foci, my semester goal was to underscore why hauntings and haunting situations were unavoidable, how they un/settle all geo-and-body politics of knowledge and understanding ("I am where I do and think"), and what *choices* are demanded of all (Mignolo 2011a, 2011c, 2013).

By week three the language of the everyday shifted from Texas-me to Utah-Utahns. We focused on hauntings and haunting situations that marked settler arrival, settlement, and expansion in Utah: the various wars between church-settlers and American Indians/Native Americans (Battle at Fort Utah, Battle Creek Massacre, Black Hawk War, Wakara's War, Tintic War); the multiple treaties (Treaty of Abiquiú of 1849, Spanish Fork Treaty of 1865,

Fort Bridger Treaty of 1868); and *coloniality of instruction-and-curriculum* (the Intermountain Indian School, the Indian Placement Program–Lamanite Placement Program, and the Relief Society). And we talked about the war on information fought on the battlefield of cultural texts (see chapter 2) that constitute the material forms of public memory in Utah (Journal of Discourses, LDS General Conference Corpus, Founders Day/Pioneer Day; Temple Square; This Is the Place Heritage Park). My goal was to excavate the *public secret* in Utah, that which remains in land, memory, knowledge, and relationality after some *things* or some *one* has passed. It is at this point that I began to contemplate the state of conversations regarding FYC.

Current issues in Utah can be understood by *returning* to and *carefully reckoning* with its past. Racism against the *other*, segregation of the *other*, and discrimination against the LGBTQ+ community can all be traced back to church-settler epistemic racism, sexism, and heterosexism inseparable from a coloniality of knowledge-being. This is not an attack on the Church or a judgement on religion, as I have no particular opinion on either, but rather an observation that is couched in historical records and contemporary reporting. Settlerizing epideictic rhetoric—"I have a little Indian body and girl . . . I knew what our duties were . . . it will be some time before they [traits] are all erased from his memory" (MRM: Young 1855, 3:64); "partakers of civilizing the Indians" (MRM: Smith 1856, 3:287)—was being echoed by students. Perhaps, though, this speaks more to what modern/colonial and settlerizing designs have done to and made of some, more than anything. Overall, my goal then was to utilize the language of the everyday to both illuminate cultural and thinking program/ings and create *friction*. Their life questions, I believed, had been contaminated and altered by their law of *what* and *who* can be *in-common* and Man-Human-Rights; by their obligation-responsibility to carry out *work-instruction* as the premise for creating a path/passage to the *other*; and by their conditional welcoming of the *other* as a wor(l)ding aspiration for a future of the Me instead of the You/We. I initially interpreted their silence and whispering positively. *Friction* was at work! But so were many of the students.

Friction cuts both ways. Students perceived their foundation of self/selves, *stories-so-far*, and community were under attack by conversations appearing as totalistic rejections of cultural and thinking programs despite the fact that students were informed constantly that the point of conversation is to unsettle the settled. The following anecdotes, based on notes and end-of-day reflections with some students, feature familiar names. Ben had his hand raised, so I called on him. "I appreciate your lecture, but you don't know everything."

I agreed because I was still learning the history. "You know," Lynn chimed in, "our ancestors came here out of persecution" (see Veracini 2010). So often such rhetoric is invoked to cloak the darker, (supposedly) hidden side of settlement. She continued, "We are proud . . . Where we come from . . . begins with them." Their awareness of their archives and their rhetorical dexterity to narrativize it in unison was truly hauntingly remarkable. Andrew, who had a habit of talking in Castilian Spanish with me in an effort to "make me feel more comfortable speaking," added, "Nostros no somos racistas." Their responses exemplify community listening-in-action. I am greatly reminded of Royster (1996) here and her line of questioning: when and how do we listen and translate listening into action (38)? Because as I accounted for at the onset of this book, what it means for me to see, feel, listen, and even *do* cannot be grasped outside the spaces, places, and people familiar to me. So I listened, *to know* and *to learn*, but definitely not to be complicit.

Candace broke the silence that had blanketed the classroom. "This is fucked up! Really? Do you really believe that? Come on, really? You have a TV right? We can't keep believing we live in a bubble." She sat resiliently knowing that, like Norma, she would be ridiculed by her peers. After class Candace tells me she was no longer *choosing* to be "aligned" with her peers. Bryan broke the second silence caused by the distaste for expletives by members of the Church, "She is not wrong!" Class ended on that note. Norma, Candace, and Bryan asked if I could chat with them in my office. Based on their own research (on Whiteness Studies), which was a surprise to me as Norma had stated previously it was important to do things in the shadows, they had ideas on how to create *friction* within the relational practices of whiteness, white privilege, and white supremacy: *erasure, distance, deflection, epistemic ignorance, silence*, and *fragility*. I tried out various activities based on their recommendations between week four and week six (see Alcoff 2006; Bonilla-Silva 2001; DiAngelo 2011; Frye 1983; Mayo 2001; McIntosh 1997; Medina 2012; Sedgwick 1998; Sue 2003; Tuana 2006).

We tried the privilege walk (if you are from Utah; if your ancestors were handcart pioneers; if your history is taught). But I found this activity too trivial because so what if students are from Utah? Should we make students feel ashamed because of that fact? Is the point to make students feel ashamed or more informed? What other history would students learn in Utah's K–12 given the war on information and domination of its mediums of circulation? With similar queries, we tried the privilege for sale activity with an added focus on how religious views or heritage are reflected in the everyday. It underscored how privilege is rooted and inherited, embodied, experienced, and practiced through *community listening*. (Both of these activities, though one faired better than the other, make assumptions and thus foreclosed on *possibilities of new stories*.) All this meant that a public record could be created from scenes of the everyday and *stories-so-far*; that an archive could be investigated for how society adheres to, interacts with, and carries out histories, cultural memories, and literacy-rhetorical practices such records represent; and that a public record could be used as a medium for intervention and means to change *contents* and *terms* (see Mills 1997). So, I left the privilege talk behind and focused on an archival approach and theory of archival impressions.

There was a messy *friction* unfolding. On the one hand, I was resistant to being perceived as the *other* (as the basis for establishing propriety) and thus as a site of and for *work-instruction*. On the other hand, many students were resistant to activities and discussions. Sometimes, *friction* is resistance, which Tsing (2005) cautioned against initially. At this point, all an educator can do is hope-struggle to be the *fly in the elephant's nose*, a different kind of friction, one that gets in the way. Norma, Candace, Bryan, and I met in the shadows several more times to continue this hope-struggle of materializing such friction in the classroom. We decided it was a good idea to invite two white colleagues to the class who, for brevity, could perhaps create *friction* in church-settler stories given their familiarity and own teachings on such matters. It was our hope.

Perhaps, we thought, conversations would fare better coming from recognizable bodies. Jon Stone and Christie Toth visited class one day after I shared with them what was going. In previous semesters, just for some background, they had co-taught a course on Mormon/ism, and the student input was positive. They started the discussion that day with a handout that contained a narrative on epistemic racism in Utah. Students were invited to read it and sit with it. The narrative set a haunting tone, because it dealt with hauntings and haunting situations from the perspective of one racialized, minoritized, and marginalized person in Utah. Eventually, Jon and Christie played a recording of students reflecting on their own *stories-so-far*, a complement of sorts to the narrative. The goal, once more, was to both create *friction* and invite students to think about their own entanglements and complicities, an invitation issued by recognizable bodies.

The narrative created *friction*. The author will remain anonymous and will be referred to only as the narrator hereafter. I include snippets of the narrative below not to capitalize on it but purely to provide insight into the conversation that day between guest speakers and students. They are not a spokesperson for all things haunting in Utah, though much of what they share is felt within the bones of many today whose ancestors predate the arrival of the church-settler. There are haunting echoes of and resonances with Frederick Douglass in the palimpsestic narratives of epistemic violence they share. So, with care, I attempt to connect those timbres along with others. The narrator reflects on their unfamiliarity with "the meaning of racism" and attribute this to a hope, "I may have chosen to believe that racism no longer existed." The narrator wrote:

> We are brought up as children in the education system to believe that we are "one Nation under God, indivisible, with liberty and justice for all"; that is, until I became a victim of a racial motivated hate crime . . . that literally shattered my life to pieces one evening in Salt Lake City.

The narrator accounted for an inheritance that in essence is captured by the utterance "liberty and justice for all." These "truths," the Declaration of Independence tells us, are "self-evident." There is a "hope" within us all that indeed these "truths" are "self-evident." But the Pledge of Allegiance, like the Declaration of Independence and the US Constitution, were formed in the crucible of colonialism, a historical nexus of racist world views, institutions, and ends, and written for and by settlers-pioneers. The narrator to an extent, recognizes this but expresses a profound hope again that they could betray rhetorics of assemblage, an objectized palimpsest of identity, and be accepted as Human.

Douglass identified hauntings and haunting situations when he referred to the "old familiar spirits of colonialization" and a "colonizing scheme." Both attempted to expel American Indians and the Black-Brown communities from the lands (Douglass 1849). The perversion here, or, "native land talk nonsense," are the ways in which "settlers" view themselves as "natives" of the New World in contrast to those whom they see as a problem (Douglass 1894). The narrator's experience of being thrown from a building illustrates the viciousness of that viewpoint and the ways "dispensable" bodies become subject to physical violence. Again, we observe in the narrative below a profound hope that it is possible to mitigate a precarious subject position of becoming a subject *in* rather than being solely a subject *of* hauntings and haunting situations:

> I never would have imagined someone, whom I'd never even met, would be filled with so much hate for me that they wanted me dead just because of my skin color. I could not understand such evil intentions, because I treated everyone I met with the teachings of compassion for one another in this world that was taught to me from a young age by my Diné [Navajo] grandmother.

The above narrative resonates with Douglass's declaration that "hope is much needed" under the "dark clouds which lower above the horizon" (Foner 2000, 189). But it is at odds with the mythos of the pronouncement "We the people," the declaration that "all men are created equal," and the proclamation "one nation under God" in the Pledge of Allegiance. Douglass underscored this with his own emphasis on "your" ("National Independence"), "their" ("country"), and I ("am not included"). For "the Negro," he argued, the rights of life, liberty, and the pursuit of happiness are neither "self-evident" nor inherited. The "propriety of the nation," indeed, has and continues to be "startled" by the disregard and violence inflected upon the *other* (194, 196).

> I remember that night and the individuals I had to fight, until the crowd got big enough to where I was overwhelmed and would be eventually thrown from a building high enough to collapse my right lung, break my left femur, and shatter a portion of my spinal cord . . . When I woke up barely breathing, I tried to call out for help . . . I finally gained the attention of a couple long enough to notice me, only to disregard my pleas. My heart sank as I overheard the couple stating that I was probably just another dumb drunk Indian . . .

The above passage underscores a hope-turned-haunting situation: "I was probably just another dumb drunk Indian." It gets at Douglass's problem-dispensable people and the darker, (supposedly) hidden side of settlement that has long "startled" the "propriety" of the US. The narrator's fears were realized in that haunting moment, that the constitution of the people did not include all people; that all men are not men, nor are they created equal; that in Baldwedian terms the flag the *other* pledges allegiance to does not pledge allegiance to them. Those documents did not have them in mind. While at the hospital clinging to life, at the edge between life and death, the narrator wanted their "savage Native American blood . . . to die." Hope can be a powerful force until the body breaks, literally and symbolically. In their darkest hours, they heard the semblances of an idea, "Hang in there." Today, they are still learning how to live otherwise (Derrida 1994b; Foner 2000). The class sat there in silence, and for a moment I thought many of them were moved by such a haunting account, an account that was but several years back.

Jon and Christie transitioned into playing a video of students reflecting on *This Is the Place Heritage Park* directly after the reading. The park commemorates Brigham Young's words, "This is the right place" ("This is the Place"). It was architected to "remember the past, entertain the present, and educate the future" (Dahl 2006). Like other material forms of public memory in Utah, it keeps alive the past and certain ghosts. The Days of '47 website provides rationales for why Mormons return to, center, and situate the past, the dead, inheritances, and dwellings to the politics of their present: "We are the beneficiaries of all the labors they [Mormon pioneers] performed"; "Let's help the rising generation to appreciate who they are, and where they come from, and what they have"; "Let's help them believe that they too can be pioneers" (Days of '47 2018). An awareness of a cultural archive and an ability to narrativize it, again, is truly hauntingly remarkable. Two narratives emerged from the video, which I have synthesized below:

> I remember going to This is the Place monument all the time when I was a little girl. We used to go and hike up to This is the Place monument up on the hill that says this is where Brigham Young decided to say this is where we are stopping as pioneers. For me that was a big deal, because I had great-great aunts and uncles who had died along the trail trying to get to the Salt Lake Valley. It was kind of a ceremonious occasion to go back every year and to celebrate our history. They settled the entire area according to the narrative I've always been raised with: they built up this area from nothing . . . the desert. That is kind of [a] cool thing about the actual land, you can turn and see the Valley and you can see what has come of it, of their works.

> I've been going there since I was a kid. I usually went with family. We would go around and read the plaques. It was more of pondering and more like reverence. These are ancestors. Whenever I went up . . . it was like remembering and reminiscing. This is Zion—this is the place; this is the promised land.

The above narratives confirm the role of stories—literacies, images-signs-sounds, rhetorics—in the epistemological, ideological, and rhetorical war on information at the micro level. The video featured students observing how "Native Americans" are depicted as "good Indians." Another called attention to how "they didn't give him [Chief Washakie] the opportunity" to tell his own narrative. One student observed how the "native village" on the park is on the opposite side, "This is the physical representation of like marginalizing a people." The student continued, "I grew up in the LDS religion and it is dear to my heart, but I know we are not perfect, and a lot of things happen . . . lots of coming here and taking over." Below is a narrative on a responsibility *otherwise*:

> I felt responsible, and not personally responsible for the deeds of others, but personally responsible for not being aware and not wanting to know because there is a part of you that goes I don't want to know this I don't want to research it . . . I want to think Indians were friends with the little cowboys

and everything was great. I felt personally responsible. I felt the land no matter where I went carried stories that I needed to know. I went through a serious identity crisis. No one wants to think that your family members, that your heritage that you're so proud of, that you take pride in, led to hurting so many people. You want to think that this land was here, and that God did design it just for you. How awesome does that feel and how sucky is it to come to realize, no, this land was stolen, and there is blood on it.

The video does four things for me. First, it highlights everyday human projects at the center of material forms of public memory in Utah extending to the micro level. Second, it confirms students' intellectual capacities to explore, investigate, analyze, interpret, determine, and translate meaning from public records of and from scenes of cultural and thinking programs. Third, it demonstrates the affordances of *friction*. And lastly, it underscores choice: *How will we choose in the now to constitute ourselves otherwise in the face of an-other set of choices, options, and obligations-responsibilities?* This activity encouraged a strong hope in me because if students in the video could recognize, acknowledge, and reflect on how they dwell in wounded/wounding spaces-places and inherit haunted/haunting *stories-so-far*, the students in my class could do the same.

Jon and Christie held a Q&A session—insight (what was thought provoking); remaining questions; identification (what resonated or did not)—directly after the video. Jon and Christie wrote three questions on the whiteboard. And then they generally asked, *What did you learn from the presentation and the video?* Much of the class did not want to participate. Norma and Candace confirmed this during my office hours. "I don't know what I was supposed to take away from all this," they reported hearing. Perhaps Bryan heard this too, because he stood up that day and shared a reflection: "I want to say that I feel uncomfortable. This makes me feel uncomfortable." Jon, Christie, and I listened, *to know* and *to learn*. But many in the class did not. Bryan continued: "But I've realized that if I am uncomfortable by this discussion, it is because I have not come to terms with it." He claimed that while "these things"—by which he meant hauntings and haunting situations—were not unique to Utah or Utahns, it was important that the class have these conversations. I ended the class there, thanked Jon and Christie, and headed to my office to decompress, reflect, and brainstorm with Norma, Candace, and Bryan, who showed up a bit after.

Students reflected in blog posts, as they had been doing throughout the semester that week. Unfortunately, they became a *gathering space* for students and a hotbed for toxic rhetoric. Again, sometimes, friction is just and solely resistance. Some notable standouts include: "I am still living in a bubble

> The issue of race and racism is an incredibly vital one for all of us to discuss. There are many people in our society that would deny its existence because it does not affect them, but this is something that is central to the problem. Some people deny the existence of this problem because it is something they are blind to. Others deny its existence because they benefit from it, and they don't want to admit that they like benefitting from this system. I don't think that either of these things are okay. It is not excusable to be ignorant to this anymore. White ignorance perpetuates racism and white supremacy. This ignorance is something that is afforded to only white people. It is not possible for people of color to be ignorant of the racism in our society. It negatively affects their daily lives. Silence about racism also perpetuates it. Many white folks purposefully ignore and do not address the subject of racism, and rationalize this by telling themselves that they are not racist, so they are not the problem. This is not as true, however, as many of us would like to believe. Being silent about a system that you benefit from at the expense of others is the problem. It is important to check your white privilege, and important to examine the ways that you may be benefiting from it. Racism and white supremacy are things that I believe are deeply woven into the fabric of this country.
>
> ↵ Reply

FIGURE 4.12. A snapshot of UofU student blog posts

> Racism definitely exists in the world we live in today and it is because of perceptions of race. I have experienced racism several times in Utah and it is horrific to go through that even as someone who isn't being targeted. Racism is definitely an issue in the Salt Lake City area and those who say it isn't an issue are just plain ignorant. They would claim it is not an issue because it is not affecting them personally. Racism is also an issue at the University of Utah, we all saw the posters, we looked at them in class. Some people at the U are clearly racist, but did those people who put the posters up suffer any consequences (I honestly don't know)? The issues on campus definitely need to be addressed.
>
> It is very important to address racism and/or discrimination because it is a very real problem. We address other problems such as climate change, poverty in third world countries, etc. but most classrooms don't usually discuss racism because it *is* so relevant and it's also a problem we can solve fairly easily in a small community. The classroom is a very effective place to start these conversations if our ultimate goal is to bring change and end racism.

FIGURE 4.13. A snapshot of UofU student blog posts

called Utah"; "I wasn't surprised to be told that Utah was stolen, I questioned why it was made as a big deal . . . I believe those that settled in Utah had a type of validation because of the circumstances America was in at the time"; "Racism is a problem in Salt Lake City and at the University. It isn't necessarily a problem that impacts my daily life"; "I have seen very little evidence of racism"; "In discussing politically-fraught topics." Norma, Bryan, and Candace

> I'd like to confirm and validate your first impression of Utah... Whether we'll all admit it or not, white people are expected to avoid interacting with people of color, unless they're serving us, below us in the social hierarchy, or (if you're Mormon) a member of your church. The only brown or Black Mormons I've ever met were adopted ("saved") from another country as babies and indoctrinated into the LDS church alongside their white siblings. That may be a cruel way of conveying that, but I have to agree with you when you say that "ignorance won't diminish if there is a lack of discussion and education on the matter", and I think that softening the reality at this point would be a lie. It's time to face ignorance and ongoing colonization.
>
> ↩ Reply

FIGURE 4.14. A snapshot of UofU student blog posts

also responded (figures 4.12, 4.13, 4.14, and 4.15). They were accompanied by Walter, a member of the Church, who together voiced concern about the behavior of their peers.

The collective responded to many of the posts. When one student argued that Utahns live "sheltered lives [not] exposed to hate crimes, racial violence or discrimination," Norma responded, "Racial slurs are constantly thrown about in daily conversations." When another student claimed racism "doesn't exist," Bryan replied by pointing out their "privilege" and discussing how they "inherit" a system "created by people who ... saw opportunities to assert social and economic power over people existing" from which they "benefit" from. Privilege, Candace (with Bryan echoing) argued, "manifests itself through the ability to ignore." In one more example, a student writes that he "did not ask for this," which Amy answered by stating, "Racism is something that is woven in with our culture and government and social interactions," and reminding others of how common it is to hear someone "divide" or "describe" the city in terms of the "races." (Amy, however, is an anomaly, who expressed later that though she was compelled to speak out then and there, she could not continue to do so because of what was at stake.) Candace's blog post stands out here as well.

Candace responded to other posts (figure 4.16). When a student wrote about being "naïve," "sheltered," taught who to "associate with," and "uncomfortable," she retorted, "Regardless of whether or not they [the conversations] feel comfortable it is important to have these conversations." In the post Candace

> This week we heard the presentation about the settlement of the Salt Lake Valley and the influence that race and racial divides played in the future of Utah and the history that was written. The discussion we had in class was different from the others we have had in the past because this one hit home in a very personal way: the focus was on the Mormon migrants and how the LDS church has effected the culture here. I personally am an active member of the LDS church and the LDS community right here in Salt Lake so I was taught church history very different from those not of my faith. I really appreciated the insights that we gained, especially that we weren't tearing down the church and teachings specifically and were talking about how we can remember those who inhabited this valley long before the Mormons arrived and be more inclusive to people of every background.
>
> From my earliest memories of being taught about those who settled the Salt Lake Valley I can recall feelings of gratitude for those in my family who crossed the plains to come here, awe in the extreme conditions they faced on their journey, and sadness for the Mormons in the Midwest who were being persecuted, murdered, raped, driven from their homes, and terrorized by government officials (see Lilburn Boggs, Missouri Executive Order 44) for what they believed. A little bit later in my days of public education we were taught about many of the peoples that had inhabited this continent for thousands of years but still saw a very White side of it. There wasn't much mention of the native tribes being robbed of lands or even the slaves that the pioneers brought with them. I felt the sense of the great injustice that had been done to these various groups of people.
>
> Racism is in the minds of individuals; the way we perceive people is reflected in how we treat them. As I mentioned in class, I felt very much a "call to arms" with the desire to see change in my community. The only was we can eradicate the racism in the individual is through education and love, to see the world from the perspective of others. I personally want to be more educated on the issues that are current and spread awareness of what needs to change in our communities.
>
> 9/26

FIGURE 4.15. A snapshot of UofU student blog posts

expressed "hope" that peers would listen to know, learn, and be *otherwise*. She understood family, community, and religion can have immense power over self, being, and agency. Candace sympathized with LDS people in the video and how "uncertainty" is intimidating. But she also leaned into critiquing peers who "blatant[ly] reject[ed]" information and relied on their "Utah culture bubble," which in other posts she titled "ridiculous." Candace called out "people

> I understood why LDS people remained with their faith even when faced with this information. As someone who grew up in an intensely religious household, I can relate to how that becomes a part of your identity, something you cannot just throw away in the face of uncertainty. However what I struggle to empathize with is the blatant rejection of the information we were given in the name of your faith. If history (facts) tell us that natives were pushed out of the land, then there needs to at least be some level of belief that natives were pushed out of the land. I get almost angry when people hear this informtion and immediatley dismiss it as garbage and then fall back on the folk stories that their grandparents told them when they were kids. That is literally the manifestation of whitewashing in contemporary culture. I think that quite frankly, our class needs to be having these discussions more often. I think that the Utah culture bubble that some people have grown up in needs to be popped and there needs to be some intense self-reflection as to how we evaluate what is true and what is false.
>
> On a side note. I also think that these discussion posts have become a breeding ground for racist microaggressions. I read through my classmates' posts today and was pretty concerned about some of the things being said. At the level that we can probably all agree that our class is not super comfortable talking about race, and is also not super educated about racism and discrimination, I think that we tread dangerous waters when we let people freely post whatever the hell they feel like on these write posts. I strongly feel that there needs to be follow up discussion with certain students about the way that they discuss race, I am not calling people racist. I understand where they are at, I grew up in an extremely conservative household raised by parents with some pretty problematic social beliefs, and the beginning of college was a scary time for me when it came to these discussions. However, I learned most when people pulled me aside in a safe environment and explained to me why some of my beliefs were not as correct as I had thought they were. I don't think that drowning students in information contrary to their current beliefs will make them change. I think it will have the opposite effect, I already see it happening on the write post, people banding together to defend their beliefs and dismiss what we are learning in class.

FIGURE 4.16. A snapshot of Candace's blog post

banding together to defend their beliefs and dismiss what we are learning in class" and those who transformed posts into a "breeding ground for racist microaggressions." This post echoed others where she called for "intense self reflection," because people "aren't born racist . . . they are taught."

The collective emailed me later in the evening when blog posts were due. Collectively, they called for continued *friction*. The throughline of each of their responses to peers was that "Racism is the system," that racism "permeates the structure[s] we function within," that racism has been "the 'norm,'" and what is demanded of all is nothing short of "an epistemological reorientation as well as a complete restructuring of the systems we function within." These, again, are their words and not mine. I agreed with their request. Candace had another request, though, that they lead a blog post anonymously. She wrote, "I am not a scholar, I am barely an undergrad," but "our class primarily struggles with issues of race." Candace was surely hesistant. I assured her that she was under no obligation to write such posts. Candace expressed concern that peers are emboldened to speak "more freely without regard for how their comments may affect other students." She wrote, "To 'listen' to an entire lecture on how individuals of color were literally slaughtered, raped, and then displaced and proceed to write a discussion post claiming that those things (1) didn't happen at all or (2) were justified because Mormons were oppressed first is gross." I agreed to Candace's request, once again, however, reminding her that at any moment she could back out.

The language of the everyday figured prominently in the classroom between week seven and the last week of the semester. I made the choice, which was hardly a choice at all, but a demand, to continue to shift and adapt. I scrapped the final project and replaced it with a new one on the fly, "Stories-So-Far and the Possibilities of New Stories," which was based on, first, my readings of Massey (2005) and Rohrer (2016); second, my orientation to *being-and-becoming* in the world; and third, my research interests on archives and archival impressions. The assignment underscored the importance of stories and storytelling from an archival approach. I felt this would jive well with students, given their keen awareness of both. The assignment, moreover, would invite students to consider the role of genre and how music speaks to social conditions in varying ways. The assignment laid bare some tenets of what would have become *deep rhetoricity*: a *return* to spaces-places where one does and thinks via memories that call; a *careful reckoning* with (*community*) *listening*; and commitments *otherwise* (*enduring tasks*). *Stories-so-far* and *possibilities of new stories* would be its anchors. It invited as much as it appealed for the initiating of archival impressions *otherwise*.

The final project was imperfect (in hindsight, it would become a vital happening in the development of an *epistemological framework for the haunted* that I return to in the last chapter). We tried out other activities to bolster emphasis on *returns* to and *careful reckonings* with hauntings, inheritances, and dwellings. The groundwork of a *corrido-ing approach* and projects of unsettling and a decolonial option returned us to genres of music (corridos, rock, rap, country) and cultural texts (*TRA*, the Digital Austin Papers, *JoD*, General Conference Corpus). Such language of the everyday would aid us in efforts to locate *community listening*, situate scenes of the everyday and *stories-so-far* (hauntings, the past, the dead, inheritances, and dwellings), and name ways we adhere to, interact with, and carry out histories, cultural memories, and literacy-rhetorical practices. These activities situated us on the role that stories and literacies, images-signs-sounds, and rhetorics have played in constructing settler sites, constituting haunted/haunting communities, and maintaining wounded/wounding spaces-places. The final assignment, overall, entered a simple premise: if literacies, images-signs-sounds, and rhetorics have been used to fashion a modern/colonial world, they can be utilized to wor(l)d a future *otherwise*.

Our focus on church-settler inventions and imaginary sparked some haunting responses. For many students, *Other-as-Same* relations were real, and they believed it was truly their obligation and responsibility to carry out *work-instruction*. "Who are you," Andrew and Christopher both asked, "to say they don't [require the word]?" For many students, racism cut both ways. "Mexicans, Blacks," Lynn exclaimed, "are racist too." She continued by telling me the course was not "meant to speak about this kind of stuff," by which she meant the rhetorics of epistemic racism. Again, at this point, all I hoped-struggled to be was the *fly in the elephant's nose*. The goal for the final project was to create an opportunity for students to gather their ancestral *stories-so-far* and collect evidence to support the verisimilitude of them. My train of thinking? That the inevitable *friction* would hopefully aid them in considering *an-other* set of choices, options, and obligations-responsibilities. And herein lies the value for me of writing and rhetoric. But human work and projects are complex, complicated, and messy, especially when other human beings are involved.

Final Projects and Literacy History Interviews

The point of the final project was to encourage students to create a public record and use it as a powerful medium for intervention and means for (re)invention. Threads emerged with a *decolonial analytic*. First, the war on information extends to the façade of a "Utah bubble" that attempts to cloak the darker, (supposedly) hidden side of a church-settler *epistemic system*, *design*, and the everyday human projects of *work-instruction*. It was from students in part that I discerned how *coloniality of instruction*-and-*curriculum* extends well beyond the classroom and the traditional image of the educator. Second, the rehearsal of corporeal exercises ensures that hauntings, the past, the dead, inheritances, and dwellings remain part of the politics of the present in Utah (in this way the living and those supposedly half-dead have something in common). Third, not by chance but by design, students adhere to, interact with, and carry out histories, cultural memories, and literacy-rhetorical practices that church-settler archives represent. People are the affective channels of rhetorical transmission of and for hauntings and haunting situations. And fourth, family, community, and religion have immense power over self, being, and agency. Because why would they not? These threads amplify the role that literacies, images-signs-sounds, and rhetorics have played at the macro level and what they have done to and made of some at the micro level.

I was not sure what to expect given the semester. I became hopeful when all twenty-three students submitted audio recordings and when I encountered audio from Jessica, who stated, "I am who I am because of my family and community." That is the import of *community listening* as a concept, theory, and methodological term. But, indeed, students echoed familiar sentiments expressed throughout the semester: "We live in a sheltered community" (Andrea); "I was never exposed to racism" (Tina); "I said this in class, but this class isn't the space" (Lynn); "I'd rather not participate in these conversations" (Andrew); and "I was always told they ['the Indian'] chose to live in a different area, that they wanted to live as far away from us as they could" (Timothy). For them, the final project was an extension of my hope-struggle that it may be possible for me to be the *fly in the elephant's nose*. And they would not stand for that. For others like Norma and Candace (and Bryan and Walter), the final project afforded the occasion to unsettle the settled and haunt back. The following are based on final projects and literacy history interviews with Norma and Candace.

NORMA

Norma is a white student who grew up in the Wasatch Back and in a very conservative family. "At least in Utah," they note, "that means very religious as well." Norma was a former member of the Church. They tell me they remember their parents always sharing stories of their ancestors, heritage, and struggles and hopes. "We are a testimony," Norma informs me, "to what they set out to accomplish way back when." They recount for me how their *stories-so-far* (of who they were, where they came from, and what they did/do) were important to their family, community, and church. "[They] were stories of us, stories that remind us of our hardships and also our accomplishments," Norma continues. "They taught us," they proceed to say, "to be proud of and celebrate our identity, heritage, and ancestors." Now, home was not the only space and place where church-settler *stories-so-far* circulated and flowed.

Norma informs me that throughout K–12 the church-settler is embraced, celebrated, and kept alive. "At my school," they share, "there is a required class called Utah history. It actually translates to Church history. In my particular case, my teacher was a local bishop." Norma looks at me in awe at this point to emphasize (*coloniality of*) settler-centered *instruction-and-curriculum*. They recount his claim, "There is nothing bad about our pioneers, they seized their God-given right, a right to the land, and moved to this land [Utah], which was already destined for them. Yes, natives were here, but after hearing the word of our pioneers, they moved out to share the land; they relocated themselves." (This is not unlike the story told throughout K–12 in Texas, where the settler pioneer is embraced, celebrated, and kept alive for their heroic triumph over "the Mexicans.") Norma was in awe because she at last understood one role of modern/colonial and settlerizing education. Hegel (1896) and others long saw pedagogy and education as a pillar to dominate the *terms* and *contents* of relation-ing, managing knowledge, and controlling epistemic obedience. Norma tells me my class was the first to go against "the status quo." They note:

> You started talking about that flier on the first day of class. Like many in the class, I didn't think twice about it. Why should I? I didn't do it. It doesn't affect me. When you asked us to think about what sound the flier made, I remember thinking to myself, what sound? You then went on to talk about how all stories are told for a reason and that all stories have some kind of effect. As class went on that day, you introduced us to all kinds of stories. The friends I was sitting with, they too told their own stories. I began to think about what you meant by stories get told for a reason. As they began to laugh about how natives were hurt and killed, I wondered why we are not told those stories and I wondered why someone getting hurt and killed was something to laugh about. So I said something both to them and the class. I was afraid. I really was.

The passage above illustrates several points. First, that even though Norma had long left the Church and applied a critical lens against it, they benefited from not having to think "twice" about racist happenings. Here we discern privilege. Second, that even though Norma was no longer part of the Church, they maintained relations with its members, however fragile they were because of their departure from the Church. Here we marginally gain insight on the ways whiteness can rally the "us" in a perceived dichotomous and oppositional context regardless of deviations. It reminds me of Ratcliffe (2005): "White functions overtly as a racial category that is privileged even if all white people do not share identical social and economic privileges" (14). Third, that though they spoke out in class, previous experiences with being publicly ridiculed made them afraid. Here we witness the perils of human work in the class.

Recall Norma wanted to remain in the shadows. Ultimately, they saw this as privilege. So they took the themes of unsettling, *friction*, and haunting back into their communities. "We didn't see eye to eye on things," Norma informs me. Their parents were dismissive of them already since their "coming out" and more so with our class discussions. "I asked them," they explain, "how can we [students] be resistant to stories that introduce us to our other histories." Norma shared with their parents, they account for me, how the history of Utah is depicted with a "nice" narrative, two populations "shar[ing] the land" and one eventually choosing to "hand over the land" so that the other could "enjoy it" and so that they could "live as far away as possible." Norma reflects for their parents on past experiences:

> We spoke about those who came here, but little time was spent on those already here. I didn't question it. I didn't question why we always spoke about pioneers first, and then, the "native" folks. I put into quotations "native" because we actually never identified these people other than "native."

Norma deviates and pivots a bit at this point to redirect their reflections to me. Something did not sit well with them that their classmates would laugh about the violence that took place in Utah. "And it feels like this is ok," Norma tells me, "because we like to believe our past is good." Norma reflects:

> We go out in the world and pretend like everyone is equal, but at home, in car rides, and amongst friends, we don't actually believe that. We tell these stories of how we are accepting of others, but we are not. I've seen how we are to people of the LGBTQ, Latino, and African American community. You know, the only brown or black church members I know were adopted from another country as babies and indoctrinated into the Church alongside their white siblings. I've grown tired of it, tired of the ignorance too; it is time to face ignorance. We tell these stories of persecution, settlement, and pioneers, but we don't tell the stories of all whom we hurt when we came to Utah. I know we did . . . And learning how to face that truth, still facing it today, that forever has changed me.

Norma's reflections above, which echo that of their class post (figure 4.14), provide crucial insights. First, that a coloniality of *instruction-and-curriculum* in the classroom both intentionally utilizes social identities ("Indians" or

"Natives") to create absences-silences and pursues epistemic obedience. Here we discern human work and projects. Second, that *instruction-and-curriculum* extends into the nuclear family. Here we gain one view both on how Utahnniceness (and politeness) and the rhetorics of persecution attempt to cloak a darker, (supposedly) hidden side of Utahn hospitality and settlement. Third, that even as Norma is no longer part of the Church, they slip into the "we" when accounting for community. This reminds me a bit of Yang (2017), because while the posterity of church-settlers may not "at all times enjoy the full privileges available" to them (10), there is most certainly a benefit gained in community contexts from such an inheritance in Utah. Fourth, that facing the truth can be both difficult and life changing. Here we can assess the affordances of the projects of unsettling and a decolonial option. Norma's work extended outward from home to classroom.

Norma requested permission to research and give a presentation on racism and segregation in Utah. They shared with me that after Trump got elected, people spray-painted "illegals" on the apartments where "the Hispanics live" in their city. Before I could ask, Norma explained to me, "There is not a big Latino population here [Park City]. So people know where nonwhite people live; they lived on their side and we lived on ours." Norma confesses it did not "bother" them at the time. Because they grew up in a community that normalized racist happenings. Norma recounts for me how family members would "mumble comments about Obama's skin color, complain about too many people of color on the [sports] field, or complain about the corn man even after buying one from him." They note, "This is the kind of story I am a part of." I can neither be sure of nor say what caused their unsettling but they had made the choice to no longer be complicit in that story. Norma gave their presentation near the end of the semester.

Norma presented a layered conversation on racism and segregation in "Mormon-land." It was a play on, they tell me, Paredes's (1958a) "Gringoland" (25), which students had read portions of as we defined early conceptualizations of settler colonialism. A central question they had the class contemplate and deliberate was, "How did we get here?" Of course, the majority of the class knew this content of their archives completely and could narrate it in an instance. But that was not the point of the question. A main appeal Norma made to peers was to be researchers of their everyday, "Do your own research." They argued that it is "not enough to not be racist" and yet "let shit happen anyway." They turn to two student blog posts they had printed. Without reading the names, Norma reads them to the class:

of [her] faith." She continues to share with me what resonated with her in Walter's class post by reading a snippet of it (see figure 4.15).

> From my earliest memories of being taught about those who settled the Salt Lake Valley I can recall feelings of gratitude for those in my family who crossed the plains to come here, awe in the extreme conditions they faced on their journey, and sadness for the Mormons in the Midwest who were being persecuted, murdered, raped, driven from their homes, and terrorized by government officials for what they believed.

The very act of reading this passage to me underscores an awareness of how one lives amid archives. Candace explains that she "never knew anything different." Many of the students I continue to work with today have this in common. She then informs me that she was taught to only "associate with other members of the same church and faith." They internalize, in other words, an us/them register and then adhere or cohere to rhetoric of *otherness* and difference. The Utahn cultural bubble was real for Candace, "I didn't need to know another way, other people, other religions, other cultures." This, however, is a bit misleading, as I reminded Candace, because part of their *work* involves a degree of knowing *other-things*. She was taught that in "God's plan, everyone started out on the [same] playing field." If others were struggling, Candace continued, "it was because of their own doing, not because others, racism, and definitely not God." A very bootstrap but also privileged outlook. She tells me, "I took these stories as truth. They were facts. That is all I knew." She rhetorically asks, "How can you be self-reflexive about contributing to a problem that you have been taught is really not a problem?"

Schooling played a pivotal role in Candace's life. She recounts for me typical discussions throughout K–12: "When he [Young] laid eyes upon the Valley, he declared 'This is the place.'" As noted previously, whether or not this is the precise phrasing attributed to Young is a moot point. The action/ing(s) of church-settlers and posterity would cement the adage into a reality. These were stories, Candace explained, "that we are taught, that tell us about who we are and of how we got here." She continued, "The one-sided story . . . is taught through[out] the curriculum." Those stories had a profound impact on her: "The stories that I had learned in school did shape the way I felt about this place [Utah] and others [beyond her community]." This is not a cop-out reflection but rather the beginning of coming to terms. Candace let me know those were the *stories-so-far* that she brought into the classroom. Like Norma, she expresses to me how my class was the first she had taken to go "against the grain." Candace notes:

> Kids in the class weren't willing to talk about or hear about racism. [Including me at first.] This upset me greatly, till I couldn't hold back. Unfortunately, people in my class are racist. I know this personally as I spoke with them during and after class. Others, only a few though, noticed it too. I even called them out in class. This made everyone uncomfortable. I quoted what they said. Without saying names, I know you know who I am talking about. Even in doing this work of calling them out, I felt bad. I didn't do it to receive a gold star.

Candace is referencing the day she spoke up-out ("This is fucked up!"). She admitted that it was unlike her to use expletives. It is sort of seen as unbecoming of a "good Mormon." In addition to what has been cited from that day, she also stated to peers, "We are only told the good things. Today, we are situated between bad things that happened and good things that happened." The passage above makes several striking points. First, there is a blatant disregard for racist happenings among those in the class. Second, membership in a church does not automatically mean all complicities are equivalent. Third, there comes a point when epistemic ignorance defies all rationality and justification and all that is left to contend with is epistemic racism. I see the expletive "this is fucked up" as the absolute limits of the spectator who realizes the spectacle unfolding before them can be unsettled if only they speak up.

Candace too took the themes of unsettling, *friction*, and haunting back into their communities. "We are part of the problem," she reflects. "I am part of this family structure," Candace recounts telling her parents, "that pushes really heavily that racism and oppression do not exist, while [we] know that it does." She wanted her parents to know that stories "affect everyone." But they did not take too kindly to it all. Candace shares with me that normally they would "ask for intellectual respect," but when it came down to dialoguing about racism, "they shrug[ed] it off." She explains to me how they began to think I was "targeting them," both because I was an "outsider" and did not understand their "complicated" life stories. Candace, at this point, begins to deviate from their reflection and pivots a bit to address me:

> You know, Dr. García, your talk on the gift of giving was right on. We are like the story of Santa Clause. He gives gifts—he provides hope. While Santa Claus is not real, our story, in [our] religion is real. We give back—we bring hope and a more positive outlook. I don't want to be in a world without hope. While giving is a truth, in the religious sense, what happens when we learn that giving is not always good?

> I agree with what you said about White Guilt. I see people letting this make them incredibly guarded and defensive about topics like this one. I was a bit alarmed listening to and reading some of the comments that people had after the guest speaker presentation this last week. I think that it is really important to acknowledge where these feelings of white guilt come from, and to let them help us to act in such a way that does not perpetuate the things that our ancestors and community members have done in the past, and I think it is equally important to make sure that your white guilt does not make you defensive or dismissive.
>
> ↩ Reply

FIGURE 4.17. Candace's response post

The passage above is significant for several reasons. First, because in the process of coming to terms with the gift of giving, Candace realizes that she has been naïve. It was almost reminiscent, one could say, of the conversation that took place at the SLC airport. Second, in contending with what the Church gives, she contends with the reality that the *ends* of that gift may not always be good. What all is involved in traveling—in moving—from one place to another to give the gift and what are the implications of the gift itself? Third, it demonstrates the affordances of *friction*. "It's hard for me to imagine," Candace tells me, "just being so unaware ... or at least we act like we are unaware." For me this brings into question—or should I say, it unsettles—the idea of epistemic ignorance. But though she informs me that she aims to change, she also reminds me that "leaving" the Church is "not an option." (I assured Candace this was not the point at all.) It is a difficult choice for Candace, but there is too much at "stake" in the face of such "uncertainty." By uncertainty, she means the potential to lose it all, and for what, for being "woke" or an "activist," as she put it. Now, I must say, critical Mormons are not uncommon, and they illustrate the possibilities of unsettling and decolonizing knowledge-being while remaining part of institutions that haunt.

Candace's work alternated between home and school. She and I chatted days after Jon and Christie's visit. Recall Candace's blog post that sounded off on peers "banding together" and creating "breeding grounds for racist microaggressions" (see figure 4.16). She was again frustrated with what she observed as white objectivity, white ignorance, and white guilt (figure 4.17).

Specifically, Candace was struck by how one student both claimed racism is "politically fraught" and argued for more "objective pieces of evidence" instead of "personal anecdotes." The whole class knew what that meant. Their post garnered support: "I strongly agree with ... your argumentation points, especially the points that talk about anecdotes and personal belief." She was taken aback by how peers ascribed to white guilt:

> "The guilt prevents us from addressing such topics."

> "White guilt just cause[s] people to not speak on sensitive topics."

> "It [the presentation] made me feel very uncomfortable"

"Privilege," Candace explains, "manifests itself through the ability to ignore the oppression that does not affect oneself," expanding on an initial thought expressed but not fully unpacked in a response to a classmate's blog post. She takes issue with epistemic standpoints cited throughout this chapter, which are noteworthy. First, they provide insight on the perception of *whom* racism affects. As if white folks are not part of a racialized society. Second, epistemic standpoints redirect the onus on the *other* to provide objective evidence. As one of Candace's response post states, "The parameters of objectivity ... justify the erasure of authors who speak to the firsthand experiences of marginalized populations." Third, they trivialize discussions. White guilt and fragility are methods of evasion. Building on Norma's and Bryan's critiques on white guilt, Candace writes a response post.

Candace's goal in meeting with me that day was to gain permission to read a statement. She interpreted Walter's "call to arms" (figures 4.12, 4.13, 4.14, and 4.15) as needing to embody and enact the change one wants to see around them. Candace stated to me she no longer wanted to "push it [racism, etc.] under the rug." She reflected on the story that Christie and Jon shared: "That story made me feel angry and hurt. And then I thought of how people didn't think racism existed ... and that made me even more angry because, to me, they are just being arrogant." I agreed, and so Candace read aloud:

> Most of us say we, even now, that we have never encountered or observed racist behavior. We are not racist. But what about the racist jokes we tell amongst each other? Sure, a racist joke doesn't hurt those targeted, because they cannot hear it. But it hurts us. It affects us. How can we be responsible to ourselves, our communities, and others differently?

"This is THE place," Candace concluded. It was a play on the words of Young. She reclaimed and reappropriated them to extend an invitation to peers to see the "there" and "now" as the space-place to mutually deliberate and determine both the meaning of a classroom and *an-other* set of choices, options, and obligations-responsibilities. Candace's reading reminded me that a space and place such as the classroom is an everyday site of human work and that human projects are always already *taking* and *making* space-place. Because, that is, students are makers of spaces-places, shapers of subjectivities, and engineers of negotiated literacies and rhetorical practices. Another goal of the end of semester archival-guided project was to encourage students to see their *archives* as a space and place they can deliberate how to *be-and-become otherwise* vis-à-vis archival impressions, precisely because they are the makers, shapers, and engineers of their everyday.

Early Days in Light of Failure

Stories from faculty of color advancing the projects of unsettling and a decolonial option at PWIs are few and far between in WRS. So I wanted to share darker, grayer stories of tension, *frictions*, adjustments, and failure in light of success stories in WRS. On the one hand, I needed to underscore how agendas do not always go as planned. It was all so simple. I perceived haunting mentalities, devised plans for students to make it out, and saw the classroom as a space and place to do human work *otherwise* than a *coloniality of instruction-and-curriculum*. Nothing could be further from the truth. Because there can be no happy narratives with the projects of unsettling and a decolonial option. Human work and projects are already complex, complicated, and messy, exasperated then by natural *friction, friction* caused by aspirations, and friction that emerges out of an obligation and responsibility to not allow hauntings and haunting situations to go unfettered (*the fly in the elephant's nose*).

I live and work within wounded/wounding spaces andplaces surrounded by haunted/haunting *stories-so-far*. It was important for me in this chapter to shed light on what haunted/haunting stories and literacies, images-signs-sounds, and rhetorics have done to and made of some Utahns. How do students of the chief demographic of Utah adhere to, interact with, and carry out histories, cultural memories, and literacy-rhetorical practices that church-settler archives represent? I approached this chapter like others—archives and archival impressions. My goal was to create a public record of rhetorics of epistemology and enter them into an *archive of knowledges, understandings, feelings*, and *doings* that is this book. For reasons outlined, public records and archives lend themselves to illuminating the immense power that family, community, and religion can have over self, being, and agency as well as animating the demand for decolonizing knowledge-being and *reintroducing invention into existence*. But as Avery Gordon (2008) would warn, it is important to "be careful not to get romantically attached" to "invention" (36). If only, however, it were that simple (see Fanon 1986).

Classroom accounts attest to students' intellectual capacities to explore, investigate, analyze, interpret, determine, and translate meaning from public records of and from scenes of *stories-so-far* and the everyday. They testify to students' familiarity with returning, centering, and situating of the past, the dead, inheritances, and dwellings to the politics of their present. Classroom accounts sound off on students' foresight to see spaces and places as a battlefield to extend an epistemological, ideological, and rhetorical war on information and ability to transform classrooms and blog posts into *gathering spaces* to carry out *work-instruction*; settlerizing epideictic rhetoric was the tool of choice. Bearing witness to what I did, it was my aim to get in the way of haunted/haunting stories and literacies, images-signs-sounds, and rhetorics that have long constructed settler sites, constituted haunted/haunting communities, and maintained wounded/wounding spaces and places.

I choose to stand at the nexus of an-other's *stories-so-far* and *possibilities of new stories* as someone had done for me in the past. So classroom accounts also speak to *friction* and how foundations of self/selves, *stories-so-far*, and community are perceived to be under attack when someone/something goes against the grain. As one student, Johnathan, says, "I trusted everything people told me about who I am and where I come from." Another student, Melissa, echoes him, "We accept them [stories]. We don't question them. They are truth. And anything that imposes upon such implies that our truths are wrong, that we are wrong. Nobody wants to be wrong." We are all settled by local histories of hauntings, inheritances, and dwellings. The question, thus, is not whether *white bodies can think decolonially* but of choice. But then again, the idea of choice is always already deceptive.

Lastly, the classroom accounts show beyond a doubt that students are not powerless. They recognize and practice the power of language, literacies, and rhetorics. My mere presence and agenda were an interruption. I learned that I occupied a unique space in their imaginary. I was an *other* but also a figment of an obligation and responsibility. Their phronetic and gnostic praxis of living were unfamiliar to me. So when Lynn told me, "I think once you know," I did not suspect I was being prepared for *work-instruction*, the gift of giving. Students were preparing an unrelenting work like I was. But my goal was not to discount or attack views but to unsettle the settled: *dispositions of the habitus* (see Bourdieu 1997). Giving is a part of relational exchanges (giving, receiving, reciprocating) (see Levinas 1969; Derrida and Ferraris 2001). But it does not have to be predicated on what another does not have to give (Derrida 1994a, 1994b) or the economy of exchange-value (Hegel 1896). The im/possibility of the gift of giving can mean becoming ready and making room to *think-feel-be-with* others (broadly conceived) *otherwise*. But a wor(l)ding of a future of the We requires mutual deliberation and determination over life questions. Such would not happen in my class that semester. And that is just another failure. But this kind of failure is understandable.

I shared my story for another reason though. On the other hand, it was important to nuance conversations on the translation of the projects of a decolonial option. In theory, it is sound and right in principle. Decolonizing being is unthinkable without decolonizing knowledge. But to apply a phrase from Žižek (2008), I was taking the *right step in the wrong direction*. The project of modernity/(de)coloniality had become a roadmap for me in graduate school and it followed me into my first year at the UofU. One of its directions was to presuppose that for a "White European body to think decolonially means to give; to give in a parallel way than a body of color formed in colonial histories" (Mignolo 2013, 145). Based on readings, I interpreted that to mean that an experiential education with a decolonial option could only be achieved if one has experienced being *thrown* into the fold, *forced* to contend with wounded/wounding spaces and places and haunted/haunting *stories-so-far*, and *imperiled* to mitigate a subject position of becoming otherwise rather than being a haunting subject to *others*. I failed by foreclosing on the *possibilities of new stories*, presupposing a proper arrivant for a decolonial option.

Another direction of the MCC is to reduce life and agency to binaries (black/white; good/bad; right/wrong) and options (surrender; assimilate; resist; confront-resignify) (see Mignolo 2007, 2011a, 2013, 2017). This is buttressed by Mignolo's (2007) claim, "There are two kinds of individuals at work in a colonizer's society" (458). I failed in clinging to out-of-touch values, presupposing that the *possibilities of new stories* could not be achieved outside of them. If the issue of reductive, dichotomous, and oppositional rhetorical structures is not apparent by now, allow me to echo a passage in Spivak's (1988a) seminal article that I amend slightly: observations, perceptions, desires, and its objects are a unity. Observatory deductions of the *other* (white bodies) and perceptions of whether bodies can give in parallel ways is an issue. Because it creates a deficit-ridden object of desire, presupposes what constitutes a proper arrival and arrivant, and hence forecloses on *possibilities of new stories*. To see entities (white bodies) rather than relations renders a decolonial option unsuitable for *anyone* who arrives at our doors.

Desire by scholars-educators has clouded what is at stake for students. Yes, Mormons need a *careful reckoning*. *How does one remain within an institution that continues to wound and haunt people and spaces and places* (see Riess 2020). Surely, the *idea of Mormon/ism* cannot be the solution for the problem it created. To change the *contents and terms*, Mormons would have to undergo a process of learning how to unlearn: abandoning an *epistemic system* and relinquishing authority over projects of territorial and epistemological (ap/ex)propriation. But life is complex, complicated, and messy. I think of Candace, who does her best to oppose and denounce not her religion or affiliation to a Church but modern/colonial and settlerizing designs. In that context, she would fall under the "kind of individual" who unsettles the "irrational myth that justifies" violence (Mignolo 2007, 458). Both in the final project and interview, Candace would say, "Through constant reminders, we are remembered in a positive light. Our stories have been heavily perpetuated." She reflects:

> [R]acism rode here on the backs of Mormon pioneers and settled it into their homes and churches. Although many people have the privilege of ignoring racism ["not my fault, not my problem"], or believing it doesn't exist ["I don't see it"], it is important to learn about the reasons and ways it is still ingrained to create a world more equitable.

But for Candace there is much at stake. There is the risk of alienation, which she has already quasi-experienced in the classroom among peers by speaking up for what she believed was right. She waited after class one day to chat with me. Candace wanted me to know her situation at home. She saw herself getting married to her partner, who like her had strong church-settler roots and ties to the Church. Candace informed me that she would never leave the Church—it is "not an option." And in this context, I am once more reminded of Mignolo (2011a), who argued one "can not think decolonially and remain within the value frame of humanitas" (90). I would be but foreclosing on her *possibilities of new stories* if I held to this position strictly. Life is too complex, complicated, and messy to reduce it to choices couched in binaries (black/white; good/bad; right/wrong) and options (surrender; assimilate; resist;

confront-resignify). I also think of Walter and his reflection about public memory for the final project:

> [T]he land belongs to the settlers, and native people could be incorporated too, but off to the side. Such a belief is reflected in how Utah state history is taught in public schools; a history that begins in 1847 only once the settler brought civilization to the wilderness.

Walter had already opened and read his mission call. Like Candace, leaving the Church was not an option. And not just because it would cause alienation. He believed in the gift of traveling to other spaces and places, chance encounters, and wor(l)ding. This would not be unlike scholars like Lugones (1987), hooks (2001a), Fabian (2007), and Maldonado-Torres (2007), who understand that difference is always already at the heart of chance encounters. The difference, of course, was that Walter was carrying out human projects and work on behalf of the Church. Still, he had hope that such human work and projects could be done *otherwise*. I informed Candace and Walter that the goal is not a total rejection but both a greater awareness of hauntings and haunting situations and a *learning-unlearning-relearning* of life question—how to hold some *things*, like a value (to live in-common, welcome, and love-another), in common, not on the basis of identity or identification but in the *non-name of all* (see Acosta 2012). Both accounts unsettled the settled-ness of a *prospective task* of a decolonial option, illuminating implicit contradictions, limitations, and inadequacies. Because it became unsuitable for *anyone, wherever they may be* and in the *non-name of all*. And yet my experiences in this classroom were most instructive, telling me something important about the demand for something else.

I am not trying to excuse behavior. I turned to *friction* to think about what happens when there is *opportunity* for people, *stories-so-far*, and words-ideas to come together, *be-with* each other, and *get to work*. Because it is troublesome to label students as problems. But their actions undermined my view of *friction*. I was teaching students raised to define themselves as Man-Human in their ethos and epistemological praxis of living. They were taught to apply self-ideas (Man), images (Human), and ends (Rights-to) that invented, devalued and dehumanized (less knowing, less human), distinguished Self from, and situated the *other* as a site of and for *work-instruction*. I gathered this much by listening, *to know* and *to learn*, to church-settler archives and students. So I hoped and struggled to be the wrench in the assembly line of knowledge production (systems, designs, and work-instruction-curriculum) at least, the *fly in the elephant's nose* at the very least. I know today, as I will discuss in the last chapter, that in the demand for something else, there is still an archival approach and theory of archival impressions to be worked out.

Can the *archives* feel? A *discourse about actions* approach would evidence that students in Utah, like their peers and family members, are at the very least maintaining archives and contributing to the *Archive*. In the same breadth it would also suggest that educators do indeed stand at the nexus of another's *stories-so-far* and *possibilities of new stories*. This confirms that the educator "has the duty of not being neutral" (Freire in Bell, Gaventa, and Peters 1990, 180; also see Mignolo 2006; Tlostanova and Mignolo 2009). Friction! An *opportunity* to *get to work* or get in the way. But friction, of course, is different from being part of the problem—a preparation of a teaching of writing and rhetoric unsuitable for *anyone* who arrives at our doors—which I make known throughout this chapter too. Now, the next chapter marks a geographic and demographic shift. Chapter 5 too underscores how decolonizing knowledge-being can be conceptually, pedagogically, and emotionally complex, complicated, messy, and to some extent impossible among those who refuse to surrender hope for the *possibilities of new stories*.

We live amid and as archives made, unmade, and remade by writing. In the next chapter, much like this one, I approach the body and Self much like Baldwin (1956, 1998), Browne (2019, 2021), Chávez (2018), Cvetkovich (2003), and Fanon (1986)—archives that can be *returned* to and *carefully reckoned* with. Ultimately, this collective, I argue, reflects an *enduring and ongoing* hope that it is possible to carry out *work* in the service of being-with "somewhere else" and being-for "something else" (Fanon 1986, 218).

Reflexión-Meditación

Returning Home

Some things have changed in writing and rhetorical studies since Mejía (1998, 1999, 2004) appealed for more research attentive to Mexicans, Mexican Americans, Latino/as, and Hispanics in their specificities and particularities. Research interests range, but nonetheless there are now more than a handful of publications (Cintron 1997; Guerra 1998; Kells 2002, 2004; Méndez Newman 2003, 2007, 2014; Enoch 2004, 2008; Kirklighter, Cardenas, and Murphy 2007; A. Martinez 2009; Lamos 2012; Medina 2014a, 2017, 2017; Enríquez-Loya and Leon 2017; I. Baca, Hinojosa, and Murphy 2019; Méndez Newman and García 2019). It would be unproductive to unpack the reservations I have on scholarship that stages a unified resistance and opposition to hegemony based on pre-commitments to idioms of resistance, that reduce ethnolinguistic identities by superimposing cohesive identity politics, and/or that frame the borderlands as an inherent site of resistance, subversion, and re-signification of hegemonic norms. I will only say this: writing and rhetorical studies still knows so little about Mexicans, Mexican Americans, Latino/as, and Hispanics. So, for over a decade, I have dedicated much of my work to returning home.

Home. The Valley air. The burning of sugar cane, the suffocating humidity, the thickness of the smell of fog. The food of the Valley. The tortillerías, panaderías, raspa-erías, taquerías. The culture of the Valley. The pulgas,

https://doi.org/10.7330/9781646426782.c005a

Basílica, teen pregnancy, single parenthood, comadres y compadres, curanderas, hope-struggle. The scholars of the Valley. The healer, hustler, dealer, pusher, single moms. Too much to unpack, but nonetheless, the Valley is my lifeblood and oxygen through and through. I left home on bad terms. I had to leave to learn how to come back *otherwise* (see Cisneros 1991). I find that I am on a path to *learn-unlearn-relearn* how to find my way back home, to relearn how to be at-home; an *archive* in an unending cycle of being made, unmade, and remade.

It was a weird feeling to be sitting in the UTRGV parking lot again. How did I get here? I had walked by that parking lot before. I slept on the floor in a small apartment right across campus during a time when I did not have a place to call home. (This was during a time, Mohanty [2003] might say, of "not being home," where I had realized "home was an illusion of coherence and safety" [90]). It was the closest I would get to being at a college, I thought to myself then. I made it out seventeen years ago. But home never quite let me go. And out of my experiences in Gringodemia a sense of obligation and responsibility materialized. I think of my first English course at Texas A&M University (TAMU). "You clearly do not understand the book, so I will be the leader of this project." That student will never know how I would come to love the works of John Milton but more hauntingly how I assented in the form of an *awaiting* because of it: one day I will read, write, speak, and be more ~~right~~ whitely (ojalá). I will have lost more than I will ever have gained out of Gringodemia in that pursuit. But it is that sense of obligation and responsibility to bring out of the shadows and below spaces, places, and people familiar to me that drives my work today both in terms of research and teaching. I had to leave to learn how to come back otherwise. I return so often today so that the bones do not ache as much (Cisneros 1991).

My sense of obligation and responsibility started at the Corpus Christi campus (TAMUCC) with an IRB-approved study, "How to Empower Hispanic Males in Higher Education, and Increase Completion, Retention, and Transition Rates: A Focus on Self-Efficacy, Social Inclusion, and Academic Inclusion." My work with first-generation Mexican, Mexican American, Latino/a, and Hispanic students carried over into two other IRB-approved studies, one conducted at UTRGV as a PhD student and the other at the UofU as an assistant professor.[1] Today I still think about the students at TAMUCC, primarily from the LRGV, who saw it as a sign of having made it out even though it is but two hours away; about the students at UTRGV, who were

---

1. For more insight on identity terms, see Kells 2002.

raised in the LRGV, who saw the school as a stepping-stone to making it out; and about the undocumented, first- and second-generation immigrants, and transfer students at the UofU who perceived the school as beyond reach, but because of the Writing Studies Scholar Program and scholars like Christie Toth and Clint Gardner they now have making it out in sight.

I have mulled over the organization of the next chapter for some time. Originally, I planned to revisit my dissertation. At UTRGV, I observed two First-year composition and rhetoric courses (hereafter FYCRCs), conducted literacy history interviews, hosted two listening group sessions, and shadowed students. Hence, why I was in the parking lot of UTRGV in 2015. Over the years, I have found that it is mostly true that Mexicans, Mexican Americans, Latino/as, and Hispanics have evolved in disparate ways (see Munoz 1989). Even under the condition of *strategic essentialism* we are not all "Chicanos" or "immigrants" (see Alberto 2016). We should resist homogenizing people and interpreting lives monolithically (Limón 2008). It does not bode well in the context of theory, curricula, instruction, and/or pedagogy (see Chabram-Dernersesian 1999). So I initially planned to separate stories to avoid conflation and erasure of difference. Yet, as I revisited the literacy history interviews it was hard to overlook how their *archives* were constellated by the archival impression of hope-struggle—a barrio mentality.

There is this hope-struggle in the students I worked with. The best way I can honor my experience with the students who participated in my studies is to highlight their collective hope-struggle to make it out by any means necessary. Once more, decolonizing knowledge-being can be conceptually, pedagogically, and emotionally complex, complicated, messy, and to some extent impossible when human beings are involved. I found this to be true among the collective of voices in the following chapter.

5
Making It Out of Haunted Mentalities

They know how to survive in the Valley. A barrio (and not a pobrecito) mentality (hope-struggle) is born out of hauntings and haunting situation not of one's making. And it is formed in some *thing* as vital as the food of poverty—carne picada, picadillo, arroz con pollo, fideo—to some *things* as powerful as the violence (broadly conceived) of poverty. They, those of haunted mentalities, who refuse to surrender hope of overcoming the odds, despite the writings on their wall and the archival impressions that have become one with their body. They feel like they do not belong outside the Valley but know they must make it out of it, and in that way, they belong to each other, the haunted. Will they ever have betrayed the archive of their brown(ed)ness—a trace of a stamped mark of inferiority and out-of-time and out-of-placeness (see Caldwell 1830, 136)—and arrived?

I was there, *to listen* and *to know*. "I can be someone." A hope and a struggle, which belonged to not one individual but to all. That they were speaking to me both confirmed that hope but also underscored their past and ongoing struggles. "I know others have it worse than me." The disposition of *mas peor que yo* becomes a way for them to cope, to keep that hope for the *possibilities of new stories* alive, to struggle to make it out of their *stories-so-far*. "I will make it out." It was said with such confidence by many at the beginning, but midway in reflecting on the contents of their *archives*, the bravado for which they spoke almost always contracted and the certainty for which they possessed most definitely dwindled. They have braved the cruelties of hauntings and haunting situations. While they were right, in a sense, *que otros lo tienen mas peor*, it did not take away from their experiences nor diminish their orientation of hope-struggle. On the contrary, it underscored a constellation in which, against the backdrop of hauntings and haunting situations, they were part of a living thread of *thinking*, *feeling*, and *being-with*: "standpoints, struggles and practices, from and with praxical theorizings, conceptual theorizings, theoretical conceptualizings, and theory-building actionings" (Mignolo and Walsh 2018, 20). They, who do their best not to surrender hope, who struggle to be resilient in spite of the wreckage of what surrounds, despite the haunt that lives within their bones. Though who I am talking about are students, they know much about life and living. We can all learn from them.

"Don't say pobrecito." It will always have mattered que uno es de ahí y no de allá for "the Mexican." This is internalized, though its meaning varies from student to student. They believe physically leaving a space and place will remove a haunted/haunting consciousness and that hauntings and haunting situations will cease presencing. And so making it out is in their minds, it haunts them in their dreams and motivates them to no end. But such students will have lost more than they will ever have gained from Gringodemia, because they will have sacrificed precisely who they are. The prospect of making it out though is all worth it to them. They are willing to *assent* in the form of an *awaiting* to ease what haunts and surrounds them: reading, writing, speaking, and being more ~~right~~ whitely. Not knowing, however, that even after obtaining some degree of success, hauntings and haunting situations will be there in one way or another. Will they ever have arrived? I learned from Mexican, Mexican American, Latino/a, and/or Hispanic students that they are keenly aware of how they have been un/settled by local histories of hauntings, inheritances, and dwellings. And how their cultural and thinking program/ings are attuned to making it out. They hope-struggle to be *otherwise* than the cards dealt to them. And even if they cannot, they assured me time after time, "We are not pobrecitos."

"I want a better life." A hope and a struggle shared among all Mexican, Mexican American, Latino/a, and/or Hispanic students I have worked with over the years. "This cannot be it." But the wreckage that surrounds them is a testament that it is more than a reality; it is an unending cycle in their communities. "I want to prove them wrong." Over the course of our discussions, they come to realize that "everyone" says that, but still holding onto hope, they assure me that they will be different and that they will end the cycle. It is something "we" say in the Valley. And people joke all the time at the sight of the many who do not make it out. Still, they hold out hope. "This is my dream." They wonder, during countless sleepless nights and the heavy fatigue of going to school, working full time, and taking care of the family, whether it will ever be more than a dream. "I can do this." Sometimes, however, it has little to do with capabilities and more to do with the cards dealt to them. "I am not sure I can do this." They struggle with the reality that sometimes one cannot be more than the cards dealt to them. "Culture," Anzaldúa (1999) reminds us, "forms our beliefs. We perceive the version of reality that it communicates" (16). They, those who refuse to surrender hope in spite of what is communicated to them and despite that which lives deep within the bones.

One might assume that the border and border(ed)landers is a natural space and place for a decolonial option to fester. But this chapter underscores the darker, grayer narratives of and from the classroom, how decolonizing knowledge-being can be conceptually, pedagogically, and emotionally complex, complicated, messy, and to some extent impossible when human beings are involved. In this chapter, such beings are the racialized, minoritized, and marginalized. Though a decolonial option is promising it is at odds with efforts to make it out. This chapter, like the previous one, does not reflect *the* story or the *whole* story. That is an impossibility alongside the reality that some stories cannot and should not be told. At times, once more, the narrative might seem fragmented or incomplete, offering only a snapshot composite or sliver of a *story-so-far* and conversation. That limitation is mine alone. Yet, it is sufficient, ultimately, for underscoring the ways our lives and bodies are *archives* and for advancing an argument for an archival approach and theory of archival impressions.

Possibilities of New Stories: Decolonizing Knowledge-Being

The students I worked with at TAMUCC, UTRGV, and the UofU were interested in decolonizing knowledge-being in theory. None had ever heard of theory much less decolonization, or so they said. But they found a *prospective vision* and epistemic disobedience promising as a people on the cusp of invisibility. They occupied a precarious space between making it out by any means necessary as subjects of hauntings and *longing* for liberation as subjects in a state of *being-and-becoming*. The projects of unsettling and a decolonial option offered students terms, concepts, and reasons to locate, identify, and name hauntings and haunting situations. It helped them make sense of *things* that made no sense. It invited them to unsettle the idea hauntings and haunting situations were inherent to the haunted. It was cliché, but to spark conversations on *coloniality of instruction-and-curriculum* and on White cultural logics informing the idea of "the Mexican," I turned to Anzaldúa's *Borderlands/La Frontera*:

> I remember being caught speaking Spanish at recess—that was good for three licks on the knuckles with a sharp ruler. I remember being sent to the corner of the classroom for talking back to the Anglo teacher when all I was trying to do was tell her how to pronounce my name. If you want to be American, speak American. If you don't like it, go back to Mexico where you belong. (Anzaldúa 1999, 75)

The first depiction observed is Anzaldúa being disciplined for speaking Spanish. This is followed by a classroom scene in which they are disciplined too for correcting the pronunciation of their name. The following are the cultural logics (see Ratcliffe 2005) in play: (1) Anglo teacher : American, (2) American identity : American language, (3) brown body : Mexico (birth of origins), and (4) Spanish language : Mexican. What *Borderlands* teaches us is that historically schools have attempted to stamp out the identity and language of and/or discipline brown(ed) students. All the students got the point. Their parents were that generation. They even shared their own experiences of being discriminated against, tolerating racist remarks, and enduring both physical and psychological violence inside and outside of the classroom (Chuck 2016; Benavides 2017; Acevedo and Fitchel 2019; Woods 2020). Such experiences conntected us all despite being raised in different counties and in different socioeconomic situations.

My next task before me was to develop conversations on a *decolonial analytic* and to invite students to see it is as practical human project. But certain students at a particular institution demanded language of the everyday, which really sparked the rise of a specific question in the trajectory of my career, *where is one at and who is one teaching*? When I was conducting research for my dissertation, I found myself initially Googling histories of South Texas (even when I was at TAMUCC) and then eventually but surrendipitously at the Special Collections and Archives at UTRGV. And I say by chance, because I happened to stumble into the archives, a space near the staircases where I was conducting interviews. All students both at UTRGV and beyond indeed exhibited their epistemic right to engage with and demonstrated their intellectual

Making It Out of Haunted Mentalities : 233

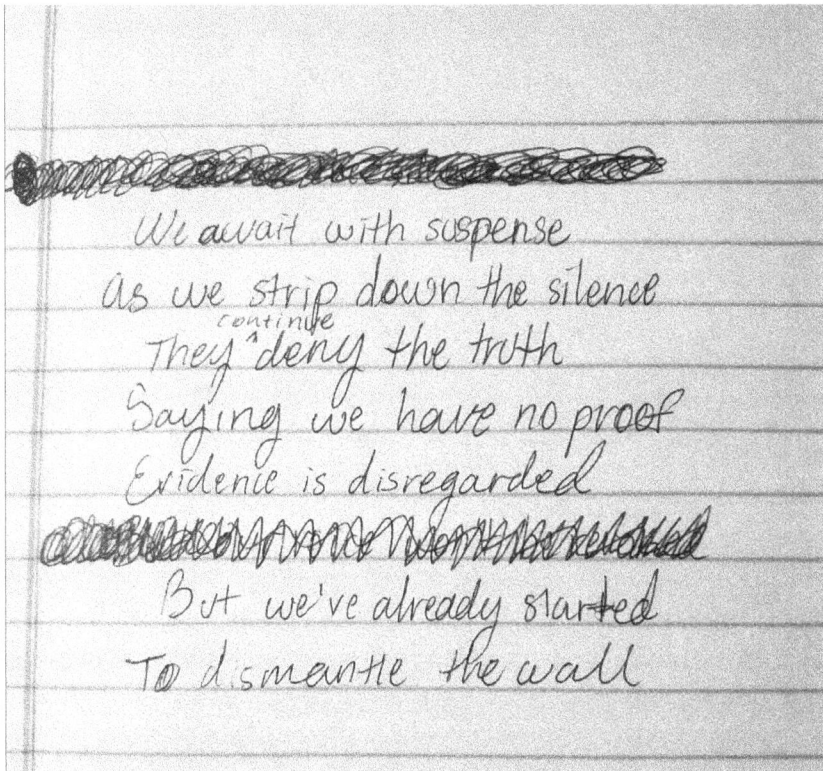

FIGURE 5.1. We Await

capacities to apply a *decolonial analytic* toward hauntings and haunting situations. One student offered a poetic response to settler archives (figure 5.1). While it is unclear as to what "the wall" refers to, it is quite apparent that "strip[ping] down" and "dismantl[ing]" are utterances meant to indicate the unsettling of the settled. Perhaps silence refers both to those who continue to deny the "truth" and the "silence" that obscures the truth? Speculation? Maybe. The tension between the "they" and the "we" is most notable. Perhaps the former refers to those who "[say] we have no proof" while the latter to those who provide it only to have their "evidence" of proof "disregarded." But this is just one example of a student response.

One student observes how "Lon Hill is looked up to as an elite or heroic man," while also commenting how the narratives of "civilizing Harlingen" and Lon C. Hill do not seem "completely true." Another student remarks, "I saw a gross disparity between the treatment and funding of Mexicans versus

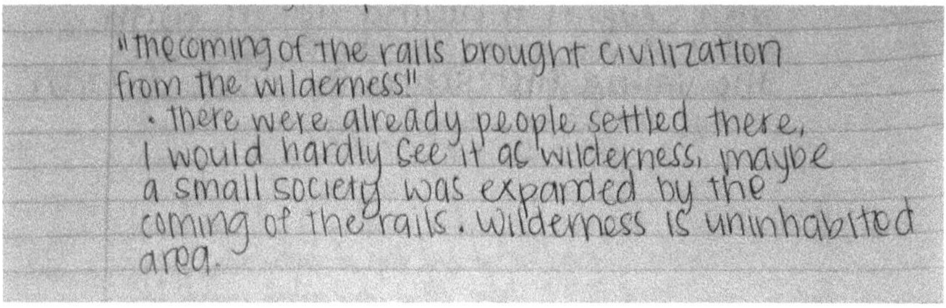

234 : MAKING IT OUT OF HAUNTED MENTALITIES

> "The coming of the rails brought civilization from the wilderness"
> - There were already people settled there, I would hardly see it as wilderness, maybe a small society was expanded by the coming of the rails. Wilderness is uninhabited area.

FIGURE 5.2. A student essay on the coming of the railroads

white," while also observing how "The publication[s] seem to skew its narrative against the injustices, as in propaganda." Another writes, "There is a recognition of civilization just not inclusive of Mexicans and Native Americans," and adds, "providing one viewpoint, it [can] lead others to assume that is the correct narrative." The depth of awareness and articulation of understanding is amazing here. But it is to be expected. These students are makers of spaces and places, shapers of subjectivities, and engineers of negotiated literacies and rhetorical practices within their everyday. They were bearing witness every day to the lived reality of history.

The response above contends with the idea that the "coming" of the railroads "brought civilization from the wilderness" (figure 5.2). How come? Perhaps because it produces absences and silences. Or perhaps because wilderness connotes "uninhabited area." As the student notes, and as settler advertisements testified to (see chapter 3), "There were already people settled there." While the student tries to empathize with how the railroads created change, he ultimately contends with the idea that a space and place was wilderness to begin with. This is an example of enacting an ethos of bearing witness in unsettling ways and praxis of unsettling the settled: a seeing without being settled with and doing of plunging into, peeling back layers of, and unsettling what is constituted as legible (Fukushima 2019; García and Kirsch 2022). Another example of this kind of work can be found below where a student centers on settler words and ideas (figure 5.3).

In figure 5.3 the student is contending with James Polk, who once argued that "the Mexican" was a problem needing to be fixed. On the other hand, she is vying with the "settler's claim" that settlers alone "own the land because of the blood, sweat, and tears." The student writes that what settlers "conveniently forgot" is the "spilling the blood, exploiting the laborious sweat, and the river of tears of the upheaval their arrival created." Both students (figures

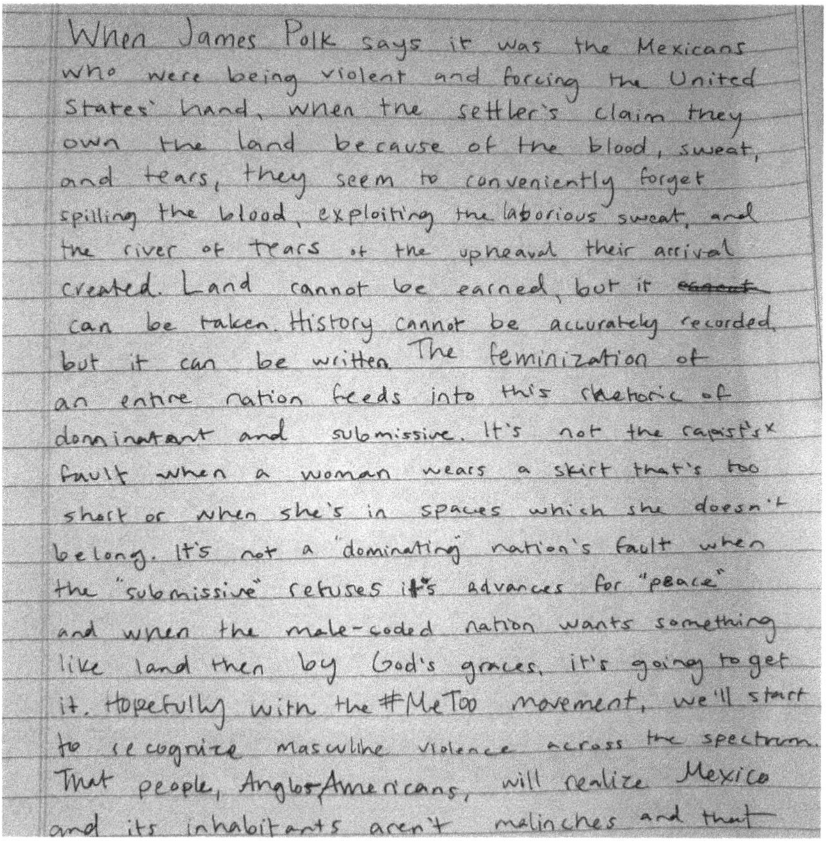

> When James Polk says it was the Mexicans who were being violent and forcing the United States' hand, when the settler's claim they own the land because of the blood, sweat, and tears, they seem to conveniently forget spilling the blood, exploiting the laborious sweat, and the river of tears of the upheaval their arrival created. Land cannot be earned, but it ~~cannot~~ can be taken. History cannot be accurately recorded, but it can be written. The feminization of an entire nation feeds into this rhetoric of dominant and submissive. It's not the rapist's fault when a woman wears a skirt that's too short or when she's in spaces which she doesn't belong. It's not a 'dominating' nation's fault when the "submissive" refuses it's advances for "peace" and when the male-coded nation wants something like land then by God's graces, it's going to get it. Hopefully with the #MeToo movement, we'll start to recognize masculine violence across the spectrum. That people, Anglo-Americans, will realize Mexico and its inhabitants aren't malinches and that

FIGURE 5.3. Conveniently forgetting

5.2 and 5.3) are unsettling an epistemology that institutes ~~ontology~~ a hegemonic narrative of Western civilization. By excavating the march toward hegemony out of the project of modernity, they reveal both an epistemological, ideological, and rhetorical war on information and the ways ~~truth~~ fictions are filtered through mediums of circulation under the management and control of modern/colonial and settlerizing mentalities and designs.

All the students who participated in conversations understood the assignment. The assignment was to apply a *decolonial analytic*. Some observed how the settler was depicted, "stern old pioneer[s], innocence, security, and modern." Other students recognized and acknowledged that when settler advertisements portrayed Indigenous peoples as "scattered Native Americans," the word "scattered" was meant to characterize them as having "no identity, because they don't follow the same culture of settlers." Other responses stood out as well, those that made concrete connections between rhetoric, superiority, and hegemonic narratives.

> "The white rhetoric gives them their own history in their own time and in their own words."

> "Subtle white superiority."

> "White domination narratives: 'We deserve it because no one was putting good use to the Valley.'"

> "A preserved message. It tells a story from a certain perspective and leaves out others. This is a white story. Does not acknowledge existence of anything besides white American story."

Students appreciated the opportunity to learn about their everyday through settler archives. It allowed them to make concrete connections to how their *stories-so-far* adhere to and interact with the projects and work settler archives represent. "We matter too," Jose tells me, dissatisfied with the focus of his writing course for the semester, "I am not sure why we had to focus so much on the African American community and their history in our course. What about ours?" Maria concurs, "We have a history too, you know." There are some haunting undertones here beyond the scope and breadth of this chapter, some of which can be summed up with anti-Blackness. Both student statements, however, underscore the importance of the question, *where is one at and who is one teaching?* It did strike me both as odd and curious why the local, whether at TAMUCC or UTRGV, was not being incorporated into the classroom given the student demographic. But while students were afforded the occasion to apply a *decolonial analytic*, it was another story to deliberate *an-other* set of choices, options, and obligations and responsibilities.

Students demonstrated their intellectual capacities to explore, investigate, analyze, interpret, determine, and translate meaning. This is important because decolonizing being is unthinkable without decolonizing knowledge. "It makes sense," Esther says of the MCC's options, "that we should not give in to what people assume of us [surrender], that forgetting who we are is bad [assimilation], and that we should confront all that does us harm [confronting]." She reflects, "Sometimes, when the days and weeks are good, and nothing has gone to shit, I can stop believing what they say [epistemic delinking], I can start rethinking who I am [epistemological decolonization], and I can plan for who I want to be [epistemic reconstitution]." This, in essence, is the *learning-unlearning-relearning* path emphasized with the brackets above. But those days are few and far between for students like Esther, who but have only one thing on their mind, making it out. They know, despite all the self-convincing, that hard times do last and that hauntings and haunting situations can break them. Their hope-struggle becomes one of simply making it out then. They believe such will ease that which lives deep within the bones. They know not otherwise for no one around them has truly made it out.

Students understood how they were perceived. Of course they would, because what it means to see, feel, listen, and even do cannot be grasped outside the spaces, places, and people familiar to them. "When people hear me say I am Mexican American," Olivia states, "all they think about is how I am Mexican, that is what they hear first." There is not a distaste for being Mexican but rather for being perceived as "the Mexican"—and there is a difference. Santana notes, "I have not forgotten where I come from. But sometimes it is hard to be proud to be Mexican." Everything around them suggests *que el Valle es un otro mundo* and yet comments and stares both by winter Texans *y los bien presumidos* reminds them that it is a world not of their own making but a by-product of modern/colonial and settlerizing designs. Many students responded, when asked what identity term they prefer to use in public and academic settings, with "Hispanic." "When I say I am Hispanic they [white people] do not look at me or treat me as differently," Olivia says, continuing, "It means I can go places." To go places underscores both academic and geographic settings. "It means," according to Santana, "we have more opportunity." "Hispanic" means academic and geographic mobility for them. But they know, as well as I do, that such is an illusion, because "The Mexican" will be gate-kept regardless of how they identify. Still, we must not ignore efforts to be resilient and to persevere (see Flynn, Sotirin, and Brady 2012; Neitch 2019). And this is different from the MCC's binaries (black/white; good/bad; right/wrong) and options (surrender; assimilate; resist; confront-resignify), which would be at odds with such practices. The irony here is that what was supposed to bring about some *thing* else instead re-entrenches Western notions of life and agency—*logics of subversion and resignification of hegemonic norms*—that fail to account for how material exchanges and relations of/with domination, management, and control enable life and create a sense of agency for the racialized, minoritized, and marginalized (see Pred 1984; Mahmood 2014). And yet for these students, choices are hardly choices at all but demands. All they know for sure is that they need to make it out by any means necessary. So despite what the MCC would say, utilizing "Hispanic" does not automatically mean they have less agency.

The catalog of hauntings and haunting situations had showed these students that there had not been and will not be any justice for them. Their bloodline of trauma is a palimpsestic narrative of epistemic violence: their immediate family members had not made it out or attended college and the family members of those members had experienced Mexican tracks, English-Only pedagogy, and second-rate learning facilitations. Students are not too far removed from any of this. Santana recalls for me a familial experience: "My dad says they use to hit him for speaking Spanish." This experience came up because he mentioned Anzaldúa's piece to his dad. It angered Santana to hear about his father's violence, but it was not unlike the psychological violence he endured being told that he would be nothing more than a "Mexican" if he continues to carry on the Spanish accent. Olivia shares a familial experience as well, "They [Mom/Dad] were told it was a waste of time because they were not going anywhere in life." This hits home for Olivia. "The Mexican" is so often told, per her accounts, that they cannot go anywhere in life. And more often than not it has much more to do with the fact that one is "Mexican" and less to do with capabilities. These students carry such haunted/haunting baggage with them. They enter Hispanic-serving institutions (HSIs) such as TAMUCC and UTRGV, which prides itself in serving its demographic, and yet students know that though enrollment is high, graduation rates continue to be low. Who is at fault? Is it the fault of students who are underprepared by the K–12 schools in Texas, or is it the fault of the university that prioritizes enrollment over the success of students? Either way, the palimpsestic narrative of epistemic violence continues (Bedolla 2009; Blanton 2007; Castellanos and Jones 2003; Guajardo and Guajardo 2004; Montejano 1987; San Miguel 1998; Spring 1996; Valencia 2000; Urrieta 2009).

The eyes were upon us as we talk near the staircase in the library. Lisa tells me, "They don't care to serve us." The "they" refers to UTRGV while the "us" reflects people like her. Brisa weighs in, "Yeah, they just want to say 'we' enroll the most gente from the Valley,' but what good is enrollment if we can't even graduate?" Santana, who will become a casualty in all this, nods his head in agreement and states, "This is why I feel stuck. Because it is inevitable that this school is going to fail me. It already has in many ways." A random student overhears our discussion in the hallways of the library at UTRGV, where again we so often held these interviews. "Can I just ask something?" he states. "Are you talking about how this school fails to serve us?" They laugh aloud, as the students with me nod in agreement and dare to laugh, knowing that they are the ones who have too just been enrolled and not served by the institution.

Sure, these students are makers, shapers, and engineers of their everyday. But their potential will have already been dampened by an institution out of touch with its demographic and faculty whose desires and objectives outweigh their needs. The students knew this. So they were going to do whatever it takes to make it out even against the numbers that suggest more enrollment over graduation rates (G. Garcia, Núñez, and Sansone 2019).

The everyday haunts these students. Lisa chimes in to amplify perceptions she and others like Esther have internalized: "We know what others [non-LRGV people] think of us, and I ain't going to lie, sometimes I believe it." Edward shares in Esther's and Lisa's sentiment, "Sometimes, I just want to say, me vale madre. Fuck everything . . . life can be shitty like that. Sometimes all our hands are tied." Mariana says what others are thinking, "This [the projects of unsettling and a decolonial option] is all good and all and we want to learn about this stuff, but I don't know, it all sounds like fluff, how is it going to help us en realidad?" I wanted to counter the "but" with my own opinion. I stopped my indiscriminate orientation to the project of modernity/(de)coloniality in me from speaking. Because then and there I recognized my privilege, but also what little I had, and the way my privilege had disconnected me from the realities racialized, minoritized, and marginalized peoples feel down in South Texas. Because I realized then, as I know now, neither life nor agency can be reduced to options: surrender; assimilate; resist; confront-resignify. Students were a haunting reminder of this. And who am I to interject with some *thing* that may indeed get in the way of them making it out.

Students made it known that while the projects of unsettling and a decolonial option were promising, they offered no concrete or tangible way to make it out of hauntings and haunting situations. It offers no perceptible outcome for them of benefit. To the contrary, the *returns* return them to a space and place they do not want to be, and the *careful reckonings* demanded with such *returns* cannot bring about happy narratives. How can that be if by the very nature of the project some *things* are being unsettled. There is this inclination in academia writ large and WRS to celebrate the cultural vitality of regions such as the LRGV, South Texas, and even segregated parts of Utah. Though I reckon a study or two can indeed illustrate vibrant *ideologies of scale* and *scale-making projects* that contribute to the (re)making of space and place, much of it tokenizes or exhibits totalistic precommitments that romanticize the resistance of border(ed)landers. But what good is cultural vitality if there has not been any justice in those areas? "You all can keep the decolonial," Marianna says, "We just want a better life for us and all those around us." The *all* implicated me, and that hurt, because much of my scholarly identity has gravitated toward the projects of unsettling and a decolonial option. Santana tells me, "We like to think and say the Valley is unique." He pauses, taking a moment to think about how he wants to say what he needs to say. "But shit, we rarely think about why the Valley is the way it is." Santana was getting at how the LRGV is the by-product of modern/colonial and settlerizing designs. Esther expands on this, "Is it really a coincidence that everything we want is beyond the Valley and that they [white folks] only come here because of cheap food, cheap labor, and warm weather?" The life they all seek is perceptibly beyond their reach because of the internal checkpoints, and for them, that is what it means to be a border(ed)lander. Mariana jokingly states, "Yeah, that's why I want to leave, because their ain't nothing here for me." All that the students know for sure is that they want to make it out. But will they ever have arrived? (also see León 1997).

Los Que Nunca Llegarán

Will the first-generation Mexican and Mexican American students I met at TAMUCC ever have arrived? I think of James, who tells me he is the "first person" in his family, and "not just immediate family," to attend college. He was both proud and scared of that fact. "Growing up," he said, "we are made to believe that while we may be able to go to college, we would not be successful." Sometimes, the haunting reality is, the people closest to us anticipate and in fact expect failure because they do not want us to make it out. "Bien presumido" or "sellout" are words often heard in secret. But James's grandpa was not one of them, and he promised him that he was indeed going to go to college. "I told him," James recalls, "I was going to make money. So much money I'll never have to worry about anything." I think of Marcos as well, aware of how some view TAMUCC: "TAMUCC [is] considered the college for students who had poor performing habits." He does not view it this way, though. For Marcos, it is an opportunity to make it out. For him, it is a "resource," noting, "I and others try to disregard the perceptions placed on us." Marcos continues, "We will try to use the resources we are provided to improve ourselves." James echoes this sentiment, "I want an education so I can have a better life." Higher education offers the *possibility of new stories* for them.

But sometimes opportunity and access are not enough. Neither can change how hauntings have worked and will continue to work and inflict upon their *stories-so-far*. I think of Isiah. "It can be tough," Isiah notes, "especially when you are worried about paying for food, clothes, bills, and other necessities." It bothers him that his friends have dropped out of school because of "financial issues or family issues." It bothers Isiah because that is his *story-so-far*: sleeping in his car and utilizing free pantries to get by. I think of Andres, who reflects on his haunting situation: "I have no money to take care of myself some nights. I go to bed hungry, because I don't have money." He is thrice conflicted: the possibility he might go hungry, the fear of going back home, the fact his family "really needs [him] back at home." Isiah admits, "Most of the time that is all I can think of." When I ask for clarification, Andres answers for him, "You know, how to get by every day." Hope is a thread that binds James's, Marcos's, Isiah's, and Andres's *stories-so-far*: "I hope to be able to stay here"; "I hope to better myself"; "I hope things will work themselves out." This hope is wedded to and couched in a haunting reality neither resistible nor decolonizable for them. They have arrived at the footsteps of higher education, where they will once more be both invented as dispensable *others* and relegated to spaces reserved for shadows. Still, they will struggle to be resilient in spite of the wreckage of what surrounds and despite the haunt that lives within the bones. *Will they ever have arrived?*

Will the first-generation Mexican and Mexican American students I met at UTRGV ever have arrived? I think of Brisa. When I initially spoke to Brisa, she affirmed to me there was no "regret staying" in the LRGV. "I lied to you," she confesses later, with mixed emotions of laughter and sadness. "I wish I could have had that experience." Brisa means the experience of making it out of the LRGV. Speaking with a sense of impending failure, she notes, "I wish I did not feel guilt for wanting to know it then and now." She is aware of how hauntings have worked and inflicted upon her *stories-so-far*, so she holds hope-struggle as two paradoxical realities. Brisa resorts to expressing hope first, "I tell myself one day." She assents then—"here I am"—in the form of an *awaiting*, hoping that UTRGV will eventually mean making it out. I think of Sandy. "I tricked myself into believing her," Sandy admits. By "her" she means her mom, and by "tricked" she means *assenting* by staying home. "I am stuck," she says. And overcome by an emotion of laughter and sadness, Sandy notes, "I am so tired sometimes"; "waitressing and doing little jobs here and there"; "I can't even think of doing school stuff." She feels stuck, because she can neither make it out of the LRGV nor the generational cycle of being *forced* into the *choice* to put family first before individual goals such as graduating from the university. Sandy assents—"I hope I will be able to finish"—in the form of an *awaiting*, against the backdrop of struggle, "pero quién sabe."

I think of Erica. "I am not happy with where I am," Erica says too with that mixed emotion of laughter and sadness. Her parents did not want to sign her financial aid papers to be able to attend higher education beyond the LRGV. Shrugging at me, holding in each and every emotion, she asks hauntingly and rhetorically, "'¿Qué puedes hacer?' I wish it was not like that. I wish shit was different." Sometimes, the haunting reality is, we are not able to make it out because there are forces working and inflicting upon us beyond our control. (Once upon a time I use to romanticize the idea of the LRGV, and when it came to the food, the best always came from women. But after these interviews, I realized that what I had romanticized was a patriarchy that had normalized and naturalized the place of women as in the household or the kitchen.) *Assent* is a thread that binds Brisa, Sandy, and Erica's *stories-so-far*: "One day"; "I hope"; "¿Qué puedes hacer?" This *assent* is wedded to and couched in a haunting reality that is neither resistible nor decolonizable for them. Hauntings have worked and inflicted upon their *stories-so-far*, doubly minoritized, racialized, and marginalized, invented and relegated to spaces reserved for shadows as *other* . . . as *women*. Still they will struggle to be resilient in spite of the wreckage of what surrounds and despite the haunt that lives within the bones. *Will they ever have arrived?*

Will the first-generation Mexican and Mexican American students I met at the UoU ever have arrived? I think of Lorena. "The car is running low in gas," she tells me one day and asks both rhetorically and quite literally, "where am I going to get money?" But gas money represents only a small part of her worries that have worked and inflicted upon her *stories-so-far* for far too long. "Tengo el bus," she says optimistically, in the face of struggle, relying on laughter to conceal her sadness. Lorena also must worry about how she and her husband are undocumented. They have been waiting for some time to receive their proper papeles. The threat of being deported haunts her daily. Still, making it out of Mexico and making it to the US is worth it. Because for her, there are no other options. "Y si me voy a México? Qué voy a hacer allá?" Lorena's dreams, though still worked and inflicted upon by hauntings, are in the US and not in Mexico. "Acaban de matar [left blank intentionally] nomas por que puso su negocio." If she goes back, impending violence is sure to be part of her everyday once more.

Lorena also worries about being able to put a roof over their heads, put food on the table, and support their family. "Todo cuesta, pero vale la pena." They must work multiple jobs, because the threat of not getting paid or not getting paid fairly is a reality they are *forced* to confront and contend with as an undocumented worker. Because Lorena wants to attend school—the university. She has expressed a sense of guilt for attending a school she cannot afford to pay for. "Of course, federal funding is only for nine-digit students. But I have to do this." But it is Lorena's dream to go to school. She believes it will be a way to make it out of her current haunting circumstances. Lorena has not made it to the university but still emails here and there to remind me that one day she will make it to the school. I tell her constantly that she is welcome to join my class via Zoom. I do so, knowing the repercussions for myself, because I try to take seriously the words of Morrison: "If you have some power, then your job is to empower somebody else" (Houston 2003, n.p.). Our role as educators is to keep hope alive.

 I think of Jake. "I can't stand . . . what I'm made of," Jake tells me. Jake is haunted by who he is. He reads me the poem he wrote for our sit-down (figure 5.4). Jake is a first-generation white-complected Mexican American college student. "Don't speak Spanish. Only speak English," Jake recalls being told throughout his K–12 education. He had no control over what his first language is. "Stand and look at the wall." That was the punishment Jake and others faced in speaking Spanish. Again, these students are not so removed from the history that remains a lived reality. "Native Spanish speakers are racialized and shunned, literally shunned for speaking Spanish," he remembers telling some "Mormon kids" after they tauntingly spoke to him in Spanish for months. "And . . . so?" That is how they responded, he recalls for me. Being of mixed races, mixed cultures, and white-complected, in addition to being taunted for being such, has worked and inflicted upon his *stories-so-far* so much so Jake cannot stand who he is. "I am still coping with what it means to be me," he says laughingly, turning away to wipe what was sure to be tears from his face. "I wish I was just white, so there was nothing to worry about. I wish I was just Brown, so there's everything to worry about," he continues to tell me.

 I think of Sara. "Your accent is not from here. You got high cheekbones. Are you Native?" Sara shares this with me as part of her haunting experience of growing up "Mexican" around "Mormon kids." Her parents never experienced such tauntings too long. "My mom got taken out of school when she was in fourth grade, and Dad dropped out by middle school." Sara is overcome by sadness because that experience has worked and inflicted upon her *stories-so-far* for too long. "I tell myself I have learned how to ignore the looks. I say ni modo, but it still fucks with me afterwards. I just can't have them see that it bothers me." On good days, these students are motivated. On good days, their surroundings and they themselves are their own motivation for making it

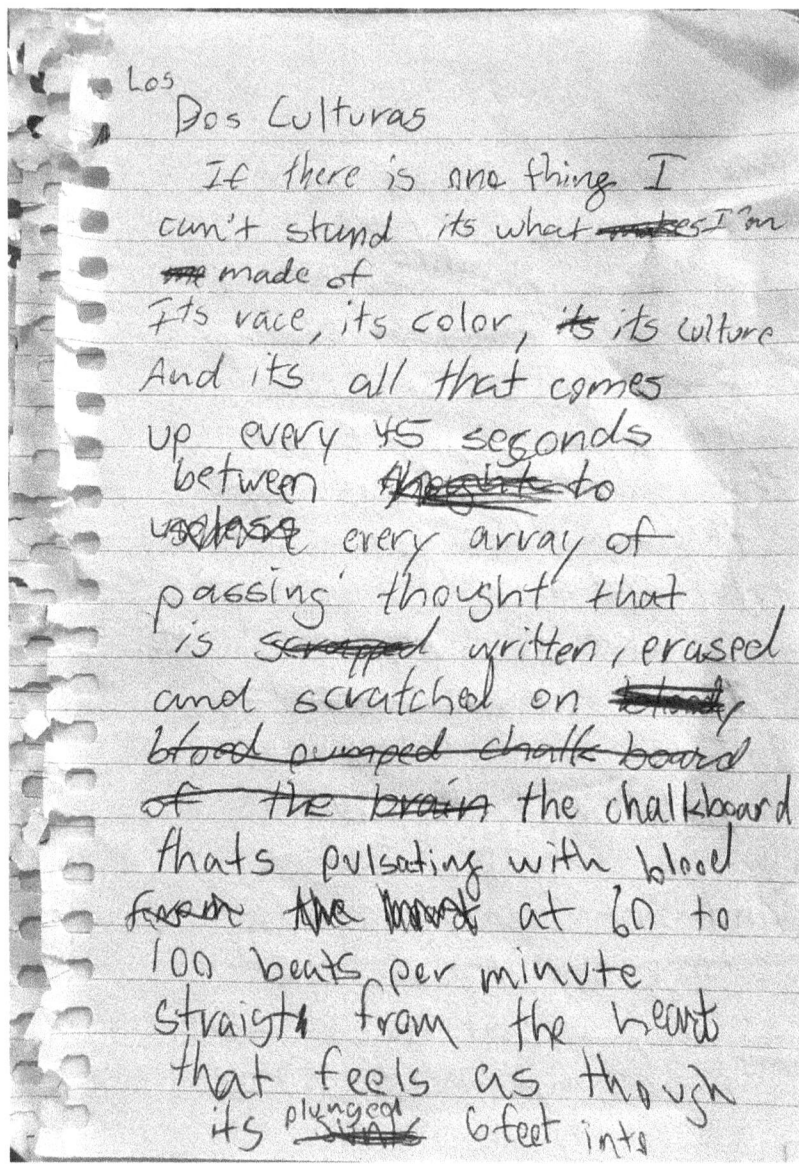

FIGURE 5.4. A student poem, "Los Dos Culturas"

out. I think of Deandra. "I keep myself motivated, because I want to see myself being something other than what I've always grown up with." I think of Amy. "I can't turn back now," she says, "because I'm already here. I can't turn back." I think of Cynthia. "No se adonde voy, pero si se a quien me voy a llegar," she tells me resolutely. This is hope!

FIGURE 5.5. No Papeles

But on bad days, and there are too many to count for them, they are haunted by how they have been *thrown* and *forced* to stand on the outside of society, relegated to spaces reserved for shadows (figure 5.5). I think of Cynthia. "No tengo papeles" (the right papers), she tells me. "Sometimes," she continues, "I close my eyes, and dream about what can be, but other times, I sit at the table knowing that 'no papeles' might mean they could only ever be just that ... dreams." On bad days, it is hard for them to be their own source of self-motivation: "Sometimes it's hard seeing myself persistently here." I broke my own protocol, as I often found myself doing during these interviews, to tell Sara to stay strong. She quickly responds, "I'm pretty weak, you just don't know." On bad days, the haunt is amplified by who their parents are. "My dad," Danny tells me, "he's been in prison most of my life." He continues, "I always thought I was gonna go to prison." On bad days, the world amplifies for them how they will never make it out. *Assent* is a thread that binds Lorena, Jake, Sara, Deandra, Amy, Cynthia, and Danny's *stories-so-far*: "Todo cuesta"; "I am still coping"; "Ni modo." This assent, spoken from a particular place (e.g., Glendale, West Valley, etc.) and from a particular history (e.g., hope-struggle), is wedded to and couched in a haunting reality that is neither resistible nor decolonizable for them. Hauntings have worked and inflicted upon their *stories-so-far*, and the university will become yet another force in their lives that both invents them as dispensable *others* and relegates them to spaces reserved for shadows. Still they will struggle to be resilient in spite of the wreckage of what surrounds and despite the haunt that lives within the bones. *Will they ever have arrived?*

They Who Do Not Surrender Hope

"I want to go to school." "I want to be here." "I want to make it out."

"I think we should take a break." I heard these words repeatedly in interviews over the course of them. But why would students need a break? Because they were being asked to *return* to and *carefully reckon* with histories, memories, and sets of *stories-so-far*. There were many haunted/haunting realizations: that hauntings lived deep within their bones; that their hopes of making it out was prearranged by and part of their cultural and thinking program because of hauntings; that their in/ability to make it out was mitigated by hauntings. "Es mucho" and "Mas pesado de lo que pensaba" were common responses. Interviews were a demanding process. They confirmed to students what they knew already. Students understood what was at stake if they failed and knew their choices to pursue higher education went against family wishes. But they desperately wanted to make it out. And so for the female student, for example, who was forced to compromise—stay in the LRGV and go to school there or figure out a way to get financial aid without her parents' help—the choice was hardly a choice at all but a demand. Students needed to make it out. We often took breaks to provide room to think, feel, be, and, yes, even cry-*with* each other off the record.

I too needed a break. Hearing the haunting words above (*"I want to go to school"; "I want to be here"; "I want to make it out"*) took its toll on me day in and day out. Because these words came with specific emotions, and I understood those emotions all too well. I too knew what it meant to be *thrown* into the world of colonial difference; *forced* to learn how to address oneself to hauntings; and *imperiled* to mitigate a precarious subject position of *becoming a subject* in rather than simply *being a subject* of hauntings. I too knew the experience of having a parent prevent my ability to make it out by withholding her signature on a FASFA form. At the time, the only discernible difference between us was that I carried the burden of knowing that hauntings are neither removed nor do they cease presencing because one leaves or makes it out of South Texas. On any given day, one could witness me and a student in the classrooms, hallways, stairways, and/or library sharing an emotional experience. The words above are haunting because students understood that behind the hope they clinched and hitched onto, it will never have been that simple to make it out. And some students would not. The reasons for students dropping out of school varied: grades, familial obligations and responsibilities, financial needs, and/or immigration issues. And yet hauntings and haunting situations are certainly the thread that binds those reasons.

The students I interviewed refused to surrender hope. That hope was steeped in struggle. Holding hope-struggle as two paradoxical realities is the hallmark of barrio literacies. I learned from surveys, interviews, and student writing that many came from single-parent households and were economically disadvantaged. But this is only part of their haunted/haunting *stories-so-far*. "My life didn't start out well," Santana shares with me. "I had to grow up pretty fast." What did he mean by "grow up"? He meant being *thrown* into "fucked-up situations," forced to address himself to those "situations that kept him up at night," and imperiled to mitigate a precarious subject position of "being like her" and having hope that one "can be more than that." Manuel shares a similar experience to Santana's: "Coming from a broken home isn't an easy thing but we had enough." Like Santana, Manuel felt obligated and responsible for helping to put food on the table by any means necessary: stealing, begging, slanging. It all echoes what Morrison (2017) wrote about the work we do, the people we are: "I was adultlike, not childlike" (n.p.). These students chose to believe it was possible to create light in the shadows and darkness, which was hardly a choice at all but a demand.

Some of the students expressed appreciation for their parents, who did the best they could for them. Karina, recognizing and acknowledging the sacrifices her parents have made, says, "Life is hard and nothing is given. I was provided with what I needed and not with what I wanted." She wanted me to know how her parents "worked hard every day in order to provide the best for the family." Danielle spoke of how her mother "never finished high school," and how her father "dropped out of middle school," but how both "did their best." Rodrigo, reflecting on the struggles and obstacles that his parents faced, tells me, "They have always been a symbol of inspiration to me." Though their *stories-so-far* would be telling of their life challenges, the ethos and praxis of holding hope-struggle as two paradoxical realities that they would inherit, embody, experience, and practice provided a foundation for persevering. "Always being expected to fail," Tony notes, "made me realize what I had to overcome." Similarly, Karina remarks, "I grew up with my mind set on success but also prepared for failure." What did they have to overcome? They had to overcome hauntings and haunting situations and what haunted/haunting literacies, images-signs-sounds, and rhetorics will have made of their *stories-so-far*. And why did Tony and Karina anticipate failure? Because their everyday communicated to them generational cycles of haunted/haunting *stories-so-far*. They knew nothing else. Still, they persisted. They refused to surrender hope. (They needed not theory or the projects of unsettling and a decolonial option. It only underscored further the looming threat of failure.) They had hope for the *possibilities of new stories*.

The experiences of their parents and their own lives would become inspiration for breaking generational cycles and making it out. Danielle shared with me, "The day of high school graduation reminded me I'm setting a new norm." Not many in her family had graduated from high school. She had hope that her accomplishment would inspire her cousins. Sandy tells me, "I am the first in my family to graduate high school, to attend college." She was proud of that too, but was also extremely concerned about what it would mean to fail. Why? Beyond the obvious, it most likely meant that the generational cycles of haunted/haunting *stories-so-far* would endure without interruption. Matthew, reflecting on how he will "go beyond what is expected of me," unwaveringly tells me, "I plan to become one of the few to have earned a degree." What did Matthew mean by the first part? Well, there is, unfortunately, an expectation of failure, both communicated and internalized, when one comes from the kind of background he does. There are countless other accounts of students celebrating. But it was all done with caution. "I finally made it," Carolina says, reflecting on being a student at UTRGV, "but I am scared of failing." She later dropped out because of grades. "God willing," Mateo notes, "I will become the first in my family." He continues, "I'm here trying to change the belief that college is not for us, not just for me, but for the younger generation." Mateo also later dropped out because of financial needs. It will never have been that simple to break generational cycles and make it out. Still, they persisted. They refused to surrender hope. They had hope for the *possibilities of new stories*.

The refusal to surrender hope kept the hope for the *possibilities of new stories* alive. Even, that is to say, in the wake of hauntings and haunting situations. Gabby, reflecting on how college had provided a new mindset for her, says, "I will not settle anymore." She struggled during her first year, but as she tells me, "I want more than with this place could offer me." Gabby continues, "I know life doesn't have to be like this [life in the LRGV]." Jose, reflecting on what college means to him, similarly states, "I definitely like the new Jose."

College gave him a renewed sense of self and being. He continues, "I feel like I can do anything, that I can make it anywhere." And Tovar, similarly, notes, "I am really looking forward to what is ahead." He expresses to me happiness that he can imagine himself in the future and plan ahead at last. I cannot say this enough: these students understood how the haunt lives deep within their bones. Still, they persisted, amid all the struggle and even the lack of familial support that cast doubts, seeded distrust, and fostered more tensions, contradictions, and paradoxes for them. They refused to surrender hope. They had hope for the *possibilities of new stories*.

There are familial ties that students have inherited, embodied, experienced, and even practiced. "The very idea of going to college," Brisa notes, "drove me." Brisa wanted to go to college outside of the LRGV. She worried, however, about leaving her family behind. "I would be a fool not to go," she shared. Ultimately, she did not go to college outside of the LRGV because her family told her they needed her close. "I do not regret staying," she says, pausing throughout those five words just to complete the sentence. Sandy shared a similar experience: "My mom influenced me to stay in the Valley." When asked if there was a reason provided, she stated, "She wanted me close and she said there were opportunities here too." Lesley, reflecting on her sister's experience, notes, "Mom and Dad didn't help her with financial aid because they didn't want her to go to college." She stayed, hoping they would not do the same to her, and they did not, and in that way, she hoped to not drop out like her sister. Each of the above students shared with me that they stayed because of familial obligations and responsibilities. What are those exactly? For students who identified as female, it was to stay home, care for the house, help family members, and if they so chose to pursue higher education, to do so nearby. What haunts them is how they can see and feel their future-to-come, the unending cycle that looms in the distance. Still, they persisted. They refused to surrender hope. They had hope for their *possibilities of new stories*.

The refusal to surrender hope is what motivates them to continue to dwell in the struggle. Katrina tells me, "Some things make us strong," but pauses here before she feels comfortable to say, "when we can overcome them." She continues, "It has been tough. You know. I work multiple jobs to make sure I stay in school." Katrina does not receive any financial help from her parents. She lives with her grandma as the condition for her parents signing FASFA, yet they have cut off communication with her as she defied their wishes. Abrienda recalls for me how her parents told her, "A university is too much for you," and how she was, "wasting [her] time." She exhibited her ethos and praxis of hope-struggle as far back as when she was thirteen years old. "This is my dream," Abrienda tells me. "I left home when I was 13 years old," she says, "because I knew my future depended on my decisions and not theirs." In the throes and face of uncertainties, she left Mexico for the US. Higher education comes at a price. But the prospect of making it out, of overcoming hauntings and what haunted/haunting literacies, images-signs-sounds, and rhetorics have made of their *stories-so-far*, is worth the struggle for these students. They persisted, refusing to surrender hope, because they had hope for their *possibilities of new stories*.

Student struggles did not end with the home or the university. Racism and discrimination also factored in, accumulated into, and constituted their haunted/haunting *stories-so-far*. "Sir, I use to hate working at Peter Pipers when the Winter Texans would come down," Erica tells me. When asked why, she stated: "One time, some guy and his wife came up to me and asked if I understood English." Adjusting herself to imitate the Winter Texan, Erica says, "DO YOU . . . UNDERSTAND . . . EN . . . GL . . . ISH [with hand gestures]." Erica continues, "When I responded that I am Mexican American and born in the U.S., she looked at me up and down first, and then, said, 'Well you don't look like it.'" Olivia reflected on a similar encounter with a Winter Texan: "The lady asked me if I was from Mexico." When asked how she responded, she laughed and said, "I asked them, are you from Germany or something?" Jacky had not experienced blatant racism and discrimination as Erica and Olivia had, but she reflected on the stories her father shared with her: "My dad wanted to know what 'research' I was part [of]. So I told him." She continues, "He took me on a drive later that afternoon to his old neighborhood. It made him emotional," Jacky says, "to talk about the things they [white people who lived on the other block] would call him and the way they treated him and his friends." Still, they persisted. They refused to surrender hope. They had hope for the *possibilities of new stories*.

ABRIENDA

Abrienda wanted to make it out. She had dreams of being a nurse. Abrienda knew this much since an early age—thirteen, to be exact. She was born in Mexico. She left home when she was thirteen years old. Abrienda stayed with an aunt in Weslaco, Texas. "My future," she shared, "depended on my decision and not theirs [parents']." So Abrienda left, with the "idea of persuading [pursuing] my dreams." The dream was more of a right she believed she had: the "right of having a better education." Mexico could not offer such an education. Abrienda dreamed of a place beyond Mexico. She had dreams that would situate her in the US and in college in the US. Abrienda knew what her decision meant. She was breaking customs, of obeying one's parents, of being a woman of Mexican descent, of being attentive to the household and/or being nurturing. "I want to be a good wife, I want to be a mother," Abrienda tells me, "but just on my own time." She had dreams, she had hope: "Everyone has their own expectations for me, but I have my own too." Abrienda recalls how she had to take care of herself and be independent, even though she was living with a family member. She felt unwanted and uncomfortable both in her new home and at school:

> My aunt gave me a mattress, not a bed. She placed it outside the restroom in the hall. I had no privacy. I put my clothes on [in] plastic bags. Her daughter used to inspect my bags and take my earrings, necklaces, or anything she liked that was mine. All she said after I found that she did that was "I'll give it back to you, don't be mean," but that never happened.

In school, Abrienda not knowing any English, did not have any friends. Classmates, though they were of Mexican descent and/or Mexican heritage, called her "wetback," "the Mexican girl," and "beaner." During lunch, she would spend her times in the restroom: "I spent the lunch hour crying." To gain the support of her parents to attend college, Abrienda moved back to Mexico. "I cross the border every single day to make it to school," she tells me. "It's hard to cross every day," Abrienda says, "because of everything that is going on in Mexico." How fitting and yet haunting it was to hear her say, "No quiero parar," for it spoke to her dispositions, an *assent* and an *awaiting*. "My dreams and goals are in the U.S.A.," she says, "and it doesn't matter how difficult it is. I know it's not impossible." Abrienda had not made it out, neither of her house or the LRGV, the last time I checked-in, but she had also not stopped moving. She persists, refusing to surrender hope, because she has hope for her *possibilities of new stories*.

ERICA

Erica wanted to make it out. She had dreams of being a journalist. Erica recalled for me her earliest of talks with her parents about college: "We don't think it is the right option for you." Her parents asked that she help by getting a job. They were struggling financially. "Maybe you will find someone," Erica recalls them saying, "Así que no tienes que preocuparte." She notes, "I am

Mexicana. I know what that means," and she continues, "I love my grandma, but I don't want to be responsible for taking care of her. I need to take care of myself." Erica struggled with what was believed to be her role as a woman: "I'm Mexicana, you know, but I know I don't want to be or feel stuck." She hesitated to apply to college; afraid that her parents would find out; afraid they would be disappointed in her; afraid they would disown her. "Why couldn't I go to college?" she asks rhetorically. "I am not easily corrupted," Erica tells me, reflecting on one of the reasons her parents told her college might not be the right option. She ended up applying to college behind her parents' back. Erica provided me with a reason:

> There was no expectation for me to continue after high school. I believed in this until I met a teacher who said I could make it in college. I struggle, and at times I want to quit school, but I remember where I come from and I remember how strong I have become because of those experiences.

Erica, at first, believed her story was fixed. "I have dreams, sir, you know," she says. When Erica received her acceptance letters, her parents found out. Right away they told her she could not attend school and should not even think about going to school outside of the LRGV. "I needed to take care of grandma, they told me, which I had done for a long time," Erica recalls. She had a big decision to make. Erica told her parents she was going to school. At first, they told her she would be at fault if something were to happen to her grandma. Then they refused to sign her financial aid paperwork. At last, they agreed to a compromise. "They demanded I stay near and visit weekly," she says. "I agreed. But this was not my dream," Erica, trying to hold her emotions in, states. Erica made it out of her house but never did make it out of the LRGV. She dropped out of school.

SANTANA

Santana wanted to make it out. He had dreams of being an engineer. Neither his mom nor his dad had a formal education; both of them worked, but this experience, according to Santana, helped him realize the importance of education. He was headstrong but dealing with so much: financial issues, familial obligations, a full-time job, and a full-time school schedule. Our last meeting was memorable. We met for lunch, and he had asked if we could talk in private, somewhere away from people. As soon as we found a space, Santana broke down. He was on the verge of failing out of school because of his grades. Santana was failing all of his classes and had stopped going to class. He asked if I could help him fill out some paperwork. While some of the paperwork consisted of appeals for school, the majority of the paperwork was for citizenship purposes for his father. Santana's father was going to be deported back to Mexico. I asked Santana, almost stupidly, what he was going to do if things did not work out for him:

> I will work. What else will I do? I will work. I will do what I have to do. I know I fucked up. I know. But it's hard, you know, having to worry about all that shit. I needed to be strong and I wasn't. What do you think I will do? What I will have to do? Where I will end up? I want to be here. It's not that I want to be a failure. My biggest accomplishment was making it here.

That day, Santana and I had a long conversation about whether or not HSIs are actually serving or merely enrolling. "Well, look how many of us are here," he tells me, "and look at how many of us graduate," he says. We ended the conversation there. It did not feel right to record or to continue with the interview business as usual. I heard from Santana a year later. He added me on Facebook. Santana's father was deported. He had indeed dropped out of school. But he assured me in a message that he was good. Santana reached out to simply ask: "If I ever needed help, can I reach out?" I assured Santana he could. Santa made it out of the LRGV, like he wanted to. Perhaps, however, not in the most ideal way. He joined the army, which allowed him to provide for his family back home and the new family he was in the process of making.

To understand what hauntings and haunting situations have done to and made of students we can turn to their *stories-so-far*. They will tell us that we are all un/settled by our local histories of hauntings, inheritances, and dwellings. But while an oppressor-oppressed environment most certainly materialized in the everyday of the students above, life and agency still cannot be reduced to binaries (black/white; good/bad; right/wrong) and options (surrender; assimilate; resist; confront-resignify) as proposed by the MCC. Because what these *stories-so-far* will tell us is that students make do with what is available to them, despite hauntings and in spite of gaining meaning from hauntings and haunting situations. That is their barrio mentality (hope-struggle) at work. Their capacity for action that is enabled and created by hauntings and haunting situations is a form of agency even as it stems from the shadows-and-below. These students cannot renew a sense of self, being, or agency if they cannot make it out; they cannot begin to heal if they have not yet made it out. Who are we to determine for them what life and agency ought to mean?

Early Days

Ellos no son pobrecitos. The students wanted me to know, so that I could one day share, that they were anything but this. They are resilient. A barrio mentality (hope-struggle) is born out of people who have survived and who, despite all the struggles, maintain hope. I only hope that in this chapter I have shed light on that dynamic between hope and struggle. Does one ever truly make it out of the "zone[s] of nonbeing" (Fanon 1986, 10) or "deaths-space[s] in the land of the living" (Taussig 1991, 133), where the "half dead" (Anzaldúa 1999, 25) and people at the "company of death" (Maldonado-Torres 2007, 257) are relegated to? They, those who refuse to surrender hope, have hope in such *possibilities of new stories*.

I initially planned for *stories-so-far* of Mexican, Mexican American, Latino/as, and Hispanic students to be separated to avoid conflation and erasure of difference. Chapters would reflect what I learned from literacy history interviews conducted. The role of women cannot be overlooked in the lives of these students. "Mrs. Brenda Rodriguez and Mrs. Mary Rodriguez," Abrienda recalls, "they used music in English to help me understand and to gain more vocabulary . . . [they] thought [taught] me how to face the American school, and society." Erica shares, "My mom would read with me the Spanish billboards off the highway [and expressway], have me record its messages on a tape player, and then when I would get home, help me translate and sound it [the message] out in English." "My grandma," Delia tells me, "would let me use the handbooks she received from the literacy centers. We would sit together and fill them out."

I have been dissatisfied with studies that fail to distinguish degrees of dominance with language use (monolingual; bilingual). Their lives are full of tensions, *frictions*, contradictions, and paradoxes. "Speaking Spanish," Andrea shares, "is a sign of respect, but for my mom, it also meant opportunities." But students felt alienated by family members who claimed they were being "fancy." Delia tells me, "I felt like I was betraying my Mexican culture, but then I felt like I was not getting to enjoy learning a new language either." But they also felt estranged by friends. "They think, 'bien presumido,'" Lorena says, "but why not learn a new language?" The interviews tell of Spanish-dominant, English-dominant, and in-between bilinguals, bilinguals who speak in a dialect that has linguistic elements reflective of their ethnolinguistic makeup. It is a dialect that weaves languages, creates friction in and unsettles language use, and (re)makes a language born out of an ethos and praxis of making do with what is available (Anzaldúa 1999).

I have been displeased too with how students are reduced to "Chicano/a" or "immigrants" in WRS. Interviews provide some insight. Marisol claimed, "I don't know what it means to speak Chicano, but I've heard of it [the identity] in movies." Efrian sarcastically remarks, "What is Chicano?" And Mariana asks skeptically, "Do people actually say Chicano?" Santana tells me he is "dissatisfied" with how some professors try to "relate to other students" through "that [Chicanismo]." He continues, "They think we are all Chicanos . . . and our histories are Chicano histories." If anything, the interviews underscored how *we are where we do and think*. Efrian offers insight, "Soy de el Valle . . . soy valle." While the reflections above are specific to a region, they underscore again the importance of the question *Where is one at and who is one teaching?* I had an agenda, but sometimes life is complex, complicated, and messy, just like research, and because of that, I had to shift, adapt, and reinterpret what my true work was to be.

I shifted from literacy history interviews to haunted/haunting *stories-so-far* because I noticed they were constellated by hauntings and haunting situations. These first-generation students were haunted by life that dealt them a tough hand, but they bucked gender scripts and roles (familial obligations-responsibilities), utilized "Hispanic" to negotiate racist and discriminatory environments, and "played the game" for the prospect of making it out. "This is my dream," recall Abrienda saying. They were haunted by faculty that attempted to mirror their everyday, but they *chose* a language and writing that was foreign to them because they wanted to make it out. Santana reflects, "We think, oh cool, the classroom is like the outside and no one will say otherwise because they too feel comfortable, but where does that get us beyond here?" He cannot quite put his finger on it, but what it touches on is the haunting by and internalization of Nott and Gliddon's (1854) words and ideas, that "no culture can eradicate" the *other-ness* that marks the *other* (283).

Students make a choice that is hardly a choice at all but a demand. Take, for example, Marisol, whom I observed writing a sentence in English with side notes in Spanish. She notes, "When I think about things, I do it unconsciously in Spanish, because that is my first language. It is the language I still think and dream in." Marisol reflects, "I appreciate that they [a professor] does not make a big deal or get mad at us like others do. I am allowed to learn the way I know how, but that's not good all the time." Abrienda shares in this sentiment, "Many of us think in Spanish but are pushing ourselves to write and speak in English." Students appreciate faculty that encourage them to practice their language and writing facilities without judgment, recourse, and/or pressure to assimilate. But for some students who struggle with financial insecurities and self-efficacy, assimilation is not a choice but a demand that carries the prospect of making it out.

The kinds of *stories-so-far* shared above are few and far between in WRS. Yes, students found the projects of unsettling and a decolonial option promising. But life and agency cannot be reduced to the MCC's binaries (black/white; good/bad; right/wrong) and options (surrender; assimilate; resist; confront-resignify). These are students made to believe they cannot be more than what time and history, circumstance and hauntings, places and experiences have done to and made of them (see Baldwin 1984a; Fanon 1986; Hall 1996). They do their best not to surrender hope and struggle to be persistent in the throes and face of hauntings. Resistance, subversion, and resignification may or may not be on their minds (see Mahmood 2014). To deliberate and judge these students on how they make do with what is available to them based on superficial options though is a grave mistake that amounts to more policing. This makes a decolonial option unsuitable for *anyone* who arrives at our doors.

So, overall, I wanted to share a story of how decolonizing knowledge-being can be conceptually, pedagogically, and emotionally complex, complicated, messy, and to some extent impossible. And yet my experiences were most instructive, telling me something important about the demand for something else. It situates me squarely on a repeated question throughout this book: Can the *archives* feel? A *discourse about actions* approach would evidence the refusal to surrender hope in the *possibilities of new stories*; they, who exist through a hope-struggle despite hauntings and haunting situations, which want nothing more than to keep them in perpetual despair. The duty of the educator thus is to stand at the nexus of another's *stories-so-far* and *possibilities of new stories*. Friction! Again, an *opportunity* to *get to work* or get in the way. But friction, of course, is different, again, from being part of the problem—a preparation of a teaching of writing and rhetoric unsuitable for *anyone* who arrives at our doors—which I make known throughout this chapter. I know today, as I will discuss in the final chapter, that in the demand for something else, there is still an archival approach and theory of archival impressions to be worked out.

Section 3

The Demand for Something Else

Reflexión-Meditación

Joining the Band

"Pa que se quite." It is an interesting phrase. The denotation can be reduced to formally mean to *remove*: "rozar la camisa pa que se le quite la mancha." Or it can mean to *take away*, "tomar las pastillas de Tylenol pa que se le quite el dolor." The connotation of *pa que se quite* can mean a lesson to be learned from *something deserved*: se cayó de la bicicleta. Ya ves, pa que se quite. Now, the unknown is the reason for falling off the bike. However, the saying "ya ves" already grounds the understood, or the culpable, the reason for falling is due in part to one's own doing.

"Pa que se quite" is a deceptive phrase that betrays and undermines its own proper meaning. (Let us recall Derrida [1997] if only to underscore the point I am getting at: "The so-called proper name, is always caught in a chain or a system of differences" [89]; "the proper name has never been ... anything but the original myth of a transparent legibility present under the obliteration" [109].) The experience never leaves us even if the lesson is learned. Because even with physically leaving a space or place, it can never *remove* or *take away* hauntings, inheritances, and/or dwellings from our *archives*. (That is the trace mark of the border[ed]lander experience—those neither wholly present nor absent, those who will have arrived in our classrooms with all the weight of hauntings, inheritances, and dwellings bearing down on them.

They hope-struggle to join the band, though, so that they can hear a different tune.) Was that ever the point, though, of pa que se quite? Pa que se quite, a praxis of knowing (¡entiendes!) and unknowing (¿entiendes?). "I am," Fanon (1986) will have written, "one who waits," which I amend slightly with "awaits," for I can never know if the lesson (or I for that matter) will ever have arrived . . . too soon . . . too late . . . or ever at all (120). Still, I/we must *go on* without knowing.

I was a child when I felt hauntings and haunting situations around me. In middle school I joined the band—it allowed me to hear a different tune than that of navigating the loss of my sense of "home." Though I often thought I was "too cool" for band, I knew then as I do now that it provided a space to escape and a place to find tranquility in the wreckage that surrounds. And for the first two years of high school, I participated in band as much as I could, given my circumstances—it allowed me to see different places, feel different attunements, hear a different tune (the tune of a future-to-come returning), and make it out of the Valley, even if only temporarily. Though I was *thrown* into my ancestral haunts in unending cycles, I had joined the band, and neither hauntings nor haunting situations could take away this new music that was in me. And though nothing can *remove* or *take away* the haunt that lives deep within the bones, I went *on*, marching to a different tune, not knowing where *there* is or whether I would ever have arrived *there*—somewhere . . . nowhere (see Gómez-Peña 1996).

Over the years I have realized that perhaps we all join the band at some point—all playing our own instruments, marching to different tunes, but harmonizing-in-difference, nonetheless. I find that I am still partly como mi tío, terco about partaking in the band, and marching to the beat of my own drum. But I am also like Grandma, who strived to see a comadre/compadre in every person and to see life in the full spectrum of matter (living, nonliving, nonhuman). I have this fond memory of Grandma humming to a *foreign* tune in the backyard while teaching me about a *foreign* relationship—"we/arth." When I left home, I had lost a sense for *it*, but since her passing, I have *longed* for *it*. Today, I go on without knowing whether we will ever have made it out of the *Archive*. "We/arth," though, is something *worth* marching to. "We/arth" is an "old" forgotten (and not lost) song—primordial and ancestral—turned a *foreign* language to some. Poetically and literally, "we" and "earth" are one; ages after and the trace marks still remain. How do we honor then what was always already our arrangement? "We/arth" *a/waits* our address, which now must be addressed in the form of a corrido-ing approach. We may not ever make it out, but we can return to, march to, and harmonize-in-difference to *an-other* archive—"We/arth." Will we ever have joined that band?

What came before the *Archive*? "We/arth" came before *it*. Will a harmony of the "we/arth"—both in the idea that humans and earth are an archive and that both think, feel, and do alike—ever have arrived? An existential question—yes, I know—but I am interested in wor(l)ding some *thing* else than this modern/colonial and settlerizing world. I *await*, a hope without guaranteed predicate, a hope for that which may or may not arrive.

Conclusion

Being-and-Becoming Recognizable to "We/arth"

There Is No Making It Out is not at all about making it out. Such a rhetoric risks reproducing the conditions of unsettling and resettling. This book, rather, is about the demand for some *thing* else. On the one hand, conversation of this book focused on the *Archive* and the ways its *epistemic system* and designs are shared-in, imported, and expanded-disputed by the archival impressions of *ideas* across scenes of history in the US. It is an *Archive* in the unending cycle of being made, unmade, and remade. On the other hand, conversations centered on how that *Archive* and its haunted/haunting *story-so-far* contaminates the *archives* of the students we teach. I invoke hauntings as a category of analysis but also as a *thing* that acts on land, memory, knowledge, and relationality after *things* or the ideas, images-signs-sounds, and ends of some *one* has passed. The essential focus of this book took shape in the form of a question: How do we reposition the contents of archives so that we can position ourselves in relation to it *otherwise*? I attempted to answer such a question, one that situates us squarely on wor(l)ding, through the projects of unsettling and a decolonial option. I demonstrated how wording is human work through a *decolonial analytic* and how the everyday involves human projects that can *take* and can *make* place or, in other words, world. The last two chapters worked toward a *prospective vision*, which proved to be conceptually, pedagogically, and emotionally complex, complicated, and messy. I say I failed in those chapters because life and agency were reduced to binaries (black/white; good/bad; right/wrong) and options (surrender; assimilate; resist; confront-resignify), and/or I failed to hold students accountable while emphasizing their capacity for transformation (see McLeod 1998). These chapters have proven to be most instructive though in telling me something important about the demand for some *thing* else.

I argued at the onset that *There Is No Making It Out* is not actually about making it out. It is about the *stories-so-far* of our *archives*; the question of obligation and responsibility if "We" are not interested in giving back to the *Archive* in the same way; the exigence for initiating decolonizing archival impressions; and the hope that impressions may give way to the *possibilities of new stories—an-other* archive. But as evidenced in the two previous chapters, decolonizing knowledge-being can be conceptually, pedagogically, and emotionally complex, complicated, messy, and to some extent impossible because human beings are involved. Decolonization might not exist. Perhaps, it ought not to, not as a proper name. There is still, however, the matter of a demand, on the one hand, for an *analytic* that can contend with modern/colonial and settlerizing designs and, on the other hand, a *prospective vision* that can imagine a future without hauntings and haunting situations unhitched from the rhetorics of deterministic binaries (black/white; good/bad; right/wrong) and options (surrender; assimilate; resist; confront-resignify). In the face of the limits of decolonizing knowledge-being, I have hope that one day we can initiate a clearing for a zone of wor(l)ding—a space and place where the doors of our everyday are open to anyone, where best practices reflect a preparation of *thinking*, *feeling*, and *being-with* everyone in the fabric of the full spectrum of matter (living, nonliving, nonhuman), and where diverse wor(l)dings can get to work. Whether or not this ultimately goes by the name *pluriversality*, I have hope that it is nonetheless a possibility to be worked out—that, indeed, we can rise to this level of obligation and responsibility. If, as I contend though, the time of proper names has reached a logical end, then what next?

It is possible both to name without revealing a proper name and to have as an orientation the thinking of some *things* under erasure. The former, a recognition of the necessity to name, and the latter, an acknowledgment that it is "already no more than a so-called proper name" (Derrida 1997, 109). What if then we were to radically reframe decolonization in the context of a crisis, critique, and unworking of knowing. By "crisis," I mean the awareness some *things* are beyond the reaches of being known and archived; by "critique," I mean that which unsettles the settled; and by "unworking," I mean a praxis of unknowing. We would be left with a proper name that has reached a logical end. Yet in that impossible yet productive space of historicity and rhetoricity, it becomes possible to think of decolonization not as the name we give to designate the arrival of some *things* but as an actioning of *being-and-becoming* that can rupture, clear, and create an opening for an-other option, obligation, and responsibility. So I call for a decolonizing archival impression thus, one that unsettles the order of the constituted, decolonizing—sharing a resemblance with decolonization only in name—and one initiated as an impression with a name (always already under erasure) that conveys an *enduring and ongoing* process. Will it ever have arrived?

What is good in theory does not always translate or bode well in practice. Now, like Fanon (1963), others warn about the the predicament of differing positions of metaphysics and of decoloniality becoming intelligible and clear to itself (Acosta 2012, 2019; Alcoff 2007; Cortez and García 2020; Cusicanqui 2012; García and Cortez 2020; Moreiras 2001). I will not rehash those conversations for it would be unproductive. I am interested in what comes after the critique (and what is to come after my own failures). I find that it is sufficient then to quote Bhabha's (1994) question here, "Is our only way out of such dualism the espousal of an implacable oppositionality or the invention of an originary counter-myth of radical purity?" (29). What is at stake in *cultivating the exceptional* is a reproduction of what constitutes a proper arrival and arrivant. Such will inevitably affect how we carry out the human work and projects of relation-ing. If a proper arrival and arrivant is known in advance, then it has already foreclosed on another's *possibilities of new stories* and made a decolonial option unsuitable for *anyone*. Life and agency cannot be reduced to binaries (black/white; good/bad; right/wrong) and options (surrender; assimilate; resist; confront-resignify). It amounts to more cultural, epistemological, ontological, and rhetorical propriety by reintroducing reductive, dichotomous, and/or oppositional rhetorical structures. Such structures would strain efforts to constellate *archives*, wor(l)d decolonizing archival impressions, and unsettle the settled-ness of the *Archive*. A decolonial option will remain unsuitable for *anyone* if we do not come to terms with truth-and-knowledge claims and rhetoricity.

The classroom is not unaffected here. The question *where is one at and who is one teaching* is good, in principle, until it is not. Humanities scholars-educators know that while they are entangled and complicit in the *idea of the University*, not all *complicities are equivalent* nor required (Baker-Bell, Butler, and Johnson 2017; hooks 2003; Peña 2022; Spivak 1994; Wynter 2003). At face value, a decolonial option appears to aid in the unsettling of the settled. One must consider, as Silvia Rivera Cusicanqui (2012) does, though that there can be no "discourse" or "theory" of decolonization "without a decolonizing practice" (100; also see Freire 2000). What constitutes the educator's praxis and how does it translate? If the previous two chapters on failure are any indication, the desire to "decolonize" knowledge and the objective to "decolonize" students on their arrival already presupposes that at the very least educators are in possession of and/or are emitting the right signs. A rhetorical analysis between the MCC's work (see Mignolo 2007, 2009, 2011b, 2013; Maldonado-Torres 2007; Tlostanova 2017b) and Latinx scholarship in WRS (see Ruiz and Sanchez 2016; Ruiz and Baca 2017; Ruiz 2018) underscores that perception—automatic equations between a position/ality and disposition that amount to what Lisa Flores (2020) might call *stoppage* (250–258). At least part of the issue in WRS stems from a *strategic essentialism*, initiated by an appeal to return to a proper space, place, and time (see Dussel 1995; Mejía 1999; Villanueva 1999; D. Baca and Villanueva 2010; García and Baca 2019), which instead of ushering in a temporary point of departure, trafficked as the actual conditions that give rise to politics (see Ritchie 1990; Pred 1995). And this is exacerbated first by presupposing a proper arrivant, and second by determining a proper arrival based on binaries and options. The same premise above applies here: if a proper arrival and arrivant is known in advance, then it has already foreclosed on another's *possibilities of new stories* and engaged in a preparation of a teaching of writing and rhetoric unsuitable for *anyone*. A decolonial option will remain unsuitable, again, if we do not come to terms with truth-and-knowledge claims and rhetoricity (also see West 2009).

It is not my intention to give the impression that the question I am asking is whether we should move past the affordances of a decolonial option. No! We ought to till the grounds on which power takes root. Rather, the question is, how do we unsettle the proper of a proper name so that it both remains an option and creates the conditions by which decolonizing knowledge-being may be possible in the classroom and beyond? Even that which was meant to unsettle can benefit from being unsettled. As Said (1983) argued, the role of the scholar-educator is to "provide resistances to theory" and "open it up toward historical reality, toward society, toward human needed and interests" (242). Alcoff (2011), Derrida (1994b), Fanon (1986), and A. Gordon (2008), among others, will continue guiding me in that endeavor. How does knowledge exist and truth emerge? Alcoff calls for a revitalization of reconstructive work in epistemology where truth is responsible to the complexities of reality

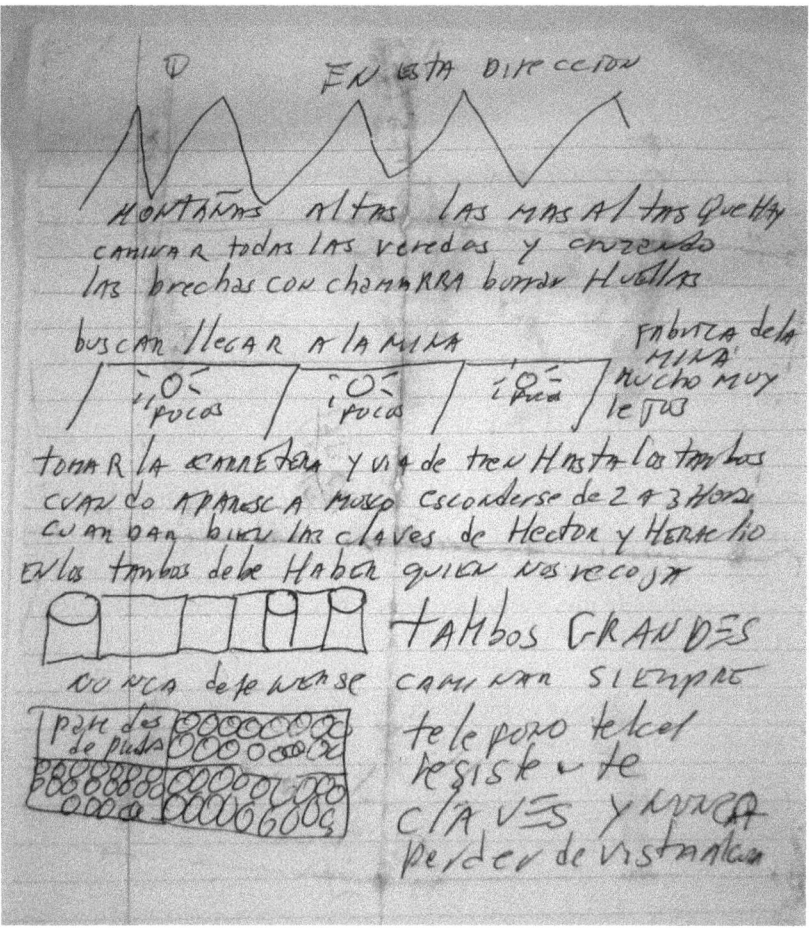

FIGURE 6.1. En Esta Dirección

and to political realities. If forgetting and conjuring away are essential to the *Archive*, then why not approach hauntings, inheritances, and responsibility as language, rhetoric, and corporeal exercise of address to remember and conjure forth. Derrida and Gordon are advancing a politics of each. How do we work toward both opening the door "of *every* consciousness" and loving another "wherever" they may be and in the *non-name of all*? Fanon to even Acosta (2012) pleaded for the world of the *You*, which the MCC might refer to as *pluriversality* (see Escobar 2020). The proper of a proper name has reached a logical end and there remains the demand for something else. What next, then?

There is an "unofficial" map that sits on my desk today (figure 6.1). It was given to a colleague and me while we were documenting experiences among dairy workers in Upstate New York (see Fox et al. 2017). The three words at the top, "En Esta Dirección," are like a sign that flashes out a warning, serendipitous given the conversations above; only, it is read as a prescriptive checklist and roadmap. The "this" in the instructions indicates a proper place of arrival. But words sometimes betray themselves, unable to deliver on their promise of direction and thus unsettling their own proper name and subsequently the knowledge and understanding of their steward. The words, like Grandma's *entiendes* at the onset of this book project, haunt me in returning to this map. I can read the map—walk all the paths, erase footprints with my jacket—that circulates within palimpsestic times (Alexander 2005), identities (Shohat 2002), narratives (A. García 2004), and an *archive of feeling* (Cvetkovich 2003) on migration and diaspora. But reading the map, listening to their story, and logicizing all of it always already marks a narratological impossibility of inscribing consciousness to experience (Acosta 2012). Still, I return to it—here and there, then and now—because of what it demands. An archival impression:

> This was their second attempt across the desert. They paid extra because they were not from Mexico nor Mexican. They were lost in the desert despite multiple payments collected. There is no grasp of time in the desert. The words on the map no longer made sense. "This" could no longer indicate a proper place. Did it ever? They drank out of cow troughs to avoid dehydration, knowing the water was contaminated. But in conditions not of one's own making, one makes a choice that is hardly a choice at all but a demand. They felt their body moving in and out of consciousness, teetering on the brink of a certain death. They saw their community in the desert, in memory and as ghosts. They would be left for dead, to become part of the desert's materiality; another trace mark of the graveyard of humanity created by inhumanity. They would be forced to address themselves to the ghosts in the desert, who neither could confirm whether they were living in a past or living in the actual present. Will they ever have arrived? They walked with a hope they were doing so at least in the right direction.

Movement is rarely just that (see Cresswell 2006, 2010). Yes, we should be "movement literate" (Cresswell 2006, 127; also see Cresswell 1996; Reynolds 2004; Sheller and Urry 2006; Pennycook 2010; Leonard 2013; Nordquist 2017). But that is different than the desire that drives the objective to archive arrivals, arrivants, and material exchanges, particularly in the context of what Anzaldúa (1999) calls *los recién llegados*. Must mobility have a proper politics of movement? What of movement when instructions demand one to erase any trace of presence—"Caminar a todas las veredas; y cruzando las brechas con chamarra borrar huellas"—or of representation and experienced and embodied practices when one will never have arrived? In this context, movement is already as misaligned and ambivalent as the markings a chamarra makes on the unsettled landscape of the desert. The praxis of knowing (¡entiendes!) and unknowing (¿entiendes?) is not lost on me. And here is the point: prescriptive checklists and roadmaps are as good as a set of directions that merely reads "in this direction." None of us are in possession of and/or are emitting the right signs, and thus, we too must be unsettled. The "unofficial" map, and the significance of "this" in the context of such a praxis, prompts me to draw out another preliminary description of a theory of unsettling and counter-writing. If we can never be certain about some *things* like writing, directions, and/or arrival, then the most ethical option is to intentionally imagine the world and thus define rhetoric and writing as misaligned and ambivalent. That is to say, it is an ethic of *doing*, whether it appears in the form of rhetoric or writing, that attends to the misalignments and ambivalences that *take* and *make* place within the un/settled grounds of wounded/wounding spaces and places.

When discourse emboldens the idea of a prescriptive checklist or roadmap, (decolonial) presuppositions of what constitutes a proper arrival and arrivant take root. The map and story demand that questions of arrival and arrivant be radically reframed in the context of a critique and unworking of knowing in general. Such a critique and unworking applies to the everyday and academia. *Must arrival and arrivant assume a proper name?* What if we understood both as sites of a crisis internal to the possibility of knowing; as signs of an impossible yet productive space of and for an *awaiting*? If we cannot ever be certain about knowledge of a proper arrival and arrivant, then both remain in aporia, in an irresolvable and paralogical limit of knowing. Who are we if not the accumulation of many arrivals? How then can we settle on a proper name as arrivant if the body is in an infinite succession of stages and junctures with each arrival? Hall (1989) wrote that we are "subject to the continuous 'play' of history, culture, and power," and thus in a state of *being-and-becoming* (70). Similarly, Derrida (1972) remarked, "I am trying, precisely, to put myself at a point so that I do not know any longer where I am going" (267). In that vein, when we radically reframe arrival and arrivant in the context of a critique and unworking of knowing in general *an-other* set of questions emerges. *What if we are all always in the process of arriving, approaching with neither a time of arrival nor a destination point given, or a given?* Such an orientation is supported by A. Gordon's (2008) and D. Davis's (2014) appeals for an epistemology or a rhetoricity for the living. But there remains the demand for some *thing* else. Each chapter demonstrates already, do they not, an *epistemological framework for the living*, which reinvents in unending cycles either through material exchanges or internalization, zones of (non)being, death spaces-space for the living, and the living-half dead? What if we were all haunted? This question is less about rhetorical effect and more about an orientation toward getting caught up *otherwise*. I argued at the onset that this book offers no definitive resolutions. It will offer only *an-other* option that presents *an-other* question that grounds *an-other* exigence. But it bears repeating: the meaning of *stories-so-far* and the *possibilities of new stories* can be found in the process of an archival approach accompanied by a theory of archival impressions. That situates us squarely on a politics and theory of wor(l)ding, of *being-and-becoming* recognizable to some *thing* else.

I take seriously Said's (1983, 242), Hall's (2019, 322), and Derrida's (2021, 6) arguments that the obligation and responsibility of the "scholar" is to be critical and thus to think of the very intellectual work we prescribe to under erasure if only to initiate a "break" and bring about something "new." That being said, I argue that a praxis of knowing (¡entiendes!) and unknowing (¿entiendes?) has implications for wor(l)ding *otherwise* and *an-other* archive. Many of us know that we do not want anything from the *Archive*. So, what next? What is our obligation and responsibility? Such a question again is the connective tissue between a *practical theorizing* and *theory building actioning*. In responding to Escobar's (2020) question of how best to "construct the archive" of decolonial thought, being, and doing (63), I claim that one way to rise to this level of obligation and responsibility is through an *epistemological framework for the haunted* facilitated by *deep rhetoricity*. In essence, an archival approach. It will take such an approach, of *archives* in assemblage with archival impressions initiated *elsewhere* and *otherwise*, to unsettle the settled-ness of the *Archive* (see Yang 2017). Such *doings* will have to involve what Guillermo Gómez-Peña (1996) and Cusicanqui (2012) call the (mega) "We" if we are to give structure to and constitute *an-other* archive (Gómez-Peña 1996, 196). The "We" though is only part of the story, a story that alone is not enough. If there is to be *an-other* archive it must necessarily include "earth."

An Epistemological Framework for the Haunted

Writing is embodied. Recognizing this, writing as an "embodied composition" (Guattari 1995, 95) and "question of becoming" (Deleuze 1997, 225) can animate how self is a space and place of multiple returns—a polylog of selves (self of the present) and others (self of the past) always but in one stage and juncture of *stories-so-far* and *possibilities of new stories* (also see Nishida 1970; Houser 1999; Vivian 2000; Guerra 2004; Phillips 2006). Rhetoric is always already about relations and life questions—how to hold some things, like a value (to live in-common, welcome, and love-another), in common. Acknowledging this, we can return rhetoric to the state of giving, receiving, and reciprocating, and by doing so, we can unsettle the settled-ness of the logic of the gift (see Levinas 1969; Caputo and Scanlon 1999; Derrida 1994a). If writing is "carving bone" (Anzaldúa 1999, 73), rhetoric is *reintroducing invention into existence* (Fanon 1986, 231). Together, writing and rhetoric can help radically reframe what it means to *be-and-become* recognizable to self/selves, others, and communities *otherwise*, and that can be a gift unhitched from the reach and grip of power. I wager that to (re)make the conditions under which decolonizing knowledge-being may be possible in the classroom and beyond will have everything to do with how we orient ourselves to hauntings, inheritances, and dwellings. The end is not to make it out—of being, of hoping, of struggling—but to bring about *an-other* orientation to a seeing, feeling, being, and doing able to rise to a wor(l)ding *otherwise* against the tension between im/possibilities. We have to unsettle the settled-ness of *things* to be capable of working out the possibilities of the impossible. An *epistemological framework for the haunted* emerges out of the demand for some *thing* else. It begins from the premise that the body is an *archive* in an unending cycle of *being-and-becoming*, made, unmade, and remade, where hope can be researched and searched for vis-à-vis a decolonizing archiving ethic, ethos, and praxis-rhetoricity. I enter it below as a decolonizing archival impression through writing and rhetoric.

An *epistemological framework for the haunted* is a wor(l)ding project of *being-and-becoming* recognizable to some *thing* else. The fabric of it, preliminarily speaking, is sketched out from my upbringing. It is necessarily weaved and textured from my experiences with *shadow work*—a love, care, healing, and learning ethic—which prioritizes, on the one hand, a *thinking*, *feeling*, and *being-with* a full spectrum of matter (living, nonliving, nonhuman) otherwise. In that way, *shadow work* advances a politics of hauntings, inheritances, and dwellings as language, rhetoric, and corporeal exercises of address. It approaches a *learning-unlearning-relearning* path as an *enduring task*. That means there is an ongoing process of getting caught up in bearing witness in unsettling ways and unsettling the settled. This reflects the inward-facing dimension of the path. On the other hand, *shadow work* has an outward-facing dimension, *being-and-becoming recognizable* to self/selves, others, and communities *otherwise*. An *epistemological framework for the haunted* holds that it is the obligation and responsibility thus of all to stand at the nexus of another's *stories-so-far* and *possibilities of new stories, wherever they may be* and in the *non-name of all-shadow work* (A. Gordon 2008; Fanon 1986). In short, the outward-facing dimension is about walking and seeing the world and interacting and exchanging meaning with others *otherwise*.

But the questions remain, what else constitutes an *epistemological framework for the haunted* and how do we rise to the level of obligation and responsibility that it demands? Aware of the risks involved here—providing a prescriptive checklist or roadmap—I propose that *deep rhetoricity* weaves and textures the fabric of such a framework. Gesa Kirsch and I (García and Kirsch 2022) conceived of it as a praxis of intervention and invention unfolding at the thresholds of politics of location, situated knowledges, and discourses of lived cultures. It also has an inward- and outward-facing dimension that strives to engage in a *doing* that is more responsible to the complexities of reality and the political realities (see Moraga and Anzaldúa 1983; Rich 1985; Haraway 1988; Giroux 1988; Hauser 1999b). Generatively, thus, it advances an *epistemological framework for the haunted*. The inward-facing dimension of *deep rhetoricity* has the epistemic principles of *returns, careful reckonings, enduring tasks*. It conceives of *stories-so-far* as archives and facilitates the repositioning of its contents to both encourage a position to it *otherwise* and to invite archival impressions *otherwise*. Here, archival impressions mean the unsettling of the settled-ness of Self, while *deep rhetoricity* means recognizing and acknowledging a polylog of selves (self of the present) and others (self of the past) always but in one stage and juncture.

There can be no inward-facing dimension without an-other. Scholars from hooks (2001a, 93) to Fabian (2007, 27) understood this. The outward-facing dimension of *deep rhetoricity* has the epistemic principle of *becoming ready* unfolding in many paths. There is becoming ready to listen, to bear witness-to, and to make room for *being-and-thinking-with*, none of which requires one to be from a proper place, speak the proper words, or identify a proper way (see Cortez and García n.d.). It conceives of humanity's *stories-so-far* as an archive and facilitates too the repositioning of its contents to both encourage a position to it *otherwise* and to invite relational archival impressions *otherwise*. Here archival impressions mean the unsettling of the settled-ness of relationality and restoration of the *logics of the gift* in *playful world-traveling* (see Maldonado-Torres 2007; Lugones 1987), while *deep rhetoricity* means recognizing and acknowledging that difference does not have to mean or signify

Man-Human-Rights (see Quijano 2007, 177; Mignolo 2007, 499). Together, the inward-outward dimensions underscore a *learning-unlearning-relearning* path of a slow and deep (de/re)compositioning of *being-and-becoming recognizable* to self/selves, others, and communities *otherwise*. To extend the meaning of archives and archival research in this way is to imagine, as Browne (2021) does, a set of rhizomatic activities within particular and different *archives*. It is to unsettle the idea of desire and its objective (to excavate memories) as reason for returning to the archive. It is to see, feel, and listen to an *epistemological framework for the haunted* that has always already been part of the *archives*. While at face value such a framework re-consigns the status of a haunted *thing* to *archives*, it does so only to underscore across all archives the global connection of hauntings. It will take a collective actioning of human relation-ing—the initiating of decolonizing archival impressions—to bring about a field of study I call "We/arth."

Deep rhetoricity helps facilitate an *epistemological framework for the haunted* in that it asks two important questions. *Where will we have chosen to stand in wholly seeing, knowing, being-with an-other? What will we have wanted from one another after we have told our stories* (Corder 1985; Fanon 1986; Lorde 1997)? A desire? No! A "longing" both for a present "enriched" by "the past and the future" (Tuck 2009, 417) and for a future of "people-possessed" rather than "individually self-possessed" (Arvin, Tuck, and Morrill 2013, 25). An *epistemological framework for the haunted* is not some utopian vision but rather a recognition that difference does not have to mean the "unequal nature of the 'other'" (Quijano 2007, 177), represent and signify "values and plus and minus degree of humanity" (Mignolo 2007, 499), or be the "basis of domination" (Quijano 2007, 177; also see Keating 2013). It is an acknowledgment that no one person has "rights" over anyone but only the right to demand the behavior of "we/arth" from another. It is a return, centering, and situating of hauntings, the past, the dead, inheritances, and dwellings to the politics of the present. Thus, no one group can claim to be in possession of and/or be emitting the right signs if we are all haunted. And extrication cannot be reserved for any one group if hauntings live deep in all our bones. Together, an *epistemological framework for the haunted* and *deep rhetoricity* intervene in the settled-ness of relation-ing and re-introduces an ethical injunction for a relational framework of ethics (see Smith 1999; Wilson 2008; Chilisa 2012; Mukavetz 2020). Here an archival approach means a *story-so-far*, while *archival impressions* means embracing the pause or hesitation—stemming from our cultural and thinking program/programing—if only to engage in a *doing otherwise* (see Derrida 1994b, 213).

"We/arth": An Assemblage

"We/arth" demands the art of turning, a politics of wor(l)ding where the doors of the everyday are open to anyone, where best practices reflect a preparation of *thinking, feeling,* and *being-with* everyone (wherever they may be and in the non-name of all), and where diverse wor(l)dings can get to work. We can never belong to "we/arth"; that would but merely reinstate Rights-to. But we can brave the cruelties of hauntings and haunting situations vis-à-vis futuristic-oriented rhetoricity and a *thinking, feeling,* and *being-with* orientation. Still the questions remain, what is "we/arth" and how do we rise to level of obligation and responsibility it demands? To call writing and rhetorical studies to a *careful reckoning,* perhaps the trap in thinking an-other option is the desire for and thus objective to invent proper names—"because the archive, if this word or this figure can be stabilized" (Derrida 1995, 14). How Spivak (1988a) unsettled the question of "can" (the subaltern speak), Derrida (1982) took to unsettling the question of "what/what is" (266). If this sounds familiar, it is because rhetoricians like Mao (2014) have also called for the unsettling of that question (450; also see R. Graff and Leff 2012). Neither Spivak nor Mao argues that some *things* do not exist but rather they break from over-totalization to shift to a theory and politics of being (historicity) and becoming (via rhetoricity). This is a long-winded way to say that what follows on "we/arth" is not meant to provide a prescriptive checklist or roadmap but an-other course of action. "We/arth" begins from a premise articulated by Fanon (1986), "Between the world and me a relation of existence was established" (128). To "arrive" here will have everything to do with how we orient ourselves to an *epistemological framework for the haunted*. It functions as and calls for the initiating of decolonizing archival impression—entries of counter-writing impressed and initiated by some *one* meant to unsettle the settled-ness of *things* and bring about decolonizing agendas that can alter the Archive/archives and wor(l)d *an-other* archive.

I am proposing that an *epistemological framework for the haunted* is one way "We" can rise to the level of obligation and responsibility "We/arth" demands. At the onset of this book, I argued that the body can function as a *technique-technology of repetition* and that through Davis's concept of a *preoriginary rhetoricity,* we can see the body-as-sensory archive before desire sets in. (This is my own interpretation.) This is important, because in breaking from the objective of a desire we can shift the "existential predicament of rhetoricity" (D. Davis 2021, 195) to a relational and inventional praxis of *thinking, feeling,* and *being-with*, grounded in historical reality, oriented toward society, and reflective of hope-struggle. I am not arguing that we can transcend the exigencies that form the existential predicament of rhetoricity: existence. But what I am saying is that it is possible to pose different questions with this break from desire and objective and shift to the condition of "any living being" (D. Davis 2014, 547):

> Is it desire that drives a return to the archive or is it a doing that can rise to the level of obligation and responsibility that "We/arth" demands?
>
> Is it the exigency to exist that spurs an archival approach or is it a *careful reckoning* with how we ought to honor what was always already our arrangement (giving, receiving, and reciprocating)?
>
> Is it the the urgency to know that prompts the initiating of archival impressions or is it the *enduring task* of a Derridean impossibility to ensure some *things* must live on *otherwise*?

Rhetoricity is experimentally sensorial, and thus, I cannot necessarily settle on a politics of (non)presence, to-come, or making it out. (Perhaps then some theories even reach their logical end?) "We/arth" would not allow it. A theory and politics of "we/arth" demand a rhetoricity of *being-and-becoming* recognizable, an orientation to a structure of living on (*sur-vie*)—"rhetoricity's irreducible and irremissible matter-ing" (D. Davis 2017, 443)—that recognizes it is simultaneously the by-product and possibly the radical rupturing of the settled from the inside. (Or perhaps, instead of a logical end, I am merely *thinking, feeling*, and *being-with* theory at the absolute limit, initiating a "break" to bring about some *thing* else.) But the weaved traces of the marks that scatter across the "we" and the "earth"—wounded/wounding and haunted/haunting—evidence how we have not risen to the level of obligation and responsibility that "we/arth" demands. The question thus remains: How might we *be-and-become* recognizable to "we/arth"? The hope-struggle for a reconciliation across the full spectrum of matter (the living, nonliving, nonhuman). At the beginning of this book, I argued that the "We" is only part of the story and that if there is to be *an-other* archive it must necessarily include "earth." "We/arth" celebrates and centers Fanon's (1986) orientation—"And long live the couple, Man and Earth!" (127)—which radically reframes the logics of the gift as it underscores an obligation and responsibility to Matter (including rhetoric) living-on (*sur-vie*) and flourishing in the *non-name of all* (see Acosta 2012). The gift of this relationship with Matter is relational and not a one-way street (D. Davis 2014; Rickert 2021).

"We/arth" is an archive. It does not begin with Man as the origins, but rather has the historicity and the rhetoricity behind the making of the earth as its reference point. "We/arth" records and stores archival impressions as much as it produces the *epistemological experiment* of it. It is delinked from Rights circumscribed by theologically and secularly structured *ideas* (divine, natural, or otherwise)—"'rights' are attributed to us by someone who has the right to attribute rights" (Mignolo 2011a, 214)—as the premise for doing *otherwise*. The "We" is not an idyllic fantasy. The "architecture of violence and of affect," Sharpe (2023) tells us, does not "reach us in the same ways"; in fact, it "fracture[s] we" (21). But, because what holds in the "we" and "earth" is our existence in-common, we ought to remember "we/arth" is a time-honored invention, a by-product of ancestral interactions and exchanges—responsivity, affectability, and rhetoric by accident—in the service of being-for (Davis 2021; Stormer 2020). The first part of "we/arth" disrupts the idea of Man-Human-Rights, orienting instead to the full spectrum of matter: the living, nonliving, and nonhuman. Here the "we" exists in Fanon's (1986) "you," entrenching not an epistemological stance predicated on supposed epistemic and ontological differences but an ethical injunction, responsibility, and relation grounded on the demand for something else. L. Gordon (2005) puts it this way: "When I speak to You, I am addressing you in your humanity" (25). Fanon (1986) did not ask, "How do I extricate myself," but rather, "How do we extricate ourselves" (12). Here "we," an unsettling of the "I" and an amendment of the "You," cannot stand alone, for it risks reproducing the reductive, dichotomous, and/or oppositional structure; rather, it is affixed with the earth standing at the nexus between a fractured "we" and a collective "we." While the "we" is indeed fractured against the backdrop of hauntings and haunting situations, it will need to be connected in times of *careful reckonings*. And "earth" can afford us that *possibility of new stories*.

The second part of "we/arth" disrupts the idea of Man-Human-Rights as the only story. Earth has a story. To paraphrase Robin Kimmerer (2013), there is a "sacred bond" between the earth and the full spectrum of matter (living, nonliving, nonhuman); it can answer questions by the way it lives and by its responses to change (158). Will earth ever have arrived as more than a waystation for the living? The tension between Kimmerer's position that "We" have the "least experience with how to live" (9) and Derrida's (1994b) exordium on what it means "to live" (xvii) is worth noting. Because both underscore a reciprocation among the body, others (broadly conceived), and the world. I neither claim to be "Indigenous" or be an expert on Indigenous practices. (My references evidence that much, a limitation that is mine alone.) But how I see, feel, and do-with today is some *thing* passed down to me, Kimmerer's (2013, 58) and Derrida's (1994b, 221) *foreign language*: "Siéntate y ayúdame con eso ... con cuidado, cuidadito ... todo con tiempo ... con cariño y amor." Every time Grandma sat *with* the earth in my presence, the inner earth within her spoke, and it healed, taught, and relinked her. She taught me how to rise to the level of obligation and responsibility that could heed the call from the earth to reciprocate that *sacred bond*. "Estoy en paz," Grandma would say. Decades after her passing, I recently heard my tío say, looking out into his garden of papaya, limes, lemons, dragon fruit, avocado, pineapple, chile de monte, grapefruit, figs, guava, prickly pear, and much more: "I found tranquility, despite and in spite of everything. This is home." His statement is not that of making it out but learning how to be at-home *otherwise* (see Fanon 1986). "We/arth" demands a healing for the full spectrum of matter (living, nonliving, and nonhuman).

"We/arth" is not deterministic and cannot be misconstrued as belonging to any one *thing* or *one*. It is akin to what Cintron (2010) refers to as *energeia*, or what I call wor(l)ding aspiration. It would seem that in all this talk of "we/arth" an archival approach and theory of archival impressions remain most promising and valuable. While both are institutionalized, neither necessarily belongs to the academy nor do they have any allegiances to any one person. An archival approach and theory of archival impressions are the connective tissue between a *praxical theorizing* of the world and bodies as archives and a *theory building actioning* toward "we/arth." Against the backdrop of *stories-so-far* and the *possibilities of new stories*, an archival approach and theory of archival impressions paint an interesting tension between Foucault's (1978) disposition that "Power is everywhere ... because it comes from everywhere" (93) and Said's (1983) claim that there is "always something beyond the reach of dominating systems" (246). Is *an-other* archive possible? Yes! But according to Browne (2021, 53), it will have to be an archive that both "exists in a [mapped] space [of a future] we cannot truly [own or] inhabit" and that endures in a state of perpetually *being-and-becoming-awaiting* the arrival of arrivants who will never have arrived. Though we can never belong to it—own or inhabit—we can all contribute to it becoming *otherwise* via a futuristic rhetoricity of initiating archival impressions *otherwise*.

There Is No Making It Out! But I refuse to give up hope on the fallacy that because *power is everywhere*, it is impossible to imagine and work toward a future without hauntings and haunting situations. Power would like nothing more than to keep people in perpetual despair without hope. But people and the earth have a way of protesting against the onslaught of modern/colonial and settlerizing designs. Even mushrooms bloom in the wake of wreckage: the "world-building proclivities of matsutake . . . they grow because of their ruins" (Tsing 2015, 211–212). How do we rise to that level of *being-and-becoming*, however precarious, where the memory of the hope is not lost in a space that is the place of ruin, spectrality, and promise? A rupture? A clearing? An opening? Whatever it is, the assemblage of "we"-in-difference must brave the wreckage of what surrounds and play as a band to the sounds of hope and struggle to create the soundscape of "we/arth" for all to see, feel, and hear. We do not have the luxury to hide it. This situates me on immortality, which is already factored into our lives and felt with everyday we wither. What will we have wanted to live-on (*sur-vie*) *otherwise*? Why not a *longing* "to rise above," in a paraphrasing of Fanon (1986), the wreckage of what surrounds (197)?

Each chapter thus far has functioned as an impression and entry submitted into this book that is an archive. The point is to connect hauntings and haunting situations with the experiences of human beings across space, place, and time. Because it can come to form the basis for a doing *otherwise*: "Coming to know the past has been part of the critical pedagogy of decolonization" (Smith 2012, 36). A book is a like a graveyard where ideas are subject to their own death and laid to rest in the ink on the pages. At the same time, a book is like an archive, this one constituted by archival impressions of the "we," a prism through which to see the past and the actions of today refracted into the present. But the pages also reflect a hope-struggle *in* assemblage with other options, pathways, and resources that *long* for the *possibilities of new stories*. This has been a long-winded way to say that when we unsettle the settledness of arrival and arrivant, what is demanded is an *epistemological framework for the haunted* that then brings up questions about *being-and-becoming* recognizable. What Tsing (2015) *longed* for as "livable collaborations" (28) and what Kimmerer (2013) called the "sacred bond" I frame as *being-and-becoming* recognizable to "we/arth." And I believe this is one option for how we might bring about a preparation of a hospitality ~~teaching of writing and rhetoric~~ suitable for *anyone* who arrives at our doors, creating the conditions under which decolonizing knowledge-being may be possible.

The Impression We Leave Behind

The classroom, as hooks (1994) saw it, can be a "radical space of possibility" (12). And I agree. We do not have the luxury to just teach. The *choices* we make on whether to stand at the nexus of an-other's *stories-so-far* and *possibilities of new stories* matters. The *work* of our *work* may not be known to us immediately. Still, it is human work. At the very least, our words and ideas will have marked a stage and juncture in ways students walk and see the world and interact and exchange meaning with others—archival impressions. Now, whether those impressions will be decolonizing will have everything to do with *choice*, which is hardly a *choice* at all but always already a demand both to unsettle the settled-ness of *things* and to *think, feel,* and *be-with* community—the dynamics of writing and rhetoric and a writing and rhetoric classroom (see Alexander and Mohanty 1997; hooks 2001a, 2003, 2010; B. Jackson and Clark 2014; Lorde 2020). We are not travel agents in possession of "official" maps or words that emit the "right" directions or signs for those arrivants who embody and carry the proper papeles. That is a classroom unsuitable for *anyone*. We are not tourists but travelers in and alongside our students, who happened to enroll in our course by chance while in one stage and juncture of their *stories-so-far*. How will our classrooms reflect a preparation of a teaching of ~~writing and rhetoric~~ life questions for everyone, *wherever they may be* and in the *non-name of all* (see Fanon 1986; Acosta 2012)? The "choices" we make today will influence and touch how future generations walk and see the world and interact and exchange meaning with others. Our work is human work. What will a future, both as an idea and as an archive-to-come *otherwise*, tell us about the *choices* we *choose* to make?

It is early days. We do not know whether the human work and projects we carry out in the humanities will amount to more than just theoretical talk. What is known is that there remains a demand for something else—an *epistemological framework for the haunted, deep rhetoricity,* "we/arth," all of which are by-products of an archival approach and theory of archival impressions. Fanon (1963) argued for language of the everyday. In his view, "Everything can be explained" on the "single condition" that one truly wants another "to understand" (189). So I return to a thematic argument in this book: if literacies, images-signs-sounds, and rhetorics have been used to construct settler sites, constitute haunted/haunting communities, and maintain wounded/wounding spaces and places, by the same token they can be used to initiate decolonizing archival impressions as stepping-stones toward *possibilities of new stories*. I argue that the demand for some *things* else is not a cultural but a global obligation and responsibility of striving to imagine and contribute toward a future without hauntings and haunting situations.

What else is there? Something else, surely. The unsettling of the settled should not be interpreted as hindering obligation and responsibility. So I *await*: a hope without guaranteed predicate, a hope for that which may or may not arrive. Will *it* ever have arrived? The haunting back of the nastiness of hauntings and haunting situations (see A. Gordon 2008)? The making it out? A *deep rhetoricity*—a slow and deep (de/re)compositioning of *being-and-becoming recognizable* to self/selves, others, and communities *otherwise*? The wor(l)ding of a theory and politics of "We/arth"? A shared obligation and responsibility of and for an *epistemological framework for the haunted*? The time is always now! Or so they say (see Baldwin 1956). *An-other* archive is possible! Somewhere, someday, right? An archival impression, at the end of a book, at the end of the world, in one stage or juncture of an unending cycle of some *things* made, unmade, and remade. "Too late . . . too late . . . You come too late, much too late" (Fanon 1986, 121–122). A researching of and searching for hope—a hope that we ought to struggle to ensure belongs to everyone.

Perhaps!

Can archives feel? I have this hope that we can all struggle to/ward the possibilities of unsettled archives and the wor(l)ding of *an-other* archive across the fabric of the full spectrum of matter (living, nonliving, nonhuman). Perhaps then, we must initiate archival impressions *otherwise* to leave behind evidence of the *work* we chose to carry out *otherwise*—to unsettle the settledness of *stories-so-far*—and to provide a pathway toward the *possibilities of new stories*. Paraphrasing Gómez-Peña (1996) and Derrida (1994b) for this context, might we begin this "heroic project" (Gómez-Peña 1996, 10)? It is a project that would require us to be "mad enough" (Derrida 1994b, 13)—loco/a—or to be unsettled-undisciplined enough to unlock the possibility of such a *project*. I may have gotten a lot of things wrong in conceiving of power as an *Archive*, but I am most certain that this *heroic project* will take a "borrowed" (Said 1983) approach. I have this hope that it is possible both to collectively carry out *work* at the absolute limit of *ends* and to initiate archival impressions *otherwise* in service of being-for some *thing* else (Fanon 1986; Davis 2010, 2017). Toward *an-other* archive? I have hope!

References

Acevedo, Nicole, and Caitlin Fichtel. 2019. "White Man Admits he's 'a racist' after telling a Latina to 'speak English'" NBC News. September 26. https://www.nbcnews.com/news/latino/white-man-admits-he-s-racist-after-telling-latina-speak-n1058826.

Achille, Mbembe. 2001. *On the Postcolony*. Berkeley: University of California Press.

Acosta, Abraham. 2012. "Hinging on Exclusion and Exception: Bare Life, the US/Mexico Border, and Los Que Nunca Llegarán." *Social Text 113* 30, no. 4: 103–123.

Acosta, Abraham. 2019. "(De)Colonial Sources: The Coloniality of Power, Reoriginalization, and the Critique of Imperialism." *FORMA* 1, no. 1: 17–36.

Adams-Campbell, Melissa, Ashley Falzetti, and Courtney Rivard. 2015. "Introduction. Indigeneity and the Work of Settler Archives." *Settler Colonial Studies* 5, no. 2: 109–116.

"Address of John H. Shary: Texas Bankers Association Convention." 1940. John H. Shary Collection, ELIBR-0002, Box 256. University of Texas Rio Grande Valley Special Collections and Archives, Edinburg Campus.

Adelsen, Charles. 1970. "A Love Affair: James Baldwin and Istanbul." *Ebony*. March 40–46.

Agnew, Lois, et al. 2011. "Octalog III: The Politics of Historiography in 2010." *Rhetoric Review* 30, no. 2: 109–134.

Ahmed, Sara. 2012. *On Being Included: Racism and Diversity in Institutional Life*. Durham, NC: Duke University Press.

Ahmed, Sara. 2017. *Living a Feminist Life*. Durham, NC: Duke University Press.

Alberto, Lourdes. 2016. "Nations, Nationalisms, and Indigenas: The 'Indian' in the Chicano Revolutionary Imaginary." *Critical Ethnic Studies* 2, no. 1: 107–127.

Alcoff, Linda. 2006. *Visible Identities: Race, Gender, and the Self.* New York: Oxford University Press.

Alcoff, Linda. 2007. "Mignolo's Epistemology of Coloniality." *New Centennial Review* 7, no. 3: 79–101.

Alcoff, Linda. 2011. "An Epistemology for the Next Revolution." *Transmodernity* 1, no. 2: 67–78.

Aldrete, Bernardo. 1674. *Del Origen y Principio de La Lengua Castellana, o Romance que oy se usa en España.* Madrid: Melchor Sánchez.

Aleman, Enrique. 2005. "Exposing the 'Niceness' in Utah's Educational Politics for What It Is." *Salt Lake Tribune*, April 24. https://archive.sltrib.com/article.php?id=2681769&itype=NGPSID&keyword=&qtype=. Accessed May 11, 2020.

Alexander, M. Jacqui. 2005. *Pedagogies of Crossing: Meditations on Feminism, Sexual Politics, Memory, and the Sacred.* Durham, NC: Duke University Press.

Alexander, M. Jacqui, and Chandra T. Mohanty. 1997. "Introduction: Genealogies, Legacies, Movements." In *Feminist Genealogies, Colonial Legacies, Democratic Futures*, edited by M. Jacqui Alexander and Chandra T. Mohanty, xiii–xlii. New York: Routledge.

Alexander, M. Jacqui, and Chandra Mohanty. 2010. "Cartographies of Knowledge and Power: Transnational Feminism as Radical Praxis." In *Critical Transnational Feminist Praxis*, edited by Amanda Swarr and Richa Nagar, 23–45. Albany: SUNY Press.

Alford, Kenneth. 2011. "Latter-day Saint Poetry and Songs of the Utah War." *Mormon Historical Studies* 12, no. 1: 1–28.

Alldredge, Ida. 1948. "They, the Builders of the Nation." Churchofjesuschrist.org. https://www.churchofjesuschrist.org/music/library/hymns/they-the-builders-of-the-nation?lang=eng. Accessed May 11, 2020.

"The American Rio Grande Land and Irrigation Company." 1923. ELIBR-0002, Box 254, Folder 42. University Library, Special Collections & Archives, University of Texas Rio Grande Valley. Edinburg, Texas.

Anderson, Emily. 2017. "Racist Posters Found on U Campus." *Daily Utah Chronicle*. August 12. https://dailyutahchronicle.com/2017/08/12/racist-posters-found-u-campus/.

Andrews, Robert. 1823. "Robert Andrews to Stephen F Austin, 03-04-1823." Digital Austin Papers. http://digitalaustinpapers.org/document?id=APB0566.xml.

Anzaldúa, Gloria. 1999. *Borderlands/La Frontera: The New Mestiza.* 2nd ed. San Francisco: Aunt Lute Books.

Aparicio, Frances. 2013. "Popular Music." In *The Routledge Companion to Latino/a Literature*, edited by Suzanne Bost and Frances Aparicio, 229–239. London: Routledge.

Arellano, Sonia, José Cortez, and Romeo García. 2022. "Shadow Work: Witnessing Latinx Crossings in Rhetoric and Composition." *Composition Studies* 49, no. 2: 31–52.

Arellano, Sonia, and Iris Ruiz. 2019. "La Cultura Nos Cura: Reclaiming Decolonial Epistemologies through Medicinal History and Quilting as Method." In *Rhetorics Elsewhere and Otherwise: Contested Modernities, Decolonial Visions*, edited by Romeo

García and Damián Baca, 141–168. Urbana, IL: NCTE/CCCC Studies in Writing and Rhetoric.
Aristotle. 2007. *On Rhetoric: A Theory of Civic Discourse*. Translated by George A. Kennedy. 2nd ed. New York: Oxford University Press.
Arvin, Maile, Eve Tuck, and Angie Morrill. 2013. "Decolonizing Feminism: Challenging Connections between Settler Colonialism and Heteropatriarchy," *Feminist Formations* 25, no. 1: 8–34.
Austin, Henry 1830a. "Henry Austin to Stephen F Austin, 01-29-1830." Digital Austin Papers. http://digitalaustinpapers.org/document?id=APB1847.xml.
Austin, Henry 1830b. "Henry Austin to Stephen F Austin, 06-03-1830." Digital Austin Papers. http://digitalaustinpapers.org/document?id=APB1951.xml.
Austin, Henry. 1830c. "Henry Austin to Stephen F Austin, 10-20-1830." Digital Austin Papers, http://digitalaustinpapers.org/document?id=APB4058.xml.
Austin, Henry. 1834. "Henry Austin to James F Perry, 11-14-1834." Digital Austin Papers. http://digitalaustinpapers.org/document?id=APB4698.xml.
Austin, J. E. B. 1829. "J. E. B Austin to Emily Perry, 05-26-1829." Digital Austin Papers, http://digitalaustinpapers.org/document?id=APB1722.xml.
Austin, Maria [B]. 1822. "Maria Austin to Stephen F Austin, 04-26-1822." Digital Austin Papers. http://digitalaustinpapers.org/document?id=APB0503.xml.
Austin, Moses. 1804. "Moses Austin to Daniel Phelps, 06-10-1804." Digital Austin Papers. http://digitalaustinpapers.org/document?id=APB0084.xml.
Austin, Moses. 1812. "Moses Austin to Stephen F Austin, 09-26-1812." Digital Austin Papers. http://digitalaustinpapers.org/document?id=APB0225.xml.
Austin, Moses. 1813. "Moses Austin to James Bryan, 01-04-1813." Digital Austin Papers. http://digitalaustinpapers.org/document?id=APB0229.xml.
Austin, Moses. 1814a. "Moses Austin to James Bryan, 09-02-1814." Digital Austin Papers. http://digitalaustinpapers.org/document?id=APB0251.xml.
Austin, Moses. 1814b. "Moses Austin to James Bryan, 11-25-1814." Digital Austin Papers. http://digitalaustinpapers.org/document?id=APB0255.xml.
Austin, Moses. 1818. "Moses Austin to Robert Wash, 02-28-1818." Digital Austin Papers. http://digitalaustinpapers.org/document?id=APB0308.xml.
Austin, Moses. 1821a. "Moses Austin to James E. B. Austin, 04-08-1821." Digital Austin Papers. http://digitalaustinpapers.org/document?id=APB0383.xml.
Austin, Moses. 1821b. "Moses Austin to Unknown, 04-22-1821." Digital Austin Papers. http://digitalaustinpapers.org/document?id=APB0387.xml.
Austin, Stephen F. 1821a. "Stephen F Austin to Antonio Martinez, 10-13-1821." Digital Austin Papers. http://digitalaustinpapers.org/document?id=APB0414.xml.
Austin, Stephen F. 1821b. "Stephen F Austin to Baron de Bastrop, 09-01-1821." Digital Austin Papers. http://digitalaustinpapers.org/document?id=APB0404.xml.
Austin, Stephen F. 1821c. "Stephen F Austin to Emigrants, 11-22-1821." Digital Austin Papers. http://digitalaustinpapers.org/document?id=APB0427.xml.
Austin, Stephen F. 1821d. "Stephen F Austin to J. H. Bell, 10-06-1821." Digital Austin Papers. http://digitalaustinpapers.org/document?id=APB0410.xml.

Austin, Stephen F. 1821e. "Stephen F Austin to Moses Austin, 07-04-1821." Digital Austin Papers. http://digitalaustinpapers.org/document?id=APB0395.xml.
Austin, Stephen F. 1821f. "Stephen F Austin to Unknown, 11-23-1821." Digital Austin Papers. http://digitalaustinpapers.org/document?id=APB0430.xml.
Austin, Stephen F. 1822a. "Stephen F Austin to Anastacio Bustamante, 05-10-1822." Digital Austin Papers. http://digitalaustinpapers.org/document?id=APB0508.xml.
Austin, Stephen F. 1822b. "Stephen F Austin to J. H. Hawkins, 05-01-1822." Digital Austin Papers. http://digitalaustinpapers.org/document?id=APB0505.xml.
Austin, Stephen F. 1822c. "Stephen F Austin to James E. B. Austin, 03-23-1822." Digital Austin Papers. http://digitalaustinpapers.org/document?id=APB0488.xml.
Austin, Stephen F. 1823a. "Stephen F Austin to Colonel Charles Caldwell, 07-17-1823." Digital Austin Papers. http://digitalaustinpapers.org/document?id=APB0604.xml.
Austin, Stephen F. 1823b. "Stephen F Austin to Luciano Garcia, 10-20-1823." Digital Austin Papers. http://digitalaustinpapers.org/document?id=APB0639.xml.
Austin, Stephen F. 1823c. "Stephen F Austin to Public, 12-05-1823." Digital Austin Papers. http://digitalaustinpapers.org/document?id=APB0662.xml.
Austin, Stephen F. 1824a. "Stephen F Austin to His Mother and Sister, 05-04-1824." Digital Austin Papers. http://digitalaustinpapers.org/document?id=APB0737.xml.
Austin, Stephen F. 1824b. "Stephen F Austin to Josiah H. Bell, 01-08-1824." Digital Austin Papers. http://digitalaustinpapers.org/document?id=APB0670.xml.
Austin, Stephen F. 1824c. "Stephen F Austin to Provincial Deputation, 05-25-1824." Digital Austin Papers. http://digitalaustinpapers.org/document?id=APB0757.xml.
Austin, Stephen F. 1824d. "Stephen F Austin to Unknown, 06-22-1824." Digital Austin Papers. http://digitalaustinpapers.org/document?id=APB0783.xml.
Austin, Stephen F. 1829. "Stephen F Austin to James W Breedlove, 11-12-1829." Digital Austin Papers. http://digitalaustinpapers.org/document?id=APB1770.xml.
Austin, Stephen F. 1830a. "Stephen F Austin to Archibald Austin, 02-24-1830." Digital Austin Papers. http://digitalaustinpapers.org/document?id=APB1858.xml.
Austin, Stephen F. 1830b. "Stephen F Austin to Thomas F Leaming, 06-14-1830." Digital Austin Papers. http://digitalaustinpapers.org/document?id=APB1961.
Austin, Stephen F. 1832a. "Stephen F Austin to General William H Ashley, 10-10-1832." Digital Austin Papers. http://digitalaustinpapers.org/document?id=APB4446.xml.
Austin, Stephen F. 1832b. "Stephen F Austin to Mary Austin Holley, 01-14-1832." Digital Austin Papers. http://digitalaustinpapers.org/document?id=APB4311.xml.
Austin, Stephen F. 1835. "Stephen F Austin to Mary Austin Holley, 08-21-1835." Digital Austin Papers. http://digitalaustinpapers.org/document?id=APB4851.xml.
Austin, Stephen F. 1836a. "Address of the Honorable S. F. Austin." *Magazine of History with Notes and Queries* 22, no. 4: 31–50.
Austin, Stephen F. 1836b. "Stephen F Austin to Senator L F Finn, 05-04-1836." Digital Austin Papers. http://digitalaustinpapers.org/document?id=APB5169.xml.
Austin, Stephen F. 1913. "Stephen Fuller Austin." In *Writers and Writings of Texas*, edited by Davis Eagleton, 21–26. New York: Broadway Publishing.
Ayala, Ramon. 1977. "Gerardo González." *Dinastía de la Muerte*.

Ayala, Ramon. 1995. "Corrido de Chita Cano." *Corridos Con Ramón Ayala y Sus Bravos Del Norte*. Universal Music Mexico.
Baca, Damián. 2008. *Mestiz@ Scripts, Digital Migrations, and the Territories of Writing*. New York: Palgrave MacMillan.
Baca, Damián. 2009a. "The Chicano Codex: Writing against Historical and Pedagogical Colonization." *College English* 71, no. 6: 564–583.
Baca, Damián. 2009b. "Rethinking Composition, Five Hundred Years Later." *JAC* 29, nos. 1–2: 229–242.
Baca, Damián. 2010. "te-ixtli: The 'Other Face' of the Americas." In *Rhetorics of the Americas: 3114 BCE to 2012 CE*, edited by Damián Baca and Victor Villanueva, 1–14. New York: Palgrave MacMillan.
Baca, Damián, and Victor Villanueva, eds. 2010. *Rhetorics of the Americas: 3114 BCE to 2012 CE*. New York: Palgrave MacMillan.
Baca, Isabel, Yndalecio I. Hinojosa, and Susan Wolff Murphy, eds. 2019. *Bordered Writers: Latinx Identities and Literacy Practices at Hispanic-Serving Institutions*. Albany: SUNY Press.
Baker-Bell, April, Tamara Butler, and Lamar Johnson. 2017. "The Pain and the Wounds: A Call for Critical Race English Education in the Wake of Racial Violence." *English Education* 49, no. 2: 116–129.
Baldwin, James. 1956. "Faulkner and Desegregation." *Partisan Review* 23, no. 4: 568–573.
Baldwin, James. 1972. *No Name in the Street*. Vintage Books.
Baldwin, James. 1979. "If Black English Isn't a Language, Then Tell Me, What Is?" *The New York Time*. July 29. https://archive.nytimes.com/www.nytimes.com/books/98/03/29/specials/baldwin-english.html?_r=1.
Baldwin, James. 1984a. *Notes of a Native Son*. Boston: Beacon Press.
Baldwin, James. 1984b. "Preface to the 1984 Edition." In *Notes of a Native Son*, ix–xvi. Boston: Beacon Press.
Baldwin, James. 1998. "The White Man's Guilt." In *Collected Essays*, edited by Toni Morrison, 722–727. New York: Library of America.
Baldwin, James. 2007. *No Name in the Street*. First Vintage International Edition. New York: New York.
Baldwin, James. 2012. *Notes of a Native Son*. Boston: Beacon Press.
Ballif, Michelle. 2014. "Regarding the Dead." *Philosophy and Rhetoric* 47, no. 4: 455–471.
Balot, Ryan. 2013. "Epideictic Rhetoric and the Foundations of Politics." *Polis* 30, no. 2: 274–304.
Banks, Adam. 2011. *Digital Griots: African American Rhetorics in a Multimedia Age*. Carbondale: Southern Illinois University Press.
Barker, Eugene. 1910. "Stephen F. Austin and the Independence of Texas." *Quarterly of the Texas State Historical Association* 13, no. 4: 257–284.
Barker Bros. Engravers. 1918. "The Treasure Land of the Lower Rio Grande." John H. Shary Collection. UTRGV Digital Library, The University of Texas Rio Grande Valley. https://scholarworks.utrgv.edu/johnshary/92/.
Barthes, Roland. 1972. *Mythologies*. Translated by Annette Lavers. New York: The Noonday Press.

Barthes, Roland. 1982. *Camera Lucida: Reflections on Photography*. Translated by Richard Howard. New York: Hill and Wang.

Bawarshi, Anis. 2003. *Genre and the Invention of the Writer: Reconsidering the Place of Invention in Composition*. Logan: Utah State University Press.

Baynham, Mike, and Mastin Prinsloo, eds. 2009. *The Future of Literacy Studies*. New York: Palgrave MacMillan.

Beaufort, Anne. 2007. *College Writing and Beyond: A New Framework for University Writing Instruction*. Logan: Utah State University Press.

Bedolla, Lisa. 2009. *Introduction to Latino Politics in the U.S.* Cambridge: Polity Press.

Bell, Brenda, John Gaventa, and John Peters, eds. 1990. *We Make the Road by Walking: Conversations on Education and Social Change*, by Myles Horton and Paulo Freire. Philadelphia: Temple University Press.

Benavides, Cristian. 2017. "Students Walk out After Teacher Orders: Speak 'American.'" October 17. https://www.nbcnews.com/news/latino/students-walk-out-after-teacher-tells-students-speak-american-n811256.

Bennett, John. 1842. *The History of the Saints; Or, an Expose of Jose Smith and Mormonism*. Boston: Leland & Whiting.

Benoit, William. 1996. "A Note on Burke on 'Motive.'" *Rhetoric Society Quarterly* 26, no. 2: 67–79.

Bergland, Renée. 2000. *The National Uncanny: Indian Ghosts and American Subjects*. Hanover, NH: University Press of New England.

Bergmann, Linda, and Janet Zepernick. 2007. "Disciplinarity and Transfer: Students' Perceptions of Learning to Write." *WPA* 31, nos. 1–2: 124–149.

Berlin, James. 1984. *Writing Instruction in the Nineteenth-Century American Colleges*. Carbondale: Southern Illinois University Press.

Bernal, Martin. 1987. *Black Athena: The Afroasiatic Roots of Classical Civilization*, Vol. 1: *The Fabrication of Ancient Greece 1785–1985*. New Brunswick, NJ: Rutgers University Press.

Bernier, François. 2001. "A New Division of the Earth." *History Workshop Journal*, no. 51: 247–250.

Berrett, William. 1969. *The Restored Church: A Brief History of the Growth and Doctrines of the Church of Jesus Christ of Latter-day Saints*. Salt Lake City: Deseret Book Company.

"The Best Crop in the Valley." n.d. John H. Shary Collection, UTRGV Digital Library, The University of Texas Rio Grande Valley. https://scholarworks.utrgv.edu/johnshary/.

Bhabha, Homi. 1994. *The Location of Culture*. New York: Routledge.

Bhambra, Gurminder. 2014. "Postcolonial and Decolonial Dialogues." *Postcolonial Studies* 17, no. 2: 115–121.

Bhambra, Gurminder, Dalia Gebrial, and Kerem Nisancioglu. 2018. *Decolonising the University*. London: Pluto Press.

Biesecker, Barbara A. 2006. "Of Historicity, Rhetoric: The Archive as Scene of Invention." *Rhetoric and Public Affairs* 9, no. 1: 124–131.

Bird, Barbara. 2008. "Writing about Writing as the Heart of a Writing Studies Approach to FYC: Response to Douglas Downs and Elizabeth Wardle, 'Teaching about Writing, Righting Misconceptions' and to Libby Miles et al., 'Thinking Vertically.'" *College Composition and Communication* 60, no. 1: 165–171.

Birkhæuser, J. A. 1893. *History of the Church, from Its First Establishment to Our Own Times*. New York: F. R. Pustet & Co.

Blackhawk, Ned. 2006. *Violence over the Land: Indians and Empires in the Early American West*. Cambridge: Harvard University Press.

Blake, Aaron, and Eugene Scott. 2021. "Joe Biden's Inauguration Speech Transcript, Annotated." *Washington Post*, January 20. https://www.washingtonpost.com/politics/interactive/2021/01/20/biden-inauguration-speech/.

Blanton, Carlos. 2007. *The Strange Career of Bilingual Education in Texas, 1836–1981*. College Station: Texas A&M University Press.

Bleich, David. 1990. "Literacy and Citizenship: Resisting Social Values." *The Right to Literacy*, edited by Andrea Lunsford, Helene Moglen, and James Slevin, 163–169. New York: Modern Language Association of America.

Bloom, Lynn. 1999. "The Essay Canon." *College English* 61, no. 4: 401–430.

Blumenbach, Johann F. 1999. "On the Natural Variety of Mankind in the Anthropological Treatise of Johann Fredrich Blumenbach." In *Slavery, Abolition, and Emancipation: Theories of Race*, vol. 8, edited by Peter Kitson, 141–214. London: Pickering & Chatto.

Blythe, James. 1810. "James Blythe to Stephen Austin, 04-04-1810." Digital Austin Papers. http://digitalaustinpapers.org/document?id=APB0167.xml.

Bonilla-Silva, Eduardo. 2001. *White Supremacy and Racism in the Post-Civil Rights Era*. Boulder, CO: Lynne Rienner Publishers.

Book of Mormon Evidence. N.d. *Moroni's America*. https://bookofmormonevidence.org/bookstore/product/moronis-america-travel-map/. Accessed May 11, 2020.

Bordo, Susan. 1993. *Unbearable Weight: Feminism, Western Culture, and the Body*. Berkeley: University of California Press.

Bourdieu, Pierre. 1997. "Marginalia—Some Additional Notes on the Gift." In *The Logic of the Gift: Toward an Ethic of Generosity*, edited by Alan Schrift, 231–243. New York: Routledge.

Bova, Gus. 2021. "The Final Frontera." *The Texas Observer*, August 30. https://www.texasobserver.org/the-final-frontera/.

Bowes, John. 1854. *Mormonism Exposed, in its Swindling and Licentious Abominations, Refuted in its Principles and in the Claims of its Head, the Modern Mohammed, Joseph Smith, who is Proved to have been a Deceiver and no Prophet of God*. London: R. Bulman.

Bowman, Matthew. 2012. *The Mormon People: The Making of an American Faith*. New York: Random House.

Bowman, Timothy. 2016. *Blood Oranges: Colonialism and Agriculture in the South Texas Borderlands*. College Station: Texas A&M University Press.

Boyle, Casey, and Jenny Rice, eds. 2018. *Inventing Place: Writing Lone Star Rhetorics*. Carbondale: Southern Illinois University Press.

Bradshaw, Jonathan. 2019. "Self-Epideictic: The Trump Presidency and Deliberative Democracy." *Present-Tense: A Journal of Rhetoric in Society* 8, no. 1. https://www.presenttensejournal.org/volume-8/self-epideictic-the-trump-presidency-and-deliberative-democracy/.

Brandt, Deborah, and Katie Clinton. 2002. "Limits of the Local: Expanding Perspectives on Literacy as a Social Practice." *Journal of Literacy Research* 34, no. 3: 337–356.

Brannstrom, Christian, and Matthew Neuman. 2009. "Inventing the 'Magic Valley' of South Texas, 1905–1941." *Geographical Review* 99, no. 2: 123–145.

Brasher, Jordan, Derek Alderman, and Joshua Inwood. 2017. "Applying Critical Race and Memory Studies to University Place Naming Controversies: Toward a Responsible Landscape Policy." *Papers in Applied Geography* 3, nos. 3–4: 292–307.

Brereton, John, ed. 1995. *The Origins of Composition Studies in the American College, 1875–1925: A Documentary History*. Pittsburgh: University of Pittsburgh Press.

Brittenham, Rebecca. 2001. "'You Say You Want a Revolution? 'Happenings' and the Legacy of the 1960s for Composition Studies." *JAC* 21, no. 3: 521–554.

Brooks, Juanita. 1944. "Indian Relations on the Mormon Frontier." *Utah Historical Quarterly* 12, nos. 1–2: 1–48.

Brown, Samuel. 2011. "The Early Mormon Chain of Belonging." *Dialogue: A Journal of Mormon Thought* 44, no. 1: 1–52.

Browne, Kevin. 2013. *Tropic Tendencies: Rhetoric, Popular Culture, and the Anglophone Caribbean*. Pittsburgh: University of Pittsburgh Press.

Browne, Kevin. 2019. "Moving the Body: Preamble to a Theory of Vernacular Rhetoric, or How a Caribbean Rhetoric[ian] Is Composed." In *Rhetorics Elsewhere and Otherwise: Contested Modernities, Decolonial Visions*, edited by Romeo García and Damián Baca, 196–222. Urbana, IL: NCTE/CCCC Studies in Writing and Rhetoric.

Browne, Kevin. 2021. "A Douen Epistemology: Caribbean Memory and the Digital Archive." *College English* 84, no. 1: 33–57.

Bruner, Jerome. 1991a. "The Narrative Construction of Reality." *Critical Inquiry* 18, no. 1: 1–21.

Bruner, Jerome. 1991b. "Self-Making and World-Making." *Journal of Aesthetic Education* 25, no. 1: 67–78.

Buchanan, Lindal, and Kathleen J. Ryan, eds. 2010. *Walking and Talking Feminist Rhetorics: Landmark Essays and Controversies*. West Lafayette, IN: Parlor Press.

Burke, Kenneth. 1945. *A Grammar of Motives*. Berkeley: University of California Press.

Burke, Kenneth. 1961. *The Rhetoric of Religion: Studies in Logology*. Berkeley: University of California Press.

Burke, Kenneth. 1969. *A Rhetoric of Motives*. Berkeley: University of California Press.

Burnet, David G. 1827. "David G. Burnet to Bustamente, 07-02-1827." Digital Austin Papers. http://digitalaustinpapers.org/document?id=APB1425.xml.

Burnett, M. Dallas. 1971. "Lamanites and the Church." *Ensign* 1, no. 7. https://www.churchofjesuschrist.org/study/ensign/1971/07/lamanites-and-the-church?lang=eng. Accessed May 11, 2017.

Butler, Judith. 1997. *Excitable Speech: A Politics of the Performative*. New York: Routledge.

Caldwell, Charles. 1830. *Thoughts on the Original Unity of the Human Race*. New York: E. Bliss.

Caldwell, Tiffany. 2017. "Racist Flyers Found on University of Utah Campus, But It's Not Clear Who Posted Them." *Salt Lake Tribune*, August 10. https://www.sltrib.com

/news/2017/08/11/racist-posters-found-on-university-of-utah-campus/. Accessed May 11, 2020.

Calhoun, John. 1848. *Speech of Mr. Calhoun, of South Carolina, on His Resolutions in Reference to The War with Mexico*. Washington, DC: John T. Towers.

Call, Tanner. 2022. "Blazing a Trail Away from the LDS Church and Toward Myself." *Salt Lake Tribune*, July 22. https://www.sltrib.com/opinion/commentary/2022/07/22/tanner-call-blazing-trail-away/.

Calleja, Remi, L. Mjenxane, Simone Oosthuizen, Charné Parrott, and Irinja Vähäkangas. 2020. "Introduction" in *Shadowlands: Expanding Being-Becoming beyond Liminality, Crossroads, and Borderlands*, edited by Remi Calleja, 1–56. Bamenda: Langaa RPCIG.

"Cameron County Named After Ill-Fated Scot." 1979. Cameron: Harlingen. F381. University Library, Special Collections & Archives, University of Texas Rio Grande Valley. Edinburg, Texas.

"Cameron History." 1978. Cameron: Harlingen. F381. University Library, Special Collections & Archives, University of Texas Rio Grande Valley. Edinburg, Texas.

"Cameron Once Called 'Wild Horse Desert.'" 1967. Cameron: Harlingen. F381. University Library, Special Collections & Archives, University of Texas Rio Grande Valley. Edinburg, Texas.

Canagarajah, Suresh. 2022. "Challenges in Decolonizing Linguistics: The Politics of Enregisterment and the Divergent Uptakes of Translingualism." *Educational Linguistics* 1, no. 1: 25–55.

Canagarajah, Suresh. 2023. "A Decolonial Crip Linguistics." *Applied Linguistics* 44, no. 3: 606–607.

Caputo, John, and Michael Scanlon, eds. 1999. *God, the Gift, and Postmodernism*. Bloomington: Indiana University Press.

Cardona, Adam. 2022. "Amazon Warehouse Brings Opportunities to the RGV." KVEO-TV, February 9. https://www.valleycentral.com/news/local-news/amazon-warehouse-brings-opportunities-to-the-rgv/.

Carrigan, William, and Clive Webb. 2003. "The Lynching of Persons of Mexican Origin or Descent in the United States, 1848 to 1928." *Journal of Social History* 37, no. 2: 411–438.

Carroll, Lee. 2002. *Rehearsing New Roles: How College Students Develop as Writers*. Carbondale: Southern Illinois University Press.

Carter, Michael. 1991. "The Ritual Functions of Epideictic Rhetoric: The Case of Socrates' Funeral Oration." *Rhetorica* 9, no. 3: 209–232.

Carus, Carl. 1849. *Denkschrift Zum Hundertjährigen Geburtsfeste Goethe's: Ueber Ungleiche Befähigung der Verschiedenen Menschheitstämme für Höhere Geistige Entwickelung*. Leipzig: F.A. Brockhaus.

Castellanos, Jeanett, and Lee Jones, eds. 2003. *The Majority in the Minority: Expanding the Representation of Latina/o Faculty, Administrators and Students in Higher Education*. Sterling, VA: Stylus Publishing.

Castro-Gomez, Santiago. 2005. *La Hybris Del Punto Cero: Ciencia, Raza E Ilustración en la Nueva Granada (1750–1816)*. Bogota: Pontificia Universidad Javeriana.

Castro-Gomez, Santiago. 2007. "The Missing Chapter of Empire: Postmodern Reorganization of Coloniality and Post-Fordist Capitalism." *Cultural Studies* 21, no. 2–3: 428–448.

Caswell, Michelle. 2021. "The Archive Is Not an Archives: On Acknowledging the Intellectual Contributions of Archival Studies." *Reconstruction* 16, no. 1: n.p. https://escholarship.org/uc/item/7bn4v1fk.

Ceraso, Steph. 2014. "(Re)educating the Senses: Multimodal Listening, Bodily Learning, and the Composition of Sonic Experiences." *College English* 77, no. 2: 102–123.

Césaire, Aimé. 2001. *Discourse on Colonialism*. Translated by Joan Pinkham. New York: Monthly Review Press.

Chabram-Dernersesian, Angie. 1999. "Chicana! Rican? No, Chicana Riqueña!: Refashioning the Transnatioanl Connection." In *Between Woman and Nation: Nationalism, Transnational Feminism, and the State*, edited by Caren Kaplan, Norma Alarcon, and Minoo Moallem, 254–295. Durham, NC: Duke University Press.

Chapman, Laura. 1979. "Research Means 'Searching Again.'" *Art Education* 32, no. 4: 6–10.

Chávez, Karma. 2018. "The Body: An Abstract and Actual Rhetorical Concept." *Rhetoric Society Quarterly* 48, no. 3: 242–250.

Child. J. 1824. "J. Child to Stephen F Austin, 02-01-1824." Digital Austin Papers. http://digitalaustinpapers.org/document?id=APB0683.xml.

Chilisa, Bagele. 2012. *Indigenous Research Methodologies*. Los Angeles: SAGE.

Chuck, Elizabeth. 2016. "Speak English. You're in America, Woman Tells Latina Shoppers in Rant Caught on Camera." NBC News. December 22. https://www.nbcnews.com/news/latino/speak-english-you-re-america-woman-tells-latina-shoppers-rant-n698776.

The Church of Jesus Christ of Latter-day Saints. 1845. *Proclamation of the Twelve Apostles of the Church of Jesus Christ of Latter-day Saints*. Liverpool: Wilford Woodruff.

The Church of Jesus Christ of Latter-day Saints. 1877. *Latter-day Saints' Millennial Star*, vol. 30. https://catalog.churchofjesuschrist.org/record/e4ef2b8e-c7ff-4902-beca-13a15c720687/0?view=browse.

The Church of Jesus Christ of Latter-day Saints. 1883. *Sacred Hymns and Spiritual Songs*, 5th ed. Salt Lake City: Deseret News Company.

The Church of Jesus Christ of Latter-day Saints. 1908. *The Doctrine and Covenants of the Church of Jesus Christ of Latter-day Saints*. Salt Lake City: The Deseret News.

The Church of Jesus Christ of Latter-day Saints. 1971. "The Lamanites (Introduction)." https://www.churchofjesuschrist.org/study/ensign/1971/07/the-lamanites-introduction?lang=eng.

The Church of Jesus Christ of Latter-day Saints. 1996. *Our Heritage: A Brief History of the Church of Jesus Christ of Latter-day Saints*. Salt Lake City: The Church of Jesus Christ of Latter-day Saints.

The Church of Jesus Christ of Latter-day Saints. 2004. *Preach My Gospel: A Guide to Missionary Service*. Salt Lake City: The Church of Jesus Christ of Latter-day Saints.

The Church of Jesus Christ of Latter-day Saints. N.d. Missionary Standards for Disciples of Jesus Christ. https://www.churchofjesuschrist.org/study/manual/missionary-handbook?lang=eng. Accessed May 11, 2017.

Cicero, Marcus T. 1967. *De Oratore*. Translated by E. W. Sutton. Cambridge: Harvard University Press.

Cintron, Ralph. 1997. *Angel's Town: Chero Ways, Gang Life, and Rhetorics of the Everyday*. Boston: Beacon Press.

Cintron, Ralph. 2010. "Democracy and Its Limitations." In *The Public Work of Rhetoric: Citizen-Scholars and Civic Engagement*, edited by John Ackerman and David Coogan, 98–114. Columbia: University of South Carolina Press.

Cisneros, Sandra. 1991. *The House on Mango Street*. New York: Vintage Contemporaries.

"City of Harlingen Founded in 1904." 1961. Cameron: Harlingen. F381. University Library, Special Collections & Archives, University of Texas Rio Grande Valley. Edinburg, Texas.

Clary-Lemon, Jennifer, and David Grant, eds. 2022. *Decolonial Conversations in Posthuman and New Material Rhetorics*. Columbus: The Ohio State University Press.

Clayton Family Association. 1921. *William Clayton's Journal: A Daily Record of the Journey of the Original Company of 'Mormon' Pioneers from Nauvoo, Illinois, to the Valley of the Great Salt Lake*. Salt Lake City: The Deseret News.

Clayton, William. N.d. "Come, Come, Ye Saints." Churchofjesuschrist.org. https://www.churchofjesuschrist.org/music/library/hymns/come-come-ye-saints?lang=eng&_r=1. Accessed May 11, 2020.

Coates, Lawrence. 1978. "Brigham Young and Mormon Indian Policies: The Formative Perdio, 1836–1851." *Brigham Young University Studies* 18, no. 3: 428–452.

Collier, Fred, ed. 1987. *The Teachings of President Brigham Young*, Vol. 3: 1852–1854. Springfield: Collier's Publishing.

"Colonizing the Valley." 1985. Cameron: Harlingen. F381. University Library, Special Collections & Archives, University of Texas Rio Grande Valley. Edinburg, Texas.

Colvin, Gina, and Joanna Brooks, eds. 2018. *Decolonizing Mormonism: Approaching a Postcolonial Zion*. Salt Lake City: University of Utah Press.

Connors, Robert. 1984. "Historical Inquiry in Composition Studies." *Writing Instructor* 3: 157–167.

Connors, Robert. 1991. "Writing the History of Our Discipline." In *An Introduction to Composition Studies*, edited by Erika Lindemann and Gary Tate, 49–71. New York: Oxford University Press.

Connors, Robert. 1992. "Dreams and Play: Historical Methods and Methodology." In *Methods and Methodology in Composition Research*, edited by Gesa E. Kirsch and Patricia Sullivan, 15–36. Carbondale: Southern Illinois University Press.

Connors, Robert. 1997. *Composition-Rhetoric: Backgrounds, Theory, and Pedagogy*. Pittsburgh: University of Pittsburgh Press.

Corbett, Edward, and Robert Connors. 1998. *Classical Rhetoric for the Modern Student*. New York: Oxford University Press.

Corder, Jim. 1985. "Argument as Emergence, Rhetoric as Love." *Rhetoric Review* 4, no. 1: 16–32.

Corrigan, Lisa. 2019. "Review." *Philosophy and Rhetoric* 52, no. 2: 163–188.
Cortez, José, and Romeo García. 2020. "The Absolute Limit of Latinx Writing." *College Composition and Communication* 71, no. 4: 566–590.
Cortez, José, and Romeo García. N.d. "Becoming Ready to Listen: Cultural Rhetorics as Emergence." Unpublished essay in author's possession.
Crandall, Brett. 2013. "RGV Least Literate Population in Texas." KVEO-TV, April 9. https://www.valleycentral.com/news/local-news/rgv-least-literate-population-in-texas/.
Cresswell, Tim. 1996. *In Place / Out of Place: Geography, Ideology, and Transgression*. Minneapolis: University of Minnesota Press.
Cresswell, Tim. 2006. *On the Move: Mobility in the Modern Western World*. New York: Routledge.
Cresswell, Tim. 2010. "Towards a Politics of Mobility." *Environment and Planning D: Society and Space* 28, no. 1: 17–31.
Crowley, Sharon. 1991. "A Personal Essay on Freshman English." *Pre/Text* 12, no. 3–4: 155–176.
Crowley, Sharon. 1998. *Composition in the University: Historical and Polemical Essays*. Pittsburgh: University of Pittsburgh Press.
C-Span. 2023. "President Biden Speaks on 'Bidenomics.'" https://www.c-span.org/video/?529028-1/president-biden-speaks-bidenomics.
Cummins, James. 1826. "James Cummins to Stephen F Austin, 07-31-1826." Digital Austin Papers. http://digitalaustinpapers.org/document?id=APB1214.xml.
Cummins, Lawrence. 1971. "Hope for the American Indian?" *Ensign* 1, no. 7. https://www.churchofjesuschrist.org/study/ensign/1971/07/hope-for-the-american-indian?lang=eng. Accessed May 11, 2017.
Cush, Forrest, ed. 2000. *A History of Utah's American Indians*. Logan: Utah State University Press.
Cushman, Ellen. 2013. "Wampum, Sequoyan, and Story: Decolonizing the Digital Archive." *College English* 76, no. 2: 115–135.
Cusicanqui, Silvia Rivera. 2012. "Ch'ixinakax utxiwa: A Reflection on the Practices and Discourses of Decolonization." *The South Atlantic Quarterly* 111, no. 1: 95–109.
Cvetkovich, Ann. 2003. *An Archive of Feelings: Trauma, Sexuality, and Lesbian Public Cultures*. Durham, NC: Duke University Press.
Dahl, Matthew. 2006. "Park Is Not LDS-Owned." *Deseret News*, October 31. https://www.deseret.com/2006/10/31/19982420/park-is-not-lds-owned. Accessed May 11, 2020.
Davenport, Frances, ed. 1917a. "The Papal Bull *Inter Caetera*, May 3, 1493." In *European Treaties Bearing on the History of the United States and Its Dependencies to 1648*, edited by Frances Davenport, 56–63. Washington, DC: Carnegie Institution of Washington.
Davenport, Frances. 1917b. "The Papal Bull *Inter Caetera*, May 4, 1493." In *European Treaties bearing on the History of the United States and Its Dependencies to 1648*, edited by Frances Davenport, 71–78. Washington, DC: Carnegie Institution of Washington.
Davenport, Frances, ed. 1917c. "The Papal Bull *Romanus Pontifex*, January 8, 1455." In *European Treaties Bearing on the History of the United States and Its Dependencies to 1648*,

edited by Frances Davenport, 9–26. Washington, DC: Carnegie Institution of Washington.

Davidson, Arnold. 1996. *Foucault and His Interlocutors*. Chicago: University of Chicago Press.

Davila, Gaige. 2022. "Housing Costs Skyrocket as SpaceX Expands in Texas City." NPR, May 13. https://www.npr.org/2022/05/13/1097981581/housing-costs-skyrocket-spacex-expands-texas.

Davis, Diane. 2010. *Inessential Solidarity: Rhetoric and Foreigner Relations*. Pittsburgh: University of Pittsburgh Press.

Davis, Diane. 2014. "Autozoography: Notes Toward a Rhetoricity of the Living." *Philosophy and Rhetoric* 47, no. 4: 533–553.

Davis, Diane. 2017. "Rhetoricity at the End of the World." *Philosophy and Rhetoric* 50, no. 4: 431–451.

Davis, Diane. 2021. "Rhetoricity, Temporality, Democratic Nonequivalence." *RSQ* 53, no. 3: 193–203.

Davis, Julie. 2018. "A Senior Republican Senator Admonishes Trump: 'America Is an Idea, Not a Race.'" *New York Times*, January 12. https://www.nytimes.com/2018/01/12/us/politics/trump-immigration-congress.html.

The Days of '47. 2018. "Pioneer Stories: Foundation for the Future." https://www.churchofjesuschrist.org/church/news/2018-days-of-47-parade-entries-embody-pioneer-stories-foundations-for-the-future-theme?lang=eng.

de Acosta, Joseph. 1604a. *The Natural and Moral History of the Indies*, vol. 1. Translated by Edward Grimston. London: The Hankluyt Society.

de Acosta, Joseph. 1604b. *The Natural and Moral History of the Indies*, vol. 2. Translated by Edward Grimston. London: The Hakluyt Society.

de Acosta, Joseph. 1670. *De Promulgando Evangelio APVD Barbaros: Sive De Procvranda*. France: Laurentius Anisson.

de Acosta, Joseph. 1987. *De Procuranda Indorum Salute: Educacion y Evangelizacion*. Madrid: Consejo Superior de Investigaciones Cientificas.

de Certeau, Michael. 1992. *The Writing of History*. Translated by Tom Conley. New York: Columbia University Press.

de Certeau, Michel. 2011. *The Practice of Everyday Life*. Berkeley: University of California Press.

de Landa, Diego. 1937. *Yucatan: Before and After the Conquest*. 2nd ed. Translated by William Gates. Baltimore: Maya Society.

Deleuze, Gilles. 1997. "Literature and Life" (translated by Daniel Smith and Michael Greco). *Critical Inquiry* 23, no. 2: 225–230.

Deleuze, Gilles, and Feliz Guattari. 2005. *A Thousand Plateau: Capitalism and Schizophrenia*. Translated by Brian Massumi. Minneapolis: University of Minnesota Press.

Delgado, Richard. 2009. "The Law of the Noose: A History of Latino Lynching." *Harvard Civil Rights–Civil Liberties Law Review* 44: 297–312.

de Mendieta, Gerónimo. 1870. *Historia Eclesiástica Indiana: Obra Escrita á Fines del Siglo XVI*. México: Antigua Libreria.

Democracy Now. 2011. "Attica Is All of Us: Cornel West on 40th Anniversary of Attica Prison Rebellion." https://www.democracynow.org/2011/9/12/attica_is_all_of_us _cornel.

Derrida, Jacques. 1972. "Structure, Signs, and Play in the Discourse of the Human Sciences." In *The Structuralist Controversy: The Language of Criticism and the Sciences of Man*, edited by Richard Macksey and Eugenio Donato, 247–272. Baltimore: The John Hopkins University Press.

Derrida, Jacques. 1982. *Margins of Philosophy*. Translated by Alan Bass. Chicago: The University of Chicago Press.

Derrida, Jacques. 1994a. *Given Time: I. Counterfeit Money*. Translated by Peggy Kamus. Chicago: University of Chicago Press.

Derrida, Jacques. 1994b. *Specters of Marx: The State of the Debt, the Work of Mourning and the New International*. Translated by Peggy Kamus. New York: Routledge.

Derrida, Jacques. 1995. "Archive Fever: A Freudian Impression." *Diacritics* 25, no. 2: 9–63.

Derrida, Jacques. 1997. *Of Grammatology* (Corrected Edition). Translated by Gayatri Chakravorty Spivak. Baltimore: The Johns Hopkins University Press.

Derrida, Jacques. 2021. *Deconstruction in a Nutshell: A Conversation with Jacques Derrida*. New York: Fordham University Press.

Derrida, Jacques, and Maurizio Ferraris. 2001. *A Taste for the Secret*. Translated by Giacomo Donis. New York: Polity.

de Sahagun, Bernardino. 1938. *Historia General de las Cosas de Nueva España*. México: Editorial Pedro Robredo.

Dewey, John. 1927. *The Public and Its Problems*. New York: Henry Holt and Company.

DiAngelo, Robin. 2011. "White Fragility." *International Journal of Critical Pedagogy* 3, no. 3: 54–70.

Doherty, William. 1906. "*Gulf Coast Line Magazine* v. 2, no. 3." UTRGV Digital Library, The University of Texas Rio Grande Valley. https://scholarworks.utrgv.edu /gulfcoastmag/21/.

Doherty, William. 1908. "*Gulf Coast Line Magazine* v. 3, no. 4." UTRGV Digital Library, The University of Texas Rio Grande Valley. https://scholarworks.utrgv.edu /gulfcoastmag/37/.

Dougherty, Timothy. 2016. "Knowing (Y)our Story: Practicing Decolonial Rhetorical History." *Enculturation* 21. n.p.

Douglass, Frederick. 1849. "Colonization." Uncle Tom's Cabin & American Culture. http://utc.iath.virginia.edu/abolitn/abar03at.html. Accessed May 11, 2020.

Douglass, Frederick. 1894. "The Folly of Colonization." Teaching American History. https://teachingamericanhistory.org/library/document/the-folly-of-colonization/. Accessed May 11, 2020.

Downs, Douglas, and Elizabeth Wardle. 2007. "Teaching about Writing, Righting Misconceptions: (Re)envisioning 'First-Year Composition' as 'Introduction to Writing Studies.'" *College Composition and Communication* 58, no. 4: 552–584.

Downs, Douglas, and Elizabeth Wardle. 2012. "Reimagining the Nature of FYC: Trends in Writing-about-Writing Pedagogies." In *Exploring Composition Studies: Sites, Issues, and Perspectives*, edited by Kelly Ritter and Paul Matsuda, 123–144. Logan: Utah State University Press.

Duffy, Bernard. 1983. "The Platonic Functions of Epideictic Rhetoric." *Philosophy and Rhetoric* 16, no. 2: 79–93.

Duffy, John. 2003. "Other Gods and Countries: The Rhetorics of Literacy." In *Towards a Rhetoric of Everyday Life: New Directions in Research on Writing, Text, and Discourse*, edited by Martin Nystrand and John Duffy, 38–57. Madison: University of Wisconsin Press.

Duffy, John. 2007. *Writing from these Roots: Literacy in a Hmong-American Community*. Honolulu: University of Hawai'i Press.

Dussel, Enrique. 1995. *The Invention of the Americas: Eclipse of 'the Other' and the Myth of Modernity*. New York: Continuum.

Dzhanova, Yelena. 2021. "House Speaker Pelosi Said the Pro-Trump Rioters Who Stormed the Capitol Chose 'Their Whiteness over Democracy.'" Business Insider, January 10. https://www.businessinsider.com/pelosi-pro-trump-rioters-chose-their-whiteness-over-democracy-2021-1.

Eberly, Rosa. 2002. "Rhetoric and the Anti-Logos Doughball: Teaching Deliberative Bodies the Practices of Participatory Democracy." *Rhetoric and Public Affairs* 5, no. 2: 287–300.

Edbauer, Jenny. 2005. "Unframing Models of Public Distribution: from Rhetorical Situation to Rhetorical Ecologies." *Rhetoric Society Quarterly* 35, no. 4: 5–24.

Elizondo, Rafael. N.d. "Corrido de Juan Cortina." Recorded by Oscar Chávez. *Interpreta Canciones*. CD. Universal Music Mexico.

Emrich, Duncan. 1952. *Songs of the Mormons and Songs of the West: From the Archive of Folk Song*. Washington, DC: Library of Congress.

Endres, Danielle, and Samantha Senda-Cook. 2011. "Location Matters: The Rhetoric of Place in Protest." *Quarterly Journal of Speech* 97, no. 3: 257–282.

Engel-Ledeboer, M. S. J., and H. Engel. 1964. *Carolus Linnaeus: Systema Natural*. Facsimile of the first edition. Nieuwkoop: B. De Graaf.

England, Eugene. 1985. "'Lamanites' and the Spirit of the Lord." *Dialogue: A Journal of Mormon Thought* 18, no. 4: 25–32.

Engleman, Allan. 1952. "*Daily Review* (Edinburg, Tex.) [Centennial Edition] 100 years of History Hidalgo County_Part 02." The Daily Review. UTRGV Digital Library, The University of Texas Rio Grande Valley. https://scholarworks.utrgv.edu/lrgv/5/.

Enoch, Jessica. 2004. "Para la Mujer: Defining a Chicana Feminist Rhetoric at the Turn of the Century." *College English* 67, no. 1: 20–37.

Enoch, Jessica. 2008. *Refiguring Rhetorical Education: Women Teaching African American, Native American, and Chicano/a Students, 1865–1911*. Carbondale: Southern Illinois University Press.

Enoch, Jessica, and Elizabeth Miller. 2021. "Historiographic Disappointment: Archival Listening and the Recovery of Politically Complex Figures." In *Ethics and Representation in Feminist Rhetorical Inquiry*, edited by Amy Dayton and Jenny Vaughn, 70–88. Pittsburgh: University of Pittsburgh Press.

Enríquez-Loya, Aydé, and Kendall Leon. 2017. "Chicanx/Latinx Rhetorics as Methodology for Writing Program Design at HSIs." *Composition Studies* 45, no. 2: 212–215.

Eppright, Mabel, and Gladys Hooper. 1961. "Yearbook of the Lower Rio Grande Valley of Texas and Norther Mexico, 1961." Rene Torres Collection. UTRGV Digital Library, The University of Texas Rio Grande Valley. https://scholarworks.utrgv.edu/renetorrespub/6/.

Ericson, Lloyd. 2019. "On 'Mormon' in Mormon Studies Publishing." *Dialogue: A Journal of Mormon Thought* 52, no. 3: 29–34.

Escobar, Arturo. 2007. "Worlds and Knowledges Otherwise: The Latin American Modernity/Coloniality Research Program." *Cultural Studies* 21, nos. 2–3: 179–210.

Escobar, Arturo. 2020. *Pluriversal Politics: The Real and the Possible*. Durham, NC: Duke University Press.

EZLN. 1997. *Documentos y Comunicados*, Vol. 3: 1995–1997. Mexico: Coleción Problemas de México.

Ezzaher, Laheen. 2008. "Alfarabi's Book of Rhetoric: An Arabic-English Translation of Alfarabi's Commentary on Aristotle's Rhetoric." *Rhetorica: A Journal of the History of Rhetoric* 26, no. 4: 347–391.

Fabian, Johannes. 2007. *Memory against Culture: Arguments and Reminders*. Durham, NC: Duke University Press.

Fabian, Johannes. 2014. *Time and the Other: How Anthropology Makes Its Objects*. New York: Colombia University Press.

Falcon, Russell. 2021. "Elon Musk: Tell Your Friends to Consider Moving to Texas' RGV, 'Starbase.'" KVEO-TV, March 30. https://www.valleycentral.com/news/elon-musk-tell-your-friends-to-consider-moving-to-texas-rgv-starbase/.

Fanon, Frantz. 1963. *The Wretched of the Earth*. Translated by Constance Farrington. New York: Grove Press.

Fanon, Frantz. 1986. *Black Skins, White Masks*. Translated by Charles Lam Markmann. London: Pluto Press.

Fanon, Frantz. 2004. *The Wretched of the Earth*. With a foreword by Homi Bhabha. New York: Grove Press.

Farberov, Snejana. 2018. "'Happy National N****r Day': Two White High School Girls Post a Racist Instagram Photo Making Fun of LYNCHING on Martin Luther King Jr Day." *DailyMail*, January 18. https://www.dailymail.co.uk/news/article-5285563/Two-white-high-school-girls-post-racist-photo-MLK-Day.html.

Farmer, Jared. 2008. *On Zion's Mount: Mormons, Indians, and the American Landscape*. Cambridge: Harvard University Press.

Felton, Lena. 2018. "Read President Trump's U.S. Naval Academy Commencement Address." *The Atlantic*, May 25. https://www.theatlantic.com/politics/archive/2018/05/read-president-trumps-us-naval-academy-commencement-address/561206/; https://www.theatlantic.com/politics/archive/2018/05/read-president-trumps-us-naval-academy-commencement-address/561206/.

Fernandez, Miriam. 2023. "Reclaiming Malintzin: Epideictic Practices of a Chicana Rhetoric." *Rhetoric Review* 42, no. 3: 139–153.

Ferreira-Buckley, Linda. 1999. "Archivists with an Attitude: Rescuing the Archives from Foucault." *College English* 61, no. 5: 577–583.

"50 Years of Progress." N.d. Cameron: Harlingen. F381. University Library, Special Collections & Archives, University of Texas Rio Grande Valley. Edinburg, Texas.

Fishman, Jenn, and Lauren Rosenberg. 2019. "Guest Editor's Introduction: Community Writing, Community Listening." *Community Literacy Journal* 13, no. 1: 1–4.

Flores, Lisa. 2016. "Between Abundance and Marginalization: The Imperative of Racial Rhetorical Criticism." *Review of Communication* 16, no. 1: 4–24.

Flores, Lisa. 2020. "Stoppage and the Racialized Rhetorics of Mobility." *Western Journal of Communication* 84, no. 3: 247–263.

Flynn, Elizabeth, Patricia Sotirin, and Ann Brady. 2012. *Feminist Rhetorical Resilience*. Boulder: Utah State University Press.

Foner, Philip, ed. 2000. *Frederick Douglas: Selected Speeches and Writings*. Chicago: Lawrence Hill Books.

Foucault, Michel. 1972. *The Archaeology of Knowledge and the Discourse on Language*. Translated by A. M. Sheridan Smith. New York: Pantheon Books.

Foucault, Michel. 1978. *The History of Sexuality*, vol. 1. Translated by Robert Hurley. New York: Pantheon Books.

Fox, Carly, Rebecca Fuentes, Fabiola Ortiz Valdez, Gretchen Purser, and Kathleen Sexsmith. 2017. "Milked: Immigrant Dairy Farmworkers in New York State." Syracuse: A Report by the Workers' Center of Central New York and the Worker Justice Center of New York.

Franklin, Benjamin. 1839. *Memoirs of Benjamin Franklin: Written by Himself*, vol. 2. New York: Harper & Brothers.

Franklin, Benjamin. 1857. *The Select Works of Benjamin Franklin: Including his Autobiography with Notes and a Memoir*. Boston: Phillips, Sampson, and Company.

Fraser, Nancy. 2007. "Transnationalizing the Public Sphere: On the Legitimacy and Efficacy of Public Opinion in a Post-Westphalian World." *Theory, Culture & Society* 24, no. 4: 7–30.

Freire, Paulo. 2000. *Pedagogy of the Oppressed*. New York: Continuum.

Frye, Marilyn. 1983. *Politics of Reality: Essays in Feminist Theory*. Toronto: Crossing Press, 1983.

Fukushima, Annie. 2019. *Migrant Crossings: Witnessing Human Trafficking in the U.S.* Stanford, CA: Stanford University Press.

Fulwider, Abrielle. 2017. "U Responds to 'Its' Okay to be White' Posters Found on Campus." *Daily Utah Chronicle*, November 10. https://dailyutahchronicle.com/2017/11/10/u-responds-to-its-okay-to-be-white-posters-found-on-campus/.

Fúnez-Flores, Jairo. 2024. "Anibal Quijano: (Dis)entangling the Geopolitics and Coloniality of Curriculum." *The Curriculum Journal* 35, 2:288–306.

Gaillet, Lynée Lewis. 2010. "Archival Survival: Navigating Historical Research." In *Working in the Archives: Practical Research Methods for Rhetoric and Composition*, edited by Alexis E. Ramsey, Wendy B. Sharer, Barbara L'Eplattenier, and Lisa S. Mastrangelo, 28–39. Carbondale: Southern Illinois University Press.

García, Alma. 2004. *Narratives of Mexican American Women: Emergent Identities of the Second Generation*. Walnut Creek, CA: AltaMira Press.

Garcia, Claudia. 2024. "Local Reaction to SpaceX Moving Headquarters to Brownsville." KRGV News. July 16. https://www.krgv.com/news/local-reaction-to-spacex-moving-headquarters-to-brownsville/.

Garcia, Gina, ed. 2020. *Hispanic Serving Institutions (HSIs) in Practice: Defining 'Servingness' at HSIs*. Charlotte, NC: Information Age Publishing.

Garcia, Gina, Anne-Marie Núñez, and Vanessa A. Sansone. 2019. "Toward a Multidimensional Conceptual Framework for Understanding 'Servingness' in Hispanic-Serving Institutions: A Synthesis of the Research." *Review of Educational Research* 89, no. 5: 745–784.

García, Romeo. 2018a. "Creating Presence from Absence and Sound from Silence." *Community Literacy Journal* 13, no. 1: 7–15.

García, Romeo. 2018b. "Corrido-ing State Violence." *Journal of Multimodal Rhetorics* 2, no. 2: http://journalofmultimodalrhetorics.com/issue-2-2-discussions.

García, Romeo. 2019a. "Haunt(ed/ing) Genealogies and Literacies." *Reflections: A Journal of Community-Engaged Writing and Rhetoric* 19, no. 1: 230–252.

García, Romeo. 2019b. "A Settler Archive. A Site for a Decolonial Praxis Project." *Constellations* 1, no. 1, https://constell8cr.com/issue-2/a-settler-archive-a-site-for-a-decolonial-praxis-project/.

García, Romeo. 2022a. "Decolonizing the Rhetoric of Church-Settlers." *Special Issue of Across the Disciplines* 18, no. 1/2: 124–144.

García, Romeo. 2022b. "Unsettling Church(-)Settler Ideas, Images, and Ends." *Rhetoric, Politics, and Culture* 1, no. 2: 1–46.

García, Romeo, and Damián Baca, eds. 2019. *Rhetorics Elsewhere and Otherwise: Contested Modernities, Decolonial Visions*. Urbana, IL: NCTE/CCCC Studies in Writing and Rhetoric.

García, Romeo, and José Cortez. 2020. "The Trace of a Mark That Scatters: The Anthropoi and the Rhetoric of Decoloniality." *Rhetoric Society Quarterly* 50, no. 2: 93–108.

García, Romeo, and Yndalecio Hinojosa. 2020. "Encounters with Friction: Engaging Resistance through Strategic Neutrality." In *On Teacher Neutrality: Praxis, Politics, and Performativity*, edited by Daniel Richards. 207–220: Logan: Utah State University Press.

García, Romeo, and Gesa Kirsch. 2022. "Deep Rhetoricity as Methodological Grounds for Unsettling the Settled." *College Composition and Communication* 74, no. 2: 229–261.

Garrett, Matthew. 2016. *Making Lamanites: Mormons, Native Americans, and the Indian Student Placement Program, 1947–2000*. Salt Lake City: University of Utah Press.

Garza, Julian. N.d. "Pistoleros Famosos." Recorded by Ramon Ayala. *Historias Norteñas: 30 Corridos*. CD. Freddie Records.

Gee, James Paul. 1989. "Literacy, Discourse, and Linguistics: Introduction." *Journal of Education* 171, no. 1: 5–17.

Geiger, T. J. 2009. "Our Work Is Our Prayer: Scholarship, Invention, and Spiritual Activism." *Peitho* 11, no. 1: 1–7.

Geiger, T. J. 2013. "Unpredictable Encounters: Religious Discourse, Sexuality, and the Free Exercise of Rhetoric." *College English* 75, no. 3: 248–269.
Gendlin, Eugene. 1982. *Focusing*. New York: Bantam Books.
Ghaddar, Jamila J. 2016. "The Spectre in the Archive: Truth, Reconciliation, and Indigenous Archival Memory." *Archivaria* 82, no. 1: 3–26.
Ghaddar, Jamila J., and Michelle Caswell. 2019. "To Go Beyond: Towards a Decolonial Archival Praxis." *Archival Science* 19: 71–85.
Giddens, Anthony. 1981. *A Contemporary Critique of Historical Materialism*, Vol. 1: *Power, Property, and the State*. Berkeley: University of California Press.
Gill, Joe. 1956–1967. *Texas Rangers in Action*, nos. 5–63. Comic Book Plus. https://comicbookplus.com/?cid=1239.
Ginés de Sepúlveda, Juan. 1987. *Tratado: Sobre Las Justas Causas de la Guerra Contra Los Indios*. México: Fondo de Cultura Economica.
Giroux, Henry. 1988. "Border Pedagogy in the Age of Postmodernism." *Journal of Education* 170, no. 3: 162–181.
Glenn, Cheryl, and Jessica Enoch. 2009. "Drama in the Archives: Rereading Methods, Rewriting History." *College Composition and Communication* 61, no. 2: 321–342.
Glenn, Cheryl, and Jessica Enoch. 2010. "Invigorating Historiographical Practices in Rhetoric and Composition Studies." In *Working in the Archives: Practical Research Methods for Rhetoric and Composition*, edited by Alexis E. Ramsey, Wendy B. Sharer, Barbara L'Eplattenier, and Lisa Mastrangelo, 11–27. Carbondale: Southern Illinois University Press.
Glissant, Edouard. 1989. *Caribbean Discourse: Selected Essays*. Translated by J. Michael Dash. Charlottesville: University Press of Virginia.
Gobineau, Arthur de. 1915. *The Inequality of Human Races*. Translated by Adrian Collins. New York: G. P. Putnam's Sons.
"Golden Groves: Lower Rio Grande Valley." N.d. John H. Shary Collection, ELIBR-0002, Box 256, Folder 52. University of Texas Rio Grande Valley Special Collections and Archives, Edinburg Campus.
"The Golden Story of Sharyland: Where Nature Produces the World's Sweetest Citrus Fruits." N.d. John H. Shary Collection, ELIBR-0002, Box 243, Folder 31. University of Texas Rio Grande Valley Special Collections and Archives, Edinburg Campus.
Gómez-Peña, Guillermo. 1996. *The New World Border: Prophecies, Poems, and Loqueras for the End of the Century*. San Francisco: City Lights.
González, Jovita, and Eve Raleigh. 1996. *Caballero: A Historical Novel*. College Station: Texas A&M University Press.
"Good Morning." 1935. Cameron: Harlingen. F381. University Library, Special Collections & Archives, University of Texas Rio Grande Valley. Edinburg, Texas.
Gordon, Avery. 2008. *Ghostly Matters: Haunting and the Sociological Imagination* Minneapolis: University of Minnesota Press.
Gordon, Lewis. 1995. *Bad Faith and Antiblack Racism*. Amherst, NY: Humanity Books.
Gordon, Lewis. 1997. *Her Majesty's Other Children: Sketches of Racism from a Neocolonial Age*. Lanham, MD: Rowman & Littlefield Publishers.

Gordon, Lewis. 2000. *Existentia: Understanding Africana Existential Thought*. New York: Routledge.
Gordon, Lewis. 2005. "Through the Zone of Nonbeing: A Reading of Black Skin, White Masks in Celebration of Fanon's Eightieth Birthday." *The C.L.R James Journal* 11, no. 1: 1–43.
Gordon, Lewis. 2007. "Problematic People and Epistemic Decolonization: Toward the Postcolonial in Africana Political Thought." In *Postcolonialism and Political Theory*, edited by Nalini Persram, 121–141. Lanham, MD: Lexington Books.
Graban, Tarez, and Wendy Hayden, eds. 2022. *Teaching through the Archives: Text, Collaboration, and Activism*. Carbondale: Southern Illinois University Press.
Graff, Harvey. 1979. *The Literacy Myth: Cultural Integration and Social Structure in the Nineteenth Century*. New York: Academic Press.
Graff, Richard, and Michael Leff. 2012. "Revisionist Historiography and Rhetorical Tradition(s)." In *The Viability of the Rhetorical Tradition*, edited by Richard Graff, Arthur Walzer, and Janet Atwill, 11–30. Albany: State University of New York Press.
Grande, Sandy. 2018. "Refusing the University." In *Toward What Justice? Describing Diverse Dreams of Justice in Education*, edited by Eve Tuck and K. Wayne Yang, 47–65. New York: Routledge.
Green, Ann. 2003. "Difficult Stories: Service-Learning, Race, Class, and Whiteness." *College Composition and Communication* 55, no. 2: 276–301.
Gries, Laurie. 2015. *Still Life with Rhetoric: A New Materialist Approach for Visual Rhetorics*. Logan: Utah State University Press.
Gries, Laurie, and Collin Brooke, eds. 2018. *Circulation, Writing, and Rhetoric*. Logan: Utah State University Press.
Groo, Katherine. 2019. *Bad Film Histories: Ethnography and the Early Archive*. Minneapolis: University of Minnesota Press.
Grosfoguel, Ramón. 2007. "The Epistemic Decolonial Turn: Beyond Political-Economy Paradigms." *Cultural Studies* 21, nos. 2–3: 211–223.
Grosfoguel, Ramón. 2013. "The Structure of Knowledge in Westernized Universities: Epistemic Racism/Sexism and the Four Genocides/Epistemicides of the Long 16th Century." *Human Architecture: Journal of the Sociology of Self-Knowledge* 11, no. 1: 73–90.
Grosfoguel, Ramón, Roberto Hernandez, and Ernesto Velasquez. 2016. *Decolonizing the Westernized University: Interventions in Philosophy of Education from Within and Without*. Lanham, MD: Lexington Books.
Guajardo, M., and Guajardo, F. 2004. "The Impact of Brown on the Brown of South Texas: A Micropolitical Perspective on the Education of Mexican Americans in a South Texas Community." *American Educational Research* 41, no. 3: 501–526.
Guattari, Félix. 1995. *Chaosmosis: An Ethico-Aesthetic Paradigm*. Translated by Paul Bains and Julian Pefanis. Bloomington: Indiana University Press.
Guerra, Juan. 1998. *Close to Home: Oral and Literate Practices in a Transnational Mexicano Community*. New York: Teachers College Press.
Guerra, Juan. 2004. "Emerging Representations, Situated Literacies, and the Practice of Transcultural Repositioning." In *Latino/a Discourses on Language, Identity, and Liter-

acy Education, edited by Michelle Hall Kells, Valerie Balester, and Victor Villanueva, 7–23. Portsmouth: Boynton/Cook Publishers.

Guevara, Emma. 2021. "What Journalists Should Know before Reporting on the SpaceX at Boca Chica Beach." *Trucha*, December 14. https://truchargv.com/what-journalists-should-know-before-reporting-on-the-spacex-at-boca-chica-beach/.

Guidotti-Hernández, Nicole. 2011. *Unspeakable Violence: Remapping U.S. and Mexican National Imaginaries.* Durham, NC: Duke University Press.

Haas, Angela. 2012. "Race, Rhetoric, and Technology: A Case Study of Decolonial Technical Communication Theory, Methodology, and Pedagogy." *Journal of Business and Technical Communication* 26, no. 3: 277–310.

Habermas, Jürgen. 1989. *Structural Transformation of the Public Sphere.* Cambridge: MIT Press.

Hall, Stuart. 1989. "Cultural Identity and Cinematic Representation." *Framework* 36: 68–81.

Hall, Stuart. 1996. "New Ethnicities." In *Black British Cultural Studies: A Reader*, edited by Houston Baker, Manthia Diawara, and Ruth Lindeborg, 163–172. Chicago: University of Chicago University Press.

Hall, Stuart. 2001. "Constituting an Archive." *Third Text* 15, no. 54: 89–92.

Hall, Stuart. 2011. "The Neo-Liberal Revolution." *Cultural Studies* 25, no. 6: 705–728.

Hall, Stuart. 2019. "Through the Prism of an Intellectual Life." In *Essential Essays*, Vol. 2: *Identity and Diaspora*, edited by David Morley, 303–324. Durham, NC: Duke University Press.

Hämäläinen, Pekka. 2008. *The Comanche Empire.* New Haven: Yale University Press.

Hanchey, Jenna. 2023. *The Center Cannot Hold: Decolonial Possibility in the Collapse of a Tanzanian NGO.* Durham, NC: Duke University Press.

Hanke, Lewis. 1937. "Pope Paul III and the American Indians." *Harvard Theological Review* 30, no. 2: 65–102.

Hanke, Lewis. 1994. *All Mankind Is One: A Study of the Disputation between Bartolomé de Las Casas and Juan Ginés de Sepúlveda in 1550 on the Intellectual and Religious Capacity of the American Indian.* DeKalb: Northern Illinois University Press.

Hansen, Kristine. 2005. "Religious Freedom in the Public Square and the Composition Classroom." *Negotiating Religious Faith in the Composition Classroom*, edited by Elizabeth Lei and Bonnie Kyburz, 24–38. Portsmouth, NH: Heinemann.

Haraway, Donna. 1988. "Situated Knowledges: The Science Question in Feminism and the Privileges of Partial Perspective." *Feminist Studies* 14, no. 3: 575–599.

Haraway, Donna. 2008. *When Species Meet.* Minneapolis: University of Minnesota Press.

Haraway, Donna. 2016a. *Manifestly Haraway.* Minneapolis: University of Minnesota Press.

Haraway, Donna. 2016b. *Staying with the Trouble: Making Kin in the Chthulucene.* Durham, NC: Duke University Press.

Harkin, Patricia. 1994. "Narrating Conflict." In *Writing Theory and Critical Pedagogy*, edited by John Clifford and John Schilb, 278–285. New York: Modern Language Association of America.

"Harlingen: Center of a Hunters Paradise." N.d. Cameron: Harlingen. F381. University Library, Special Collections & Archives, University of Texas Rio Grande Valley. Edinburg, Texas.

"Harlingen: The City That Citrus Built." 1931. Series 5. Reference Files, ELIBR-0062. University Library, Special Collections & Archives, University of Texas Rio Grande Valley. Edinburg, Texas.

Harlingen Chamber of Commerce. 1932. "Information about Harlingen and the Lower Rio Grande Valley." John H. Shary Collection. UTRGV Digital Library, The University of Texas Rio Grande Valley. https://scholarworks.utrgv.edu/johnshary/78/.

"Harlingen Gateway to the Valley 'Wants You.'" 1925. Series 5. Reference Files, ELIBR-0062. University Library, Special Collections & Archives, University of Texas Rio Grande Valley. Edinburg, Texas.

"Harlingen Heritage Trail." N.d. Cameron: Harlingen. F381. University Library, Special Collections & Archives, University of Texas Rio Grande Valley. Edinburg, Texas.

"Harlingen Proud of Its Modern School System." N.d. Series 5. Reference Files, ELIBR-0062. University Library, Special Collections & Archives, University of Texas Rio Grande Valley. Edinburg, Texas.

"Harlingen's Location Makes It Key City of 'World's Garden Spot.'" N.d. Series 5. Reference Files, ELIBR-0062. University Library, Special Collections & Archives, University of Texas Rio Grande Valley. Edinburg, Texas.

"Harlingen the Geographical and Trade Center of the Lower Rio Grande Valley of Texas." N.d. Cameron: Harlingen. F381. University Library, Special Collections & Archives, University of Texas Rio Grande Valley. Edinburg, Texas.

Harris, Matthew, and Newell Bringhurst, eds. 2015. *The Mormon Church and Blacks: A Documentary History*. Urbana: University of Illinois Press.

Hartley, William. 2001. "Missouri's 1838 Extermination Order and the Mormon's Forced Removal to Illinois." *Mormon Historical Studies* 2, no. 1: 5–27.

Harwell, William, and Fred Collier. 1997. *Manuscript History of Brigham Young, 1847–1850*. Salt Lake City: Collier's Publishing Co.

Hauser, Gerard. 1998. "Vernacular Dialogue and the Rhetoricality of Public Opinion." *Communications Monographs* 65, no. 2: 83–107.

Hauser, Gerard. 1999a. "Aristotle on Epideictic: The Formation of Public Morality." *Rhetoric Society Quarterly* 29, no. 1: 5–23.

Hauser, Gerard. 1999b. *Vernacular Voices: The Rhetoric of Publics and Public Spheres*. Columbia: University of South Carolina Press.

Hawkins, Joseph H. 1821. "Joseph H. Hawkins to Maria Austin, 06-27-1821." Digital Austin Papers. http://digitalaustinpapers.org/document?id=APB0393.xml.

Hegel, G. W. F. 1857. *Lectures on the Philosophy of History*. Translated by J. Sibree. London: Henry G. Bohn.

Hegel, G. W. F. 1886. *The Introduction to Hegel's Philosophy of Fine Art*. Translated by Bernard Bosanquet. London: Kegal Paul, Trench & Co.

Hegel, G. W. F. 1894. *Hegel's Philosophy of Mind*. Translated by William Wallace. Oxford: Clarendon Press.

Hegel, G. W. F. 1896. *Hegel's Philosophy of Right*. Translated by S. W. Dyde. London: George Bell & Sons.

Hegel, G. W. F. 1902. *Philosophy of History*. Translated by J. Sibree. New York: American Home Library Company.

Hegel, G. W. F. 1977. *Phenomenology of Spirit*. Translated by A. V. Miller. New York: Oxford University Press.

Heidegger, Martin. 1962. *Being and Time*. Translated by John Macquarrie and Edward Robinson. Hoboken, NJ: Blackwell.

Heineccius, Johann. 1741. *A Methodical System of Universal Law: Or, the Laws of Nature and Nations Deduced from Certain Principles, and Applied to Proper Cases*. Translated by George Turnbull. London: J. Noon.

Herrera-Sobek, Maria. 1993. *The Mexican Corrido: A Feminist Analysis*. Bloomington: Indiana University Press.

Hidalgo County Centennial Corp. 1952. "The Centennial Celebration of the Organization of Hidalgo Country in Texas, December 7–13, 1952: Official Program." John H. Shary Collection. UTRGV Digital Library, The University of Texas Rio Grande Valley. https://scholarworks.utrgv.edu/johnshary/6/.

"His Faith in Harlingen's Future a Factor in Its Growth." N.d. Cameron: Harlingen. F381. University Library, Special Collections & Archives, University of Texas Rio Grande Valley. Edinburg, Texas.

Hodge, Robert, and Gunther Kress. 1993. *Language as Ideology*. New York: Routledge.

Holland, Sharon. 2000. *Raising the Dead: Readings of Death and (Black) Subjectivity*. Durham, NC: Duke University Press.

hooks, bell. 1989. *Talking Back: Thinking Feminist, Thinking Black*. Boston: South End Press.

hooks, bell. 1994. *Teaching to Transgress: Education as the Practice of Freedom*. New York: Routledge.

hooks, bell. 2001a. *All About Love: New Visions*. New York: Harper Perennial.

hooks, bell. 2001b. "Homeplace (a Site of Resistance)." In *Available Means: An Anthology of Women's Rhetorics*, edited by Joy Ritchie and Kate Ronald, 382–390. Pittsburgh: University of Pittsburgh Press.

hooks, bell. 2003. *Teaching Community: A Pedagogy of Hope*. New York: Routledge.

hooks, bell. 2009. *Belonging: A Culture of Place*. New York: Routledge.

hooks, bell. 2010. *Teaching Critical Thinking: Practical Wisdom*. New York: Routledge.

hooks, bell. 2015. *Talking Back: Thinking Feminist, Thinking Black*. New York: Routledge.

Houser, Gerald. 1999. *Vernacular Voices: The Rhetoric of Publics and Public Spheres*. Columbia: University of South Carolina Press.

Houston, Pam. 2003. "The Truest Eye." Oprah.com. https://www.oprah.com/omagazine/toni-morrison-talks-love/all.

Howard, Jane. 1963. "Doom and Glory of Knowing Who You Are." *Life Magazine*, 86–90. May 24.

Howe, E. D. 1834. *Mormonism Unvailed [sic]: Or, a Faithful Account of That Singular Imposition and Delusion, From Its Rise to the Present Time*. Painesville, OH: E. D. Howe.

Howett, Benjamin. 1885. *The Politics of Aristotle*. Oxford: Clarendon Press.

Huang, Yu-Ting, and Rebecca Weaver-Hightower, eds. 2019. *Archiving Settler Colonialism: Culture, Space, and Race*. New York: Routledge.
Hume, David. 1822. *Essays and Treatises on Several Subjects*. A New Edition. Vol. 1. London: J. Jones.
Hunt, Dallas. 2016. "Nikîkîwân: Contesting Settler Colonial Archives through Indigenous Oral History," *Canadian Literature*, nos. 230–231: 25–42.
Icazbalceta, Joaquín. 1889. *Nueva Coleción de Documentos para la Historia de México*, vol. 2. México: Francisco Diaz de Leon.
Inoue, Asao. 2017. *Antiracist Writing Assessment Ecologies: Teaching and Assessing Writing for a Socially Just Future*. Fort Collins: WAC Clearinghouse.
Ismael M. 2021. "Rio Grande Valley against SpaceX." *Trucha*, April 5. https://truchargv.com/rio_grande_valley_against_spacex/.
Ivey, Darren. 2010. *The Texas Rangers: A Registry and History*. Jefferson, NC: McFarland & Company.
Jackson, Brian, and Gregory Clark, eds. 2014. *John Dewey, Rhetoric, and Democratic Practice: Trained Capacities*. Columbia: University of South Carolina Press.
Jackson, Jay. 1913. "The True Story of the Lower Rio Grande Valley of Texas: Where Crops Never Fail." ELIBR-0151. UTRGV Digital Library, The University of Texas Rio Grande Valley. https://scholarworks.utrgv.edu/lrgv/26/.
Jackson, Rachel. 2017. "Decolonizing Place and Race: Racial Resentments, Local Histories, and Transrhetorical Analysis." *Rhetoric Review* 36, no. 4: 255–347.
Jefferson, Thomas. 1825. *Notes on the State of Virginia*. Philadelphia: H. C. Carey & I. Lea.
Jimenez, Freddy. 2022. "Commentary: On the Shoulders of Giants." *Trucha*, March 21. https://truchargv.com/social-justice-template-2/.
Johnson, Benjamin. 2003. *Revolution in Texas: How a Forgotten Rebellion and Its Bloody Suppression Turned Mexicans into Americas*. New Haven: Yale University Press.
Johnson, Francis W. 1831. "Francis W. Johnson to Stephen F Austin, 03-21-1831." Digital Austin Papers. http://digitalaustinpapers.org/document?id=APB4179.
Johnson, Lane. 1975. "Who and Where Are the Lamanites." *Ensign* 5, no. 12. https://www.churchofjesuschrist.org/study/ensign/1975/12/who-and-where-are-the-lamanites?lang=eng. Accessed May 11, 2017.
Jones, Abigail. 2023. "Report: Elon Musk Plans to Build His Own Town in Texas." *Valley Central*, March 10. https://www.valleycentral.com/news/report-elon-musk-plans-to-build-his-own-town-in-texas/.
Kanngieser, A. M. 2023. "Sonic Colonialities: Listening, Dispossession, and the (Re)making of Anglo-European Nature." *Transactions of the Institute of British Geographers* 48, no. 4: 690–702.
Kant, Immanuel. 1819. *Logic from the German*. Translated by Jonn Richardson. London: W. Simpkin and R. Marshall.
Kant, Immanuel. 1996a. "An Answer to the Question: What Is Enlightenment?" In *Practical Philosophy*, edited by Mary Gregor, 11–22. Cambridge: Cambridge University Press.
Kant, Immanuel. 1996b. *Anthropology from a Pragmatic Point of View*, edited by Victor L. Dowdell. Carbondale: Southern Illinois University Press.

Kant, Immanuel. 1996c. "Critique of Practical Reason." In *Practical Philosophy*, edited by Mary Gregor, 133–272. Cambridge: Cambridge University Press.

Kant, Immanuel. 1996d. "Groundwork of the Metaphysics of Morals." In *Practical Philosophy*, edited by Mary Gregor, 37–108. Cambridge: Cambridge University Press.

Kant, Immanuel. 1996e. "The Metaphysics of Morals." In *Practical Philosophy*, edited by Mary Gregor, 353–604. Cambridge: Cambridge University Press.

Kant, Immanuel. 1996f. "Toward Perpetual Peace." In *Practical Philosophy*, edited by Mary Gregor, 311-352. Cambridge: Cambridge University Press.

Kant, Immanuel. 1997. "Moral Philosophy: Collins's Lecture Notes." In *Lectures on Ethics*, edited by Peter Heath, 37–222. Cambridge: Cambridge University Press.

Kant, Immanuel. 1998a. "Idea for a Universal History from a Cosmopolitan Point of View." In *Classical Readings in Culture and Civilization*, edited by John Rundell and Stephen Mennell, 39–47. New York: Routledge.

Kant, Immanuel. 1998b. *Critique of Pure Reason*, edited by Paul Guyer and Allen Wood. Cambridge: Cambridge University Press.

Kant, Immanuel. 2011. *Observations on the Feeling of the Beautiful and Sublime and Other Writings*, edited by Patrick Frierson and Paul Guyer. Cambridge: Cambridge University Press.

Kant, Immanuel. 2012. "Physical Geography." In *Natural Science*, edited by Eric Watkins, 434–679. Translated by Lewis Beck, Jeffrey Edwards, Olaf Reinhardt, Martin Schönfeld, and Eric Watkins. Cambrdige: Cambridge University Press.

Kant, Immanuel. 2013a. "Of the Different Human Races." In *Kant and the Concept of Race: Late Eighteenth-Century Writings*, edited by Jon Mikkelsen, 55–72. Albany: SUNY Press.

Kant, Immanuel. 2013b. "Determination of the Concept of a Human Race." In *Kant and the Concept of Race: Late Eighteenth-Century Writings*, edited by Jon Mikkelsen, 125–142. New York: SUNY Press.

Kant, Immanuel. 2013c. "On the Use of Teleological Principles in Philosophy." In *Kant and the Concept of Race: Late Eighteenth-Century Writings*, edited by Jon Mikkelsen, 169–194. New York: SUNY Press.

Karami, Iris. 2021. "Elon Musk Looking to Create a City in the RGV." KVEO-TV, March 5. https://www.valleycentral.com/news/local-news/elon-musk-looking-to-create-a-city-in-the-rgv/.

Kearney, Richard. 1984. *Dialogues with Contemporary Continental Thinkers: The Phenomenological Heritage: Paul Ricoeur, Emmanuel Levinas, Herbert Marcuse, Stanislas Breton, Jacques Derrida*. Manchester: Manchester University Press.

Keates, Nancy, and Mark Maremont. 2021. "Elon Musk's SpaceX Is Buying Up a Texas Village. Homeowners Cry Foul." *Wall Street Journal*, May 7. https://www.wsj.com/articles/elon-musk-spacex-rocket-boca-chica-texas-starbase-11620353687.

Keating, AnaLouise. 2013. *Transformation Now: Toward a Post-Opposition Politics of Change*. Urbana: University of Illinois Press.

Kells, Michelle Hall. 2002. "Linguistic Contact Zones in the College Writing Classroom: An Examination of Ethnolinguistic Identity and Language Attitudes." *Written Communication* 19, no. 1: 5–43.

Kells, Michelle Hall. 2004. "Understanding the Rhetorical Value of Tejano Codeswitching." In *Latino/a Discourses on Language, Identity, and Literacy Education*, edited by Michelle Hall Kells, Valerie Balester, and Victor Villanueva, 24–39. Portsmouth, NH: Boynton/Cook Publishers.

Kells, Michelle Hall. 2006. *Hector P. Garcia: Everyday Rhetoric and Mexican American Civil Rights*. Carbondale: Southern Illinois University Press.

Kelly, Casey, and Jason Edward Black, eds. 2018. *Decolonizing Native American Rhetoric: Communicating Self-Determination*. New York: Peter Lang.

Kenan, Randall, ed. 2011. *James Baldwin: The Cross of Redemption: Uncollected Writings*. New York: Vintage Books.

Kennedy, George. 1998. *Comparative Rhetoric: An Historical and Cross-Cultural Introduction*. New York: Oxford University Press.

Kerbey, McFall. 1939. "The Texas Delta of an American Nile: Orchards and Gardens Replace Thorny Jungle in the Southmost Tip of the Lone Star State /Rio Grande Cornucopia Under a Winter Sun." *National Geographic* 75, no. 1: 51–96.

Kimball, Spencer. 1954. "No Title." In *124th Annual Conference of the Church of Jesus Christ of Latter-day Saints*, 102–108. Salt Lake City: Church of Jesus Christ of Latter-day Saints.

Kimball, Spencer. 1960. "No Title." *130th Semi-Annual Conference*, 32–37. Salt Lake City: Church of Jesus Christ of Latter-day Saints.

Kimball, Spencer. 1984. "And the Lord Called His People Zion." *Ensign* 14, no. 8. https://www.churchofjesuschrist.org/study/ensign/1984/08/and-the-lord-called-his-people-zion?lang=eng. Accessed May 11, 2017.

Kimmerer, Robin Wall. 2013. *Braiding Sweetgrass: Indigenous Wisdom, Scientific Knowledge, and the Teachings of Plants*. Minneapolis: Milkweed Editions.

King, Lisa. 2023. "Gaining Indigenous Ground in a European Museum? Colonial Logics and Decolonial Possibilities at the Humboldt Forum." *Pluriversal Literacies: Tool for Perseverance and Livable Futures*, edited by Romeo García, Ellen Cushman, and Damián Baca. 48-70. Pittsburgh: University of Pittsburgh Press.

King, Lisa, Rose Gubele, and Joyce Rain Anderson, eds. 2015. *Survivance, Sovereignty, and Story: Teaching American Indian Rhetorics*. Logan: Utah State University Press.

Kirklighter, Cristina, Diana Cardenas, and Susan Wolf Murphy, eds, 2007. *Teaching Writing with Latino/a Students: Lessons Learned at Hispanic-Serving Institutions*. Albany: SUNY Press.

Kirsch, Gesa, and Peter Mortensen. 1996. "Introduction: Reflections on Methodology in Literacy Studies." In *Ethics and Representation in Qualitative Studies of Literacy*, edited by Peter Mortensen and Gesa Kirsch, xix–xxxiv. Urbana: National Council of Teachers of English.

Kirsch, Gesa, and Liz Rohan, eds. 2008. *Beyond the Archives: Research as a Lived Process*. Carbondale: Southern Illinois University Press.

Klopfenstein, Jacob. 2021. "U. Condemns Racism as Investigators Review Reports of KKK on Campus, Feces on Student's Door." KSL, December 21. https://www.ksl.com/article/50315575/us-racism-investigators-reviewing-reports-of-kkk-on-campus-feces-found-on-students-door.

Knox, Annie. 2017. "White Nationalist Posters Appear on Weber State Campus." *Deseret News*, August 28. https://www.deseret.com/2017/8/28/20618389/white-nationalist-posters-appear-on-weber-state-campus.

Kruks, Sonia. 1995. "Identity Politics and Dialectical Reason: Beyond an Epistemology of Provenance." *Hypatia* 10, no. 2: 1–22.

Kump, Eileen. 1973. "'L Is for Indian'—And Other Family Projects." *Ensign* 3, no. 8. https://www.churchofjesuschrist.org/study/ensign/1973/08/l-is-for-indian-and-other-family-projects?lang=eng. Accessed May 11, 2017.

Lamos, Steve. 2012. "Minority-Serving Institutions, Race-Conscious 'Dwelling,' and Possible Futures for Basic Writing at Predominately White Institutions." *Journal of Basic Writing* 31, no. 1: 4–35.

Lamp, Kathleen. 2019. "Building Praise: Augustan Rome and Epideictic." *Advances in the History of Rhetoric* 22, no. 2: 153–166.

"Land of Hearts Delight." N.d. Cameron: Harlingen. F381. University Library, Special Collections & Archives, University of Texas Rio Grande Valley. Edinburg, Texas.

Las Casas, Bartolomé de. 1566. *Apologética Historia Sumaria*. Colombia: Fundación El Libro Total. https://www.ellibrototal.com/ltotal/?t=1&d=4072.

Las Casas, Bartolomé de. 1877. *Biblioteca Mexicana: Historia de las Indias*. Edited by Jose Vigil. México: Ireneo Paz.

Las Casas, Bartolomé de. 1958. *Biblioteca de Autores Españoles: Desde la Formacion del Lenguaje Hasta Nuestros Dias*. Madrid: M. Rivadeneyra.

Las Casas, Bartolomé de. 1965. *Tratados*, vol. 1. México: Fondo de Cultura Económica.

Las Casas, Bartolomé de. 1974. *In Defense of the Indians: The Defense of the Most Reverend Lord, Don Fray Bartolomé de las Casas, of the Order of Preachers, Last Bishop of Chiapa, Against the Persecutors and Slanderers of the Peoples of the New World Discovered Across the Seas*. Translated by Stafford Poole. DeKalb: Northern Illinois University Press.

Latina Feminist Group. 2001. *Telling to Live: Latina Feminist Testimonios*. Durham, NC: Duke University Press.

Lawrence, William. 1848. *Lectures on Comparative Anatomy, Physiology, Zoology, and the Natural History of Man*. London: Henry Bohn.

Legg, Emily. 2023. *Stories of Our Living Ephemera: Storytelling Methodologies in the Archives of the Cherokee National Seminaries, 1846–1907*. Logan: Utah State University Press.

León, Arnoldo de. 1997. *The Tejano Community, 1836–1990*. University Park: Southern Methodist University Press.

León, Arnoldo de. 2010. *They Called Them Greasers: Anglo Attitudes toward Mexicans in Texas, 1821–1900*. Austin: University of Texas Press.

Leonard, Rebecca Lorimer. 2013. "Travelling Literacies: Multilingual Writing on the Move." *Research in the Teaching of English* 48, no. 1: 13–39.

L'Eplattenier, Barbara. 2009. "An Argument for Archival Research Methods: Thinking beyond Methodology." *College English* 72, no. 1: 67–79.

Levinas, Emmanuel. 1969. *Totality and Infinity: An Essay on Exteriority*. Pittsburgh: Duquesne University Press.

Lewis, Pierce. 1979. "Axioms for Reading Landscape." In *The Interpretation of Ordinary Landscapes*, edited by D. W. Meinig, 11–32. New York: Oxford University Press.

Liew, Jamie. 2024. *Ghost Citizens: Decolonial Apparitions of Stateless, Foreign and Wayward Figures in Law*. Halifax: Fernwood Publishing.

Limón, José. 1992. *Mexican Ballads, Chicano Poems: History and Influence in Mexican-American Social Poetry*. Berkeley: University of California Press.

Limón, José. 2008. "Border Literary Histories, Globalization, and Critical Regionalism." *American Literary History* 20, no. 1–2: 160–182.

Linnaeus, Carolus. 1759. *Animalium Specierum in Classes, Ordines, Genera, Species Methodica Dispositio, Additis Characteribus, Differetiis atque Synonymis*. Lugduni Batavorum: Theodorum Haak.

Livesey, Richard. 1838. *An Exposure of Mormonism, Being a Statement of Facts Relating to the Self-Styled "Latter Day Saints," And the Origin of the Book of Mormon*. Preston: J. Livesky.

Lloyd, Everett. 1924. "*Lloyd's Magazine*—The Story of the Rio Grande Valley and Other Big Features." John H. Shary Collection. UTRGV Digital Library, The University of Texas Rio Grande Valley. https://scholarworks.utrgv.edu/johnshary/5/.

Lloyd, Keith. 2011. "Culture and Rhetorical Patterns: Mining the Rich Relations between Aristotle's Enthymem and Example and India's Nyāya Method." *Rhetorica: A Journal of the History of Rhetoric* 29, no. 1: 76–105.

Lloyd, Keith. 2013. "Learning from India's Nyāya Rhetoric: Debating Analogically through Vāda's Fruitful Dialogue." *Rhetoric Society Quarterly* 43, no. 3: 285–299.

Locke, John. (1689) 1821. *Two Treatises on Government*. London: R. Butler.

"Lon Hill, Sr., Had Vision to Found Empire in Valley." 1950. Cameron: Harlingen. F381. University Library, Special Collections & Archives, University of Texas Rio Grande Valley. Edinburg, Texas.

López, Willie. 1967. "Los Rinches de Tejas." Recorded by Dueto Reynosa. *Chulas Fronteras*. Videocassette. Brazos Films. http://www.laits.utexas.edu/jaime/cwp2/ccg/los_rinches_de_texas.html.

Loraux, Nicole. 1986. *The Invention of Athens: The Funeral Oration in the Classical City*. Translated by Alan Sheridan. Cambridge: Harvard University Press.

Lorde, Audre. 1997. "There Are No Honest Poems about Dead Women." In *The Collected Poems of Audre Lorde*, 409–410. New York: W. W. Norton & Company.

Lorde, Audre. 2020. *Sister Outsider*. New York: Penguin.

Lovejoy, Arthur. 1933. *The Great Chain of Being: A Study of the History of an Idea*. Cambridge: Harvard University Press.

"Lower Rio Grande Valley Magazine." 1928. John H. Shary Collection, ELIBR-0002, Box 256, Folder 52. University of Texas Rio Grande Valley Special Collections and Archives, Edinburg Campus.

Lu, Min-Zhan. 1992. "Conflict and Struggle: The Enemies or Preconditions of Basic Writing?" *College English* 54, no. 8: 887–913.

Lueck, Amy. 2021. "Haunting Women's Public Memory: Ethos, Space, and Gender in the Winchester Mystery House." *Rhetoric Review* 40, no. 2: 107–122.

Lugones, María. 1987. "Playfulness, 'World'-Travelling, and Loving Perception." *Hypatia* 2, no. 2: 3–19.

Lugones, María. 2008. "The Coloniality of Gender." *Worlds and Knowledges Otherwise* 2: 1–17.

Lugones, María, 2010. "Toward a Decolonial Feminism." *Hypatia* 25, no. 4: 742–759.
Lyon, Arabella. 2010. "Writing an Empire: Cross-Talk on Authority, Act, and Relationships with the Other in the Analects, Daodejing, and HanFeizi." *College English* 72, no. 4: 350–366.
Lyons, Scott. 2010. *X-Marks: Native Signatures of Assent*. Minneapolis: University of Minnesota Press.
Mahmood, Saba. 2014. "Feminist Theory, Agency, and the Liberatory Subject." In *On Shifting Ground: Muslim Women in the Global Era*, edited by Fereshteh Nouraie-Simone, 111–152. New York: The Feminist Press.
Maidenberg, Micha. 2023. "Elon Musk's Starbase is Starting to Transform Part of Texas." *Wall Street Journal*, December 5. https://www.wsj.com/story/elon-musks-starbase-is-starting-to-transform-part-of-texas-4ec0c949.
Maldonado-Torres, Nelson. 2007. "On the Coloniality of Being." *Cultural Studies* 21, nos. 2–3: 240–270.
Maldonado-Torres, Nelson. 2008. *Against War: Views from the Underside of Modernity*. Durham, NC: Duke University Press.
"Man of Action—Man of Dreams." N.d. Cameron: Harlingen. F381. University Library, Special Collections & Archives, University of Texas Rio Grande Valley. Edinburg, Texas.
Mao, LuMing. 2014. "Thinking beyond Aristotle: The Turn to How in Comparative Rhetoric." *PMLA* 129, no. 3: 448–455.
Martinez, Aja. 2009. "'The American Way': Resisting the Empire of Force and Color-Blind Racism." *College English* 71, no. 6: 584–595.
Martinez, George. 2011. *Mexican Americans and Whiteness*. In *The Latino/a Condition: A Critical Reader*, edited by Richard Delgado & Jean Stefancic, 364–368. New York: New York University Press.
Martinez, Monica. 2018. *The Injustice Never Leaves You: Anti-Mexican Violence in Texas*. Cambridge, MA: Harvard University Press.
Massey, Doreen. 2005. *For Space*. London: SAGE Publications.
Mayo, Cris. 2001. "Civility and Its Discontents: Sexuality, Race, and the Lure of Beautiful Manners." *Philosophy of Education* 57: 78–87.
McAllen Chamber of Commerce. 1927. "McAllen, Texas, the City of Palms." John H. Shary Collection. UTRGV Digital Library. University of Texas Rio Grande Valley. https://scholarworks.utrgv.edu/johnshary/2/.
M'Chesney, James. 1838. *An Antidote to Mormonism; A Warning Voice to the Church and Nation; The Purity of Christian Principles Defended; and Truth Disentangled from Error and Delusion*. New York: Burnett & Pollard.
McIntosh, Peggy. 1997. "White Privilege and Male Privilege: A Personal Account of Coming to See Correspondences through Work in Women's Studies." In *Critical White Studies: Looking behind the Mirror*, edited by Richard Delgado and Jean Stefancic, 291–299. Philadelphia: Temple University Press.
McKenna, Verna. 1960. "Harlingen Golden Anniversary Celebration, April 24–30, 1960." Rene Torres Collection. UTRGV Digital Library, The University of Texas Rio Grande Valley. https://scholarworks.utrgv.edu/renetorrespub/12/.

McKittrick, Katherine, ed. 2015. *Sylvia Wynter: On Being Human as Praxis*. Durham, NC: Duke University Press.

McLeod, Melvin. "There's No Place to Go but Up—bell hooks and Maya Angelou in Conversation." January 1. Lions Roar. https://www.lionsroar.com/theres-no-place-to-go-but-up/.

McMullen. Ken. 1983. *Ghost Dance*. Directed by Ken McMullen. https://www.youtube.com/watch?v=SwkjAuN-_-k.

Meader, John, ed. 1912. *Americana: American Historical Magazine*, vol. 7. New York: The National Americana Society.

Medina, Cruz. 2014a. *Reclaiming Poch@ Pop: Examining the Rhetoric of Cultural Deficiency*. New York: Palgrave MacMillan.

Medina, Cruz. 2014b. "'(Who Discovered) America': Ozomatli and the Mestiz@ Rhetoric of Hip Hop." *alter/nativas* 2: 1–24. https://alternativas.osu.edu/en/issues/spring-2014/essays1/medina.html.

Medina, Cruz. 2017. "Identity, Decolonialism, and Digital Archives." *Composition Studies* 45, no. 2: 222–225.

Medina, Cruz. 2019. "Decolonial Potential in a Multilingual FYC." *Composition Studies* 47, no. 1: 74–95.

Mejía, Jaime. 1998. "Tejano Arts of the U.S.-Mexico Contact Zone." *JAC* 18, no. 1: 123–135.

Mejía, Jaime. 1999. "Latina and Latino Rhetorical Issues." In *Rhetoric, the Polis, and the Global Village: Selected Papers from the 1998 Thirtieth Anniversary Rhetoric Society of America Conference*, edited by C. Jan Swearingen and Dave Pruett, 15–18. Mahway, NJ: Lawrence Erlbaum Associates.

Mejía, Jaime. 2004. "Bridging Rhetoric and Composition Studies with Chicano and Chicana Studies: A Critical Turn to Critical Pedagogy." In *Latino/a Discourses on Language, Identity, and Literacy Education*, edited by Michelle Hall Kells, Valerie Balester, and Victor Villanueva, 40–56. Portsmouth, NH: Boynton/Cook Publishers.

Memmi, Albert. 1991. *The Colonizer and the Colonized*. Boston: Beacon Press.

Méndez Newman, Beatrice. 2003. "Centering in the Borderlands: Lessons from Hispanic Student Writers." *Writing Center Journal* 23, no. 2: 43–62.

Méndez Newman, Beatrice. 2007. "Teaching Writing at Hispanic-Serving Institutions." In *Teaching Writing with Latino/a Students: Lessons Learned at Hispanic-Serving Institutions*, edited by Cristina Kirklighter, Diana Cardenas, and Susan Wolf Murphy, 17–36. Albany: SUNY Press.

Méndez Newman, Beatrice. 2014. "The Discourse of First Year Writers at Border Sites: Discerning the Transcultural, Bilinguistic Strategies of English Language Learners in College." *Rhetoric, Professional Communication, and Globalization* 6, no. 1: 1–21. https://docs.lib.purdue.edu/rpcg/vol6/iss1/1/.

Méndez Newman, Beatrice, and Romeo García. 2019. "Teaching with Bordered Writers: Reconstructing Narratives of Difference, Mobility, and Translingualism." In *Bordered Writers: Latinx Identities and Literacy Practices at Hispanic-Serving Institutions*, edited by Isabel Baca, Yndalecio I. Hinojosa, and Susan Wolff Murphy, edited by 125–146. Albany: SUNY Press.

Mignolo, Walter. 1989. "Literacy and Colonization: The New World Experience." In *1492–1992: Re/Discovering Colonial Writing*, edited by René Jara and Nicholas Spadaccini, 51–96. Minneapolis: Prisma Institute.

Mignolo, Walter. 1992. "On the Colonization of Amerindian Languages and Memories: Renaissance Theories of Writing and the Discontinuity of the Classical Tradition." *Comparative Studies in Society and History* 34, no. 2: 301–330.

Mignolo, Walter. 1994. "Signs and Their Transmission: The Question of the Book in the New World." In *Writing without Words: Alternative Literacies in Mesoamerica and the Andes*, edited by Elizabeth Boone and Walter Mignolo, 220–270. Durham, NC: Duke University Press.

Mignolo, Walter. 2000a. *Local Histories/Global Designs: Coloniality, Subaltern Knowledges, and Border Thinking*. Princeton, NJ: Princeton University Press, 2000.

Mignolo, Walter. 2000b. "The Role of the Humanities in the Corporate University." *PMLA* 115, no. 5: 1238–1245.

Mignolo, Walter, 2002. "The Geopolitics of Knowledge and the Colonial Difference." *South Atlantic Quarterly* 101, no. 1: 57–96.

Mignolo, Walter. 2003. *The Darker Side of the Renaissance: Literacy, Territoriality, and Colonization*. Ann Arbor: University of Michigan Press.

Mignolo, Walter. 2005. *The Idea of Latin America*. Malden, MA: Blackwell Publishing.

Mignolo, Walter. 2006. "Citizenship, Knowledge, and the Limits of Humanity." *American Literary History* 18, no. 2: 312–331.

Mignolo, Walter. 2007. "Delinking." *Cultural Studies* 21, no. 3: 449–514.

Mignolo, Walter. 2008. "Racism As We Sense It Today." *PMLA* 123, no. 5: 1737–1742.

Mignolo, Walter. 2009. "Epistemic Disobedience, Independent Thought and De-Colonial Freedom." *Theory, Culture & Society* 26, no. 7–8: 159–181.

Mignolo, Walter. 2011a. *The Darker Side of Western Modernity: Global Futures, Decolonial Options*. Durham, NC: Duke University Press.

Mignolo, Walter. 2011b "Epistemic Disobedience and the Decolonial Option: A Manifesto." *Transmodernity* 1: 44–66.

Mignolo, Walter. 2011c. "I Am Where I Think: Remapping the Order of Knowing." In *The Creolization of Theory*, edited by Françoise Lionnet and Shu-mei Shih, 159–192. Durham, NC: Duke University Press.

Mignolo, Walter. 2013. "Geopolitics of Sensing and Knowing: On (De)coloniality, Border Thinking, and Epistemic Disobedience." *Confero* 1, no. 1: 129–150.

Mignolo, Walter. 2017. "Coloniality Is Far from Over, and So Must Be Decoloniality." *Afterall: A Journal of Art, Context and Enquiry* 43: 38–45.

Mignolo, Walter. 2018. "Decoloniality and Phenomenology: The Geopolitics of Knowing and Epistemic/Ontological Colonial Differences." *Journal of Speculative Philosophy* 32, no. 3: 360–387.

Mignolo, Walter, and Catherine Walsh. 2018. *On Decoloniality: Concepts, Analytics, Praxis*. Durham, NC: Duke University Press.

Miles, Libby, Michael Pennell, Kim Owens, Jeremiah Dyehouse, Helen O'Grady, Nedra Reynolds, Robert Schwegler, and Linda Shamoon. 2008. "Interchanges: Commenting on Douglas Downs and Elizabeth Wardle's 'Teaching about Writing, Righting Misconceptions.'" *College Composition and Communication* 59, no. 3: 503–511.

Mills, Charles. 1997. *The Racial Contract*. Ithaca: Cornell University Press.

Mirzoeff, Nicholas. 2011. *The Right to Look: A Counterhistory of Visuality*. Durham, NC: Duke University Press.

The Missionite. 1909. John H. Sharyland Collection, ELIBR-0002, Box 254, Folder 17. University Library, Special Collections & Archives, University of Texas Rio Grande Valley. Edinburg, Texas.

Missouri Pacific Lines. 1927. "The Service of a Great Railway." ELIBR-0151. UTRGV Digital Library, The University of Texas Rio Grande Valley. https://scholarworks.utrgv.edu/lrgv/27/.

Missouri Pacific Railroad Company. 1925. "The Beautiful Valley of the Lower Rio Grande." John H. Shary Collection. UTRGV Digital Library, The University of Texas Rio Grande Valley. https://scholarworks.utrgv.edu/johnshary/4/.

Missouri Pacific Railroad Company. 1930. "The Lower Rio Grande Valley of Texas." Rene Torres Collection. UTRGV Digital Library, The University of Texas Rio Grande Valley. https://scholarworks.utrgv.edu/renetorrespub/1/.

Missouri Pacific Railroad Company. N.d. "Facts about the Lower Rio Grande Valley of Texas." N.d. John H. Shary Collection, ELIBR-0002, Box 256. University of Texas Rio Grande Valley Special Collections and Archives, Edinburg Campus.

Mohanty, Chandra. 1984. "Under Western Eyes: Feminist Scholarship and Colonial Discourses." *boundary2* 12/13: 333–358.

Mohanty, Chandra. 2003. *Feminism without Borders: Decolonizing Theory, Practicing Solidarity*. Durham, NC: Duke University Press.

Monroe, Rachel. 2020. "Elon Musk, His Rocket and Scheme That Tore Apart Boca Chica." *Esquire Magazine*, February 27. https://www.esquire.com/news-politics/a30709877/elon-musk-space-x-boca-chica-residents/.

Montejano, David. 1987. *Anglos and Mexicanos in the Making of Texas, 1836–1986*. Austin: University of Texas Press.

Montesano, Mark, and Duane Roen. 2005. "Religious Faith, Learning, and Writing: Challenges in the Classroom." In *Negotiating Religious Faith in the Composition Classroom*, edited by Elizabeth Lei and Bonnie Kyburz, 84–98. Portsmouth, NH: Boynton/Cook-Heinemann.

Montgomery, Julia. 1922. "The Citrus Tree: Facts and Potentials of the Lower Rio Grande Valley's Great Industry." Brownsville, TX: Monty's Monthly News.

Montgomery, Julia. 1928. *A Little Journey through the Lower Valley of the Rio Grande: The Magic Valley of Texas*. Houston: Rein.

Montgomery, Julia. 1929. "A Camera Journey through the Lower Valley of the Rio Grande." Brownsville: Monty's Monthly News.

Montgomery, Julia. 1930. "The Grapefruit Special." Vol. 1, no. 3. Brownsville: Monty's Monthly News. John H. Shary Collection. UTRGV Digital Library, The University of Texas Rio Grande Valley. https://scholarworks.utrgv.edu/johnshary/20/.

Montgomery, Julia. N.d. "The Greatest Opportunity Yet Presented to Valley Citrus Growers." John H. Shary Collection, ELIBR-0002, Box 256. University of Texas Rio Grande Valley Special Collections and Archives, Edinburg Campus.

Moraga, Cherríe, and Gloria Anzaldúa, eds. 1983. *This Bridge Called My Back: Writings by Radical Women of Color.* Women of Color Press.

Moreiras, Alberto. 2001. *The Exhaustion of Difference: The Politics of Latin American Cultural Studies.* Durham, NC: Duke University Press.

Mormonism Research Ministry. 1851–1886. *Journal of Discourses: Public Sermons by Mormon Leaders from 1851–1886.* https://jod.mrm.org/.

Morris, Charles. 2006. "The Archival Turn in Rhetorical Studies; Or, the Archive's Rhetorical (Re)Turn." *Rhetoric and Public Affairs* 9, no. 1: 113–115.

Morris, Charles. 2010. "(Self-)Portrait of Prof. R.C.: A Retrospective." *Western Journal of Communication* 74, no. 1: 4–42.

Morrison, Toni. 1987. *Beloved.* New York: Alfred A. Knopf.

Morrison, Toni. 1992. *Playing in the Dark: Whiteness and the Literary Imagination.* Cambridge, MA: Harvard University Press.

Morrison, Toni. 2017. "The Work You Do, the Person You Are." *The New Yorker.* May 29. https://www.newyorker.com/magazine/2017/06/05/toni-morrison-the-work-you-do-the-person-you-are.

Mortensen, Peter, and Gesa Kirsch, eds. 1996. *Ethics and Representation in Qualitative Studies of Literacy.* Urbana, IL: National Council of Teachers of English.

Morton, Samuel. 1839. *Crania Americana: A Comparative View of the Skulls of Various Aboriginal Nations of North and South America.* Philadelphia: John Penington.

Mukavetz, Andrea. 2018. "Decolonial Theory and Methodology." *Composition Studies* 46, no. 1: 1–24.

Mukavetz, Andrea. 2020. "Developing a Relational Scholarly Practice: Snakes, Dreams, and Grandmothers." *College Composition and Communication* 71, no. 4: 545–565.

Muniz, Aldolfo. 2023. "Claiming Gentrification, Brownsville Residents Protest SpaceX." Spectrum News 1, December 22. https://spectrumlocalnews.com/tx/south-texas-el-paso/news/2023/02/10/claiming-gentrification-brownsville-residents-protest-spacex#.

Munoz, Carlos. 1989. *Youth, Identity, Power: The Chicano Movement.* London: Verso.

Murphy, James, James Berlin, Robert J. Connors, Sharon Crowley, Victor Vitanza, Susa Jarratt, Nan Johnson, Jan Swearingen, Richard Enos. 1988. "The Politics of Historiography." *Rhetoric Review* 7, no. 1: 5–49.

Musk, Elon. 2021a. "Am Donating $20M to Cameron County Schools & $10M to City of Brownsville for Downtown Revitalization . . ." Twitter, March 30. https://twitter.com/elonmusk/status/1376903913564160002?s=20.

Musk, Elon. 2021b. "Creating the City of Starbase, Texas." Twitter, March 02. https://x.com/elonmusk/status/1366848696298561536?lang=en.

Mutnick, Deborah. 1998. "The Rhetorics of Race and Racism: Teaching Writing in an Age of Colorblindness." *Literacy in Composition Studies* 3, no. 1: 71–81.

Na'puti, Tiara. 2020. "Rhetorical Contexts of Colonization and Decolonization." *Oxford Research Encyclopedia*, 1–53. New York: Oxford University Press.

National Archives. 2024. "America's Founding Documents: Declaration of Independence: A Transcription." *National Archives*. July 3, 2024. https://www.archives.gov/founding-docs/declaration-transcript.

National Humanities Center Resource Toolbox. 2007. "Requerimiento." In *American Beginnings: The European Presence in North America, 1492–1690*. https://nationalhumanitiescenter.org/pds/amerbegin/amerbegin.htm.

Neitch, Kenna. 2019. "Indigenous Persistence: Challenging the Rhetoric of Anti-Colonial Resistance." *Feminist Studies* 45, nos. 2–3: 426–454.

Nelms, Gerald, and Ronda Dively. 2007. "Perceived Roadblocks to Transferring Knowledge from First-Year Composition to Writing-Intensive Major Courses: A Pilot Study." *WPA* 31, nos. 1–2: 214–233.

Nelson, Russell. 2018. "The Correct Name of the Church." https://www.churchofjesuschrist.org/study/general-conference/2018/10/the-correct-name-of-the-church?lang=eng.

Nishida, Kitarō. 1970. *Fundamental Problems of Philosophy: The World of Action and the Dialectical World*. Translated by David Dilworth. Tokyo: Sophia University Press.

Nishida, Kitarō. 1986. "The Logic of Topos and the Religious Worldview," *Eastern Buddhist* 19, no. 2: 1–29.

Nishida. Kitarō. 1998. "The Historical Body." In *Sourcebook for Modern Japanese Philosophy: Selected Documents*, edited by David Dilworth, V. H. Viglielmo, and Augustín Zavala, 27–53. Westport, CT: Greenwood Press.

Noe, Mark. 2009. "The Corrido: A Border Rhetoric." *College English* 71, no. 6: 596–605.

Nora, Pierre. 1989. "Between Memory and History: Les Lieux de Mémoire." *Representations* 26: 7–24.

Nordquist, Brice. 2017. *Literacy and Mobility: Complexity, Uncertainty, and Agency at the Nexus of High School and College*. New York: Routledge.

Nott, Josiah, and George Gliddon. 1854. *Types of Mankind: Or, Ethnological Researches, Based Upon the Ancient Monuments, Paintings, Sculptures, and Crania of Races, and Upon their Natural, Geographical, Philological, and Biblical History*. Philadelphia: Lippincott, Grambo & CO.

Nystrand, Martin, and John Duffy, eds. 2003. *Towards a Rhetoric of Everyday Life: New Directions in Research on Writing, Text, and Discourse*. Madison: University of Wisconsin Press.

O'Gorman, Edmundo. 1961. *The Invention of America: An Inquiry into the Historical Nature of the New World and the Meaning of Its History*. Bloomington: Indiana University Press.

Oliver-Jackson Investment Company. 1919. "Letters from Your Northern Neighbors Who Are Now Satisfied and Prosperous: Lower Rio Grande Valley Farmers." ELIBR-0151. University Library, University of Texas Rio Grande Valley. https://scholarworks.utrgv.edu/lrgv/30/.

Olson, Christa. 2021. *American Magnitude: Hemispheric Vision and Public Feeling in the United States*. Columbus: Ohio State University Press.

Olson, Gary. 1998. "Encountering the Other: Postcolonial Theory and Composition Scholarship." *JAC* 18, no. 1: 45–55.

Oravec, Christine. 1976. "'Observation' in Aristotle's Theory of Epideictic." *Philosophy and Rhetoric* 9, no. 3: 162–174.

Osamu, Nishitani. 2006. "Anthropos and Humanitas: Two Western Concepts of 'Human Being.'" In *Translation, Biopolitical, Colonial Difference*, edited by Naoki Sakai and John Solomon, 259–273. Hong Kong: Hong Kong University Press.

"Our Lower Rio Grande Valley." 1985. Series 5. Reference Files, ELIBR-0062. University Library, Special Collections & Archives, University of Texas Rio Grande Valley. Edinburg, Texas.

Paredes, Américo. 1958a. *George Washington Gomez: A Mexicotexan Novel*. Houston: Arte Publico Press.

Paredes, Américo. 1958b. *With His Pistol in His Hand: A Border Ballad and Its Hero*. Austin: University of Texas Press.

Parrott, William S. 1831. "William S. Parrott to Stephen F Austin, 02-16-1831." Digital Austin Papers. http://digitalaustinpapers.org/document?id=APB4151.xml.

Parson, Tyler. 1841. *Mormon Fanaticism Exposed: A Compendium of the Book of Mormon, or Joseph Smith's Golden Bible*. Boston: T. Parson.

Patel, Leigh. 2016. *Decolonizing Educational Research: From Ownership to Answerability*. New York: Routledge.

Patel, Leigh. 2021. *No Study without Struggle: Confronting Settler Colonialism in Higher Education*. Boston: Beacon Press.

Paulsen, Michael, and Kenneth Feldman. 1999. "Student Motivation and Epistemological Beliefs." *New Directions for Teaching and Learning* 78: 17–25.

Pauszek, Jessica. 2017. "'Biscit' Politics: Building Working-Class Educational Spaces from the Ground Up." *CCC* 68, no. 4: 655–683.

Peña, Lorgia García. 2022. *Community as Rebellion: A Syllabus for Surviving Academia as a Woman of Color*. Chicago: Haymarket Books.

Pennycook, Alastair. 2010. *Language as a Local Practice*. New York: Routledge.

Perelman, Chaim, and Lucie Olbrechts-Tyteca. 1969. *The New Rhetoric: A Treatise on Argumentation*. Translated by John Wilkinson and Purcell Weaver. Notre Dame: University of Notre Dame Press.

Peters, Evelyn. 1998. "Subversive Spaces: First Nations Women and the City." *Environment and Planning D* 16, no. 6: 665–685.

Petersen, Mark. 1954. "Race Problems—As They Affect the Church." In *The Convention of Teachers of Religion on the College Level*, 1–21. https://archive.org/details/RaceProblemsAsTheyAffectTheChurchMarkEPetersen/page/n1/mode/1up.

Phillips, Kendall. 2006. "Rhetorical Maneuvers: Subjectivity, Power, and Resistance." *Philosophy and Rhetoric* 39, no. 4: 310–332.

Pink, Sarah. 2012. *Situating Everyday Life*. Los Angeles: Sage.

Plato. 1864. *Plato's Gorgias*. Translated by E. M. Cope. Cambridge: Deighton, Bell, and Co.

Powell, Malea. 2008. "Dreaming Charles Eastman: Cultural Memory, Autobiography, and Geography in Indigenous Rhetorical Histories." In *Beyond the Archives: Research as a Lived Process*, edited by Gesa Kirsch and Liz Rohan, 115–127. Carbondale: Southern Illinois University Press.

Pratt, P. P. 1842. *A Voice of Warning, and Instruction to All People; Or, an Introduction to the Faith and Doctrine of the Church of Jesus Christ, of Latter-day Saints.* New York: J. W. Harrison.

Pred, Allan. 1981. "Social Reproduction and the Time-Geography of Everyday Life." *Geografiska Annaler* 63, no. 1: 5–22.

Pred, Allan. 1984. "Place as Historically Contingent Process: Structuration and the Time-Geography of Becoming Place." *Annals of the Association of American Geographers* 74, no. 2: 279–297.

Pred, Alan. 1995. "Out of Bounds and Undisciplined: Social Inquiry and the Current Moment of Danger." *Social Research* 62, no. 4: 1065–1091.

Prendergast, Catherine. 1998. "Race: The Absent Presence in Composition Studies." *College Composition and Communication* 50, no. 1: 36–53.

"Proclamation." N.d. Cameron: Harlingen. F381. University Library, Special Collections & Archives, University of Texas Rio Grande Valley. Edinburg, Texas.

Progreso Development Company. N.d. "Progreso Haciendas: Citrus Fruit and Farm Lands in the Lower Rio Grande Valley of Texas." John H. Shary Collection, ELIBR-0002, Box 256, Folder 48. University of Texas Rio Grande Valley Special Collections and Archives, Edinburg Campus.

"Prominent Factor in Harlingen's Growth." N.d. Cameron: Harlingen. F381. University Library, Special Collections & Archives, University of Texas Rio Grande Valley. Edinburg, Texas.

"Prosperity." N.d. John H. Sharyland Collection. Box 223. University Library, Special Collections & Archives, University of Texas Rio Grande Valley. Edinburg, Texas.

Quijano, Aníbal. 2000a. "Coloniality of Power and Eurocentrism in Latin America." *International Sociology* 15, no. 2: 215–232.

Quijano, Aníbal. 2000b. "Coloniality of Power, Eurocentrism, and Latin America." *Nepantla* 1, no. 3: 533–80.

Quijano, Aníbal. 2007. "Coloniality and Modernity/Rationality." *Cultural Studies* 21, nos. 2–3: 168–178.

Quijano, Anibal, and Immanuel Wallerstein. 1992. "Americanity as a Concept, or the Americas in the Modern World-System." *International Social Science* 134: 549–557.

Quintanilla, Beto. 2015. "Piquete de Ojos." *Pobreza Infeliz.* Regio Norte.

Quintanilla, Beto. 2019. "La Klika." *Ayer y Hoy: 15 Corridos Y Mas.* Regio Norte.

Ramirez, Josue. 2021. "Opinion: Mural Madness." *Trucha*, October 13. https://truchargv.com/opinion-mural-madness/.

Ramirez, Josue. 2022. "Space Exed, a Forced Rebranding." *Trucha*, January 13. https://truchargv.com/space-exed/.

Ramirez, Josue. 2023a. "Commentary: In Solidarity with Bekah Hinojosa against SpaceX." *Trucha*, January 31. https://truchargv.com/bekah/.

Ramirez, Josue. 2023b. "Nuestra Delta Mágica: Settler Imaginaries and Community Resistance." *Trucha*, March 22. https://truchargv.com/nuestra-delta-magica-settler-imaginaries-community-resistance/.

Ratcliffe, Krista. 2005. *Rhetorical Listening: Identification, Gender, Whiteness*. Carbondale: Southern Illinois University Press.

Rawson, K. J. 2018. "The Rhetorical Power of Archival Description: Classifying Images of Gender Transgression." *Rhetoric Society Quarterly* 48, no. 4: 327–351.

Reeve, Paul. 2015. *Religion of a Different Color: Race and the Mormon Struggle for Whiteness*. Oxford: Oxford University Press.

Reichstein, Andrea. 1985. "The Austin-Leaming Correspondence, 1828–1836." *Southwestern Historical Quarterly* 88, no. 3: 247–282.

Rev. 2020. "Donald Trump Rally Speech Transcript, Reading, PA October 31." *Rev.* November 1, https://www.rev.com/blog/transcripts/donald-trump-rally-speech-transcript-reading-pa-october-31.

Reynolds, Nedra. 2004. *Geographies of Writing: Inhabiting Places and Encountering Difference*. Carbondale: Southern Illinois University Press.

Rice, Jenny. 2012. *Distant Publics: Development Rhetoric and the Subject of Crisis*. Pittsburgh: University of Pittsburgh Press.

Rich, Adrienne. 1973. *Diving into the Wreck: Poems 1971–1972*. New York: W. W. Norton.

Rich, Adrienne. 1985. "Notes Toward a Politics of Location." In *Women, Feminist Identity, and Society in the 1980s: Selected Papers*, edited by Myriam Diaz-Diocaretz and Iris Zavala. 7–22. Amsterdam: John Benjamins Publishing Company.

Rickert, Thomas. 2007. "Invention in the Wild: On Locating Kairos in Space-Time." In *The Locations of Composition*, edited by Christopher Keller and Christian Weisser, 71–90. Albany: SUNY Press.

Rickert, Thomas. 2013. *Ambient Rhetoric: The Attunements of Rhetoric Being*. Pittsburgh: University of Pittsburgh Press.

Rickert, Thomas. 2021. "Preliminary Steps Towards a General Rhetoric: Existence, Thrivation, Transformation." *The Routledge Handbook of Comparative World Rhetorics*, edited by Keith Lloyd, 414–421. New York: Routledge.

Rickert, Thomas, and Michael Salvo. 2006. "The Distributed Gesamptkunstwerk: Sound, Worlding, and New Media Culture." *Computers and Composition* 23, 3:296–316.

Riess, Jana. 2020. "What Does an LDS Pioneer Day Look Like in the Context of Black Lives Matter?" *Salt Lake Tribune*, July 24. https://www.sltrib.com/religion/2020/07/24/jana-riess-what-does-an/.

Ríos, Cati de los. 2017. "Toward a Corridista Consciousness: Learning from One Transnational Youth's Critical Reading, Writing, and Performance of Mexican Corridos." *Reading Research Quarterly* 53, no. 4: 455–471.

Ritchie, Joy. 1990. "Confronting the Essential Problem: Reconnecting Feminist Theory and Pedagogy." *Journal of Advanced Composition* 10: 249–271.

Rivera, Tomás. 1992. *Y no se lo tragó la tierra/And the Earth Did Not Devour Him*. Houston: Arte Publico Press.

Roberts-Miller, Patricia. 2017. *Demagoguery and Democracy*. New York: The Experiment.

Rodriguez, Luis. 2015. "From Trauma to Transformation." *LAPL Blog*. https://www.lapl.org/collections-resources/blogs/lapl/trauma-transformation.

Roemer, Marjorie, Lucille Schultz, and Russel Durst. 1999. "Reframing the Great Debate on First-Year Writing." *College Composition and Communication* 50, no. 3: 377–392.

Rohan, Liz. 2010. "The Personal as Method and Place as Archive: A Synthesis." *Working in the Archives: Practical Research Methods for Rhetoric and Composition*, edited by Alexis E. Ramsey, Wendy B. Sharer, Barbara L'Eplattenier, and Lisa S. Mastrangelo, 232–247. Carbondale: Southern Illinois University Press.

Rohrer, Judy. 2016. *Staking Claims: Settler Colonialism and Racialization in Hawai'i*. Tucson: University of Arizona Press.

Roosevelt, Theodore. 1901. First Annual Message. The American Presidency Project. https://www.presidency.ucsb.edu/documents/first-annual-message-16.

Rousseau, Jean-Jacques. 1973. "Discours sur l'origine de l'inégalité." In *The Enlightenment: A Comprehensive Anthology*, edited by Peter Gay, 175–195. New York: Simon and Schuster.

Roy, Arundhati. 2014. *Capitalism: A Ghost Story*. Chicago: Haymarket Books.

Roy, Arundhati. 2020. *Azadi: Freedom. Fascism. Fiction*. Chicago: Haymarket Books.

Royall, R. R. 1835. "R. R. Royall to Stephen F Austin, 10-18-1835." Digital Austin Papers. http://digitalaustinpapers.org/document?id=APB4962.

Royster, Jacqueline Jones. 1996. "When the First Voice You Hear is not Your Own." *CCC* 47, no. 1: 29–40.

Royster, Jacqueline Jones. 2000. *Traces of a Stream: Literacy and Social Change among African American Women*. Pittsburgh: University of Pittsburgh Press.

Royster, Jacqueline Jones, and Gesa E. Kirsch. 2012. *Feminist Rhetorical Practices: New Horizons for Rhetoric, Composition, and Literacy Studies*. Carbondale: Southern Illinois University Press.

Ruiz, Iris. 2018. "La indigena: Risky Identity Politics and Decolonial Agency as Indigenous Consciousness." *Africology: The Journal of Pan African Studies* 11, no. 6: 221–230.

Ruiz, Iris. 2021. "Critiquing the Critical: The Politics of Race and Coloniality in Rhetoric, Composition, and Writing Studies Research Traditions." In *Race, Rhetoric, and Research Methods*, edited by Alexandria Lockett, Iris Ruiz, James Chase Sanchez, and Christopher Carter, 39–79. Perspectives on Writing. Fort Collins, CO: WAC Clearinghouse.

Ruiz, Iris, and Damián Baca. 2017. "Decolonial Options and Writing Studies." *Composition Studies* 45, no. 2: 226–229.

Ruiz, Iris, and Raúl Sanchez. 2016. *Decolonizing Rhetoric and Composition Studies: New Latinx Keywords for Theory and Pedagogy*. New York: Palgrave MacMillan.

Rushdy, Ashraf. 2012. *The End of American Lynching*. New Brunswick: Rutgers University Press.

Russel, David. 1991. *Writing in the Academic Disciplines, 1870–1990: A Curricular History*. Carbondale: Southern Illinois University Press.

Rutledge, Jack. 1935. "Good Morning." Cameron: Harlingen. F381. University Library, Special Collections & Archives, University of Texas Rio Grande Valley. Edinburg, Texas.

Said, Edward. 1979. *Orientalism*. New York: Vintage Books.

Said, Edward. 1983. *The World, the Text, and the Critic*. Cambridge, MA: Harvard University Press.

Said, Edward. 1985. "Orientalism Reconsidered." *Cultural Critique*, no. 1: 89–107.

"San Benito: A Statement of Facts about the Lands and Irrigation Canal of the San Benito Land and Water Company." N.d. Cameron: Harlingen. F381. University Library, Special Collections & Archives, University of Texas Rio Grande Valley. Edinburg, Texas.

San Benito Light. 1921. Cameron: Harlingen. F381.University Library, Special Collections & Archives, University of Texas Rio Grande Valley. Edinburg, Texas.

Sánchez, Martha. 2006. *Corridos in Migrant Memory*. Albuquerque: University of New Mexico Press.

San Miguel, Guadalupe. 1998. "Roused from our Slumbers." In *Latinos and Education: A Critical Reader*, edited by Antonia Darder, Rodolfo Torres, and Henry Gutierrez, 135–157. New York: Routledge.

Santos, Boaventura de Sousa. 2017. *Decolonising the University: The Challenge of Deep Cognitive Justice*. Newcastle upon Tyne: Cambridge Scholars Publishing.

Schaff, Erin. 2020. "Full Transcript: Trump's 2020 State of the Union Address." *New York Times*, February 5. 2020, https://www.nytimes.com/2020/02/05/us/politics/state-of-union-transcript.html.

Schilb, John. 1994. "Getting Disciplined?" *Rhetoric Review* 12, no. 2: 398–405.

Schwartz, J. M., and T. Cook. 2002. "Archives, Records, and Power: The Making of Modern Memory." *Archives and Museum Informatics* 2: 1–19.

Sealey-Ruiz, Yolanda. 2013. "Building Racial Literacy in First-Year Composition." *Teaching English in the Two-Year College* 40, no. 4: 384–398.

Sedgwick, Eve. 1998. "Privilege of Unknowing." *Genders* 1: 102–124.

Sela, Rona. 2016. "The Hump of Colonialism, or the Archive as a Site of Resistance." February 17. https://www.internationaleonline.org/research/decolonising_practices/60_the_hump_of_colonialism_or_the_archive_as_a_site_of_resistance/.

Sepúlveda, Juan Ginés de. 1987. *Tratado: Sobre Las Justas Causas de la Guerra Contra Los Indios*. México: Fondo de Cultura Economica.

Shapiro, Sherry. 1999. *Pedagogy and the Politics of the Body*. New York: Garland Publishing.

Sharpe, Christina. 2010. *Monstrous Intimacies: Making Post-Slavery Subjects*. Durham, NC: Duke University Press.

Sharpe, Christina. 2023. *Ordinary Notes*. Toronto: Alfred A. Knopf Canada.

"Sharyland: Citrus Fruit Orchards." N.d. John H. Shary Collection, ELIBR-0002, Box 256, Folder 41. University of Texas Rio Grande Valley Special Collections and Archives, Edinburg Campus.

"Sharyland as a Place to Live." 1931. John H. Shary Collection, ELIBR-0002, Box 223. University of Texas Rio Grande Valley Special Collections and Archives, Edinburg Campus.

Shary Organization. 1948. "The Shary Organization: 35 Years of Progress, 1913–1948." John H. Shary Collection. UTRGV Digital Library, The University of Texas Rio Grande Valley. https://scholarworks.utrgv.edu/johnshary/7/.

Sheard, Cynthia. 1996. "The Public Value of Epideictic Rhetoric." *College English* 58, no. 7: 765–794.

Sheller, Mimi. 2012. *Citizenship from Below: Erotic Agency and Caribbean Freedom*. Durham, NC: Duke University Press.

Sheller, Mimi, and John Urry. 2006. "The New Mobilities Paradigm." *Environment and Planning A* 38, no. 2: 207–226.

Sheridan, Erin. 2022. "The Fine Print: Exploring Musk's Impact, Local Leaders' Complacency, and the Community's Struggle." *Trucha*, May 24. https://truchargv.com/the-fine-print-spacex/.

Shohat, Ella. 2002. "The Shaping of Mizrahi Studies: A Relational Approach." *Israel Studies Forum* 17, no. 2: 86–93.

Sibley, David. 1995. *Geographies of Exclusion: Society and Difference in the West*. London: Routledge.

"Six-Shooter Junction." 1946. Cameron: Harlingen. F381. University Library, Special Collections & Archives, University of Texas Rio Grande Valley. Edinburg, Texas.

Smith, Daniel. 2003. "Intensifying Phronesis: Heidegger, Aristotle, and Rhetorical Culture." *Philosophy and Rhetoric* 36, no. 1: 77–102.

Smith, Joseph. 1833. Plat of the City of Zion. May 18 2017. https://history.churchofjesuschrist.org/article/revised-plat-of-the-city-of-zion-circa-early-august-1833?lang=eng.

Smith, Joseph. 1879. *The Book of Mormon: An Account Written by the Hand of Mormon, Upon Plates Taken from the Plates of Nephi*. Translated by Joseph Smith. Liverpool: William Budge.

Smith, Joseph. 1908. *The Doctrine and Covenants of the Church of Jesus Christ of Latter-day Saints*. Bedford, MA: Applewood Books.

Smith, Joseph. 1917. *The Pearl of Great Price: A Selection from the Revelations, Translations, and Narrations of Joseph Smith*. Salt Lake City: The Deseret News.

Smith, Joseph. 2016. *History of the Church*, Vol. 1: 1805–1833. The Joseph Smith Papers. https://www.josephsmithpapers.org/paper-summary/history-1838-1856-volume-a-1-23-december-1805-30-august-1834/23#facts.

Smith, Linda. 1999. *Decolonizing Methodologies: Research and Indigenous Peoples*. London: Zed Books.

Smith, Linda. 2012. *Decolonizing Methodologies: Research and Indigenous Peoples*. London: Zed Books.

Smith, Linda, Eve Tuck, and K. Wayne Yang. 2019. *Indigenous and Decolonizing Studies in Education*. New York: Routledge.

Solomon, Dan. 2021. "Will Elon Musk Austin-ify Brownsville?" *Texas Monthly*, December 27. https://www.texasmonthly.com/news-politics/is-brownsville-becoming-btx/.

Sommers, Nancy, and Laura Saltz. 2004. "The Novice as Expert: Writing the Freshman Year." *College Composition and Communication* 56, no. 1: 124–149.

Soto Vega, Karrieann. 2020. "Colonial Causes and Consequences: Climate Change and Climate Chaos in Puerto Rico." *enculturation: A Journal of Rhetoric, Writing, and Culture* 32. November 10. https://enculturation.net/colonial_causes_consequences.

Southern Pacific Lines. 1930. "The Magic Valley of the Lower Rio Grande: The Land of Golden Fruit." John H. Shary Collection, ELIBR-0002, Box 256. University of Texas Rio Grande Valley Special Collections and Archives, Edinburg Campus.

Southwestern Land Company. 1933. "In Rio Grande Valley Paradise: Sharyland; Where Nature Produces the World's Sweetest Citrus Fruits." John H. Shary Collection. UTRGV Digital Library, The University of Texas Rio Grande Valley. https://scholarworks.utrgv.edu/johnshary/3/.

Spivak, Gayatri. 1985a. "The Rani of Sirmur: An Essay in Reading the Archives." *History and Theory* 24, 3:247–272.

Spivak, Gayatri. 1985b. "Three Women's Texts and a Critique of Imperialism." *Critical Inquiry* 12, 1:243–261.

Spivak, Gayatri. 1988a. "Can the Subaltern Speak?" In *Marxism and the Interpretation of Culture*, edited by Cary Nelson and Lawrence Grossberg, 271–313. Urbana: University of Illinois Press.

Spivak, Gayatri. 1988b. "Subaltern Studies: Deconstructing Historiography." In *Selected Subaltern Studies*, edited by Ranajit Guja and Gayatri Chakravorty Spivak, 4–33. New York: Oxford University Press.

Spivak, Gayatri. 1994. "Responsibility." *Boundary 2* 21, no. 3: 19–64.

Spivak, Gayatri Chakravorty, trans. 1997. "Translator's Preface." In *Of Grammatology*, Corrected ed., by Jacques Derrida, ix–lxxxvii. Baltimore: The Johns Hopkins University Press.

Spivak, Gayatri. 1999. *A Critique of Postcolonial Reason: Toward a History of the Vanishing Present*. Cambridge: Harvard University Press.

Spring, Joel. 1996. *Deculturalization and the Struggle for Equality: A Brief History of the Education of Dominated Cultures in the United States*. New York: Routledge.

"Standard Blue Book. U.S.A. (South Texas Edition, Deluxe)." 1926. John H. Shary Collection, ELIBR-0002, Box 256. University of Texas Rio Grande Valley Special Collections and Archives, Edinburg Campus.

Starbase Brewing. N.d. "Starbase Texas Jobs." https://starbasebrewery.com/pages/starbase-texas-jobs.

Steedman, Carolyn. 2002. *Dust: The Archive and Cultural History*. New Brunswick: Rutgers University Press.

Steedman, Carolyn. 2005. "Archival Methods." In *Research Methods for English Studies*, edited by Gabriele Griffin, 17–30. Edinburgh: Edinburgh University Press.

Stewart, Ruth. 2001. "Teaching Critical Thinking in First-Year Composition: Sometimes More Is More." *Teaching English in the Two-Year College* 29, no. 2: 162–171.

Stoler, Ann. 2002. "Colonial Archives and the Arts of Governance." *Archival Science* 2, nos. 1–2: 87–109.

Stormer, Nathan. 2020. "Rhetoric by Accident." *Philosophy & Rhetoric* 53, 4:353–376.

"Story of Lon Hill Is Story of Early Valley Growth." 1950. Cameron: Harlingen. F381. University Library, Special Collections & Archives, University of Texas Rio Grande Valley. Edinburg, Texas.

Street, Brian. 1994. *Literacy in Theory and Practice*. Cambridge: Cambridge University Press.

Sue, Derald. 2003. *Overcoming Our Racism: The Journey to Liberation*. San Francisco: Jossey-Bass.

Sunderland, La Roy. 1842. *Mormonism Exposed: In Which Is Shown the Monstrous Imposture, the Blasphemy, and the Wicked Tendency, of that Enormous Delusion Advocated by a Professedly Religious Sect, Calling Themselves "Latter-day Saints"* New York: Office of the NY Watchman.

Tamez, Margo Garcia. 2011. "'Our Way of Life Is Our Resistance': Indigenous Women and Anti-Imperialist Challenges to Militarization along the U.S.-Mexico Border." *Works and Days* 29, nos. 57–58: 281–318.

Taussig, Michael. 1991. *Shamanism, Colonialism, and the Wild Man: A Study in Terror and Healing*. Chicago: University of Chicago Press.

Taussig, Michael. 1999. *Defacement: Public Secret and the Labor of the Negative*. Stanford: Stanford University Press.

"The Land of Continuous Crops." N.d. John H. Shary Collection, ELIBR-0002, Box 256. University of Texas Rio Grande Valley Special Collections and Archives, Edinburg Campus.

Thiong'o, Ngũgĩ wa. 2004. *Decolonising the Mind: The Politics of Language in African Literature*. Nairobi: East African Educational Publishers.

Thiong'o, Ngũgĩ wa. 2011. *Dreams in a Time of War: A Childhood Memoir*. New York: Anchor Books.

Thiong'o, Ngũgĩ wa. 2013. *In the Name of the Mother: Reflections on Writers and Empires*. Nairobi: East African Educational Publishers.

Thorpe, Francis Newton, ed. 1909. *The Statesmanship of Andrew Jackson as Told in His Writings and Speeches*. New York: The Tandy-Thomas Company.

Till, Karen. 2012. "Wounded Cities: Memory-Work and a Place-Based Ethics of Care." *Political Geography* 31, no. 1: 3–14.

Tinberg, Howard. 1990. "A Model of Theory-Making for Writing Teachers: Local Knowledge." *Teaching English in the Two-Year College* 17, no. 1: 18–23.

Tinoco, Lizbett, Sonya Eddy, and Scott Gage. 2020. "Developing an Antiracist, Decolonial Program to Serve Students in a Socially Just Manner: Program Profile of the FYC Program at Texas A&M University–San Antonio." *Composition Forum* 44. https://compositionforum.com/issue/44/tamu-sa.php.

Tlostanova, Madina. 2017a. "Can the Post-Soviet Think? On Coloniality of Knowledge, External Imperial and Double Colonial Difference." *Intersections* 1, no. 2: 38–58.

Tlostanova, Madina. 2017b. "Transcending the Human/Non-Human Divide." *Angelaki* 22, no. 2: 25–37.

Tlostanova, Madina, and Walter Mignolo. 2009. "Global Coloniality and the Decolonial Option." *Kult* 6: 130–147.

Tlostanova, Madina, and Walter Mignolo. 2012. *Learning to Unlearn: Decolonial Reflections from Eurasia and the Americas*. Columbus: Ohio State University Press.

"To Lon C. Hill IV." 1960. Cameron: Harlingen. F381. University Library, Special Collections & Archives, University of Texas Rio Grande Valley. Edinburg, Texas.

Trainor, Jennifer. 2005. "My Ancestors Didn't Own Slaves: Understanding White Talk about Race." *Research in the Teaching of English* 40, no. 2: 140–167.

Trouillot, Michel-Rolph. 1995. *Silencing the Past: Power and the Production of History*. Boston: Beacon Press.
Trucha. N.d. "District Attorney, Facing Community Pressure, Reduces Charges against Brownsville Environmental Activist." *Trucha*. https://truchargv.com/rgv-free-bekah-hinojosa/.
Trucha. 2023. "Op-Ed: El Cucuy y El Chupacabra Are Very Much Alive in the Rio Grande Valley." *Trucha*, October 31. https://truchargv.com/cucuy-chupacabra-are-alive-rgv/.
Tsing, Anna. 1993. *In the Realm of the Diamond Queen: Marginality in an Out-of-the-Way Place*. Princeton, NJ: Princeton University Press.
Tsing, Anna. 2000. "The Global Situation." *Cultural Anthropology* 15, no. 3: 327–360.
Tsing, Anna. 2005. *Friction: An Ethnography of Global Connection*. Princeton, NJ: Princeton University Press.
Tsing, Anna. 2015. *The Mushroom at the End of the World: On the Possibility of Life in Capitalist Ruins*. Princeton, NJ: Princeton University Press.
Tuana, Nancy. 2006. "The Speculum of Ignorance: The Women's Health Movement and Epistemologies of Ignorance." *Hypatia* 21, no. 3: 1–19.
Tuck, Eve. 2009. "Suspending Damage: A Letter to Communities." *Harvard Educational Review* 79, no. 3: 409–428.
Tuck, Eve, and K. Wayne Yang. 2012. "Decolonization Is Not a Metaphor." *Decolonization: Indigeneity, Education & Society* 1, no. 1: 1–40.
Tuck, Eve, and K. Wayne Yang. 2017. "Late Identity." *Critical Ethnic Studies* 3, no. 1: 1–19.
Turner, Jared, and Arielle Harrison. 2022. "Teens Caught on Video in Blackface Costumes at Cedar City Walmart." 2KUTV. https://kutv.com/newsletter-daily/investigations-underway-after-viral-video-showing-group-wearing-blackface-costumes-cedar-city-utah-tiktok-instagram.
University of Utah. 2021. "Inauguration." University of Utah. https://president.utah.edu/inauguration/.
University of Utah Communications. 2020. "Two Flyers Promoting Racist and Anti-Diversity Ideologies Found Near Student Services Building." University of Utah Communications. https://attheu.utah.edu/university-statements/two-flyers-promoting-racist-and-anti-diversity-ideologies-found-near-student-services-building/.
Urrieta, Luis. 2009. *Working from Within: Chicana and Chicano Activist Educators in Whitestream Schools*. Tucson: University of Arizona Press.
US Senate. 2021. "Proceedings and Debates of the 117th Congress, First Session." *Congressional Record* 164, no. 24: S589–D108.
Valencia, Richard. 2000. "Inequalities and the Schooling of Minority Students in Texas." *Hispanic Journal of Behavioral Sciences* 22, no. 4: 445–459.
Vallette, Marc. 1917. "An Unwritten Page in the History of Education." *American Catholic Quarterly Review* 42: 623–642.
"Valley Pioneer and Founder of Harlingen." N.d. Cameron: Harlingen. F381. University Library, Special Collections & Archives, University of Texas Rio Grande Valley. Edinburg, Texas.

Veracini, Lorenzo. 2010. *Settler Colonialism: A Theoretical Overview*. New York: Palgrave Macmillan.

Veracini, Lorenzo. 2011. "Introducing Settler Colonial Studies." *Settler Colonial Studies* 1, no. 1: 1–12.

Vieira, Kate. 2016. "Writing Remittances: Migration-Driven Literacy Learning in a Brazilian Homeland." *Research in the Teaching of English* 50, no. 4: 422–449.

"View of Jackson Avenue Taken from the Same Spot in 1915." N.d. Cameron: Harlingen. F381. University Library, Special Collections & Archives, University of Texas Rio Grande Valley. Edinburg, Texas.

Villa, Brenda. 2024. "New Marketing Campaign Aims to Rebrand the Valley as 'Rioplex.'" KRGV News. July 18. https://www.krgv.com/news/new-marketing-campaign-aims-to-rebrand-the-valley-as-rioplex-/.

Villanueva, Victor. 1993. *Bootstraps: From an American Academic of Color*. Urbana, IL: National Council of Teachers of English.

Villanueva, Victor. 1997. "Maybe a Colony: And Still another Critique of the Comp Community." *JAC* 17, no. 2: 183–190.

Villanueva, Victor. 1999. "On the Rhetoric and Precedents of Racism." *College Composition and Communication* 50, no. 4: 645–661.

Villanueva, Victor. 2004. "'Memoria' Is a Friend of Ours: On the Discourse of Color." *College English* 67, no. 1: 9–19.

Villanueva, Victor. 2006. "Blind: Talking about the New Racism." *Writing Center Journal* 26, no. 1: 3–19.

Villanueva, Victor. 2008. "Colonial Memory, Colonial Research: A Preamble to a Case Study." In *Beyond the Archives: Research as a Lived Process*, edited by Gesa Kirsch and Liz Rohan, 83–92. Carbondale: Southern Illinois University Press.

Vivian, Bradford. 2000. "The Threshold of the Self." *Philosophy and Rhetoric* 33, no. 4: 303–318.

Vizenor, Gerald. 1999. *Manifest Manners: Narratives on Postindian Survivance*. Lincoln: University of Nebraska Press.

Voltaire, François-Marie. 1780. *The Works of M. de Voltaire*. London: Fielding and Walker.

W. E. Stewart Land Company. 1929. "Souvenir of the Lower Rio Grande Valley of Texas: Original Poems of the Valley and Songs." UTRGV Digital Library, The University of Texas Rio Grande Valley. https://scholarworks.utrgv.edu/lrgv/1/.

Wagner, Meg. 2017. "Blood and Soil: Protesters Chant Nazi Slogan in Charlottesville." CNN, August 12. https://www.cnn.com/2017/08/12/us/charlottesville-unite-the-right-rally/index.html.

Walker, Jeffrey. 1989. "Aristotle's Lyric: Re-Imagining the Rhetoric of Epideictic Song." *College English* 51, no. 1: 5–28.

Wardle, Elizabeth. 2007. "Understanding Transfer from FYC: Preliminary Results." *WPA* 31, nos. 1–2: 65–85.

Wardle, Elizabeth. 2009. "'Mutt Genres' and the Goal of FYC: Can We Help Students Write the Genres of the University?" *College Composition and Communication* 60, no. 4: 765–789.

Warner, Michael. 2002. "Publics and Counterpublics." *Public Culture* 14, no. 1: 49–90.
Wanzer-Serrano, Darrel. 2018. "Decolonial Rhetoric and a Future Yet-to-Become: A Loving Response." *Advances in the History of Rhetoric* 21, no. 3: 326–330.
Weaver, Richard. 1953. *The Ethics of Rhetoric*. https://www.gutenberg.org/ebooks/68421.
Webb, Walter. 2008. *The Texas Rangers: A Century of Frontier Defense*. Austin: University of Texas Press.
"Welcome to Mission: Home of the Grapefruit." N.d. John H. Shary Collection, ELIBR-0002, Box 256. University of Texas Rio Grande Valley Special Collections and Archives, Edinburg Campus.
West, Cornel. 2009. "Truth." In *Examined Life: Excursions with Contemporary Thinkers*, edited by Astra Taylor, 1–24. New York: New Press.
West, Cornel. 2009. "Truth." *Examined Life: Excursions with Contemporary Thinkers*, edited by Astra Taylor, 1–24. New York: The New Press.
Wetmore, Alphonso. 1837. *Gazetteer of the State of Missouri*. St. Louis: C. Keemle.
Wharton, William. 1836. "Address of the Honorable WM. H. Wharton." *Magazine of History with Notes and Queries* 22, no. 4: 7–30.
Whittaker, David. 1985. "Mormons and Native Americas: A Historical and Bibliographical Introduction." *Dialogue: A Journal of Mormon Thought* 18, no. 4: 33–64.
Wideman, John. 2001. "In Praise of Silence." *Callaloo* 24, no. 2: 641–643.
"William Jennings Bryant Helped Valley to Grow." N.d. Cameron: Harlingen. F381. University Library, Special Collections & Archives, University of Texas Rio Grande Valley. Edinburg, Texas.
Williams, Raymond. 1977. *Marxism and Literature*. New York: Oxford University Press.
Wilson, Shawn. 2008. *Research Is Ceremony: Indigenous Research Methods*. Halifax, Nova Scotia: Fernwood Publishing.
Wingard, Jennifer. 2013. *Branded Bodies, Rhetoric, and the Neoliberal Nation-State*. Lanham, MD: Lexington Books.
Wolf, Zachary, and Curt Merrill. 2021. "Biden's Congressional Address, Annotated and Fact-Checked." CNN, April 28. https://www.cnn.com/interactive/2021/04/politics/biden-address-annotated/.
Wolfe, Patrick. 2006. "Settler Colonialism and the Elimination of the Native." *Journal of Genocide Research* 8, no. 4: 387–409.
Woodruff, Wilford. 1845. *Proclamation of the Twelve Apostles of the Church of Jesus Christ of Latter-day Saints*. Liverpool: Wilford Woodruff.
Woods, Amanda. 2020. "Arizona 'Karen' Slapped Across the Face for Telling Woman to 'Go Back to Mexico.'" *New York Post*. June 8. https://nypost.com/2020/06/08/arizona-karen-slapped-for-telling-woman-to-go-back-to-mexico/.
Wordsworth, William. 1898. *Selections from the Poems of William Wordsworth*. Edited by W. H. Venable. New York: American Book Company.
Writers' Program. 1941. *Utah: A Guide to the State*. New York: Hastings House.
Wynter, Sylvia. 2003. "Unsettling the Coloniality of Being/Power/Truth/Freedom: Towards the Human, After Man, Its Overrepresentation—An Argument." *CR: The New Centennial Review* 3, no. 3: 257–337.

Wynter, Sylvia. "Human Being as Noun? Or Being Human as Praxis? Towards the Autopoetic Turn/Overturn: A Manifesto." Unpublished essay. https://bcrw.barnard.edu/wp-content/uploads/2015/10/Wynter_TheAutopoeticTurn.pdf.

Yancy, George. 2008. "Colonial Gazing: The Production of the Body as Other." *Western Journal of Black Studies* 32, no. 1: 1–15.

Yang, K. Wayne. 2017. *A Third University Is Possible*. Minneapolis: University of Minnesota Press.

You, Xiaoye. 2006. "The Way, Multimodality of Ritual Symbols, and Social Change: Reading Confucius's Analects as a Rhetoric." *Rhetoric Society Quarterly* 36, no. 4: 425–448.

You, Xiaoye. 2023. *Genre Networks and Empire: Rhetoric in Early Imperial China*. Carbondale: Southern Illinois University Press.

Žižek, Slavoj. 2008. *In Defense of Lost Causes*. New York: Verso.

Permissions

García, Romeo. 2018. "Corrido-ing State Violence." *Journal of Multimodal Rhetorics* 2, no. 2: 51–69.

García, Romeo. 2018. "Creating Presence from Absence and Sound from Silence." *Community Literacy Journal* 13, no. 1: 7–15.

García, Romeo. 2022. "Decolonizing the Rhetoric of Church-Settlers." In *Unsettling Archival Research: Engaging Critical, Communal, and Digital Archives*, edited by Gesa Kirsch, Romeo García, Dakota Smith, and Caitlin Burns. Special Issue of *Across the Disciplines* 18, no. 1/2: 124–144.

García, Romeo. 2019. "Haunt(ed/ing) Genealogies and Literacies." *Reflections: A Journal of Community-Engaged Writing and Rhetoric* 19, no. 1: 230–252.

García, Romeo. 2017. "On the Cusp of Invisibility: Opportunities and Possibilities of Literacy Narratives." *Open Words: Access and English Studies*, n.p.

García, Romeo. 2024. "Re/searching (for) Hope: Archives and Archival Impressions." *The Writing Center Journal* 41, no. 1: 1–52.

García, Romeo. 2019. "A Settler Archive: A Site for a Decolonial Praxis Project." *constellations: A Cultural Rhetorics Publishing Space* 1, no. 2: n.p.

García, Romeo. 2022. "Unsettling Church(-)Settler Ideas, Images, and Ends." *Rhetoric, Politics, and Culture* 1, no. 2: 1–46.

García, Romeo, and Gesa Kirsch. 2023. "Addressing the Barriers Between Us and that Future via Deep Rhetoricity." *Peitho* 26, no. 1: 250–292.

Index

Page numbers followed by f indicate figures. Page numbers followed by n indicate notes.

absences-silences, 13, 17, 39, 55, 87, 89, 103, 108, 160, 211–12, 234
academia, 30, 33, 40, 239, 246, 269
academic struggles, first-generation students, 252–53
Acosta, Abraham, 56, 267
Acosta, José de, 56
addressing and being addressed, 112
aesthetic issues, Eurocentrism, 16, 47–52
affective value and rhetorical force (*pesado-ness*), 6, 94, 103, 140
Alcoff, Linda, 33, 266
Aldrete, Bernardo, 56–57
Alexander, M. Jacqui, 41
Alexander VI (Pope), 53–54
Alfonso (King), 53
alienation, 10, 38, 193, 197, 213, 222–23, 254
alphabetic writing, 4, 17, 55, 56, 96–97
Amazon.com, 110
American Indians/Native Americans: archival research, 38; dehumanization, 58, 91, 127f, 200, 209; displacement, 91, 92, 112, 123, 126, 157, 195, 199, 234f; *otherness*, 38, 82, 124, 143, 183, 189f, 211; portrayal of, 43, 80, 88–89, 95–97, 125, 201–2, 235; religious conversion, 54, 87, 90; *thingification*, 47–52, 86, 185; treaties, 195–96; *work-instruction*, 55, 56, 57, 96, 210
Americanity: *Archive*, 59, 60; decolonial analytic, 19; Eurocentrism, 44, 47–52; exploitation, 121; modernity, 18, 19, 20, 46, 59; settler advertisement, 112, 113f, 114f, 115f
Americas, idea of. See *idea of the Americas*
an-other archive: arrival and arrivant, 269, 277; bearing witness, 23, 47, 64, 101, 194; *being-and-becoming-awaiting*, 34, 273, 277; choices, options, obligations-responsibilities, 166, 168, 172, 195, 202, 208, 213, 219, 236; inward-facing dimension, 272; possibilities of new stories, 264; proper names, 274; public records, 101; space, place, and time, 22, 47, 100, 165, 177; *stories-so-far*, 214, 220, 270; we/arth, 260–61, 275; "Weism," 13, 27, 29, 270; wor(l)ding, 4, 8, 10, 26–27, 39, 167, 271, 281
analytic tasks and prospective visions, 9, 11–13, 27, 264
Anglo-American/Anglo-Saxon settler-pioneers, 88–89, 112, 115, 118, 123–25, 132, 149, 157, 232
Animalium Specierum, 49
anonymous response surveys, 188f–93f

anti-Blackness within the Mexican, Mexican American, Latino communities, 236
any living being, condition of, 275
Anzaldúa, Gloria, 140, 231, 232, 238, 268
(ap/ex)propriation: careful reckoning, 222; deficiency, racism, 51; *ghosting* of citizens, 98, 150–52; homesteading, 83; invention, 94; justification, 54, 82, 89, 164, 195; myth, 138, 153; Rights-to, 109–10; visuality, 140; *work-instruction*, 85, 95. *See also* land as inheritance
Apaches, 126, 157
Apologética, 55–56
archival approach and theory of archival impression: careful reckonings, 13, 275; classroom, 278–79; decolonial analytic, 166–67; decolonizing, 27, 28, 32, 29, 34, 101, 171–72, 265, 266, 274; logistics of the gift, 272; making/unmaking/remaking 10, 14–15, 21–25, 29, 41, 224, 280; *otherwise*, 26, 29, 32, 75, 101, 159–62; *possibilities of new stories*, 256, 270, 277; power, 41, 277; *praxical theorizing*, 4, 20, 23, 26, 172, 230, 270, 277; public memory, 39, 87, 97, 126, 140; race, 124, 163; rehabilitated humanity and society, 9–10; rhetoricity, 26, 30, 42, 67, 87, 107, 154–56, 168; space, place, and time, 165; *stories-so-far*, 8, 178, 198, 207, 231, 273; structural, 107; *theory-building actioning*, 23, 172, 230, 270, 277; we/arth, 276, 279; words and ideas, 44, 59–60, 263; writing and rhetoric studies (WRS), 30, 106
archival research, 5–7, 16, 30–32, 37–39, 71, 121, 163, 171, 187, 273
Archive: adding to, 8–12; archival impressions, 67, 99, 108, 194; assemblage, 79, 85, 89, 123, 131–34; decolonizing, 29, 61, 64, 102, 104, 171; discourse about actions, 224; epistemic system, 26, 30, 172, 263; *friction*, 185, 186f, 187; human work and projects, 70; *humanitas*, 47, 52–53; *idea of the University*, 3, 27–28, 59; inferiority/superiority, 47–52, 86–88, 124; literacies, images-signs-sounds, and rhetorics, 41, 167; making/unmaking/remaking, 6, 10–14, 24, 42, 53, 60, 160–62, 168–69, 195; modernity, 20, 22; power of, 7, 25, 281; proper naming concepts, 274; public memory, 28, 39, 63, 97, 126, 140; (re)writing, 41, 58, 62, 69, 72, 75, 107, 111, 147, 163, 164, 177, 195, 271; repositioning content, 159, 161–62; sonic coloniality, 115–16; space, place, and time, 63, 69, 71, 73–74, 100, 103, 109, 165, 188–93; *stories-so-far*, 31–32, 101, 264, 281; unsettling, 9, 33, 65, 105, 121, 265, 270; we/arth, 260–61; wor(l)ding aspiration, 166; *working parts*, 34, 42, 65, 68, 105, 177, 195. *See also* modern/colonial and settlerizing designs; rhetorics of modernity
archive of feeling, 6, 9, 268
Archive-archives, 6–8, 23, 26–29, 37, 39, 64–65, 178, 274
archives: *an-other*, 8f, 10, 100, 275, 277, 280, 281; awareness of, 201; brown(ed)ness, 229–30; construct, 270; death-space, 39; discourse about actions, 224; everyday, 105; film, 67; ideas, 47; influence on self, being, and agency, 220; *otherwise*, 159, 166, 279; relation to, 34; returning to, 273; (re)writing, 111; *stories-so-far*, 7, 172, 212, 214, 272; unsettling, 12, 39, 281; we/arth, 261, 274–76
archives (body-as-sensory), 101, 172, 178, 219, 224, 227, 230–31, 256, 259, 263–65, 270–71, 273–74
archivization of memories, 39, 107
Aristotelian philosophy, 4, 27–28, 56, 57
arrival and arrivant, decolonizing, 27, 222, 239, 241, 245–46, 265–66, 267f, 269
art of turning, 274
Arvin, Maile, 76, 91, 149
aseptic cleanliness trope, 62, 122, 165f, 166
assemblage, branding, and recasting work: *Archive*, 25, 26; divine and natural design, 123; enunciations, 163; *ghosting of citizens*, 85, 111, 131; invention, 43, 68, 75, 107–8; land as inheritance, 87, 124, 132; privilege, 89; settler advertisements, 113f, 114f, 134, 147; *visuality*, 79, 92, 118, 129, 159; we/arth, 274–78; *working parts*, 3, 26, 34, 60, 65, 169
assent, first-generation students, 230, 241–42, 245
assimilation, 221–22, 232, 236–37, 239, 253, 256, 264–65
association of social interests, 17–20, 30, 45, 61, 99, 164, 179
attributed rights, 276
Austin-ification, 151, 159–60, 162
Austin (TX), 126, 154, 161
Austin, Moses, 122–23
Austin, Stephen F., 123–26, 128, 134
Austin's Colony, 123
autobiographies, 65
awaiting, 12, 13, 58, 120, 166, 226, 230, 233f, 241
awareness, haunted/hauntings, 26, 37, 104, 160, 197, 201, 207, 215, 223, 234, 265

Baldwin, James, 5, 118
Ballif, Michelle, 147
Balot, Ryan, 72
Bandit Wars, 143, 144f
barrio mentality (hope-struggle), 226–30, 240–41, 244, 247–50, 251–54, 275
Barthes, Roland, 87, 94, 138, 145
Baynham, Mike, 6, 77
bearing witness in unsettling ways, 23, 63, 74, 171–72, 180, 213, 220, 234, 271–72
being-and-becoming, 7, 33, 69, 74, 231–32, 265, 271, 273, 275, 277–78, 280
Being of Being, 51
being-with, 6, 9, 11, 21, 33, 72, 110, 178, 223, 264, 272, 274, 279
belonging-to, 52, 74, 77, 84, 97, 111, 148, 274
Beloved, 12
Benoit, William, 25, 26, 60, 72
Bergland, Renée, 76
Bernier, Johann, 49
Beyond the Archives (Kirsch and Rohan), 5
Bhabha, Homi, 265
Biden, Joe (President), 42, 43, 45–46
Biesecker, Barbara, 37
bilingual dominant language, 232, 238, 243, 254
binaries, 221, 222, 237, 253, 256, 264–66
Black communities: anti-Blackness within the Mexican, Mexican American, Latino communities, 236; displacement, 199; *otherness*, 200; *possibilities of new stories*, 181; racism, 47–52, 87, 88; Utah, University of, 178–82
Black Skin, White Masks, 10
black/white binary, 221, 222, 237, 253, 256, 264
blog posts, students, 202, 203f, 204–7, 212, 217–18, 220
Blumenbach, Johann Friedrich, 49–50
Boca Chica (TX), 110, 120–21
The Book of Mormon, 78–83, 86, 87, 89, 90, 93, 94, 96, 98
border(ed)land, 109, 159, 163, 231, 239, 240
Borderlands/La Frontera, 232
Bordo, Susan, 6–7
Bova, Gus, 120
Boyle, Casey, 121
Bradshaw, Jonathan, 72
branding. *See* assemblage, branding, and recasting work
Brandt, Deborah, 6
Brannstrom, Christian, 111
Brazos River, 123
break/shift initiation, 4, 11, 14, 20, 33, 270, 274–75

brown(ed)ness, 162, 181, 199, 211, 229–30, 232, 243
Browne, Kevin, 6, 72, 273, 277
Brownsville (TX), 159, 160
Bryan, William Jennings, 141–42
bulls, papal, 53–54

Caldwell, Charles, 48, 49, 94, 126
Calhoun, John, 46, 124
calling out/calling up, 13
Cameron County, 133, 142, 145
Campacuas, 145
capitalism, 19, 20, 148, 162
careful reckonings, 11–13, 105, 196, 207, 222, 239, 272, 274–76
Carson, Ben, 42
Castro, Joaquin, 42, 43
Castro-Gomez, Santiago, 17
Catholic Church. *See* Christianity
Certeau, Michel de, 73
Césaire, Aimé, 13
Chain of Being model, 17, 18, 45, 48, 49, 52, 87
chantwells, 105
Chicano/a students, 227, 255
choices, options, obligations, and responsibilities, 11, 13, 29, 39, 54, 101, 165, 168, 195, 202, 208, 279
Chomsky, Noam, 38
Christianity, 19, 44, 49, 53–57, 59, 88, 111, 213. *See also Mormon/ism*
church-settler archives: citizen/ship, 31, 125, 131–32; *coloniality of instruction-and-curriculum*, 80, 82, 96–97, 115, 187, 210; divine and natural design, 77, 81, 86, 88–89, 91–95, 99; final classroom project, 208, 209; historical records, 196; hymns, 83, 85, 87, 89, 90; information as truth, 100; knowledge production, 223; land as inheritance, 82, 85, 86, 92, 95, 99, 199–202, 212; literacies, images-signs, sounds, and rhetorics, 100; *otherwise*, 201–2; physical/spiritual work, 78–79, 88–94; public memory, 63, 97, 200–201; *stories-so-far*, 209–10, 214–15; unsettling, 87, 101; Utah, 98, 195. *See also Mormon/ism*
Cicero, 187
Cintron, Ralph, 7, 277
Circulation of rhetoric, 16, 26, 44–45, 77, 112, 180, 197, 235
citizen/ship / uncivilized, 31, 47–52, 86, 107, 113f, 114f, 124, 125, 131–32, 140, 145, 148–51, 155–57, 164–65
class, embodied experiences, 5

classification, name-giving, 49
classroom environment: alienation, 197, 213, 222; archival impressions, 278–79; assignments, 182, 207–9; decolonial option, 32, 172, 187, 271; friction, 198–206, 217, 220; gathering space, 183; group discussions, 185, 186f, 194–95, 213, 216–18, 222; human work and projects, 219; knowledge-being, 32, 33, 266; language of the everyday, 76, 207; meaning of, 101, 219; observation, 227; *otherwise*, 205, 206f, 207; *possibilities of new stories*, 278; racist happenings, 216–18; rhetorical exchange, 194–95; settler archives, 188; site of inquiry, 172; unsettling, 196–97; violence, 52, 126, 232; vulnerability, 187; white privilege, 185, 186f; *work-instruction*, 183
Clinton, Katie, 6
Closner, John, 134
coded words, tropes, and ideas, 61–62, 92, 122, 142, 151–52, 165, 166, 171
colonial mother theory, 154
coloniality of instruction-and-curriculum, 55–59, 77, 80, 82, 94, 115, 144, 154, 163, 172–73, 183, 187, 196, 210–12, 219, 223, 232
coloniality: archival impressions, 38, 163; being, 45, 100; *ends of*, 81, 120–21, 181; gender, 58; knowledge, 45, 52, 61, 71, 101, 129, 151–52, 167; local-regional histories, 14; logic of, 21, 60; matrix of power, 4, 20, 22–23, 30, 41, 42; modernity/rationality, 14, 49, 59; myths, 183; *otherness*, 96, 246; *sonic coloniality*, 114–15
colonization, 9, 10, 195
colonization business, 125
Colorado River, 123
Comanches, 124, 157
community listening, 103–4, 207–9
community, influence on self, being, and agency, 160–61, 182, 209, 210
"company of death" (Maldonado-Torres), 140, 254
conditional hospitality, 184–85
confront-resignify option, 109, 221–22, 236–37, 253, 256, 264–66
conjuration, 11, 13, 100, 168
Connors, Robert, 37, 72
consciousness, 268
construct the archive, 6, 270, 279
containment, 159
contents and terms, 10, 222
contents reposition, 263
contradictions, 61, 101, 171

conversion of Indigenous peoples to Christianity, 55–56, 71, 81, 88, 96, 185
Corbett, Edward, 72
corridistas, 105
corridos, 65, 103–5, 187
counter-writing, 8, 25, 27, 167, 169, 274
Cresswell, Tim, 70
critical method, 24
critical thinking, 202
critique and unworking of knowing, 269
Cueros Cruds, 157
cultural displacement, 4, 91, 96, 110–12, 147, 152, 255
cultural texts, 83, 96, 101, 196, 208
Cushman, Ellen, 38
Cusicanqui, Silvia Rivera, 3–4, 266, 270
Cvetkovich, Ann, 6, 9

Davis, Diane, 269–70, 274
Days of '47 website, 201
De Oratore, 187
De Promulgando Evangelio APVD Barbaros, 56
death-space, 39, 80, 159, 163, 254, 270
decolonial analytic: *association of social interests*, 24; careful reckonings, 59; ecological rhetoric, 121; final projects, 208; hegemonic architecture, 16–17; *humanitas*, 52–53; *idea of the Americas*, 19, 58; invisibility, 59; irrational discourse, 50–53, 82, 108; rhetorics of settler colonialism, 28, 30, 31; *semiotic apparatus of enunciations*, 30, 74; settler archives, 233f, 235–36; space, place, and time, 74–75, 166–67; *stories-so-far*, 181; truth-and-knowledge claims, 28, 68, 266; W/H questions, 16, 70; words and ideas, 47, 263; writing and rhetoric studies (WRS), 178, 181–82, 195, 208, 232–36
decolonial option: academic responsibility, 33, 213, 219, 266; bearing witness, 74, 213; border(ed)landers, 231; choice, 166–67, 202; coursework, 3, 5, 172–73, 181, 187, 221–23; cultural texts, 208; first-generation students, 239–40, 248; language of the everyday, 187; musical genres, 207–8; non-name of all, 33; presuppositions, 269; prospective vision, 21, 23, 172; scholarship, 3, 5; thought, being, and doing, 270; white students, 195, 220–21
decolonizing: alphabetic writing, 4, 17, 55, 56, 96–97; archival impressions, 13, 27–29, 34, 101, 166–67, 273, 279; awakening, 10; *being-and-becoming*, 265; counter-writing, 3, 27, 274; discourse, 50–53, 82, 231, 236; Eurocentrism, 29, 47–52; haunted/hauntings, 23,

277; knowledge-being, 31–33, 100, 121–22, 168, 171–73, 187, 220–21, 231, 256; praxis, 264, 265, 266, 278; projects, 3, 108; public records, 28; rhetoricity, 23, 27; *stories-so-far*, 76, 168; unsettledness, 263
deep rhetoricity, 34, 207, 270–73, 279, 280
deficiency, racism, 86, 87, 88, 89, 123–25
Del Origen y Principio de la Lengua Castellana, 57
democracy, idea of, 45–47
denialism, *Archive*, 61, 101, 171, 183
deportation issues, 242, 245f, 253
Derrida, Jacques: archivization, 107; *being-and-becoming*, 269; break/shift, 33; conditional hospitality, 185; conjuration, 267; critiques, 39; enduring tasks, 12; future-to-come, 29; hauntings, 8, 38; proper names, 259; role of scholar-educator, 266, 270; unsettling, 274, 276, 281
Derridean impossibility, 275
Deseret News, 75
desire and objective, 10, 18, 24, 44, 60, 72, 73, 91, 100, 134, 239, 273–75
development of land, 96, 125, 129, 136f, 137f, 138, 140–41, 153–54, 160
dichotomous rhetorical structure, 184, 276
differences, recognition of, 42–43, 80, 87, 89, 94, 95, 123–24, 125, 140, 272–73
Digital Austin Papers (DAP), 122, 208
discourse about actions approach, 25, 26, 60, 72, 111, 184, 224, 256
discourse: assemblage, branding, and recasting, 108; coursework, 194–95; decolonization, 266; *humanitas*, 47, 50–53; irrational, 48, 50, 51, 52, 58, 68, 82; lived cultures, 272; praxis, 266; *semiotic apparatus of enunciations*, 75, 111–12; unsettling, 58, 269
discovery of land, 44, 53, 62, 77, 79, 93, 122, 134, 147–48. *See also* invention praxis
discrimination. *See* racism
dispensability, 17, 18, 53, 58, 92, 150–52, 199–200, 241, 246
displacement, cultural, 91, 110–12, 147, 152, 160–61, 210
divine and natural design, 18, 49–53, 57–58, 62, 77, 81, 86, 88, 91–95, 99, 122–25
doings. *See* decolonizing
dominant narrative: absences-silences, 39, 55, 87, 89, 103, 108, 160, 211–12; *Archive*, 10, 60; language of the everyday, 188, 189f–93f, 232, 238, 243, 254; settler archives, 233, 234f–35f, 236. *See also* information as truth
domination/exploitation, 18, 48, 120–21, 125, 138, 140

Douglass, Frederick, 199, 200
dualism. *See* binaries
Duffy, John, 6
Dussel, Enrique, 15, 17, 19, 20

ecocide, 23, 61, 110–11
ecological rhetoric, 121
Edbauer, Jenny, 6, 25, 121
Edinburg (TX), 153f, 154
education: assimilation, 232; dominant narrative, 73, 210, 211, 212; epistemic obedience, 55, 59, 90, 172; privilege, 239; right to pursue, 250–51; segregation, 151, 154, 155f
educators, 180–81, 183, 219, 224, 243, 255, 256, 265
effects and consequences, 28
elsewhere and otherwise, 7
embodied experiences, 5, 32, 270
emotional labor, 246–47
empire builder myth, 153
empowering students, 243
empty landscape trope, 44–45, 53, 85–87, 99, 125, 127f, 134, 139–40, 142–46, 148, 150
enabling *stories-so-far*, 177
end-of discourse, 181
Endres, Danielle, 69, 71
ends (Rights-to), 77, 79–82, 84, 85, 87, 110, 120–22, 152, 181, 223
enduring tasks, 12, 71, 105, 207, 271, 272
engagement, 9, 13, 32
English-dominant language use, 232, 238, 243, 254
Enoch, Jessica, 37
Ensign, 95
environmental issues, 110–11, 159, 160–61
epideictic rhetoric, 72–73, 75, 92, 131
epistemic murk, 26, 109
epistemic racism, 16, 20, 45, 47–48, 52, 53, 59, 98, 147, 163, 179–80, 214
epistemic system (of ideas, images, and ends), 9–10, 17–18, 30–31, 41, 46–47, 53, 59–60, 64, 71–73, 76, 78, 91
epistemic system, design, and epistemological framework for the living, 13, 57, 70–72, 82, 84, 89, 95–97, 101, 110–12, 167
epistemic zero point and provenance, 87, 93, 122
epistemological experiments, 21, 24, 26, 149, 151–52, 276
epistemological framework for the haunted, 33–34, 270–75, 278, 279, 280
epistemological war on knowledge. *See* information as truth

epistemological zero point, 17, 20, 47, 49, 50, 52, 53, 55–57, 62, 77, 79, 87–89, 93, 97, 119–20, 122
epistemology, 180, 201, 208, 219–20, 266–67
equality/inequality, idea of, 48, 78–80, 111
Escobar, Arturo, 21, 270
Essays and Treatises on Several Subjects, 49
Esto'k Gna (Carrizo/Comecrudo), 105, 108, 157, 160
ethno-and-epistemicide, 23, 61, 165
ethos and praxis, 13, 181, 213, 223, 247, 250, 254, 272
Eurocentrism, 15–16, 19, 20, 29, 30, 41, 44, 47–52, 58–59
everyday language. *See* language of the everyday
exaggeration of crises, 22, 47, 99
excursion parties, gaze, 141, 152, 153f
expands-disputes, *Archive*, 42, 61, 177, 195
expectations of/for first-generation students, 182, 238, 240, 247–48, 250–51, 256
exploitation, 18, 48, 120–21, 125, 138, 140, 149
expropriation. *See* (ap/ex)propriation

Fabian, Johannes, 223, 272
faculty of color (PWIs), 178, 219
FAFSA (Federal Student Aid), 249
failure in the classroom, 178, 219, 240
fake news, 61
familial obligations, first-generation students, 241–43, 247, 249, 251–52
family, influence on self, being, and agency, 209, 210
Fanon, Frantz, 6–10, 13, 33, 44, 118, 154, 181, 187, 265–67, 274–79
feeling, 39, 264
Feild, Caroline, 153
feminist rhetorical frameworks, 37
Feminist Rhetorical Practices, 5
Ferdinand (King), 54
Fernandez, Miriam, 72
Ferreira-Buckley, Linda, 37
final classroom projects, 208–10
first-generation students: cultural influences, 231; decolonial option, 239–40; generational cycles, 238, 248; haunted/hauntings, 246, 253, 255; hope-struggle (barrio mentality), 229–30, 242–44, 247–49; making it out, 241, 250–53; *otherwise*, 226; *possibilities of new stories*, 240, 250; *stories-so-far*, 236–37, 246
first-year composition (FYC) courses, 182, 196, 227
flash staking, 70, 71, 73

fliers as visual rhetoric, 178–82
Flores, Lisa, 266
forced rebranding, 85, 87, 92, 111, 123–25, 129, 131–34, 159–62
forgetting or conjuration, 11, 13, 100, 151, 167, 179, 235f, 267
Foucault, Michel, 5, 38, 277
foundational rhetorical practices, 182
friction: archival research, 37; *Archive*, 185, 186f, 187; *be-with* situations, 178, 223; classroom discussions, 198–206, 217, 220; human work and projects, 219; language of the everyday, 196; unsettledness, 181; whiteness, 197
frontier/tamed wilderness, 45, 115, 163
fuckable earth trope, 122, 166
future-to-come, 29, 110, 118, 274

Gante, Pedro de, 54–55
Garden of Eden trope, 43, 78–79, 92, 99–100, 113f, 114f, 122, 140–44, 165
Gardner, Clint, 227
gatekeeping, 182, 237
gathering space, 183
gaze, excursion parties, 141, 152, 153f
gender scripts and roles, 5, 58, 255
generational cycles of first-generation students, 230–31, 238–39, 241, 248
genocide, 23, 61
gentrification, 110–11, 151–52, 160
geographies of power, 108
get to work, 223
ghosting of citizens, 79, 85, 107–8, 110, 123–25, 129, 131, 133–34, 140, 147, 150, 151, 152, 156f, 157, 159
Ghostly Matters, 13
Giddens, Anthony, 5
gift of giving teaching method, 216, 217
Glenn, Cheryl, 37
Gliddon, George, 49, 126, 255
global modernities-colonialities, 20, 61
Gobineau, Arthur de, 22–23, 43, 48, 62, 126
goings-on, 77f, 107–8
"The Golden Story of Sharyland," 142–43
Gomez-Pena, Guillermo, 270, 281
good/bad binary, 221–22, 237, 253, 256, 264–66
Gordon, Avery, 11, 13, 33, 75, 121, 220, 266–67, 269–70
Gordon, Lewis, 16, 118, 276
Goshute, 65
graduation rates, 238
Graff, Harvey, 6
Graham, Lindsey, 42

Gries, Laurie, 121
Gringoland, idea of, 139, 147, 148, 212
griots, 105
Groo, Katherine, 67
Grosfoguel, Ramon, 17
group classroom discussions, 185, 186f, 194–97, 198–205, 206f, 207, 213, 216–18, 222, 227
Guadalupe Hidalgo, Treaty of, 112, 113f, 158
Guevara, Emma, 160–61

half-dead, 80, 163, 254
Hall, Stuart, 33, 269
Hämäläinen, Pekka, 91, 149
Harices, 157
Harlingen Star, 143f
Harlingen (TX): education system, 154, 155f; founding, 132, 133, 142; Magic Valley myth, 143f, 157; settler advertisements, 134, 150f; settler archives, 190, 191f, 192f
haunted/hauntings: *Archive*, 7; awareness, 223; binaries, 264; "company of death," 140, 254; corridos, 65, 104; decolonial analytic, 232–33, 277; epistemological frameworks, 273–75, 279–80; first-generation students, 239, 253; forgetting or conjuration, 11–13, 100–101, 151, 167–68, 179, 193, 235f, 267; fractured "we," 276; ghosting of citizens, 79, 85, 103–8, 110–12, 123–25, 129, 131–34, 147, 156f, 157, 159–61, 210; hope-struggle (barrio mentality), 229; incarceration, 245; land, effects and consequences, 28; language of the everyday, 188–193; lived experience, 278; memory, 263; past/present connection, 105; Pledge of Allegiance, 199, 200; racism, 95, 178–82, 243; realizations, 246; rhetoricity, 6, 29, 208; space, place, and time, 34, 163–64, 182, 230, 259–60; *stories-so-far*, 8f, 177, 180–82, 248, 255; students, 256; unsettledness, 68; violence, 52, 81, 91, 126, 127f, 128, 242
haunting back, 23
hauntology, 9, 11, 38–39
healing, 13, 277
Hegel, Georg W.F., 43, 51, 58, 60, 88, 210
hegemonic architecture of knowledge, 164: *Americanity*, 18, 44, 59, 60, 112, 113f–15f, 121; *association of social interests*, 17–20, 30, 45, 61, 99, 164, 179; contents and terms, 10; Eurocentrism, 15–17, 44, 47–52; forgetting or conjuration, 11, 13, 100, 151, 167, 179, 235f, 267; identity, 108–9, 237; literacies, images-signs-sounds, and rhetorics, 17, 180, 201, 208; modernity, 31, 45, 46, 59, 64, 68. *See also* knowledge

heritage, 197–98
heroism, 128, 281
Hidalgo County, 133, 145
Hill, Lon C., 134, 142–45, 153–54, 192f, 193f, 195, 233
Hinojosa, Rebekah, 159–60
Hispanic Serving Institutions (HSIs), 238–39, 253
Hispanic people: generational cycles, 230–31; identity, 227, 237; Lower Rio Grande Valley (LRGV), 109; *stories-so-far*, 254; students, 32, 226; unsettledness, 230
Historia de las Indias, 58
Historia Eclesiástica Indiana, 55
Historia General de las Cosas de Nueva España, 57
historical contexts, 4, 7, 13, 25, 196, 208, 209
historicity, 22–24, 274
histories of power, 13, 24, 108
historiography, 112, 113f
Holley, Mary Austin, 125
homesteading, 83, 84, 85
hooks, bell, 172, 223, 272, 278
hope-struggle (barrio mentality), 226–30, 240–41, 244, 247–50, 251–54, 275
horizontal cross-chain, 87, 165
hospitality, conditional, 184, 185
hubris, settler colonialism, 97–98
human progress, 125, 129, 150, 195
human work and projects, 13, 23, 34, 76, 100, 181, 219, 223
humanitas, 47, 52–53
humanities, 3, 9–10, 28
"humanity of the settler," 168
humanization/dehumanization, 55–56, 81, 91
Hume, David, 49
hymns, as rhetoric, 83, 85, 87, 89, 90

idea of Gringoland, 139, 147, 148, 212
idea of race, 53, 95, 123–24, 179, 181
idea of Texas, 60, 105
idea of the Americas: American enterprise, 19, 99, 123, 124, 132; careful reckoning, 59, 64; coloniality of knowledge, 53, 151; dualistic idea of the Americas, 43–44; local forms and conditions, 39, 67–68; modernity, 14, 26; myth, 120; *Rights-to*, 53–58, 75; settler colonialism, 14, 22–24, 46, 98, 163; unsettling, 105; whiteness, 158
idea of the University, 27–28, 265
idea of Utah, 29, 30, 60–61, 64, 67, 93, 222
ideas as knowledge, 20, 27, 30, 62, 152, 263, 276
identity: church settlers, 88, 95, 145; first-generation students, 255; haunted/haunt-

ings, 230; hegemonic norms, 237; life questions, 185; logics of subversion and resignification, 109, 237; public memory, 26, 63; students, 227, 237, 255; writing and rhetorical studies (WRS), 225, 255
ideological war on information. *See* information as truth
im/possibilities, prospective vision, 33
image-and-myth, 92, 164
images-signs-sounds, 7, 28, 41, 107, 152, 164, 166, 183, 223, 263
immigration, dominant narrative, 190f, 227
imperial archives, 24, 26, 38
importing *Archive*, 61, 177, 195
impressions. *See* archival approach and theory of archival impression
in/actions, 13
incarceration, 245
Indigenous peoples, 47–52, 56–59, 86–90, 96, 123–27, 157–58, 235–36. *See also* American Indians/Native Americans; *individual tribes by name*
individual self-possessed, 273
indoctrination, first-year composition (FYC), 182
inferiority/superiority, justification, 47–52, 81, 86–88, 91, 95, 123–24
information as truth: church-settler archives, 100, 187; circulation, 44–45, 180; dominant narrative, 60, 188, 189f–93f; fake news, 61; ideology, 93, 94, 179, 201; invention, 91, 111; language of the everyday, 197–98; modern/colonial and settlerizing designs, 235; otherness, 55, 82, 125; power, 59; public memory, 63, 87, 97, 122n, 126–28, 140, 196, 208; settler advertisements, 112, 113f, 114f, 140, 149, 151–52; truth-and-knowledge claims, 28, 42, 80, 265
inheritance, rights of, 11–13, 32, 42–45, 64, 78–79, 84–86, 87, 91, 92, 95, 98, 212, 259
initiating a break, prospective vision, 11, 33
Inoue, Asao, 121
Institutional Review Board (IRB), 32, 226
instruction-and-curriculum, coloniality, 58, 59, 82, 94, 115, 144, 154–55, 163
intellectual work, unsettling, 11–12, 33, 270
interpretation of public records, 12, 25, 202
intervention praxis, 272
interview research method, 227, 246–47, 254, 255
invention praxis, 15, 58, 107–8, 111, 120, 129, 142, 145–48, 150, 167, 272, 274–75
invisible histories, 59, 159, 161

inward-facing dimension, 272
IRB (Institutional Review Board), 32, 226
irrigation in Magic Valley, 151–52
iterative writing, 94, 112

January 6, 2021, 46
Jefferson, Thomas, 47
Joint Committee of the Senate and the House in the Investigation of the Texas State Ranger Force (1919), 158
Journal of Discourses (*JoD*), 81, 82–84, 86, 89, 94, 96, 208
justification of colonialism, 25, 41, 47–48, 52, 57, 81, 91, 95, 150, 195, 222

Kannigieser, A.M., 114, 116
Kant, Immanuel, 43, 50–52, 58, 125
Karankawa, 105, 108, 145, 157
Keates, Nancy, 120
Kells, Michelle Hall, 73
Kelly, Ted, 159, 160
Kerby, McFall, 134
Kimbell, Spencer (Elder), 95–96
Kimmerer, Robin, 276, 278
Kirsch, Gesa, 5, 272
Kleberg, Robert, 160
know-learn, 104
knowing and unknowing praxis, 269
knowing-subjects, 16, 45–46, 53–59
knowledge: *Archive*, 8, 25, 27; coloniality, 19, 20, 30, 45, 47, 52–57, 100–101, 151, 152; decolonizing, 23, 28–31, 42, 76, 121–22, 171, 221, 236, 278; hauntings, 263; making/unmaking, 10, 26, 59, 172, 210, 211, 212; politics, 21; production, 223; pursuit of, 275; Rights-to, 77–80, 86, 122–24, 152; theo-and-ego structure, 129; writing and rhetoric studies (WRS), 71. *See also* hegemonic architecture of knowledge; information as truth; *working parts*
knowledge-being, 32–34, 59, 61, 94, 144, 173, 187, 220, 231, 256, 264, 266
knowledges, understandings, feelings, and *doings*, 178
Ku Klux Klan, 158–59
Kump, Eileen, 96–97, 184

L'Eplattenier, Barbara, 37
La Matanza, 158
labeling/mislabeling, 177, 223
labor exploitation, 110, 125, 138, 149
Ladd, Chas F.C., 141–42
Lamp, Kathleen, 72

land as inheritance, 10, 43, 52, 78–79, 82–86, 91, 92, 95, 98, 140, 145. *See also* (ap/ex)propriation
land, memory, knowledge, and relation-ing, 23, 25, 61–62
Landa, Diego de, 57
language barriers, first-generation students, 251
language of the everyday: classroom group discussions, 76, 207; community listening, 208, 209; corridos, 105; dominant narrative, 188, 189f, 190f, 191f, 192f, 193f, 232, 238, 243, 254; haunted/hauntings, 182, 195–96; information as truth, 69–72, 197–98; literacies, images, and rhetorics, 7, 214, 220; modern/colonial and settlerizing designs, 28; unsettling, 187
Las Casas, Bartolomé de, 55–58
last frontier, 114
Latin America, 14
Latino/a students, 4, 226, 227, 230–31, 254
Latter-day Saints, Church of Jesus Christ of. *See Mormon/ism*
laws of nature/reason, 42–43
Lawrence, William (Sir), 48–49, 58
LDS. *See Mormon/ism*
league of nations-friendships, 52
learning-unlearning-relearning path, 3, 5–6, 21, 213, 222, 223, 226, 236–37, 271, 273
León, Arnoldo de, 109
Leonard, Rebecca, 6
Lewis Gaillet, Lynee, 37
Lewis, Pierce, 5, 65, 70
LGBTQ+ community, 196, 211
Liew, Jamie, 76, 110
life questions, 185, 279
linguistic implications, 4
Linnaeus, Carl, 49
Lipan, 145, 157
listening, 39, 227, 272
literacies, images-signs-sounds, and rhetorics: academic responsibility, 28–29; *Archive*, 41; church-settler archives, 100–102; dominant narrative, 201; *coloniality of instruction-and-curriculum*, 82, 97; epistemic racism, 214; haunted/hauntings, 4–7, 167–68, 179–81, 208–9, 219–20; hegemonic architecture, 16–18; language of the everyday, 46, 188; *semiotic apparatus of enunciations*, 70–71; *thingification*, 86; unsettling, 10, 87; whiteness, 158; wor(l)ding, 21, 112, 166
literacy history interview research method, 32, 227, 254, 255

Little Journey through the Lower Valley of the Rio Grande, 129, 130f, 131f, 132
lived experience, 6, 25, 159, 178, 264, 268, 271, 272, 278
living on (sur-vie) structure, 275
Lloyd, Everett, 142, 151–52
Lloyd's Magazine, 140, 148, 151–52
local culture, 161
local forms and conditions, 25, 28, 29, 61, 67–68
local-regional histories, 14
Locke, John, 42–43, 99, 164
logic of coloniality of, 21, 60, 76
logic of the gift, 271, 272
logics of subversions and resignification, 109, 237
los recién llegados, 268
Lott, Uriah, 142
Lower Rio Grande Valley (LRGV): border(ed)land, 109, 231, 239, 240; Cameron Country, 142; colonization of new settlers, 145; *ghosting* of citizens, 110, 123–25, 129, 131–34, 140, 147, 150, 159; Hill, Lon C., 153–54; *idea of Texas*, 31, 122, 164; Musk, Elon, 110–11, 118, 119f, 152, 160, 162–63; mythmaking/mystification, 60, 144, 145, 147–48, 149, 152; rhetoric of place, 108–9; settler advertisements, 112, 113f, 114f, 115f, 135f, 136f, 138–41, 151–52, 155, 156f, 157–58, 161–62; Sharyland, 145, 146f, 147; SpaceX, 110, 120, 159, 160; visuality, 108, 111, 123–24, 129–34, 159. *See also* "The Magic Valley"
Lugones, Maria, 18, 21, 223

making/unmaking/remaking, 29, 171, 280
"The Magic Valley": divine and natural design, 122, 123, 125; empty landscape, 125, 127f, 134, 139, 140, 141, 142, 144; exploitation, 120; invention of, 111, 129–30, 157, 164; mythmaking/mystification, 115, 133–35, 139, 141–42, 157, 158; rebranding, 161–62; Rights-to, 109–10; settler-pioneers, 45, 60, 89, 113f–17f, 122, 129, 149; sonic coloniality, 114–15. *See also* Lower Rio Grande Valley (LRGV)
making it out, 229–30, 239–41, 250–53
making/unmaking/remaking, 26
Maldonado-Torres, Nelson, 10, 18, 21, 140, 223
Man-Human-Rights, 18, 42–44, 51, 53, 57, 77–80, 86, 94, 122–25, 147, 152, 167, 223, 273, 276–77
management of knowledge, 41, 59, 172, 210–12
Mao, LuMing, 274
mapping, 131f, 132
Maremont, Mark, 120

marginalized knowledge-being, 231, 237
martyrdom, 163
Massey, Doreen, 5–6, 207
materialism, 13
matter (living, nonliving, and nonhuman), 28, 29, 33, 260–61, 275–77
McAllen (TX), 110
McLeod, Wimberly, 141–42
meaning of place, 31, 107, 270
meaning of the classroom, 101, 219
media. *See* settler advertisements
mega "We," 270
Mejía, Jaime, 4, 121, 225
Memmi, Albert, 13
memory. *See* public memory
Mendez, Trey (Mayor), 160–62
Méndez Newman, Beatrice, 121
Mendieta, Gerónimo de, 55
Mercedes (TX), 134, 154
Mescaleros, 157
metaphysics, 265
Mexican/Mexican American students, 151, 154, 226–27, 230–31, 237–39, 241, 254
Mexican peoples, 108–9, 124–26, 129, 143, 144*f*, 148, 149, 157–58, 189*f*, 190, 193*f*, 194*f*
Mexico, Republic of, 123–25
Mignolo, Walter: academic responsibility, 3, 28; *coloniality of knowledge-being*, 94; decolonial analytic, 19, 21, 61, 68, 108, 221, 222; ideas as reality, 24, 30, 75, 111, 144; literacies, images-signs-sounds, and rhetorics, 17; mapping, 132; modern/colonial situations, 72, 87; myths, 145; unsettling, 16; visuality, 76
migration, 268
Miller, Elizabeth, 37
Milton, John, 226
mind subjective/mind objective/mind absolute, 51
minoritized knowledge-being, 231, 237
Mirzoeff, Nicholas, 76
mislabeling students, 177, 223
Mission (TX), 156*f*, 157
The Missionite, 132–33, 140–41
mobility movement, politics of, 70, 73, 268
modern/colonial and settlerizing designs: Americanity, 18, 19, 20, 59, 60; (ap/ex)propriation of land, 43, 82–85, 93–94, 109, 156–57; citizen/ship, 125, 131–32, 140; death-space, 39, 80; democracy, idea of, 45–47; disputing, 177; engagements, 9; environmental issues, 110–11, 159–61; epideictic rhetoric, 72–73, 75, 92; Eurocentrism, 16, 47–52; forms and conditions, 67–68; *goings-on*, 77, 107–8; information, 235; interactions, 9, 150; justification/legitimacy, 3, 26, 41, 81, 91, 95, 99, 144, 195; obedience/disobedience, 55, 90, 172, 231; primitive/modern, 131*f*, 132–34, 139*f*; principles, 44; racism, 95, 163, 178–83, 198, 214; violence, 52, 81, 91, 126, 127*f*, 128, 238; whiteness, 166. *See also Archive*; rhetorics of modernity
Modernity/Coloniality Collective (MCC): binaries/options, 109, 221, 222, 237, 253, 256, 264–66; criticism, 3–4; decolonial analytic, 24, 30; divine and natural design, 18, 49, 50, 51, 52, 53, 57, 58, 62, 95; hegemonic Europe, 15–16, 47–52; *idea of the Americas*, 67–68, 120; myth of modernity, 19; praxical theorizing actioning, 4; prospective vision, 33; theo- and-ego politics, 20, 51, 88, 89, 97; theses and propositions, 14, 20, 22, 30
Mohanty, Chandra T., 41
Montgomery, Julia, 129, 130*f*, 131*f*, 132, 164
Mormon students, 75, 100–101, 202, 204*f*, 205*f*, 214–18
Mormon/ism: *The Book of Mormon*, 78–83, 86, 87, 89, 90, 93, 94, 98; careful reckoning, 29, 222; cultural texts, 96, 99; *idea of Utah*, 30, 60, 64, 67, 70, 75, 76, 99, 100; *Journal of Discourses* (*JoD*), 81, 82–84, 86, 89, 94, 96, 208; narrative, 191; persecution, 83–85; preexistence, 87–88; *system* of philosophy and *superstructure*, 93, 94; whiteness, 74, 88; wor(l)ding aspiration, 93. *See also* church-settler archives
Morrill, Angie, 76, 91, 149
Morrison, Toni, 11, 12, 247
Morton, Samuel, 48
movement, settlerizing, 73
multiculturalism, 225, 239, 244*f*
multilingual students, 232, 238, 243, 254–56
musical genres, 207–8
Musk, Elon, 110–11, 118, 119*f*, 152, 160–63
Musk Foundation, 160
mythmaking/mystification: *Archive*, 61, 171; coloniality, 183; haunted/hauntings, 101; Hill, Lon C., 142, 144, 145; heroism, 128; human progress, 125, 129, 150; invention, 107; land dispossession, 110, 152; literacies, images-signs-sounds, and rhetorics, 82, 101; Magic Valley, 111, 115, 133–35, 138, 139; modernity, 19; *Mormon/ism*, 31, 78–81, 87, 92, 99; promised land, 115–18; settler advertisements, 113*f*, 114*f*, 140, 145, 147; settler colonialism, 115, 149, 151, 183; space, place, and time, 75–76, 157; Texas Rangers, 126–28

naming convention, 49, 264, 274
narcissism, 61, 101, 171, 183
narrative, 26, 183
Narrative of America, 191, 192f
nation-states, 52
Native Americans. *See* American Indians/ Native Americans; Indigenous peoples
native to a place, invention, 91
The Natural and Moral History of the Indies, 56
natural design. *See* divine and natural design
nature, law of, 42–43, 47–52
nature/natural resources, land exploitation, 30, 91, 92, 110–11, 120–21, 125, 132, 138, 145, 148
Nazan, 157
Ndé Kónitsąąíí Gokíyaa, 105, 108
Neuman, Matthew, 111
A New Division of the Earth, 49
new stories, 278
newness, 160
Nicholas V (Pope), 53
Nishida, Kitarō, 6–7
"no papeles," 245f
non-name of all, 21, 33, 223, 272, 274, 275
nonbeing, zone(s) of. *See* "zone(s) of nonbeing"
Nordquist, Brice, 6
normalization of modern/colonial and settlerizing designs, 3, 144, 211, 212
not-in-Utahisms, 183
Notes on the State of Virginia, 47
nothingness, 164
Nott, Josiah, 49, 126, 255
Nystrand, Martin, 6

objective of a desire, 273–75
obligation demands, 33, 270, 272, 274, 275
observation research method, 227
observatory deductions, 221–22
Olson, Christa, 121
On The Natural Varieties of Mankind, 49
ontological system of ideas. *See* epistemic racism; hegemonic architecture of knowledge; Man-Human-Rights
operation with/out colonies, 22
opposition to SpaceX, 120, 159, 160
oppositional structure, 184, 276
options, 221, 222, 237, 253, 256, 264, 265, 266
organizing systems of power, 13
"Orientalism Reconsidered," 24
origin stories, 15
original impulse, visuality, 43
Oravec, Christine, 72
other-as-possessions-of-the-Same, 54

other-as-Same, 43, 54, 73, 80, 82, 84, 86, 163, 183, 184, 185
other-things, 112
otherness: alienation, 10, 193, 197, 213, 254; arrival and arrivant, 245–46; border(ed)land, 109, 231, 239, 240; cultural, 4, 255; first-generation students, 237; humanization/dehumanization, 55–56, 91; Mexican peoples, 125, 129–30; multiculturalism, 244f; Native Americans/Indigenous people, 38, 96, 124, 157–58; observatory deductions, 221–22; racialization, 74; racism, 95, 243; rhetoric, 184; segregation in education, 154; Self/Selves, 223, 271; *stories-so-far*, 243; *thingification*, 86, 87, 90, 91, 112, 127, 128, 143; violence, 52, 81, 91, 126, 127f, 128, 199, 200
otherwise: any living being, 275; archival impressions, 7, 13, 29, 32, 75, 121, 159–61; at-home, 277; classroom group discussions, 205, 206f, 207, 226; human projects, 223; literacies, images, and rhetorics, 101, 166, 208; public memory, 63, 201–2; students of color, 230; wor(l)ding, 101, 166
outward-facing dimension, 272

Paiute, 65
Pajaritos, 157
palimpsestic narrative, 12, 26, 158, 238
papal bulls, 53–54
Paredes, Américo, 139, 147–48, 212
parents of first-generation students, 247–48
past, knowing, 75, 105, 278
past/present, 75, 121, 130f, 278
patriarchy, 242
Paysanos, 157
peaceful settlers, 167
pedagogy: decolonization, 4, 278; dominant narrative, 59, 210, 211; epistemic obedience, 55, 59, 90, 172; placed-based, 32
Pelosi, Nancy, 46
Pennycook, Alastair, 7
people-earth-and-future *longing*, 6
people-possessed future, 273
performative rhetoric, 71–72
permissions/prohibitions, 13
pesado-ness (affective value and rhetorical force), 6, 94, 103, 140
Peterson, Mark (Elder), 95
Philip (King), 54–55
philosophy of rights, 58
physical violence, 52, 81, 91, 126, 127f, 128, 199, 232

342 : INDEX

physical work, 78–79, 89, 91–94
Pink, Sarah, 7
pioneering. *See* settler-pioneers
Pintas, 157
place image-and-myth, 102, 118, 120, 152, 157
place. *See* space, place, and time
playful world-traveling, 21, 272
Pledge of Allegiance, 199, 200
pluriversality, 21, 100, 167, 264, 267
policing, 56–57, 126, 127*f*
politics of hauntings, inheritances, and dwellings, 13, 104
politics of location, 272
politics of mobility, 70, 72, 73, 268
Polk, James, 234, 235*f*
polylogs, 270–71
possibilities of new stories: archival approach and theory of archival impressions, 277; arrival and arrivant, 265, 266; classroom assignments, 207, 278; collective ethos, 181; educators, 224; expectations, 251, 256; first-generation students, 32, 240, 248–50; generational cycles, 248; haunted/hauntings, 6, 8; human work and projects, 181; *idea of the Americas*, 24, 120; literacies, 29; making it out, 229–30; meaning, 270; Mormon students, 204*f*, 205*f*, 214–18; praxis, 173; prospective vision, 182; Self/Selves, 271; we/arth, 276
poverty/prosperity, 111, 129, 133–35, 137*f*, 139, 161, 229
Powell, Malea, 38
power, as an *Archive*, 13, 22–25, 30, 38, 58, 59, 68, 101, 108, 277, 281
praxical theorizing actioning, 4, 23, 26, 269, 270, 277
praxis, *thinking, feeling,* and *being-with*, 13, 265, 272, 274–75
Pred, Alan, 70
predominantly white institutions (PWIs), 178, 219
prejudice, 189, 192*f*, 193*f*, 194*f*
preoriginary rhetoricity, 274
present/future, 110, 118, 121
present/past, 75, 121, 130*f*, 105, 278
primitive/modern, 131*f*, 132–34, 139*f*, 140
Prinsloo, Martin, 6, 77
privilege, 88, 89, 93, 197–98, 204, 210–11, 239
productive space, 159
promised land, 115–18
promotional materials, settler advertisements, 112, 113*f*, 114*f*
propaganda, 234

proper arrival and arrivant. *See* arrival and arrivant
proper names, 259, 264, 266, 268, 274
proselytizing, 71
prospective vision: decolonial option, 21, 23, 172, 231; haunted/hauntings, 11, 264; im/possibilities, 33; language, 12; *learning-unlearning-relearning*, 5–6; *possibilities of new stories*, 182; "Weism," 13, 27, 29, 270
prosperity/poverty, 111, 129, 133–35, 137*f*, 139, 161, 229
protest, forms of, 159–60
psychological violence, 52, 81, 91, 232
public memory: archival impressions, 87, 159; *Archive*, 25; bearing witness, 63, 74; corridos, 104; frontiers, 163; information as truth, 112, 196; modern/colonial and settlerizing mentality, 39; narratives, 26; *otherwise* narrative, 200–202; racist happenings, 179; settler archives, 223; settler colonialism, 126, 140, 145; Utah, 63, 97, 99, 200–201
public murals, 159–60, 161, 162
public places, rhetoric, 73–74
public records, 28, 30, 61, 101, 166, 202, 219–20
publications, *otherwise* archival impressions, 160–61
pursuit of knowledge, 275

Quijano, Anibal, 15, 17, 18, 20, 21, 157, 158–59

race, idea of, 5, 88, 95, 123–24, 163, 179, 181
race/labor, 48, 110, 125, 129, 140, 147, 148, 149
racialization, 18, 74, 231, 237
racism: *association of social interests*, 179; deficiency, idea of, 86, 87, 88, 89, 123, 124, 125; displacement, 111; *ends* of coloniality, 181; epistemic, 178–83; instruction-and-curriculum, 82, 115, 154; language, literacies, and rhetorics, 214; mindset, 4; *Mormon/ism*, 95; Native Americans/Indigenous, 96, 123–24, 199–202, 222; *otherness*, 125, 243; *stories-so-far*, 250; students of color, 197, 202, 203*f*, 204–7, 217–18, 232, 238, 250; unsettling, 214; Utah, 198, 204, 212; violence, 52, 81, 91, 126, 127*f*, 128, 204, 238
racist happenings: bearing witness, 180–82; *end-of discourse*, 181; group discussion, 216–18; haunted/hauntings, 179; hegemonic narrative, 180; Mormon students, 214–18; normalization, 211; physical violence, 52, 81, 126, 127*f*, 128, 199; racist fliers, 178–82, 190, 210, 211
railroads, 190*f*, 234*f*

Ramirez, Josue, 162–63
Randall, Taylor (University of Utah President), 97–98
Ratcliffe, Krista, 210–11
rationalization of *archival impressions*, 25
Rayados/Borrados, 105, 108
reap what you sow trope, 122, 166
reason, law of, 42–43, 51
rebranding invention, 85, 87, 92, 107–8, 111, 123–25, 129, 131–34, 152
receptive generosity, 21
reclaiming terms and concepts, 4, 109
recognition of differences, 80, 87, 89, 94, 95, 123–24, 125, 271–73
reconciliation, 275
reconstitution, epistemic, 236
reconstructive work, 266–67
recovery work, modern/colonial contexts, 4, 6
recycled writing, 94
reductive rhetorical structures, 184, 276
Reeves, Paul, 74
reflexivity, 48
reframing decolonization, 264–65
rehabilitated humanity and society, 9–10
reinscribing rhetorics and rhetorical practices, 4
relation of existence, 274
relation to archives, 34
relational framework of ethics, 273–75
religion, influence on self, being, and agency, 74, 197–98, 209, 210
religious persecution of Mormons, 83–85
(re)making space and place, 7, 239
remapping, 131f, 132
remembering, process of, 11, 12
reorientation, archival impressions, 67
repositioning contents of the *Archive*, 27, 158–63, 263
repressions/exclusions, 13
Requerimiento, 54
research methods, 30, 37, 226, 227, 254
researchers, emotional labor, 246–47
resistance option, 38, 221, 222, 237, 253, 256, 264, 265, 266
responsibility of scholar-educator, 33, 270
responsibility of we/arth, 201–2, 272, 274, 275
reterritorialization, 161
return to spaces and places, 59, 105, 207, 239, 272
(re)writing the *Archive*, 25–26, 42, 62, 69, 75, 111, 140–41
Reynolds, Nedra, 6
rhetoric of epistemology, 28, 42, 61, 219–20

rhetoric of modernity: archival research, 37, 103; *association of social interests*, 10, 17–20, 24, 60, 179; branding, 85, 87, 123–25, 161, 162; coded words/tropes, 61–62, 122, 151, 164, 165, 166; counter-writing, 27; education system, 154–55; empty landscape, 44–45, 127f, 131–34, 139, 140, 141, 144, 150; invention, 271; logic of coloniality, 4, 21–23; mythmaking/mystification, 76, 142, 171; *otherness*, 96, 184; performative, 71–72; protest, forms of, 159–60; semiotic apparatus of enunciation, 111–12; visuality, 78–79, 92, 97, 107–8, 129–34, 178–82; words and ideas, 46, 47; writing and rhetoric studies (WRS), 22, 28, 30, 105–6, 169. See also *Archive*; modern/colonial and settlerizing designs
rhetoric of process, 92
rhetoric of the sublime, 58
rhetorical studies. *See* writing and rhetoric studies (WRS)
rhetorical war on information. *See* information as truth
right/wrong binary, 221, 222, 237, 253, 256, 264–66
Rights-and-belonging-to, 43, 69, 70, 71, 88, 113, 148
rhizomatic activities, 273
Rice, Jenny, 121
Rickert, Thomas, 71
right to education, 250–51
right/wrong binary, 264
rights of inheritance, 42, 92
Rights-to, 69, 77, 79, 80, 81, 84, 85, 87, 112, 122, 152, 223, 276
Roberts-Miller, Patricia, 160
Rohan, Liz, 5, 37
Rohrer, Judy, 6, 7, 207
role of educators, 28, 31, 180–81, 266
Roosevelt, Theodore, 45
Royster, Jacqueline Jones, 5, 197
ruler/ruled, 56
Rushdy, Ashraf, 158
Rutledge, Jack, 153

sacred bond, 278
Safford, H.R., 139
Sahagún, Bernardino de, 57
Said, Edward, 5, 9, 24, 33, 266, 270, 277
Salt Lake City, racist happenings, 203f
Salt Lake Tribune, 180
San Benito (TX), 151, 153, 157
scalemaking projects, 239
Schoen, David, 42–43

scholar-educator, 11, 28, 31, 33, 265, 266, 270
scholarship, 3, 5
secularly-structured terms, 17
seeing, knowing, 39, 273
segregation, 95, 151, 154, 158, 190, 193f, 194f, 212
self of the past/present, 270–72
self-awareness, 37
self-ideas (Man), 223
self-motivation, 243–45
self, being, and agency: binaries/options, 109, 221, 239, 253, 256, 264, 265; influence of family, community, and religion, 205, 209, 210, 220; racialized, 237; us/them, 8
Self/Selves, 13, 21, 37, 223, 270–72, 273, 280
semiotic apparatus of enunciation, 16, 28–30, 42, 61, 74, 75, 111–12, 129–34
Senda-Cook, Samantha, 69, 71
Sepúlveda, Juan Ginés de, 57, 58
settled-ness: counter-writing, 8; *friction*, 181; present, 75; *stories-so-far*, 281; unsettling, 23, 27, 38–39, 213, 271, 272, 274, 279; unworking, 265
settler advertisements: assemblage, branding, and recasting work, 92, 108, 111, 123–25, 129, 131–34; circulation, 112; citizen/ship, 148, 151, 155–57; coded words/tropes, 62, 122, 151–52, 165f, 166; coloniality, 115, 151; corporations, 157; differences, 140; *ghosting* of citizens, 110, 129, 131, 133–34, 147, 150, 156–57; Harlingen, 150f, 190, 191f, 192f; Lower Rio Grande Valley (LRGV), 135f, 136f, 150f, 151–52, 155, 156f, 157–58; mythmaking/mystification, 133–34, 138, 140, 142, 145; primitive/modern, 131f, 132–34, 139f, 140; promotional materials, 112, 113f, 114f; prosperity/poverty, 129, 133–35, 137f, 151–52; public murals, 161, 162; race/labor, 110, 125, 129, 138, 147–49; *Rights-and-belonging-to*, 148; Sharyland, 145, 146f, 147; slogans, 138; social media, 118, 119f, 120, 152–53; visuality, 129–34, 154–57
settler archives: anonymous student responses, 188f–93f; decolonial analytic, 23, 233f, 234–36; decolonizing knowledge, 168; epistemological experiments, 31, 149, 151–52; *epistemological framework for the living*, 84, 112, 167; haunted/hauntings, 167–68, 193; historical contexts, 25; identity, 95, 145, 235; information as truth, 100, 112, 151–52; lived contexts, 25; museums, role of, 4; public memory, 30, 63, 126, 145, 223; (re)writing, 25–26, 75, 140–41; space, place, and time, 188–93; *stories-so-far*, 101, 236; temporal contexts, 25

settler colonialism: anonymous student responses, 188f–93f; classroom, 188; decolonial analytic, 23, 168, 233f, 234–36; epistemological experiments, 31, 149, 151–52; *epistemological framework for the living*, 84, 112, 167; railroads, 234f
settler-pioneers, 45, 60, 89, 113f–17f, 122, 129, 149
shadow research method, 227
shadow work, 33, 34, 103, 271–72
shared-in epistemic system, 42, 61, 195, 263
Sharpe, Christina, 76, 276
Shary, John, 134
Sharyland, 133, 134, 142–45, 146f, 147, 157
Shary Organization, 145–47
Sheard, Cynthia, 72, 74
Sheller, Mimi, 70, 76
Sheridan, Erin, 161–62
shift, existential predicament of rhetoricity, 274–75
Shoshone, 65
sites of inquiry, 172
situated knowledge, 32, 105, 272
slavery in the Americas, 47–48, 58
slogans, 138
smaller archives of knowledges, understandings, feelings, and doings. See Archive; working parts
Smith, Joseph, 74, 78, 83, 85
Smith, Linda, 16
social interest association. *See* association of social interests
social media, 118, 119f, 120, 152–53
sociopolitical thought and action, 5
sonic coloniality, 114–15
space, place, and time: archival impressions, 22, 165; *Archive*, 100, 165, 168; border(ed)land, 109, 231, 239, 240; classroom, meaning of, 219; decolonial analytic, 166–67; embodied experiences, 5; empty landscape trope, 44–45, 53, 85, 86, 99, 125, 127f, 133–34, 139–42, 144–46, 150, 148; epideictic rhetoric, 72–73, 75, 92, 112, 131; forced rebranding, 85, 92, 108, 111, 123–25, 129, 131–34, 161, 162; haunted/hauntings, 34, 163–64, 182, 230, 259–60; homesteading, 83–85; *idea of the Americas*, 42, 56, 120; image-and-myth, 75–76, 138, 164; inclusion, 264; meanings of, 107; pedagogies, 32; public places, 73–75; (re)making, 239; return to, 207; rhetorics, 63, 69, 71–74; self/selves, 270; *stories-so-far*, 5–6; visuality, 78–79, 85, 92, 97, 111, 123–24, 129–34; wor(l)ding, 84, 264; wounded/wounding, 167, 208, 279

SpaceX, 110, 120, 159–62
Spanish conquest, 30, 41, 53–59, 145, 157–58
Spanish-dominant language use, 232, 238, 254. *See also* bilingual dominant language
Specters of Marx, 11
spiritual work, 78–79, 89
Spivak, Gayatri, 26, 39, 221, 274
Starbase (TX), 118, 119*f*
status quo, epistemic system and design, 161–62
Steedman, Carolyn, 37, 39
stoppage, 266
stories-so-far: archival approach and theory of archival impressions, 273, 277; *Archive*, 7, 32, 101, 263, 281; assent, 109, 242, 245; becoming ready, 272; classroom assignments, 207, 208; educators, 224; final classroom project, 209–10; financial difficulties, 240–41; first-generation students, 236, 246, 251–53; friction, 196, 223; haunted/hauntings, 8, 12, 167, 182, 241; hope-struggle, 240–41; idea of the Americas, 24, 120; inheritances, 12, 92; inward-facing dimension, 272; making it out, 229–30; meaning, 270; *otherness*, 96, 243; praxis, 173; racism, 180, 250; Self/selves, 271; settledness, 281; settler archives, 101, 209–10; students, 32, 168, 196, 199–202, 214–15, 254, 278, 279; unsettledness, 281; Zion, Utah, 177
storytelling, 71, 103–4
strategic essentialism, 227, 266
Street, Brian, 6, 70
strengthening the stakes, 71
structural racism, 178–82
structure of feelings and thought, 6, 13, 14, 26
structuring principles of settler colonialism, 158–59
students: anonymous survey responses, 188*f*–93*f*; archives, 5, 31, 263; assimilation, 232, 238, 255–56; *being-and-becoming*, 231–32; blog posts, 202, 203*f*, 204–7; hauntings, 256; labeling/mislabeling, 177, 223; language, literacies, and rhetorics, 220; learning-unlearning-relearning, 213; Mormons, 100–101, 182; multilingual, 232, 238, 255–56; *possibilities of new stories*, 32; privilege, 197–98; racism of peers, 197, 217–18; research participants, 227, 246, 252–53; rhetoric, 194–95; *stories-so-far*, 32, 168, 278, 279; transformation, 264; writing and rhetoric studies (WRS), 236
subaltern speak, 274
subjectivities, 13

subsume, ontological differences, 26
surrender option, 221, 222, 237, 253, 256, 264, 265, 266
surveillance, 159
surveys, anonymous responses, 188*f*–93*f*
System Naturae, 49
system of philosophy and *superstructure*, 93, 94

take away, proper names, 259
taking/making spaces and places, 101
Tamez, Margo, 109
TAMUCC, 226, 240
teaching methods: decolonial analytic, 181–82; disposition of the habitus, 221; first-generation students, 238, 255; *friction*, 185; gift of giving, 216, 217; group discussions, 185, 186*f*; language of the everyday, 187; life questions, 279; work-instruction, 221; writing and rhetoric studies (WRS), 236, 256
technique-technology of repetition, 274
technology, decolonial analytic, 24, 159
Tejano Cultural Zone, 109
Tejones, 157
Temple Square, 64
temporal contexts, settler archives, 25
terms of the conversation, unsettling, 16
territorial (ap/ex)propriation. *See* (ap/ex)propriation
Texas: archival impression, 105, 108; future-to-come, 110, 118; *idea of Texas*, 105; settler advertisements, 112, 113*f*, 114*f*; settler-pioneers, 23, 123–26, 163. *See also* Lower Rio Grande Valley; "the Magic Valley"
Texas A&M University (TAMU), 226
Texas Rangers, 126–28, 143, 144*f*, 158
Texas Rangers in Action (TRA), 122, 126, 127*f*, 128
Texas Revolution (1835–1836), 122–24
Texas Rio Grande Valley, University of (UTRGV), 122, 226, 227, 238
Texas, Republic of, 122
theo-and-ego politics, 20, 51, 79, 88, 89, 97, 126, 129
theologically-structured terms, 17
theory building actioning, 26, 270, 277
theses and proposition, MCC, 22, 30
thingification, 18, 48, 50, 51, 53, 54, 80, 82, 86, 87, 90, 91, 112, 126, 127*f*, 128
things of mere nature, 86, 87, 127, 128, 143
things otherwise, (de/re)compositioning, 6, 26, 29, 264, 274
thinking, feeling, and *being-with*, 13, 21, 33, 72, 230, 264, 271, 274–75
This Is the Place Heritage Park, 200–201

time, archival impressions, 34, 165
Tlostanova, Madina, 3, 21, 132
Toreguanos, 157
Toth, Christie (Dr.), 181, 198, 227
Traces of a Stream, 5
Tratado: Sobre las Justas Causas de la Guerra Contra los Indios, 57
transfer, first-year composition (FYC), 182, 264
translation of public records, 12, 202
traveling, non-name of all, 21
treaties, 158, 195–96
tropes, 43, 62, 92, 122, 142, 151–52, 165, 166, 171
Tropic Tendencies, 6
Trouillot, Michel-Rolph, 76
Trucha, 160, 161, 162
"The True Story of the Lower Rio Grande Valley," 151–52
Trump, Donald, 44–46
truth-and-knowledge claims, 28, 42, 80, 151–52, 265
Tsing, Anna, 68, 108, 177–78, 198, 278
Tuck, Eve, 68, 76, 91, 108, 149

uncivilized/citizen/ship, 86, 113f, 114f, 124, 125, 131–32, 139, 140
underscore differences, 26, 80
undocumented individuals, 159, 242–43
United States, 30
universality of hegemonic architecture, 17
University, as *working part* of *Archive*, 3, 59, 265
unknowing, as praxis, 259, 265
unknown/known, 45
unmaking knowledge, 10
unsettled: bearing witness, 23, 74, 171–72, 234f; decolonialism, 10, 263; discourse, 50–53, 58; faculty of color, 219; first-year composition (FYC), 182; group discussions in the classroom, 196–97; hauntology, 38–39; hegemonic architecture, 15, 16; idea of desire and objective, 273; intellectual thought, 11–12; justification of violence, 81, 91, 126, 127f, 128, 222; language of the everyday, 187; literacies, images, and rhetorics, 87, 101, 208; past, 75; power, 68; proper names, 266, 268; racism, 214; settled-ness, 8, 27, 39, 181, 213, 271, 272, 279; settler archives, 233f; *stories-so-far*, 281; students, 230; things, 126, 127, 274; Western narrative, 29; unworking of knowing, 264–65
Urry, John, 70
us/them, 184, 210, 215
Utah, University of, 185–86, anti-immigration fliers, 179; *Archive*, 185, 186f; invention, 75;
racism, 95, 178–82, 203f; Randall, Taylor (President), 97–98; research participation, 227; Writing and Rhetoric Studies, Department of, 181
Utah: careful reckonings, 63–65, 196; church-settlers, 195–96; Garden of Eden trope, 78–79, 86, 92, 99–100, 113f, 114f, 115f, 140, 141; idea of, 60–61, 64, 75, 85–87, 93, 98, 99, 100; language of the everyday, 69–70; literacies, images, and rhetorics, 82, 208, 219–20; public memory, 63, 97, 196, 200–201; racism, 95, 179, 198, 203f, 204, 212; state history, 223; Temple Square, 64; Utah bubble, 208
Ute, 65

Valladolid debate, 55
Valley Morning Star, 153
value/difference, 13
values, learning-unlearning-relearning path, 223
Vanguard of Utah, 181
Veach, Don, 157
Veracini, Lorenzo, 68, 108
vertical cross-chain, 87, 165
Villanueva, Victor, 4, 38
violence, 52, 57, 81, 91, 126, 127f, 128, 199, 222, 229, 238, 242
visuality: (ap/ex)propriation of land, 43, 92, 140, 147–48; *The Book of Mormon*, 78–79; Lower Rio Grande Valley (LRGV), 111, 129–34, 151, 159; racist fliers, 178–82, 190, 210, 211; rhetoric, 97, 124, 178–82; settler rhetoricity, 75–76, 107–8, 154–57, 161, 162
vulnerability, classroom environment, 187

W.E. Stewart Land Company, 113f, 114f, 115f
[W]-[H] questions, 14, 16, 21, 24, 41, 159
walking exigencies, xxviii, 73
Wallerstein, Immanuel, 15, 18, 20
Walsh, Catherine, 16, 21, 61
war on information. *See* information as truth
Warner, Michael, 74
waste place, 43, 164
wasteland. *See* empty landscape trope
we/arth, 33, 34, 247, 260–61, 273–79; collective/fractured "we," 276
"Weism," 13, 27, 29, 270
Western narrative, 4, 15, 18, 19, 20, 235f
Wharton, William, 123–24, 162
"what/what is," question of, 274
White cultural logics, 232
white ignorance, 203f, 204f, 210, 213, 214, 217f
white perception, 49–50, 58

white privilege, 74, 93, 185, 186f, 218
white spaces-places, 25, 165
white students, 195, 220–22
whiteness, 46, 74, 96, 100, 158, 166, 197, 210, 232, 243
Whittaker, David, 68
Wild West/modern world, 45
wilderness. *See* empty landscape trope
wildlife. *See* environmental issues; nature/natural resources, land exploitation
Williams, Raymond, 6, 13, 15
Wingard, Jennifer, 75, 108, 121
Wolfe, Patrick, 70, 158–59
wording, 13, 34, 263
words-ideas, 42–43, 223
work agenda, 78–79
work-instruction, 82, 84, 85, 88, 183, 184, 185, 221, 223; physical/spiritual work, 90, 91, 92, 93, 94
working parts, 9, 77, 96, 219–20; *Archive*, 25, 26, 65, 68, 105, 171, 177, 195; assemblage, 60, 79, 85, 89, 111, 131–34; (re)writing, 42, 111
world history, 14, 20, 22–24
wor(l)ding: archives, 8, 12, 27, 34, 39, 274; aspiration, 72, 74, 277; *being-and-becoming*, 271; best practices, 274; decolonialization, 4; humanization/dehumanization, 55–56, 81, 91; invention, 75; *Mormon/ism*, 93; *otherwise*, 13, 21, 26, 101, 166, 208; physical/spiritual work, 78–79, 89, 91, 92, 93; space, place, and time, 74, 84, 129–34, 263, 264; *work-instruction*, 82, 84, 85, 183
wounded/wounding, 29, 65, 71, 104, 167, 177, 180–82, 208, 275, 279

The Wretched of the Earth, 9, 10
wretched/civilized, 43
writing and rhetoric studies (WRS): analytical methods, 28; archival research, 30, 37–39, 106; *Aristotelian syndrome*, 27–28; careful reckoning, 64, 65, 274; "carving bone," 271; *coloniality of instruction-and-curriculum*, 115, 232; criticism, 105; cultural vitality, 225, 239; decolonial analytic, 4, 5, 181–82; embodiment, 270; Eurocentrism, 4, 47–52, 56–57; faculty of color, 178; first-year composition (FYC), 182; idea of, 27; identity, 225, 255; imperial archives, 38; knowledge, 71; modern/colonial and settlerizing designs, 105, 139, 169; multilanguage students, 255–56; naming concepts, 247, 274; predominantly white institutions (PWIs), 219; recycled/iterative writing, 94, 112; rhetorical exchange, 194–95; teaching methods, 236, 256
writing, alphabetic, 4, 17, 55, 56, 96–97
written record. *See Archive*
Wynter, Sylvia, 21, 27

Yang, K. Wayne, 68, 76, 91, 108, 149, 168, 180, 212
Young, Brigham, 85, 183, 200–201, 215, 219
Yucatan, 57

zero-point epistemology, 17, 20, 47, 49, 50, 52, 53, 55–57, 62, 77, 79, 87–89, 93, 97, 119–20, 122
Žižek, Slavoj, 221
"zone(s) of nonbeing," 254

www.ingramcontent.com/pod-product-compliance
Lightning Source LLC
Chambersburg PA
CBHW040639100526
44585CB00039B/2790